John Croumbie Brown

Hydrology of South Africa

Details of the former hydrographic condition of the Cape of Good Hope

John Croumbie Brown

Hydrology of South Africa
Details of the former hydrographic condition of the Cape of Good Hope

ISBN/EAN: 9783337123970

Printed in Europe, USA, Canada, Australia, Japan

Cover: Foto ©Andreas Hilbeck / pixelio.de

More available books at **www.hansebooks.com**

HYDROLOGY OF SOUTH AFRICA.

INTERNATIONAL FORESTRY EXHIBITION.

WORKS ON FOREST SCIENCE.

By the REV. J. C. BROWN, LL.D.

Edinburgh: OLIVER & BOYD.
London: SIMPKIN, MARSHALL, & CO., and W. RIDER & SON.
Montreal: DAWSON, BROTHERS.

I.—**Introduction to the Study of Modern Forest Economy. Price 5s.**

In this there are brought under consideration the extensive destruction of forests which has taken place in Europe and elsewhere, with notices of disastrous consequences which have followed—diminished supply of timber and firewood, droughts, floods, landslips, and sand-drifts—and notices of the appliances of Modern Forest Science successfully to counteract these evils by conservation, planting, and improved exploitation, under scientific administration and management.

Extract from Preface.—'At a meeting held on the 28th of March last year (1883), presided over by the Marquis of Lothian, while the assemblage was representative of all interests—scientific, practical, and professional—it was resolved :—"That it is expedient in the interests of forestry, and to promote a movement for the establishment of a National School of Forestry in Scotland, as well as with a view of furthering and stimulating a greater improvement in the scientific management of woods in Scotland and the sister countries which has manifested itself during recent years, that there should be held in Edinburgh, during 1884, and at such season of the year as may be arranged, an International Exhibition of forest products and other objects of interest connected with forestry." It was then moved, seconded, and agreed :—"That this meeting pledges itself to give its hearty co-operation and patronage to the promotion of an International Forestry Exhibition in Edinburgh in 1884; and those present resolve to give their best efforts and endeavours to render the Exhibition a success, and of such importance and general interest as to make it worthy of the name of International."

'It is in accordance with this resolution, and in discharge of obligations which it imposed, that this volume has been prepared.'

II.—The Forests of England; and the Management of them in Bye-gone Times. Price 6s.

Ancient forests, chases, parks, warrens, and woods, are described; details are given of destructive treatment to which they have been subjected, and of legislation and literature relating to them previous to the present century.

EXTRACT FROM PREFACE.—' Contrast with this [the paucity of works in English on Forest Science], the richness of Continental languages in literature on such subjects. I have had sent to me lately *Ofversight of Svenska Skogsliteraturen, Bibliografiska Studieren of Axel Cnattingius*, a list of many books and papers on Forest Science published in Sweden; I have also had sent to me a work by Don José Jordana y Morera, Ingenero de Montes, under the title of *Apuntes Bibliographico Forestale*, a *catalogue raisonné* of 1126 printed books, MSS., &c., in Spanish, on subjects connected with Forest Science.

'I am at present preparing for the press a report on measures adopted in France, Germany, Hungary, and elsewhere, to arrest and utilise driftsand by planting them with grasses and trees; and in *Der Europaeische Flug-sand und Seine Cultur, von Josef Wessely General Domaenen-Inspecktor, und Forst-Academie-Direktor*, published in Vienna in 1873, I find a list of upwards of 100 books and papers on that one department of the subject, of which 30, in Hungarian, Latin, and German, were published in Hungary alone.

'According to the statement of one gentleman, to whom application was made by a representative of the Government at the Cape, for information in regard to what suitable works on Forest Economy could be procured from Germany, the works on *Forst-Wissenchaft*, Forest Science, and *Forst-Wirthchaft*, Forest Economy, in the German language may be reckoned by cartloads. From what I know of the abundance of works in German, on subjects connected with Forestry, I am not surprised that such a report should have been given. And with the works in German may be reckoned the works in French.

'In Hermann Schmidt's *Fach Katalogue*, published in Prague last year (1876), there were given the titles, &c., of German works in *Forst und Jagd-Literatur*, published from 1870 to 1875 inclusive, to the 31st of October of the latter year, amounting in all to 650, exclusive of others given in an appendix, containing a selection of the works published prior to 1870. They are classified thus :—General Forest Economy, 93; Forest Botany, 60; Forest History and Statistics, 50; Forest Legislation and Game Laws, 56; Forest Mathematics, 25; Forest Tables and Measurements, &c., 148; Forest Technology, 6; Forest Zoology, 19; Peat and Bog Treatment, 14; Forest Calendars, 6; Forest and Game Periodicals, 27; Forest Union and Year Books, 13; Game, 91; Forest and Game in Bohemian, 44. In all, 652. Upwards of a hundred new works had been published annually. Amongst the works mentioned is a volume entitled *Die Literatur der letzten sieben Jahre* (1862-1872) *aus* dem *Gesammtgebiete der Land-und Forst-wirthschaft mit Einschluss der landw. Geweber u. der Jagd, in deutscher, französischer u englisher Sprache Herausg. v. d. Buchandl*, v. Gerold and Co., *in Wein*, 1873, a valuable catalogue filling 278 pages in large octavo.

'This volume is published as a small contribution to the literature of Britain, on subjects pertaining to Forest Science.

'It is after due consideration that the form given to the work—that of a compilation of what has been stated in works previously published —has been adopted.

III.—Forestry of Norway. Price 5s.

There are described in successive chapters the general features of the country. Details are given of the geographical distribution of forest trees, followed by discussions of conditions by which this has been determined—heat, moisture, soil, and exposure. The effects of glacial action on the contour of the country are noticed, with accounts of existing glaciers and snow-fields. And information is supplied in regard to forest exploitation and the transport of timber, in regard to the export timber trade, to public instruction in sylviculture, and to forest administration, and to ship-building and shipping.

EXTRACT FROM PREFACE.—'In the spring of 1877, while measures were being taken for the formation of an Arboretum in Edinburgh, I issued a pamplet entitled *The Schools of Forestry in Europe: a Plea for the Creation of a School of Forestry in connection with the Arboretum in Edinburgh.* After it was made known that arrangements were being carried out for the formation of an International Exhibition of forest products, and other objects of interest connected with forestry, in Edinburgh with a view to promoting the movement for the establishment of a National School of Forestry in Scotland, and with a view of furthering and stimulating a greater improvement in the scientific management of woods in Scotland, and the sister countries, which has manifested itself during recent years, the council of the East Lothian Naturalists' Club resolved on having a course of lectures or popular readings on some subject connected with forestry, which might enable the members and others better to profit by visits to the projected Exhibition, and which should be open to the public at a moderate charge. The conducting of these was devolved upon me, who happened to be vice-president of the club. The following treatise was compiled from information then in my possession, or within my reach, and it constituted the basis of these lectures.'

IV.—Finland: its Forests and Forest Management.
Price 6s 6d.

In this volume is supplied information in regard to the lakes and rivers of Finland, known as *The Land of a Thousand Lakes*, and as *The Last-born Daughter of the Sea;* in regard to its physical geography, including notices of the contour of the country, its geological formations and indications of glacial action, its flora, fauna, and climate; and in regard to its forest economy, embracing a discussion of the advantages and disadvantages of *Svedjande*, the *Sartage* of France, and the *Koomaree* of India; and details of the development of Modern Forest Economy in Finland, with notices of its School of Forestry, of its forests and forest trees, of the disposal of its forest products, and of its legislation and literature in forestry are given.

EXTRACT FROM PREFACE.—' I happened to spend the summer of 1879 in St. Petersburg, ministering in the British and American Chapel in that city, while the pastor sought relaxation for a few months at home. I was for years the minister of the congregation worshipping there, and I had subsequently repeatedly spent the summer among them in similar circumstances. I was at the time studying the Forestry of Europe; and I availed myself of opportunities afforded by my journey thither through Norway, Sweden, and Finland, by my stay in Russia, and by my return through Germany and France, to collect information bearing upon the enquiries in which I was engaged. On my return to Scotland I contributed to the *Journal of Forestry* a series of papers which were afterwards reprinted under the title *Glances at the Forests of Northern Europe*. In the preface to this pamphlet I stated that in Denmark may be studied the remains of forests in pre-historic times; in Norway, luxuriant forests managed by each proprietor as seemeth good in his own eyes; in Sweden, sustained systematic endeavours to regulate the management of forests in accordance with the latest deliverances of modern science; in Finland, *Sartage* disappearing before the most advanced forest economy of the day; and in Russia, *Jardinage* in the north, merging into more scientific management in Central Russia, and *Réboisement* in the south. This volume is a study of information which I then collected, together with information which I previously possessed, or have subsequently obtained, in regard to the Forests and Forestry of Finland.'

Translation of Extracts from Letters from DR A. BLOMQVIST, Director of the Finnish National School of Forestry at Evois:—' On my return from Salmos three weeks ago I had the great pleasure to receive your volume on the Forests and Forest Management in Finland. I return you grateful thanks for the gift, and no less for publishing a description of the forestal condition of our country. It is with sentiments of true gratitude I learn that you had previously taken part in a work so important to our country as the preparation of a new edition of the New Testament in Finnish. Your descriptions of our natural scenery are most excellent and interesting. Personally I feel most interest in your accounts of *Koomaree*. I value it much, and not less so your concurrent final conclusion in regard to the effects of the exercise of it in Finland.'

Translation of Statement by M. DE LA GRYE, in the *Revue des Eaux et Fôrets* of January 1884 :—'In an address delivered some weeks since at a banquet of exhibitors in the French section at Amsterdam, M. Herisson, Minister of Commerce, expressed an intention to publish a series of small books designed to make known to French merchants foreign lands in a commercial point of view. If the Minister of Commerce wishes to show to our merchants the resources possessed by Finland, he need not go far to seek information which may be useful to them, they will be found in a small volume which has just been published by Mr John Croumbie Brown.

'Mr Brown is one of those English ministers, who, travelling over the world in all directions [some at their own cost], seeking to spread the Word of the Lord in the form of Bibles translated into all languages, know how to utilise the leisure left to them at times while prosecuting this mission. Some occupy themselves with physical science, others with archæology, some with philology, many with commerce; Mr Brown has made a special study of sylviculture. He has already published on this subject many works, from amongst which we may cite these : *Hydrology of South Africa; The Forests of England; The Schools of Forestry in Europe; Réboisement in France; Pine Plantations on Sand Wastes in France.*

'His last book on Finland is the fruit of many journeys made in that country, which he visited for the first time in 1833, but whither he has returned frequently since that time. Mr Brown gives narratives of his voyages on the lakes which abound in Finland, and his excursions in the immense forests, the exploitation of which constitutes the principal industry of the country. The School of Forestry at Evois has furnished to him much precise information in regard to the organisation of the service, and the legislation and the statistics of forests, which, added to what he had procured by his own observation, has enabled him to make a very complete study of this country, poetically designated *The Land of a Thousand Lakes*, and which might also justly be called *The Kingdom of the Forest*, for there this reigns sovereign.'

V.—Forest Lands and Forestry of Northern Russia.
Price 6s 6d.

Details are given of a trip from St. Petersburg to the forests around Petrozavodsk on Lake Onega, in the government of Olonetz; a description of the forests on that government by Mr Judrae, a forest official of high position, and of the forests of Archangel by Mr Hepworth Dixon, of Lapland, of the land of the Samoides and of Nova Zembla; of the exploitation of the forests by *Jardinage*, and of the evils of such exploitation; and of the export timber trade, and disposal of forest products. In connection with discussions of the physical geography of the region information is supplied in regard to the contour and general appearance of the country; its flora, its forests, and the palaeontological botany of the regions beyond, as viewed by Professor Heer and Count Saporta; its fauna, with notices of game, and with copious lists of coleoptera and lepidoptera, by Forst-Meister Gunther, of Petrozavodsk.

EXTRACT FROM PREFACE.—'In the spring of 1877 I published a brochure entitled *The Schools of Forestry in Europe: a Plea for the Creation of a School of Forestry in connection with the Arboretum in Edinburgh*, in which with details of the arrangements made for instruction in Forest Science in Schools of Forestry in Prussia, Saxony, Hanover, Hesse, Darmstadt, Wurtemburg, Bavaria, Austria, Poland, Russia, Finland, Sweden, France, Italy, and in Spain, and details of arrangements existing in Edinburgh for instruction in most of the subjects included amongst preliminary studies, I submitted for consideration the opinion, "that with the acquisition of this Arboretum, and with the existing arrangements for study in the University of Edinburgh, and in the Watt Institution and School of Arts, there are required only facilities for the study of what is known on the Continent as Forest Science to enable these Institutions conjointly, or any one of them, with the help of the other, to take a place amongst the most completely equipped Schools of Forestry in Europe, and to undertake the training of foresters for the discharge of such duties as are now required of them in India, in our Colonies, and at home."

'This year has seen world-wide arrangements for an International Exhibition of forest products and other objects of interest connected with forestry in Edinburgh, "In the interests of forestry, and to promote a movement for the establishment of a School of Forestry in Scotland, as well as with a view of furthering and stimulating a greater improvement in the scientific management of woods in Scotland and the sister countries which has manifested itself during recent years."

'The following is one of a series of volumes published with a view to introduce into English forestal literature detailed information on some of the points on which information is supplied to students at Schools of Forestry on the Continent; and to make better known the breadth of study which is embraced in what is known there as *Forstwissenscaft*, or Forest Science.'

VI.—**French Forest Ordinance of 1669; with Historical Sketch of Previous Treatment of Forests in France. Price 4s.**

The early history of forests in France is given, with details of devastations of these going on in the first half of the seventeenth century; with a translation of the Ordinance of 1669, which is the basis of modern forest economy; and notices of forest exploitation in *Jardinage*, in *La Methode à Tire et Aire*, and in *La Methode des Compartiments*.

EXTRACT FROM PREFACE.—' "The Celebrated Forest Ordinance of 1669;" Such is the character and designation generally given at the present day to the Ordinance in question. It is known, by reputation at least, in every country on the Continent of Europe; but, so far as is known to me, it has never before been published in English dress. It may possibly be considered antiquated; but, on its first promulgation, it was welcomed, far beyond the bounds of France, as bringing life to the dead; and I know of no modern system of Forest Exploitation, based on modern Forest Science, in which I cannot trace its influence. In the most advanced of these—that for which we are indebted to Hartig and Cotta of Saxony—I see a development of it like to the development of the butterfly from what may be seen in the structure of the chrysalis; and thus am I encouraged to hope that it may prove suggestive of beneficial arrangements, even where it does not detail what it may be deemed desirable to adopt.

' In my translation I have followed an edition issued with Royal approval in 1753, with one verbal alteration to bring it into accordance with certain older approved editions, and with another verbal alteration to bring it into accordance with editions issued in 1699, 1723, 1734, and 1747.'

Translation of notice by M. DE LA GRYE for July 1883 in the *Revue des Eaux et Fôrets:* ' England, which with her immense possessions in India, in Canada, and in the Cape of Good Hope, is beyond all question a State rich in forests, has never up to the present time given to this portion of her domains more than a very moderate share of her attention; but for some years past public opinion is becoming alarmed, in view of the immense devastations which have been committed in them, and the forest question coming forward spontaneously has become the subject of numerous publications : amongst which, after the excellent monthly collection, the *Journal of Forestry and Estate Management*, comes the Translation of the Ordinance of 1669, which has just been published by Mr John Croumbie Brown. This translation of a monument of jurisprudence, well known in France, but which has never before been reproduced in English, has furnished to Mr Brown an opportunity of giving a historical sketch of French Forest Legislation, and an exposition of the different methods of exploitation followed in our country. Drawn from the best sources, and commented on with talent, these documents form an elegant volume, which the author has made the more complete by binding with it a summary of the treatise he has published on the Forests of England.'

VII. —Pine Plantations on Sand Wastes in France. Price 7s.

In this are detailed the appearances presented by the Landes of the Gironde before and after culture, and the Landes of La Sologne; the legislation and literature of France in regard to the planting of the Landes with trees; the characteristics of the sand wastes; the natural history, culture, and exploitation of the maritime pine, and of the Scots fir; and the diseases and injurious influences to which the maritime pine is subject.

EXTRACTS FROM PREFACE.—'The preparation of this volume for the press was undertaken in consequence of a statement in the *Standard and Mail*, a Capetown paper, of the 22d July 1876, to the effect that in the estimates submitted to Parliament £1000 had been put down for the Cape Flats, it was supposed with a view to its being employed in carrying out planting operations as a means of reclaiming the sandy tracts beyond Salt River.

'This volume was originally compiled in view of what seemed to be required at the Cape of Good Hope. It has been revised and printed now, as a contribution towards a renewed enterprise to arrest and utilise sand-wastes which stretch from Table Mountain to the Hottentot Holland Mountains; and additional information is forthcoming if it should be desired.'

VIII.—Reboisement in France; or, Records of the Replanting of the Alps, the Cevennes, and the Pyrenees, with Trees, Herbage, and Bush, with a view to arresting and preventing the destructive consequences of torrents. Price 12s.

In this are given a *résume* of Surell's study of Alpine torrents, of the literature of France relative to Alpine torrents, and of remedial measures which have been proposed for adoption to prevent the disastrous consequences following from them—translations of documents and enactments, showing what legislative and executive measures have been taken by the Government of France in connection with *réboisement* as a remedial application against destructive torrents—and details in regard to the past, present, and prospective aspects of the work.

EXTRACT FROM PREFACE.—' In a treatise on the Hydrology of South Africa I have given details of destructive effects of torrential floods at the Cape of Good Hope and Natal, and referred to the measures adopted in France to prevent the occurrence of similar disastrous floods there. The attention of the Legislative Assembly at the Cape of Good Hope was, last year, called by one of the members of the Assembly to the importance of planting trees on unproductive Crown lands. On learning that this had been done I addressed to the editor of the *Cape Argus* a communication, of which the following is a copy :—

' "I have before me details of destructive effects of torrents which have occurred since I left the Colony in the beginning of 1867. Towards the close of that year there occurred one, the damage occasioned by which to roads and to house property at Port Elizabeth alone was estimated at from £25,000 to £30,000. Within a year thereafter a similar destructive torrent occurred at Natal, in regard to which it was stated that the damage done to public works alone was estimated at £50,000, while the loss to private persons was estimated variously from £50,000 to £100,000. In the following year, 1869, a torrent in the Western Province occasioned the fall of a railway bridge, which issued in loss of life and loss of property, and personal injuries, for one case alone of which the railway proprietors were prosecuted for damages amounting to £5000. In Beaufort West a deluge of rain washed down the dam, and the next year the town was flooded by the waters of the Gamko; and the next year, 1871, Victoria West was visited with a similar disaster. Such are the sums and the damages with which we have to deal in connection with this question, as it affects the case; and these are only the most remarkable torrents of the several years referred to. I have spoken of millions of francs being spent on *réboisement* in France, and some may be ready to cry out, ' Nothing like such an expenditure can be undertaken at the Cape!' Perhaps not; but the losses occasioned by the torrents seem to amount at present to about a million of francs *in the year*. This falls in a great measure on individuals, that would fall on the community; and the community in return would benefit by water retained to fertilize the earth, instead of being lost in the sea, and by firewood and timber being grown where now there is none. These are facts well deserving of consideration in the discussion of the expediency of planting Crown lands with trees."

'Towards the close of last year, 1874, still more disastrous effects were produced by torrential floods. According to the report given by one of the Colonial newspapers, the damages done could not be estimated at much less than £300,000. According to the report given by another, the damage done to public works alone was estimated at £350,000,—*eight millions, seven hundred and fifty thousand francs.* And my attention was called anew to the subject.

'On addressing myself to M. Faré, Director-General of the Administration of Forests in France, there was afforded to me every facility I could desire for extending and verifying the information I had previously collected in regard to the works of *reboisement* to which I have referred. Copies of additional documents were supplied to me, with copies of works sanctioned by the Administration, and arrangements were made for my visiting and inspecting, with every assistance required, the works begun and the works completed; and thus I have been enabled to submit a much more complete report than it would otherwise have been in my power to produce.

'While the compilation I have prepared owes its publication at this time to the occurrence of the inundations of last year at the Cape of Good Hope, the publication has been undertaken in the hope that in other countries besides South Africa the information may be turned to practical account.'

Translation of extract from letter to the author by M. ALEXANDRE SURELL, *Ingenieur des Ponts et Chausses*, chairman of the *Compagnie des Chemins des Fer du Midi et du Canal lateral à la Garonne*, and author of *Etude sur les Torrents des Hautes-Alps, Ouvrage Couronne par l'Academie des Sciences en 1842* :—' You are rendering an eminent service to society in calling the attention of serious thinkers to the subject of *reboisements* and *gazonnements*. It is a vital question affecting our descendants, specially in southern climates, there are useful truths which have to be diffused there, and you have fulfilled this duty amongst your countrymen.

'In France public opinion, long indifferent, is now sufficiently enlightened on the question, and much has been done.

'I have been able to establish in the course of a recent journey that, throughout a great part of Switzerland, in Styria, in Carinthia, and in the Tyrol, the same phenomena which have issued in the desolation of our French Alps are beginning to produce the same effects. There have been recognised a number of extinct torrents which had originated in the destruction of the forests. If people go on sleeping, and the administration or the communes do nothing to arrest the evil, posterity will have a sad inheritance devolved upon it.

'You have given, with very great clearness, a *résumé* of what I have done in France, be it by my works, or be it by my workings, for the regeneration of our mountains.'

Translation of extract from letter by the late M. Ernest Cézanne, *Ingenieur des Ponts et Chausses, Représentant des Hautes Alpes à l'Assemblée Nationale*, and author of *Une Suite* to the work of M. Surell. 'The post brought to me yesterday your very interesting volume on *Réboisement*. I at once betook myself to the perusal of it; and I am surprised that a foreigner could digest so completely such a collection of our French documents drawn from so many diverse sources. The problem of *réboisement and the regeneration of the mountains* is one of the most interesting which man has to solve, but it requires time and money, and with the authorities and political assemblies, technical knowledge which is as yet but very sparingly possessed. It is by books so substantial as yours, sir, that public opinion can be prepared to face the importance of this great work.'

IX.—Hydrology of South Africa; or Details of the Former Hydrographic Condition of Cape of Good Hope, and of Causes of its Present Aridity, with Suggestions of Appropriate Remedies for this Aridity. Price 10s.

In this the desiccation of South Africa, from pre-Adamic times to the present day, is traced by indications supplied by geological formations, by the physical geography or the general contour of the country, and by arborescent productions in the interior, with results confirmatory of the opinion that the appropriate remedies are irrigation, arboriculture, and an improved forest economy: or the erection of dams to prevent the escape of a portion of the rainfall to the sea—the abandonment or restriction of the burning of the herbage and bush in connection with pastoral and agricultural operations—the conservation and extension of existing forests—and the adoption of measures similar to the *réboisement* and *gazonnement* carried out in France, with a view to prevent the formation of torrents, and the destruction of property occasioned by them.

M. Jules Clavé, of world-wide reputation as a student of Forest Science, wrote in the *Revue des Deux Mondes* of 1st May 1882:—

[*Translated.*] 'Since the first travels of Livingstone, the African continent, hitherto inaccessible, has been attacked on all points at once. By the north, and by the south, by the east, and by the west, hardy explorers have penetrated it, traversed it, and have dragged from it some of its secrets. Travellers have paid tribute and done their work in opening up a path; it is now for science and civilisation to do theirs, in studying the problems which present themselves for investigation; and in drawing in the current of general circulations the peoples and lands, which appear as if destined to stand outside; and in causing to contribute to the increase of social wealth the elements of production previously unknown. Thus are we led to receive with interest works which can throw a new light on the condition of regions which may have been known for a long time, and which make known the conditions of their prosperity. It is under this title that the work of the Rev. J. C. Brown on the *Hydrology of South Africa* appears deserving of notice ; but it is so also from other points of view. Mr Brown, after a previous residence in the colony of the Cape, whither he had been sent in 1844 as a missionary and head of a religious congregation, returned thither in 1863 as Professor of Botany in the College of South Africa, and he remained there some years. In both of these positions he had occasion to travel through the colony in all directions, and had opportunities to collect most valuable information in regard to its physical geography. Mr Brown on going out to the Cape knew nothing of the works which had for their object to determine the influence of forests on the climate, on the quantity of rain, and on the river-courses in Europe ; he had never heard mention of the work of M. Surell on the torrents of the Alps, or of that of M. Mathieu on forest meteorology, nor of those of M. Domontzey, Costa de Bastelica, and so many others on the subject of *reboisement ;* and yet in studying by himself, and without bias, the climatic condition of South Africa, he came to perceive that the disturbances in the regularity of the flow of rivers within the historic period should be attributed in a large measure to the destruction of forests ; and he meets in agreement on this point the *savants* whose names have been mentioned. We have thought it might not be without interest to readers of the *Revue* to have in the lines of Mr Brown a collection of phenomena which, in their manifestation at any specified point are not less due to general causes, the effects of which may be to make themselves felt everywhere where there may be existent the same conditions than to aught else.' And there follows a lengthened article in illustration.

X.—Water Supply of South Africa, and Facilities for the Storage of it. Price 18s 6d.

In this volume are detailed meteorological observations on the humidity of the air and the rainfall, on clouds, and winds, and thunder-storms; sources from which is derived the supply of moisture which is at present available for agricultural operations in the Colony of the Cape of Good Hope and regions beyond, embracing the atmosphere, the rainfall, rivers, fountains, subterranean streams and reservoirs, and the sea ; and the supply of water and facilities for the storage of it in each of the divisions of the colony

—in Basutoland, in the Orange River Free State, in Griqualand West, in the Transvaal Territory, in Zululand, at Natal, and in the Transkei Territory.

EXTRACT FROM PREFACE.—'Appended to the Report of the Colonial Botanist at the Cape of Good Hope for 1866 was an abstract of a Memoir prepared on the Hydrology of South Africa, which has since been embodied in a volume which has been published on that subject, and an abstract of a Memoir prepared on Irrigation and its application to agricultural operations in South Africa, which embraced a Report on the Water Supply of the Colony; its sources, its quantity, the modes of irrigation required in different circumstances, the facilities for the adoption of these in different districts, and the difficulties, physical and other, in the way of works of extensive irrigation being carried out there, and the means of accomplishing these which are at command.

'In the following volume is embodied that portion of the Memoir which related to the water supply, and the existing facilities for the storage of this, with reports relative to this which were subsequently received, and similar information in regard to lands beyond the Colony of the Cape of Good Hope, which it has been sought to connect with the Colony by federation, or otherwise; and the information relative to irrigation has been transferred to a Report on the Rivers of the Colony, and the means of controlling floods, of preventing inundations, of regulating the flow of rivers, and utilising the water by irrigation otherwise.

'In the series of volumes to which this belongs its place is immediately after that on the *Hydrology of South Africa*, which contains details of the former hydrographic condition of the Cape of Good Hope, and of causes of its present aridity, *with suggestions of appropriate remedies for this aridity;* and it has been prepared to show that, not in a vague and general use of the terms, but in strict accordance with the statement, the severe, protracted, and extensive droughts, and destructive floods and inundations, recorded in the former volume, find their counterpart in constantly alternating droughts and deluges in every district of the Colony,—and that, in every so-called division of it, notwithstanding the deluges, there were protracted sufferings from drought, and, notwithstanding the aridity, there is a supply of water at command, with existing facilities for the storage of the superabundant supply which at present proves productive of more evil than good.'

Statement by Reviewer in *European Mail:*—' Dr Brown is well known at the Cape, for in the exercise of his duties he travelled over the principal part of it, and much, if not indeed the substance, of the bulky volume before us, has been before the Cape public in the form of Reports to the local Government. As these reports have been commented upon over and over again by the local press there is little left for us to say beyond the fact that the author reiterates his opinion that the only panacea for the drought is to erect dams and other irrigation works for the storage of water when the rains come down. There can be no doubt that this is sage and wholesome advice, and the only question is, who is to sustain the expense? Not long ago, somewhere about the time that Dr Brown was prosecuting his labours, it will be remembered that General Wynard said that "Nature had furnished the cups if only science would take the trouble to make them secure." It is but to repeat an oft-told story that with a good supply of water South Africa would be one of the finest of nature's gardens, and would be capable of producing two crops a year, in addition to furnishing fodder for sheep and cattle. The question of the water supply for irrigation and other purposes has been staved off year after year, and nothing has been done. It is not too much to say, however, that the question must make itself felt, as it is one of the chief factors in the ultimate prosperity of South Africa. The author is evidently in love with his subject, and has contributed a mass of facts to Hydrology which will be useful to all countries of an arid character.'

XI.—Forests and Moisture; or Effects of Forests on Humidity of Climate. Price 10s.

In this are given details of phenomena of vegetation on which the meteorological effects of forests affecting the humidity of climate depend—of the effects of forests on the humidity of the atmosphere, and on the humidity of the ground, on marshes, on the moisture of a wide expanse of country, on the local rainfall, and on rivers—and of the correspondence between the distribution of the rainfall and of forests—the measure of correspondence between the distribution of the rainfall and that of forests—the distribution of the rainfall dependent on geographical position, or determined by the contour of a country—the distribution of forests affected by the distribution of the rainfall—and the local effects of forests on the distribution of the rainfall within the forest district.

EXTRACTS FROM PREFACE.—' This volume is one of a series. In the first of the series—a volume entitled—published last year, *Hydrology of South Africa; or, Details of the Former Hydrographic Condition of the Cape of Good Hope and of Causes of its recent Aridity, with Suggestions of appropriate Remedies for this Aridity.*

'This volume, on the effects of forests on the humidity of the atmosphere and the ground, follows supplying illustrations of the reasonableness of the suggestion made in regard to the conservation and extension of forests as a subordinate means of arresting and counteracting the deseccation and aridity of the country.'

EXTRACTS FROM LETTERS to the author from the late Hon. George P. Marsh, Minister of the United States at Rome, and author of *The Earth as Modified by Human Action*:—'I am extremely obliged to you for a copy of your *Réboisement in France*, just received by post. I hope the work may have a wide circulation. . . . Few things are more needed in the economy of our time than the judicious administration of the forest, and your very valuable writings cannot fail to excite a powerful influence in the right direction. . . .

'I have received your interesting letter of the 5th inst., with the valuable MSS. which accompanied it. I will make excerpts from the latter, and return it to you soon. I hope the very important facts you mention concerning the effect of plantations on the island of Ascension will be duly verified.

. . . 'I put very little faith in *old* meteorological observations, and, for that matter, not much in *new*. So much depends on local circumstances, on the position of instruments, &c.—on *station*, in short, that it is only on the principle of the tendency of some to balance each other that we can trust to the registers of observers not *known* to be trained to scientific accuracy. Even in observatories of repute, meteorological instruments are seldom properly hung and guarded from disturbing causes. Beyond all, the observations on the absorption of heat and vapour at small distances from the ground show that thermometers are almost always hung too high to be of any value as indicating the temperature of the stratum of the atmosphere in which men live and plants grow, and in most tables, particularly old ones, we have no information as to whether the thermometer was hung five feet or fifty feet from the ground, or whether it was in any way protected from heat radiated from near objects.'

EXTRACT LETTER from the late Professor Henry, of the Smithsonian Institution, Washington:—'The subject of Forest Culture and its influence on rainfall is, just at this time, attracting much attention in the United States. At the last meeting of the American Association for the advancement of science a committee was appointed to memorialise Congress with reference to it. Several of the Western States Governments have enacted laws and offered premiums in regard to it. The United States Agricultural Department has collected statistics bearing on the question, and we have referred your letter to that establishment.

'The only contribution that the Smithsonian Institution has made to the subject is that of a series of rain-fall tables, comprising all the observations that have been made in regard to the rainfall in the United States since the settlement of the country; a copy of this we have sent to your address.

'It may be proper to state that we have commenced a new epoch, and have, since the publication of the tables in question, distributed several hundred rain gauges in addition to those previously used, and to those which have been provided by the Government in connection with the signal service.'

These notices and remarks are cited as indicative of the importance which is being attached to the subject discussed.

EXTRACT FROM LETTER to the author from Lieut.-Col. J. Campbell Walker, Conservator of Forests, Madras, then Conservator-in-Chief of Forests, New Zealand; author of *Report on State Forests and Forest Management in Germany and Austria* :—' I am in receipt of yours, along with the notices of your works on Forestry, by book post. I think very highly of the scope of the works, and feel sure that they and similar works will supply a want much felt by the Indian forest officers.

' It contains many important data which I should have vainly sought elsewhere, and it will be regarded by all competent judges as a real substantial contribution to a knowledge of the existing surface, and the changes which, from known or unknown causes, that surface is fast undergoing.'

Copies of any of these Works will be sent post-paid to any address within direct Postal communication with Britain, on receipt by Dr JOHN C. BROWN, Haddington, of a Post-Office Order for the price.

HYDROLOGY OF SOUTH AFRICA;

OR DETAILS OF THE FORMER HYDROGRAPHIC CONDITION OF THE CAPE OF GOOD HOPE,

AND OF CAUSES OF ITS PRESENT ARIDITY,

WITH SUGGESTIONS OF APPROPRIATE REMEDIES FOR THIS ARIDITY.

COMPILED BY

JOHN CROUMBIE BROWN, LL.D.,

*Formerly Government Botanist at the Cape of Good Hope and Professor of
Botany in the South African College, Capetown,
Honorary Vice-President of the African Institute of Paris,
Fellow of the Royal Geographical Society,
Fellow of the Linnean Society, &c.*

HENRY S. KING & CO.,
65 CORNHILL, AND 12 PATERNOSTER ROW, LONDON.
1875.

ALL RIGHTS RESERVED.

CONTENTS AND ARGUMENT.

	PAGE
PREFACE,	1

INTRODUCTION 7
    States how the subject of the Hydrology of South Africa came under the consideration of the Author, gives his experience of drought at the Cape (p. 8); and of deluges (p. 12); and observations of the similarity of several districts to features of the Lake Districts of North America and of Finland (p. 14).

PART I.—FORMER HYDROGRAPHIC CONDITION OF SOUTH AFRICA, . 18

CHAPTER I.—*Testimony supplied by the Physical Geography of South Africa,* 18
    Describes the general contour of South Africa (p. 18); specifies at greater length similarities to features of the Lake Districts of North America and to Finland (p. 21); adduces indications that the land had been long under water, and that valleys specified had been created by the flow of ocean-currents (p. 27); describes the composition of Table Mountain (p. 31); and draws the conclusion from the physical geography of the locality that the land must have upheaven from the bottom of the ocean, and, it may be, have been again submerged and subsequently upheaven, and this done oftener than once (p. 33).

CHAPTER II.—*Testimony in regard to the former Geographical condition of South Africa supplied by Geological Observations,* . 35

SECTION I.—*Geological Formations of Table Mountain,* . . 37
    States that these belong to the Primary, Metamorphic, Silurian, and Devonian formations (p. 38); supplies indications of the land having been for ages of untold duration at the bottom of the ocean (p. 47); and quotes descriptions given by Hugh Miller of what may be supposed to have then been the state of the ocean (p. 57).

SECTION II.—*Geological Formations less ancient than those of Table Mountain,* 62
    Refers successively to the lower and upper karoo shales, with imbedded fossils, indicative of the existence of dry land (p. 62); to trap conglomerate rocks, indicative of volcanic eruptions (p. 64); and dicynodon fossils, indicative of the existence of extensive lakes—quotes description given by Hugh Miller of the supposed condition of land at this period (p. 68), and description given by Page of coal deposits (p. 69); cites account given by Dr Grey, of Cradock, of carboniferous deposits in the vicinity of dicynodon beds (p. 75); and refers successively to new red sand stone formations (p. 78), oolitic formations (p. 80), tertiary deposits (p. 82), boulder formations (p. 85), and the drying up of the Great Sahara (p. 88).

PREFACE.

This Volume owes its publication in some measure to the phrase Postal University having come under my notice in a passage in a review, which appeared in the *Spectator*, of a work by Mr George Baden-Powell, entitled "New Homes for the Old Country," of which the following is an extract :—

"The squatters or landed proprietors of Australia are mainly drawn from the highest class of immigrants, and have generally received some, at least, of the elements of a liberal education; but they enter, many of them, on their new work very young, and find themselves at certain seasons of the year with ample leisure, but, as Mr Baden-Powell remarks, separated by their new life from all the centres of learning:

"'Could they but bridge over this separation by means of the post, they might continue to do a modified amount of work on some useful subject. A Board of professors forms the centre of the system, and all the instruction is carried on by letter. The idea might further be elaborated into examinations, and even to the granting of degrees. Peculiarly and immediately useful would be the study of engineering, and of veterinary science, of natural history, of law, and many other matters of immense benefit to the dwellers in the bush. And a young "super," by devoting any leisure hours, more especially of his first three or four years, to the study of veterinary science, would assuredly become a far better manager of cattle, sheep, and horses, than if his knowledge of the subject were confined to limited personal experience. The value of runs, again, is greatly enhanced by the proper storage of water, by the erection of dams, and by judicious clearing and planting. For such purposes engineering, geology, and botany, practical and to the point, may prove of immense use. In short, many are the branches of knowledge which might be successfully studied by the means of such instructors, and which in the end would prove invaluable to the success of the squatter. A postal university might be made to form an efficient substitute for training colleges, which would be of little use in a country where the requisite amount of leisure time at the disposal of the would-be students is so broken and uncertain that their attendance would be an impossibility, even though we leave out of the question altogether the immense distance they would have to journey to any fixed centre. *Reading by post* could be carried on at any available opportunity, and at any distance from the central courts.'"

In connection with this it is said :—

"Sydney possesses a University of its own, at which, however, at present, it is impossible to get that real University education whose chief charm lies not so much in the book-learning that it gives as in that mutual intercourse and rubbing together of those of every character with learned, clever, and good men, which proves so useful in after life. New South Wales, though fortunate in possessing the services of several clever professors, is as yet too young to provide a sufficiently large number of undergraduates.

"Situated on the top of a neighbouring eminence, the University Buildings form a conspicuous and handsome feature in the Sydney landscape, and closer inspection will show them to be of very high order with regard to size, plan, material, and finish.

"The happy idea of starting what may be called a *Postal University* has lately claimed attention. Such method of education should prove an immense boon to Australia. Thousands and thousands of miles of bush country are held by the squatters, and their work, necessarily of a very isolated character, is mainly in the hands of young men, most of whom have entered on its life fresh from school and full of aspirations. At times they have a great amount of leisure on their hands, and this a large majority of them would probably be very glad to devote to self-improvement. At school their minds have been trained; thus they know the way of working, but their new life separates them from all centres of learning."

Such was the statement of Mr Baden-Powell. On seeing this I addressed to the editor of the *Colonies* a letter on the subject, of which the following is the substance :—

"The term Postal University is new to me, but the desideratum is not. For some years I held the chair of Botany in the South African College, Capetown, and in professional tours which I made throughout the colony and districts beyond its limits, I met with not a few men such as are referred to, giving thought in their isolated homes to the requirements of the country for the development of its resources and its capabilities, and giving willing labour to the perfecting of devices which could only be entertained in ignorance of what was well known to practical and scientific men in Europe.

"On some of the tours which I made, I gave field-lectures on the vegetable products of the locality, which were attended by numbers varying from fifteen to eighty; and not a few availed themselves of the opportunity thus afforded to them to propound questions of considerable importance to the interests of the colony—questions relating not only to economic botany, but to mining, to metallurgy, to motive force developed in connection with magnetism and electricity, and to other subjects.

"On other tours I encouraged arrangements being made for open public conferences on subjects connected with agriculture, arboriculture, and irrigation. These were attended by still greater numbers; and information was given and obtained on a wide range of subjects. On one occasion, at an isolated farm, some twelve or fifteen miles from Montague, from twenty to thirty farmers met me, and the conference was continued, with a short intermission for refreshments, from 10 a.m. till 5 p.m. At these conferences there occurred sometimes an adjournment in a body to the vineyard, the water leading, or the dam, for the purpose of testing information given, and continuing the discussion in view of facts and phenomena referred to.

"Subjects broached at the field lectures and conferences were discussed more fully in letters, which were franked at the Colonial Office. Copies of these letters were appended to annual reports to the government which I made as Colonial Botanist. These were printed and submitted to both Houses of Parliament, by command of the governor, and a number of copies were put into circulation on loan, while copies were sent to officials and others, who might desire to possess copies for reference.

"The following list of these shows the kind of subjects upon which information was sought :—

"Appended to Report of Colonial Botanist for 1863—(1) Memoir on the Conservation and Extension of the Forests as a means of counteracting disastrous consequences following the destruction of Bush and Herbage by Fire. (2) Report on the Capetown Botanic Gardens. (3) Copies of Letters to and from the Colonial Botanist on subjects connected with the Development of the Resources of the Colony, viz.: 1. Letters from and to the Rev. T. D. Philip Hankey on Destruction of Orange Trees; 2. Letter to the Rev. P. Smail, Bathurst, on the Rust in Wheat; 3. Letter, sent in triplicate, to A. N. Ella, Esq., Queen's Town, F. W. Hopley, Esq., Burgersdorp, and D. Arnot, Esq., Colesberg, on Grasses and Pasture Herbs; 4. Letter to J. Mosel, Esq., Uitenhage, on the possibility of obtaining a substitute for India-Rubber or Gutta-Percha from the Milk Sap of the Euphorbia; 5. Letter to W. Lemark, Esq., Port Elizabeth, on the Growth of Chicory; 6. Letter to Mr Titterton, Kracha Kama, on the Cultivation of the Prickly Pear, with a view to the Preparation of Cochineal; 7. Letter to the Rev. T. Merrington, Bethelsdorp, on the Cultivation of the Sococtrine Aloe, and the Preparation of the Drug; 8. Letter to Mr Buckley, Knysna Forest, on the Cultivation of the Olive and Kei Apple; 9. Letter to the Rev. W. Stegmann, Adelaide, on the Spread of the Rhenoster Bush; 10. Letter to Mr Hayward, Swellendam, on the Planting of Trees by Water-Courses; 11. Letter to the Rev. J. Brownlee, King William's Town, on Plants found by him in British Kaffraria; 12. Letter to Dr Harvey, Professor of Botany, Trinity College, Dublin, on South African Plants; 13. Letter to John A. Merrington, Esq., on Irrigation, Arboriculture, Wine-Making, the Utilization of Night-Soil, and the Collecting of Salt as supplying Remunerative Employment for Capital.

PREFACE.

'Appended to Report of Colonial Botanist for 1864.—(1) Letter to J. A. Merrington, Esq., London, on the Sour, the Sweet, and the Mixed Veldts, and the Karoo, on their Agricultural Capabilities, and on the Employment of Irrigation, Arboriculture, Agricultural Machinery, and Manure, as means of developing these. (2) Letter to the same, in answer to the question —Can we increase the number of Vegetable Productions of South Africa, or can we render those already obtained more valuable?—including notices of Lindseed Oil, Colza Oil, Mustard, Chicory, Beet, Tobacco, Wine, Euphorbia Sap, Aloes, Timber, Maize-Fibre, Olives, Castor Oil, Myrtle-Berry, Wax, Keurboom Gum, Buchu, and Indigo. (3) Letter to the same, on the improvement of the manufacture of Cape Aloes. (4) Letter to the same, on the preparation of Ebonite and Vulcanite from the milk sap of the Euphorbia. (5) Letter to the same, on the improvement of the Cape Wines. (6) Letter to the same, on the importance of the establishment of an experimental farm, with a view to the development of the agricultural resources of the Colony. (7) Letter to J. H. Davis, Esq., J.P., Coleaberg, on Grasses and Herbage, found on the Sour, the Sweet, and the Mixed Veldts, and the Karoo. (8) Letter to F. W. Hoply, Esq., M.L.A., Burghersdorp, sent in duplicate to A. N. Ella, Esq., Queen's Town, on Pasture Herbs and Grasses of the districts of Albert and Queen's Town. (9) Letter to John Dickson, Esq., Port Elizabeth, on Grasses adapted to arrest drifting sands. (10) Letter to F. Tudhope, Esq., Graham's Town, on the question—Whether good or evil preponderates in the results obtained by burning the veldt? embodying an illustration of the improbability of the pastoral condition of the Colony being perpetuated by the practice. (11) Letter to Dr Harvey, Professor of Botany, Trinity College, Dublin, on South African Plants. (12) Letter to James Chapman, Esq., Cape Town, on the Welwitschia mirabilis. (13) Circular addressed to Missionaries labouring in South Africa beyond the Colony, requesting their co-operation in extending the acquaintance of botanists with the flora of South Africa. (14) Report on the accommodation provided for the herbarium of the late Dr Pappe, and on the expediency of providing accommodation for a museum of South African Vegetable Economic Products. (15) Letter to the Honourable the Colonial Secretary on measures calculated to develope the vegetable resources of the Colony.

"Appended to Report of Colonial Botanist for 1865.—(1) Letter to G. A. T. de Graaff, Esq., Hon. Secretary to Mossel Bay Agricultural Society, on Experimental Farms adapted to the wants of the Colony. (2) Report on the Potato Disease, submitted in accordance with the desire of Select Committees of Legislative Council. (3) Report on Rusts and other destructive growths on Cereals. (4) Report on the Destruction of Orange Trees in the Colony, with special notices of the Scale, the Soot-like substance, and the Ants and other Insects found upon diseased Orange Trees, and of the probable cause of the evil, and the remedy. (5) Report on the Destruction of Chesnut Trees and Walnut Trees in different parts of the Colony. (6) Report on the Blight affecting Apple Trees in the Colony. (7) Letter to E. V. Williams, Esq., Simon's Town, on the affection of Peach Trees. (8) Letters to Albert Kennedy, Esq., Land Surveyor, Humansdorp, on the arrest of Drifting Sand, and on planting the same with Trees. (9) Letter to J. F. J. Wrensch, Esq., Sec. to Divisional Council of district of Albert, on Trees deemed suitable for culture in that and similar districts. (10) Letter to J. H. L Schumann, Esq., Aberdeen, South Africa, on Trees deemed suitable for culture in the Karoo and Sweetveldt, and on raising Trees from Seeds. (11) Letter to E. L. Layard, Esq., Cape Town, on Trees deemed suitable for culture at Cape L'Agulhas and other districts exposed to a strong sea breeze. (12) Letter to Dr Mueller, Government Botanist and Director of Melbourne Botanic Gardens, relative to Shrubs and Trees used at the Cape for Fences, Avenues, and Burying-grounds. (13) Letter to Walter G. Fry, Esq., Victoria Tanery, Bristol relative to Tannin-yielding Plants growing in the Colony. (14) Letter to D. D. Williamson, Esq., Manager of the North British Rubber Company, Edinburgh, on the utilisation of Milk-sap of the Euphorbia. (15) Letter to the Rev. Mr Rousseau, Clanwilliam, on the Culture and Manufacture of Indigo. (16) Circular relative to facilities for Irrigation in different parts of the colony.

Appended to Report of Colonial Botanist for 1866.—(1) List of South African Trees, Shrubs, and Arborescent Herbs—upon the natural history, or botanic characters, or economic uses of which a report is forthcoming if necessary. (2) Abstract of memoir prepared on the Forests and Forest Lands of Southern Africa. (3) Abstract of memoir prepared on the Forest Economy of the Colony. (4) Abstract of memoir prepared on Arboriculture in the Colony. (5) Abstract of memoir prepared on the Hydrology of Southern Africa. (6) Abstract of memoir prepared on Irrigation, and its application to agricultural operations in South Africa. (7) Observations on the agricultural capabilities of the Colony, and requirements for the development of these: A resumé of the results and observations made during tenure of office in the years 1863, 1864, 1865, and 1866. (8) Copy of circular relative to South African Plants desired by the Directors of Botanic Gardens in Europe and elsewhere.

"Such are subjects on which information has been desired and transmitted by post in one colony, and it may be inferred that corresponding information will be desired in others.

"The desideratum might be supplied in part by the publication of a series of treatises on discoveries of modern science applicable to the development of colonial settlements, printed in small type and on thin paper, that they may be transmitted by book-post from the place of publication if need be to wherever they may be required. In such treatises it would be desirable that all statements in other works cited should be quoted in full, as those for whose perusal they are designed live far from cities, have not access to works of reference, and rarely have an opportunity of entering a bookseller's shop.

"More efficiently would the desideratum be supplied if arrangements were also made for answering queries. This might easily be done by combining with the publication of such treatises as have been referred to the publication of other works calculated to meet the craving of colonists having little access to general literature, issuing the whole periodically, keeping each number within a specified postal weight, and bringing each up to this by appended sheets appropriated to answers to correspondents, and by encouraging subscriptions for the whole by annual pre-payment by post-office orders. There is not an outstation to which letters can be sent to which these could not be sent from London, the postage being substituted, if necessary, for the trade allowance to booksellers.

"In the absence of any such arrangements, may I submit to your consideration the expediency of making the *Colonies* a medium for such communication? What I attempted to do single-handed at the Cape might be done much more efficiently and extensively by the editor of a newspaper or periodical extensively circulated in the colonies, published in London, where access could be had to sources of valuable information on subjects connected with the practical application of science to the physical development of nature. I do not conceal from myself that it would be unreasonable to expect that professional counsel would always be obtained by the conductors simply for the asking; and I question whether any increase of circulation which would result from arrangements for obtaining information from professional men on all subjects, on which information might be desired, would cover the expenditure which would be incurred in procuring this.

"This is one of the considerations on the ground of which I would recommend the publication of treatises with the provision for answering queries."

Practical effect has not been given to the suggestion, nor is it deemed probable that it would be found remunerative to do so; but it may be some one may be able to give a practicable and remunerative form to the idea suggested to me by the proposal of Mr Baden-Powell; and having had of late some time at my command, I have, partly with a view to supply an indication of the kind of treatises which I consider to be likely to meet the case of such colonists, of the character described by him, with whom I have had correspondence or personal intercourse, recast the materials I had collected on the Hydrology of Southern Africa and embodied in the Memoir on that subject referred to above, in which the desiccation of South Africa from pre-Adamic times to the present day is traced by indications supplied by geological formations, by the physical geography or general contour of the country, and by arborescent productions in the interior, with results confirmatory of the opinion that the appropriate remedies are irrigation, arboriculture, and an improved forest economy; and in recasting this I have added information which has in the interval come into my possession. The treatise, even in its present form, is designed primarily for the benefit of colonists at the Cape of Good Hope, but it embodies information which may be useful in other lands beside South Africa. In view of what I have stated in regard to the difficulties experienced about stations and getting access to works cited, I have quoted in full many passages to which it might have sufficed to refer in a treatise designed primarily for readers otherwise situated. In doing so, I have availed myself gladly of permission given to me by the Hon. George P. Marsh, minister of the United States of America at Rome, to quote freely from his valuable work, "The Earth as

Modified by Human Action," and of permission to do so from a valuable paper by Mr J. Fox Wilson on the desiccation of the Valley of the Orange River, read before a Meeting of the Royal Geographical Society. I have also quoted largely from the works of Dr Livingstone and others.

If encouragement offers, the publication of this will be followed by the publication of one or more of similar treatises on the following subjects, which have been prepared with a view to being ultimately deposited in manuscript in the Public Library in Capetown, Cape of Good Hope, for consultation by scientific and practical men desiring the information they contain, but which will admit of introduction into the text, or of additions in the form of foot-notes, of such illustrations or explanations as may appear to be desirable to meet the requirements of colonists and residents in localities in which it is difficult to get access to the various sources of information open to those who dwell in towns and older settled lands :

1. *Reboisement* in France : or, the Replanting of Forests on the Alps and Pyrenees and Mountains of Central France, with a view thereby to prevent the occurrence or the destructive effects and consequences of torrents.

2. *Sylviculture* in Belgium, with a study of the Dunes or Sand-hills in Belgium, Holland, and France, and of the arrest and utilization of the drift-sands of the Gironde by plantations of trees.

3. *Die Bewaldung* of the Karst, in Illyria : or, the re-foresting of the country, with a view thereby to restore fertility to a land reduced to sterility through the destruction of trees.

4. The Forest Economy of Russia, and the arrangements which are there being made to introduce the improved forest mangement of the day.

5. The Forest Economy of Finland, and arrangements which have there been made to carry out a systematic management of forests, in accordance with the requirements of Forest Science.

6. The Forest Economy of Sweden, in which country the latest arrangements suggested by discourses of Forest Science are being introduced and vigorously carried out.

7. Forest Science and Forest Economy of France.

8. Forest Administration in Germany.

9. Improved Forest Management in India and Burmah, illustrative of the practicability of introducing with success into the management of colonial forests measures suggested by the most advanced Forest Science of the day.

10. Forest Lands and Forest Management in Great Britain and Ireland.

11. American Forests, and treatment of forests in the United States, in the British Dominion of Canada, in Honduras, and in British Guiana.

On the subject of Forest Science, which these treatises were designed to unfold, I find the following statement by Dr Hooker quoted in a number of the "Journal of Applied Science" for August 1872 :—

"Forestry, a subject so utterly neglected in this country that we are forced to send all candidates for forest appointments in India to France or Germany for instruction, both in theory and practice, holds on the continent an honourable and even a distinguished place amongst the branches of a liberal education. In the estimation of an average Briton, forests are of infinitely less importance than the game they shelter, and it is not long since the wanton destruction of a fine young tree was considered a venial offence compared with the snaring of a pheasant or rabbit. Wherever the English rule extends, with the single exception of India, the same apathy, or at least inaction, prevails. In South Africa, according to the colonial botanists' report, millions of acres have been made desert, and more are being made desert annually, through the destruction of the indigenous forests; in Demerara the useful timber trees have all been removed from accessible regions, and no care or thought given to planting others; from Trinidad we have the same story; in New Zealand there is not now a good Kauri pine to be found near the coast, and 1 believe that the annals of almost every English colony would repeat the tale of wilful wanton waste and improvidence. On the other hand, in France, Prussia, Switzerland, Austria, and Russia, the forests and waste lands are the subjects of devoted attention on the part of the Government, and colleges, provided with a complete staff of accomplished professors, train youths of good birth and education to the duties of state foresters. Nor, in the case of France is this law confined to the mother country; the Algerian forests are worked with scrupulous solicitude, and the collections of vegetable produce from the French colonies of New Caledonia, &c., in the permanent museum at Paris contain specimens which abound in evidence of their forest products being all diligently explored."

I accept the statement of what has occurred and of what is going on in South Africa as a legitimate inference from what is stated in the reports in question, by any one looking only to the effects of trees by retaining humidity in the soil and atmosphere, and modulating the rainfall; but I hold that herbage and grass produce similar effects, less only in degree to those produced by arborescent vegetation, which, I doubt not, will be generally admitted; and in accepting the statement cited, I do so on the understanding that the effects referred to are attributable to the destruction of indigenous forests, together with the destruction of herbage and grass, effected both chiefly by fire—chiefly, but not exclusively, the axe having aided the fire in the destruction of forests, and sheep having aided the fire in the destruction of herbage and grass.

Besides the treatises mentioned, memoirs or treatises on the following subjects have been placed at the command of the Government at the Cape of Good Hope, any or all of which are forthcoming if ever publication should be desired:—

1. The Water Supply of South Africa: Its sources, its quantity, the modes of irrigation required in different circumstances, the facilities for the adoption of these in different districts, and the difficulties, physical and other, in the way of works of extensive irrigation being carried out at the Cape, and the means of accomplishing these which are at command.

2. Forests and forest lands of South Africa.

3. South African trees, arborescent shrubs, and bushes described under their popular names in English, Dutch, Kaffir, Sechuana, and Hottentot, arranged alphabetically, with notices designed to present in phraseology intelligible to readers unacquainted with botanic terms what has been learned in regard to the natural history of each, and in regard to the economical uses to which it is applied.

4. Arboriculture in South Africa, with details of what has been done, and of what might be done in planting trees in the Cape colony, with notices of the natural history of Australian and European trees which have been recommended by arboriculturists for plantation there.

5. Agricultural capabilities of the Cape of Good Hope, and measures adapted to the development of these.

6. The Herbage and Grasses of the Cape of Good Hope, with notices of economic uses to which many may be applied, and Guide to the Study of Botany in newly-settled lands.

Haddington,   JOHN C. BROWN.

HYDROLOGY OF SOUTH AFRICA.

INTRODUCTION.

THE conclusions at which I have arrived, from a somewhat extensive knowledge of the physical geography and of the history of South Africa, is, that after having been long a portion of the basin of the sea, and after, it may be, repeated upheavals and submersions of the land, in whole or in part, it has been upheaved from the depth of the sea, drained, dried by evaporation, and covered with vegetation, much of which has been destroyed by man, and the removal of this has permitted a freer evaporation, the effect of which has been a drying up of lakes, and a diminished flow of streamlets and streams within the memory of the present inhabitants, with the somewhat frequent occurrence of destructive torrents carrying off to the sea water hurriedly precipitated from the atmosphere in thunder showers, leaving an arid atmosphere and a desiccated land.

The aridity which has been thus produced is unfavourable to the culture of cereal and other plants, which those who now inhabit the land desire to raise, and it is sought by artificial means to secure the moisture desired. Experience has proved the efficiency of some of these, and it is proposed greatly to extend the application of them. I think it probable that the diffusion of the knowledge of observations by which the views stated have been suggested, or confirmed, may tend to give confidence in the measures proposed—suggest, it may be, modifications of these, whereby their efficiency may be increased—and suggest the adoption also of other measures, whereby the accomplishment of the end in view may be promoted. Under this impression the following statements have been prepared for the press. I do not consider a knowledge of the past former condition of the country requisite to enable a man of intelligence to devise means of turning to account, in horticultural or agricultural operations, what water and moisture are still at command, or to enable legislators and others to form a trustworthy opinion in regard to the expediency of giving or withholding the assistance of the Government, as representative of the community, in the carrying out of measures of extensive application proposed as means of so doing. But such knowledge, though not absolutely required, may be useful, and, though not desired, it may be acceptable and valued when freely given; and provision having been made by Parliament for the employment of a hydraulic engineer, with a view to irrigation works being afterwards undertaken, I offer the information I possess as a contribution towards the formation of an enlightened public opinion on the subject.

The information thus submitted should be tested by its accordance with fact, and I have no desire it should be treated otherwise; it is the truth alone which I desire should be discovered. But in view of the importance which I attach to the discovery of the truth, whatever the truth may be, I would fain secure for my statements an attentive perusal and calm consideration; and for the information of those who are interested in the measure proposed but know me not, I shall state the circumstances in which I gave attention to the subject, and thus indicate the oportunities I have had of studying some of the phases which it presents.

In the autumn of 1844 I went to the Cape of Good Hope, at the instance of the directors of the London Missionary Society, to take the pastoral charge of a congregation in Cape Town, while passing through the transition from their connection with that Society to a position of self-reliance and independence which they wished to acquire—the Congregational Church now meeting for worship in Caledon Square.

This being accomplished, I took occasion in 1847 to make the tour of the Colony. While passing through the Karroo, I witnessed the privations to which the inhabitants were subjected through the aridity of the climate.

My recollections of the journey call up vividly even now oft-recurring visions of bones of oxen at varying distances along the road—the bones of oxen which had succumbed by the way travelling in a land where no water is. And they call up incidents more definitely declarative of the characteristic of the land, amongst which are the following:

At one place at which we arrived on a Saturday we learned that beyond that place there was no water to be obtained within a distance of 84 miles on the road to Beaufort—whither we were bound—and we found this to be the case. Resting the horses on the Sabbath, when we resumed our journey we started before day-break, and managed by night-fall to reach the fountain, but water the horses touched not by the way.

The day following we had at midday to send our horses six miles off the road to slake their thirst while we rested, letting them browse by the way in going and coming, the *achter reiters* driving them slowly, very slowly along, that they might not be unfitted for resuming the journey on their return.

At a farm house, at which towards evening we were, in accordance with colonial hospitality, welcomed and served with tea, I, inconsiderately perhaps, but stay-at-home travellers will say very naturally, said I would be obliged if they would give me also a little bread. "Bread," said the farmer, "we have not seen bread for nearly three years." "Why, how is that?" said I. "Because of the drought," was the reply, "we cannot raise corn" (the name given in the Colony to wheat). "Then what do you raise?" I asked, "Nothing," said the farmer, "we have occasionally had showers, and after these we have sown beans and they grew; but scarcely were they above the ground when they died away." "Then what do you eat?" "Mutton." "But what do you eat with the mutton." "Mutton." "What do you mean?" "I mean what I say, we eat the fat with the lean and the lean with the fat, and so do the best we can."

A more extended acquaintance with the Colony showed me that though such privations as thus indicated might be rare, they were not unknown in other parts. From a missionary of the Wesleyan body, who had been stationed in Great Namaqualand, I learned that while he was there it was only by a six weeks journey that he could procure flour for his family, and *that* a journey made with difficulty. The statement with which this was followed is now recalled, eight-and-twenty years after it was made, and there may be slight inaccuracies in my report of it, though I do not see this to be possible. It was substantially this, that they could not grow wheat and had to send into the Colony for flour, and in doing so their waggons had to be got across the Orange River, where there was neither ford nor ferry. They sent on the waggon a boat; the waggon was taken to pieces on the bank of the river; the boat was launched; the waggon was carried across piece by piece, and when reconstructed on the colonial side of the river, the journey to the nearest village was resumed. Supplies having been obtained, in returning the same operation had to be gone through in re-crossing the Orange River, and the supplies carried across in a similar way; six weeks in all being in general consumed in the journey to and from the Colony.

Dry and arid as was the Karroo, I was told that within a few days after a thundershower it is clothed with verdure on every spot on which this may have fallen; and if the rain were copious, within perhaps three weeks thereafter it would be studded with flowers, many of them of exquisite beauty, delicate in structure, and brilliant in hue. So copious at times, I was told, are the showers which fall in connection with a thunderstorm, that they deluge the land. Shortly before it had happened, I was told, that the inhabitants of a village which was named to me, but the name of which I have forgotten, were roused during the night by the noise of a rush of waters threatening to carry all before them, and one man stepping to the door to see what it might be, found himself on crossing the threshold more than knee deep in the stream, and scarcely able to maintain his footing against its flow. And I subsequently witnessed what satisfied me of the verisimilitude of what I had heard. I was on one of my journeys overtaken in a Kloof by a thunderstorm, in little more than five minutes the road was a river, the waters rushing along with a rapidity such as is seldom seen in a river-bed, and from six to ten inches in depth from bank to bank.

In accordance with this is the testimony of others. The late Dr Rubidge, of Port Elizabeth, in a paper on Irrigation and tree planting, which appeared in a volume entitled *The Cape and its People*, published in 1869, says, " In October 1866, I passed over the bare plains between the Milk River and Graaffreinnet just after a heavy shower of rain. The "by-road" was running knee-deep, in every hollow was a fine running stream, while the gullies were great torrents now, which in a few hours you could pass dry shod. Yet most of these channels presented spots where much of the water that was rushing uselessly and destructively to the sea might have been stored.

" It was sad to contrast the beautiful orchards, vineyards, and corn fields we had just left with the dreary monotonous flats, and to reflect that all that was wanting to convert that wilderness into a smiling garden, was speeding away to swell the rivers into dangerous torrents, and carrying along with it some of the most fertile soil of the country."

Similar were my feelings in witnessing what I did on the journey to which I am now referring. While I witnessed what I have detailed, it appeared to me, that it was quite practicable greatly to modify the condition of the Colony and of its inhabitants, by a proper storage of the waters which fell from the heavens during the rainy seasons in districts in which these annually occur, and the water which fell in thunder showers, and tropical torrents of rain in districts in which annual rainy seasons were unknown.

It seemed to me that the country offered considerable facilities for storing up such waters. There might be difficulties to be overcome, but I knew of nothing great which has been accomplished by man without difficulty. It might be difficult to get labourers; it might be difficult to carry to them needed provisions for their support while engaged in the work; it might be difficult to find the money required; and it might be difficult to do a hundred other things. But the practical questions resolved themselves into two, Was it practicable? and, Would it pay? On the latter point I was not then, nor am I now, in possession of the data necessary for a solution of the question, and therefore I could not speak. But in answer to the first I could say I see no physical hindrance which may not with reasonable effort be overcome; and on my return to Capetown I communicated to others the impressions I had received of the practicability of greatly modifying the effects there produced by the aridity of the climate.

It was known to many that I had given attention to several branches of physical science, and before I left the colony I received a communication from the Secretary of the South African College, stating that he was instructed by the Committee of Council to offer to me the appointment of interim Professor in the College. The number and nature of my engagements at the time prevented me from accepting the appointment; but in 1863, on the death of the Colonial Botanist, who was also Professor of Botany in the South African College, I was invited to return and undertake the duties of these offices, which I did.

While in Scotland I had for years filled the chair of Botany in University and King's College, Aberdeen; and I was pleased to have an opportunity of studying the rich flora of the Cape, with the facilities for doing so which such appointments supplied.

I had scarcely entered upon the discharge of the duties of my office as Colonial Botanist at the Cape,—which office, originally established in the year 1858, was created with the two-fold object, 1st, Of ascertaining and making generally known the economic resources of the Colony as regards its indigenous vegetable productions and its fitness for the growth of valuable exotic trees and other plants; and 2nd, Of perfecting our knowledge of the flora of South Africa, and thus contributing to the advance of botanical science—when I found it necessary to make an extensive tour of observation, that I might acquire a general idea of the physical geography of the Colony, its capabilities and its productions, make the acquaintance of practical and scientific men resident in different districts, and endeavour to raise up everywhere a body of intelligent observers of the vegetation of the country.

In the course of this tour I passed through the divisions of Stellenbosch, Paarl, Tulbagh, Caledon, Swellendam, Riversdale, Mossel Bay, George, Knysna, Humansdorp, Uitenbage, Albany, and Victoria East, British Kaffraria, the divisions of Queen's Town and Burghersdorp, the landdrosdy of Philippolis, and the divisions of Colesberg, Middleburg, Cradock, Bedford, Alexandria, and Port Elizabeth, whence I returned by sea, having been prevented by the state of the Fish River from carrying out arrangements I had made for visiting Somerset East, Pearston, Graaff-Reinet, Aberdeen, Beaufort, Dyselsdorp, Oudtshoorn, Amandelboom, Montagu, Robertson, and Worcester.

The villages, of which the three last named villages are centres, and the district of Clanwilliam, I had afterwards an opportunity of visiting, some of them oftener than once, and most of the others I had previously visited.

In the course of that tour I found in very many places—I had almost said everywhere—lamentations over the consequences of a severe and long-continued drought from which the Colony was suffering, though rain had then fallen and was falling in torrents, and reviving hope was beginning to cheer the drooping spirits of the community.

Of this drought, which had reached its climax in the preceding year, I received the most saddening accounts. It prevailed not only throughout the Colony, but far beyond it. In the tropical regions of the Great Lakes it was felt. In the district of the Lesuto, which is generally blessed with abundance of rain, it was severely felt,—the vast grassy plains being changed into deserts of sand. Clouds which appeared passed away, and clouds of dust took their place. The largest streams ceased to flow. At one place the Orange River could be stepped across by a child, and after a time it ran dry in some parts of its course, exposing in its bed near Hopetown the remains of a waggon which had been lost in a sudden flood while crossing the river some thirty years before.

Within the Colony cattle died by the thousand, and many of the farmers had lost more than half their substance. I heard of lambs being killed in hundreds, lest both they and the dams should perish if these were allowed to suckle them.

At Colesberg cabbage was sold at a penny the leaf; and there was shown to me a bundle of fodder, which I grasped with my forefinger and thumb, which was kept as a memorial specimen of what had been sold for *half-a-crown* each. I was there told of travellers—one of them a personal friend of my own—having had, on a journey to Hopetown, to stop again and again and rest, till by a few handfuls of grass roots, gathered from the ground, the horses were refreshed. I was told that at Bloomfontein emaciated horses had been seen—by my informant, if I remember aright,—hanging about the doors of stores while the floors of these were being swept, returning again and again when driven away, and afterwards tearing and eating old gunny bags and sheets of paper swept to the street.

I was told that many were anticipating absolute ruin, and possibly death by starvation, as the probable effects of the drought, when the rain came to their relief.

My previous experiences in Africa enabled me to enter into the feelings which were described to me; and sometimes while listening to details of privation and suffering I was reminded of the Word of the Lord that came to Jeremiah concerning the dearth—"Judah mourneth, and the gates thereof languish; they are black unto the ground; and the cry of Jerusalem is gone up. And their nobles have sent their little ones to the waters; they came to the pits, and found no water; they returned with their vessels empty; they were ashamed and confounded, and covered their heads. Because the ground is chapt, for there was no rain in the earth, the plowmen were ashamed, they covered their heads. Yea, the hind also calved in the field and forsook it, because there was no grass. And the wild asses did stand in the high places, they snuffed up the wind like dragons; their eyes did fail, because there was no grass."—Jer. xiv. 2–6.

At other times I was reminded of what is recorded of the sufferings endured during the three years drought which occurred in the reign of Ahab, illustrated, incidentally as they are, by the reply of the widow woman whom Elijah saw gathering sticks, and to whom he called and said,—"Fetch me, I pray thee, a little water in a vessel, that I may drink. And as she was going to fetch it, he called to her, and said, Bring me, I pray thee, a morsel of bread in thine hand. And she said, As the Lord thy God liveth, I have not a cake, but a handful of meal in a barrel, and a little oil in a cruise: and, behold, I am gathering two sticks, that I may go in and dress it for me and my son, that we may eat it and die."—1 Kings xvii. 10–12. In connection with this we read that after three years and six months of continued drought, during which there seemed to be neither rain nor dew, "Ahab the king called Obadiah, who was the governor of his house, and said unto him, Go into the land, unto all fountains of water, unto all brooks; peradventure we may find grass to save the horses and mules alive, that we lose not all the beasts. So they divided the land between them, to pass throughout it: Ahab went one way by himself, and Obadiah went another way by himself."—1 Kings xviii. 5–6. These are life-pictures to one who is conversant with farm life in South Africa, and with the droughts which prevail; and the narrative is suggestive of details of what many a farmer at the Cape had to say to his sons, and his sons-in-law, and his herds, during the drought to which reference is made.

But the similarity does not stop here. In the one case as in the other, the long-continued drought issued in torrents of rain. In the one case, as we read, in the hour of extremity "Elijah said to Ahab, get thee up, eat and drink; for there is a sound of abundance of rain. So Ahab went up to eat and drink: and Elijah went up to the top of Carmel; and he cast himself down upon the earth, and put his face between his knees, and said to his servant, Go up now look towards the sea. And he went up, and looked, and said, there is nothing. And he said, Go again seven times. And it came to pass, at the seventh time, that he said, Behold, there ariseth a little cloud out of the sea, like a man's hand. And he said, Go up, say unto Ahab, Prepare thy chariot and get thee down, that the rain stop thee not. And it came to pass, in the meanwhile, that the heaven was black with clouds and wind, and there was a great rain."—1 Kings xvii. 41–45.

So was it then, and so has it often been seen at the Cape, after the drought, a deluge. Some cases of this I shall afterwards have occasion to detail, at present I confine myself to what I experienced and witnessed on the tour which I then made.

Everywhere I found that there had been copious rains, in some places torrents. For days I was confined to the house by drenching rains, which made the roads rivers. I met the Government Railway Engineer returning from the Eastern Province, at a farm house near Caledon at which we both outspanned, by whom I was told that I should find the roads in the Lang Kloof impassable for the vehicle in which I travelled, the clay in many places having been converted into mud three feet deep, the surface of which caked and hardened would in all probability, like rotten ice, again and again give way, and my horses would be unable to drag out my conveyance. My informant had himself only got through by the strength of his team, which was double that which I drove, and his vehicle lighter by one-half.

I did get safely through, but I saw evidence of the correctness of my informant's observations.

At Riversdale I was detained forty-eight hours by the state of the river. The crossings of the Kroom River I found to be not unaccompanied with danger.

In approaching Van Staden's River I found one-half of the breadth of the road converted into a deep gully, leaving not breadth enough for my cart; and we passed it by letting one horse drag the cart, with one wheel on the road, the driver and I holding it level by bearing up the other. The Van Staden's River I found in flood, and I got through only by the help of a hired team.

At Grahamstown I was prevented day after day by rains from making excursions for botanical observations in the neighbourhood; and I learned that the Fish River was so full that to go to Kaffraria by Fort Peddie, as was my intention, was impracticable.

Leaving Grahamstown for Fort Beaufort I passed a streamlet where, during my sojourn of a few days at Grahamstown, a post-rider had been drowned in attempting to cross.

Further on my way, I found the Fish River had so flooded the road by its side that in the middle of the highway the water was some eighteen or twenty inches above the axle of my cart.

The Buffalo River I crossed with difficulty at a ford where a few hours before, and again a few hours later, it was impassable for man and beast.

Leaving Queenstown for Burghersdorp, I travelled over ground high and dry, where within a few weeks before two farmers had been drowned.

I had adventures more ludicrous than perilous in the course of my tour. One of these occurred shortly after this in my ascent of Pen Hoek. The surface of the road was soft clay, which had been brought to something like the consistency of cream, by the abundant or rather superabundant rain, and some three inches deep covered clay, somewhat more tenacious but not less slippery to the foot. Ere we reached the top of the pass, my horses, tired of sprawling, the four feet of each going sometimes in as many directions, refused to go one step further. A friend from Queenstown, who had kindly accompanied me so far, to see me beyond all danger, asked me to mount his horse while he tried what could be done with mine. I had scarcely mounted when his horse quietly and deliberately lay down on its side, giving me time to withdraw my foot from the stirrup, but then throwing me flat on my back in the mud. It was raining hard, and happily I had on a waterproof topcoat and waterproof splatterdashes. But the horses in the cart would neither be coaxed nor scolded, fondled nor flogged, to put forth another effort; and we made the hills around to ring again with the noise of our laughter. "Stop," said my friend, "I'll make them go!" and tying the tail of his horse to the head of one of mine in such a way that if his advanced mine must either follow or die; causing my driver to mount the cart and take the reins; and taking his horses by the head, he and the driver gave simultaneously a tremendous shout, shook the reins and made an unearthly commotion, under which the horses took to their feet as if the cry had been, "Woe betides the hindmost!" I followed, encased in clay, and we stopped not till in this fashion we cleared the pass! Whatever may have been the drought and however long it may have lasted, there was no lack of rain then! At Burghersdorp I found the Civil Commissioner, after having been twice to the river, had given up all expectation of my being able to cross it.

On my return from beyond the Orange River, I re-crossed the Fish River, but within forty-eight hours after I had done so and was safely housed in Cradock, it was tearing along full from bank to bank impassable.

In proceeding to Bedford I had to cross the Tarka. But on the banks of the Tarka I was, along with many others, detained several days, the river which the day before that on which I was to have crossed might almost have been crossed dryshod, having come down in the afternoon, and continuing day after day to rush and roar and tear along in a torrent, ranging in depth as shown by the figures on the unfinished bridge from twenty to four-and-twenty feet. Not deeming it expedient to remain longer, I was at length conveyed across in something like an old soap-box suspended from a strong rope attached to trees on the opposite banks, and to which were attached cords by which it could be drawn from the one bank to the other, conveying the mails when the river was in such a condition.

My sensations, when suspended between heaven and earth above a roaring torrent, were something different from any I had previously experienced. But a gentleman well-known in the Eastern Province, who left Grahamstown for King William's Town about the same time I did, but by another route, must have had more to tell of his sensations than I, if what was told me be true. I was informed that he had to cross the Buffalo in a way similar to that in which I had to cross the Tarka; but there the conveyance was a basket and not a box, and there were no cords attached to it whereby it could be drawn from the one bank to the other, but the passenger had by a hand-over-hand movement, on the suspending rope, to pull himself and the basket across; and this rope was not quite so tight as that by which I was suspended. Getting into the basket and being somewhat corpulent, his weight distended the rope into a beautiful curve, and the basket and he almost flew half way towards the further shore; but there it stopped! the slope of the rope made it equally difficult to go forward or to return, the weight of the aerial voyager, which so greatly facilitated his passage thither, seemed to say to his basket or to himself, what Canute is said to have said to the sea, "Thus far but no further, and here shall thy proud course be stayed." At length, by strenuous effort, the further bank was reached in safety. My transit was comparatively a pleasant flight; but both speak of the abundance of rain which had fallen.

I proceeded to Adelaide and Bedford *en route* for Somerset and Graaff-Reinet. But at Bedford I was again detained through the Fish River being again impassable. It had come down and had continued to flow for a great many days, I think ten days or a fortnight, and that with a current so impetuous that the ferrymen had refused a fare of £10 to carry across a medical practitioner, whose services were required on the further side; and there being no appearance of subsidence, I had to abandon my purpose of crossing it, and to change entirely my route in returning to the Western Province.

Hearing everywhere of the drought, and seeing the deluges of water rushing in torrents to the sea, I was often ready to cry out, Wherefore is this waste? and the feeling prompting to this was the more intense that almost everywhere I saw facilities for preventing this, and indications that formerly the water was not so lost to the land. In elucidation of this remark, I must state I had previously travelled both in Finland and in the lake district of North America, and in many of the districts through which I passed in the Colony of the Cape I was reminded by what I then saw of what I had seen in these lands; in these lands were lakes of water—some of them like inland seas in extent,—in the country through which I was passing there were none; but there were what looked like basins of lakes, which it required no effort of the imagination to picture as filled with water, though then drained and dry.

The lakes of North America cover an area of 84,000 square miles; nearly a fourth part of the whole area of Canada; and two-fifths of the whole area of Finland are covered by lakes, a hundred of which may sometimes be seen in the course of a single day's journey. Lake Superior, in America, covers an area of 31,000 square miles, the others are of corresponding extent. In Finland—called by its inhabitants, The Land of a Thousand Lakes, and The Lost Daughter of the Sea—they are smaller, but of a magnitude not to be despised : one measures nearly 30 miles long by 30 miles broad, and Lake Ladoga, through which its waters flow in their progress to the sea, covers 6190 square miles, an area equal nearly to the whole principality of Wales. And such were the scenes recalled by what I saw of the general contour of the colony as I journed from place to place; but what was seen spoke of this as having been the case long, long ago. Now all was changed; the waters had all escaped and the dry basin alone remained, with, in some cases, gorges through which the waters had poured in seeking a lower level, and finally made their escape.

I considered that it not only came within the sphere of my duties as Colonial Botanist to give attention to such subjects, but that, in accordance with the primary object for which that office was created, as stated in the communication made to me when I received the appointment, and which I have quoted,—that "of ascertaining and making generally known the economic resources of the Colony as regards its indigenous vegetable productions, and its fitness for the growth of valuable exotic trees and other plants,"—the moisture and supply of water available, or which might be made available, for agricultural and horticultural purposes, was one to which, in the peculiar circumstances of the Colony, I ought to give special attention; and I did so in all my tours in the Colony.

In my official report for 1866 I reported—"In my capacity of Professor of Botany in the South African College, I am required to deliver, annually, a course of lectures on Botany at that season of the year which is least favourable to the prosecution of my other official duties. I have twice in the course of the year reported myself ready to do this if a class could be formed; but on neither occasion did a class offer. I also publicly intimated during the severe drought which prevailed in the beginning of the year that I was prepared to lecture in any place in the Colony, however remote it might be, on the causes of the aridity of South Africa, and on the remedies which could be applied, and to hold conferences on the subject, either in the lecture-room or on the veldt, on condition that my travelling expenses should be met, either by several applicants for my services conjointly, or by one and another as I moved from place to place. This measure was carried out in whole or in part at Capetown, Wynberg, Koeberg, Stellenbosch, Frensche Hoek, Worcester, Robertson, and Montagu.

"At Cradock and some other places my services were desired if I should come within the bounds of the Eastern Province. Arrangements were made for my free conveyance through the district of Namaqualand, if I could get to Clanwilliam. An offer was made to me of free conveyance throughout an extensive tour from Mossel Bay, if I could find my way thither. And on the occasion of a conference on irrigation being held at George a letter was addressed to the Colonial Office by the Civil Commissioner of Mossel Bay, in which that officer wrote as follows:—

"'By a resolution of the Mossel Bay Agricultural Society I have been desired to solicit the official attendance of Dr Brown, the Colonial Botanist, if he would kindly come, at the meeting of delegates from other societies at George, invited for the purpose of discussing a scheme for irrigation, and model farms which the Mossel Bay Society intends to offer for criticism and improvement. This meeting will take place about the 7th March, during the combined agricultural show for George, Oudtshoorn, and Mossel Bay divisions.

"'Such a suitable opportunity rarely occurs for the hearing of that gentleman's scientific views and suggestions for the increase of products founded on the practical observations of others. Considering that many of the farmers from four important divisions will be congregated on the occasion, the committee trust that the general benefit to be derived will justify His Excellency the Governor in graciously acceding to the request, and in incurring the small expense which will be incurred thereby. The committee had hoped to be in a position to afford the expense, but unfortunately find that the show will necessitate again an extra subscription on the part of the members. The hospitality which will be gladly shown to Dr Brown will limit his expenditure to the transport alone between Capetown and Mossel Bay.

"'In my official capacity I am of opinion that incalculable advantage to the central part of the Colony is likely to be derived from his *viva voce* lectures by the agriculturalists, who are keenly alive to their present critical state, and anxious for some practical scheme whereby labour will be made remunerative in the production of better and other articles for export and for home consumption.'

"It was intimated, in reply from the Colonial Office, that no provision was made for meeting such expense. And having thus an opportunity of showing what I have experienced in many other ways, that the salary and allowance of £400 per annum is insufficient to meet the expenses which are necessarily incurred in the discharge of the duties to which I have been called as Colonial Botanist, I presented to the Honourable the House of Assembly a petition, praying that adequate provision might be made for the discharge of these duties; but it was deemed more expedient, with a view to retrenchment, to abolish the office.

"In the report of the Colonial Botanist for 1863 in reference to a lengthened tour through the Colony which had been made that year with a view to the study of the physical geography of the Colony, and to the raising up everywhere a body of intelligent observers of the vegetation of the country, and of phenomena connected with agriculture, it is stated that having visited the more populous districts of the Colony, it was my intention to visit also the more sparsely peopled districts, and some of the missionary stations beyond the Orange River, in accordance at once with my own views of what was desirable, and with the corresponding views of the late Dr Harvey communicated in letters quoted in that report; but that the outlay I had incurred in making the tour then completed would prevent me from carrying out my intention at that time.

"When the recommendation of the select committee on retrenchment appointed by the Honourable the House of Assembly, that the office I hold should be abolished, was adopted by the House, I was engaged in correspondence relative to a journey towards the Limpopo, to be undertaken in like manner, at my own expense, in the beginning of the year, provided His Excellency the Governor should approve my going so far beyond the boundary of the Colony. This journey would have taken me through the Karroo, the country intermediate between that and the Orange River, the **Orange River Free State, the State of the Transvaal Republic** to the advanced northern limit in lat. 22° S., and either through the colony of Natal or through the country of Moselekatze and the district of the Kuruman on my return to the Colony.

"The proposed object of this journey was to obtain verifications or corrections of observations and conclusions embodied in the memoranda prepared on the Hydrology of Southern Africa, on the forest and forest lands of Southern Africa, and on the natural history of South African trees, before these should be published, and at the same time to secure a more extensive observation of South African flora. But the resolution of the Assembly to abolish, at the close of the year, the office of Colonial Botanist rendered it necessary for me to abandon at once all thoughts of prosecuting this enterprise."

Appended to this report were abstracts of several memoirs on subjects connected with the development of the agricultural capabilities of the Colony, and amongst these one on the Hydrology of South Africa,—the substance of this recast, with the addition of details of facts which have subsequently come under my notice, constitutes the substance of the following treatise.

PART I.—FORMER HYDROGRAPHIC CONDITIONS OF SOUTH AFRICA.

CHAPTER I.

TESTIMONY SUPPLIED BY THE PHYSICAL GEOGRAPHY OF SOUTH AFRICA TO THE FORMER HYDROGRAPHIC CONDITION OF THE COUNTRY.

By physical geography I understand the general contour and superficial condition of the face of the country, marked as this is by hills, and kloofs, and pláins, passes, forests, and watercourses, or what may be remarked by an intelligent traveller,—though, on the one hand, he may know nothing of geology or the structure of the earth's crust, and, on the other hand, know nothing of botany or of the characteristics of the vegetation with which it is clothed,—travelling, it may be, in pursuit of health, or in pursuit of wealth, or in pursuit of pleasure, or in pursuit of game, and of nothing else, but travelling with his eyes open and looking intelligently upon what he sees.

To derive from the physical geography of South Africa, or of any land, all the information it may be made to yield in regard to the previous hydrographic condition of the country, it is necessary to look upon it in the light of observations previously made—made, it may be, in childhood, on the muddy basin of a tidal harbour emptied by the ebb of the tide—or made, it may be by others and read of in advancing youth, or at a riper age. But there is much that is told by physical geography which may command the assent of one who has not consciously gone through any such training when what is seen is read off by another; and this is what I propose to do.

In my mind, and in the minds of many others, what is chiefly and most powerfully associated in thought with the mention of South Africa is the Cape of Good Hope, and associated with this Table Mountain, and the Devil's Hill, and the Lion's Head. We must commence our survey at some point, and we may as well commence at this point as at any other.

The tabular outline of the summit of Table Mountain, and the conical outline of the summit of the Lion's Head, as these are seen from Table Bay, are characteristic of the summits of many other isolated mountains throughout extensive districts of South Africa.

The summits of such mountains, and the summits of mountain ranges ten, twenty, or forty miles distant, are not unfrequently found to be, or they appear to be, of the same deposit. In some instances—as is the case with the so-called Gates of the Oomzimvooboo and the next mountain range beyond—they are either at the same elevation or at an elevation indicative of a continuous dip. All of these appearances are suggestive of the land having been tilted up in a mass from a subaqueous depth, the stratification or other indications of deposit from water being strongly marked, and of the intervening level valleys having been, either previously or subsequently, scooped out by the erosive action of currents.

Besides linean level valleys of great extent, there are numerous level valleys of circular outline of considerable extent, from which there is a narrow cleft-like outlet as in Tulbagh Kloof, or one less marked as at Colesberg.

These, together with much more extensive beds of deposit characterised by fossil remains of the *Dicynodon*, speak of the subsequent silting up or escape and drying up of lacustrine sheets of water.

By Bain, who gave much attention to the geology of South Africa before it commanded the attention which it has received of late years, the *Dicynodon* beds were conjectured to have been the bottom of an ancient lake or inland sea, which extended north as far at least as the Zambesi; and this now is supposed to have been one of the outlets by which its waters escaped. According to Professor Owen, there are good reasons for referring this formation to the age of the New Red Sand Stone, of which age I shall afterwards have occasion to speak.

But the draining off of the waters from the estuaries between the mountain ranges in the south, and the drying up of the lakes and filling the level valleys of circular outline, to which reference has been made, may have occurred—the former perhaps, but the latter certainly—long subsequent to that remote era. On these points we may afterwards enquire what may be learned from the records to which we are directing our attention; but that pertains to geology, and it is physical geography alone with which we have at present to do.

Dr Livingstone has read off for us much of what may be learned from the country further to the north; and there is a pleasure in being able to cite the observations of such a man.

One supposition in regard to the general contour of Southern Africa is, that it is a succession of table-lands, at several successive elevations, from the coast to the interior of the continent, where level deserts of sand, dry as dust through the effects of torrid heat, bid defiance to vegetation. But of late years this supposition has been by many abandoned, and by others it has been modified to bring it into accordance with the recorded observations of travellers and the reasonings of men of science.

Dr Livingstone, in his Narrative of an Expedition to the Zambesi and its tributaries, describing what he saw in the district of Lake Nyassa at Ndonda, where the boiling point of water showed an altitude of 3440 feet above the sea, says—"Looking westwards we perceived that which from below had the appearance of mountains was only the edge of a table-land, which, though at first undulating, soon became smooth and sloped towards the centre of the country."

Of the country in that district, after discussing the water-shed as indicated by the alleged and by the observed courses of known rivers, he says—"Some parts of the continent have been said to resemble an inverted dinner-plate. This portion seems more of the shape, if shape it has, of a wide-awake hat, with the crown a little depressed. The altitude of the brim is in some parts considerable, in others, as at Tette and the bottom of Murchison's Cataracts, it is so small that it could only be ascertained by eliminating the daily observations of the barometer by simultaneous observations on the coast and at points two or three hundred miles inland. So long as African rivers remain in what we may call the brim, they present no obstructions; but no sooner do they emerge from the higher lands than their utility is impaired by cataracts. The low-lying belt is very irregular, at times sloping up in the manner of the rim of an inverted dinner-plate, while in other cases a high ridge rises near the sea, to be succeeded by a lower district inland before we reach the central plateau. The breadth of the lowlands is sometimes as much as 300 miles, and that breadth determines the limits of navigation from the seaward."

Dr Livingstone was very careful to ascertain as certainly as possible the fact of the inclination or dip of the land towards the interior of the continent.

Not only does he record the observation made from the summit at Ndonda, where the boiling point of water showed an altitude of 3440 feet above the sea, that looking westward they perceived that what from below had the appearance of mountains was only the edge of a table-land, which, though at first undulating, soon became smooth, and sloped towards the centre of the country; "but," he subsequently writes, "We have taken pains to ascertain from the travelled Bapessa and Arabs as much as possible about the country in front, which, from the lessening time we had at our disposal, we feared we could scarcely reach, and had heard a good deal of a small lake called Bemba. As we proceeded west, we passed over the courses not only of the Loangwa, but of another stream called Moitawa or Moitala, which was represented to be the main feeder of Lake Bemba. This would be of little importance but for the fact that the considerable river Luapula, or Loapula, is said to flow out of Bemba to the westward, and then to spread out into another and much larger lake, named Moero, or Moelo. Flowing still further in the same direction, the Loapula forms Lake Mofue, or Mofu, and after this it is said to pass the town of Cazembe, bend to the north, and enter Lake Tanganyika. Whither the water went after it entered the last lake, no one would venture an assertion. But that the course indicated is the true water-shed of the whole country, we believe from the unvarying opinion of native travellers. There could be no doubt that our informants had been in the country beyond Cazembe, for they knew and described Chiefs whom we afterwards met about thirty-five or forty miles west of his town. The Lualaba is said to flow into the Loapula, and when, for the sake of testing the accuracy of the native travellers, it was asserted that all the water of the region round the town of Cazembe flowed into the Luambadzi, or Luambezi (Zambesi), they remarked with a smile, "He says that the Loapula flows into Zambesi—did you ever hear such nonsense,"—or words to that effect. We were forced to admit, that, according to native accounts, our previous impression of the Zambesi's draining the country about Cazembe's had been a mistake. Their geographical opinions are now only stated, without any further comment than that the itinerary given by the Arabs and others shows that the Loapula is twice crossed on the way to Cazembe's. We may add that we have never found any difficulty from the alleged incapacity of a negro to tell which way a river flows.

"The boiling point of water shows a descent, from the edge of the plateau to our farthest point west, of 170 feet; but this can only be considered as an approximation, and no dependence could have been placed on it, had we not had the courses of the streams to confirm this rather rough mode of ascertaining altitudes. The slope, as shown by the water-shed, was to the Loangwa of the Maravi, and towards the Moitala, or south-west west, and north-west. After we leave the feeders of Lake Nyassa, the water drains towards the centre of the continent. The course of the Kasai, a river seen during Dr Livingstone's journey to the west coast, and its feeder, was to the north-east or somewhat in the same direction. Whether the water thus drained off finds its way out by the Congo, or by the Nile, has not yet been ascertained."

The question thus raised has commanded the attention of others besides that noble man; and perhaps there has not been an observation in connection with its solution which does not add to data which may be used in determining the former hydrographical condition of South Africa, but in what has been cited there is enough for the purpose for which this has been done.

In accordance with the illustration of the contour of South Africa, as observed by Dr Livingstone, is much which may be seen within the colony of the Cape of Good Hope.

In almost every map of the colony may be seen indications of the position of successive mountain ranges, more or less parallel to one another, and more or less parallel to the coast. Between these lie plateaux of seeming level ground; and it may have been remarked, or it may be recollected when mentioned, that the mountain ranges are frequently precipitous on the seaward side, but much less, if at all, on the further side,—sometimes slanting away or sloping gradually towards the level land beyond.

Thus it is with Table Mountain—almost perpendicular where it faces Table Bay, and scarcely less so where it overlooks the camp-ground, Rondebosch and Newlands, but sloping away towards False Bay. Thus it is with the Hottentot Holland range of mountains—somewhat precipitous towards False Bay and the Atlantic, much less so towards the interior. Thus is it with many of the mountain ranges in the colony. Thus is it with the mountain range carried across the mouth of the Oomzimvooboo, in Kaffir land. The celebrated Gates of the Oomzimvooboo, or the St John's, through which the river emerges from the country behind, rise almost perpendicularly by two successive precipices of 600 feet each, to a height ascertained by measurement to be 1263 feet, but the land behind is only 1000 feet above the level of the sea, while beyond it stretches away a broken mountainous country, varying in elevation above the sea from 1000 to 800 feet. And from the descriptions I have had of mountain ranges in Natal I am led to conclude that so is it also with these. In all this there is much which is in accordance with the idea gained by Dr Livingstone from more extensive observations.

At present this is adduced as in accordance with the illustration of a wide-awake hat with the crown slightly depressed, to which I shall afterwards have occasion to revert, and which I therefore deem it expedient thus to nail down for future use, while I proceed to make another use of some of the corroborative observations which I have cited.

In all the regions near to the colony, as in the colony itself, we find the rivers flowing from the interior of the country to the sea, and there is no truer indication of the comparative elevation of land than is afforded by the waterflow, as it always flows from a higher to a lower level. But when, as is the case with the Oomsimboovoo, the river flows through an opening in a mountain range, while this gives proof that the shore is at a lower level than is the land behind, it affects not the evidence otherwise supplied that the summit of the range is at an elevation still higher than is the country through which that river has flowed in its course to the sea, and higher even than are the mountains there.

Ere that river fell into a course leading directly towards the sea, many a streamlet flowing into it must have flowed in what seemed a landward direction; and but for this outlet by the Gates, as they are called, the waters must have accumulated behind that mountain range, forming a vast inland lake, rising and increasing in depth till it began to overflow some mountain neck, when, abrading and washing away, and thus, as it were, sawing down, as doth the overflowing water of a reservoir the dam by which it is confined, and, it may be, undermining by the swirl of its waters at the outer base of the neck over which it flows—as the waters of the Niagara have done through many miles of rock—the barrier was lowered, whereby a freer and yet freer and more destructive flow of water was allowed, to the still further lowering of the restraining neck at that part over which the water flowed, and the consequent lowering of the water behind, until the barriers being swept away—ages, it may be, being required for the work—the lake became drained and its basin converted into dry land, through which the river-bed sufficed to carry off the superfluous rainfall of the district; and there is nothing improbable in the supposition that what it is likely would have been the case if this outlet had not existed may have been what actually occurred in the formation of this outlet—a lake or inland sea shut up behind finding here a way of escape, lowered the level of the outlet, and silted up the basin till the sheet of water disappeared.

The contour of many, if not of all, the plateaux lying between the mountain ranges of the Cape presents indications of something similar to this having given to them their form. I say something similar, for in many of them are indications of oceanic—as well as of lacustrine sheets of water —*floes*—as well as lakes, having at sometime filled these vales, indications of the draining off of the ocean from these ocean beds, and of the silting up of the lacustrine beds till the raising of the bottom of the lake by earthy deposits met the frotting away of the confining neck of land, and of the level required for the conversion of the lake into dry land having thus been produced.

And here a more detailed reference to the lake district of North America and to Finland may illustrate both what may temporarily—though for centuries—have been the condition of the country, and the operations or process by which this state of things was changed.

In the lake country of America to which I have referred, we have Lake Superior pouring its waters through a somewhat lengthened vale into Lake Huron, into which flow also the waters of Lake Michigan with its Green Bay—itself a lesser lake,—the waters of Nipissing Lake, and the waters of Lake Simcoe. From Lake Huron, the superabundant waters flow by the River St Clair into Lake Erie; whence, with such accessions as they have there received, they pour themselves over the falls of Niagara and flow by the Niagara River into Lake Ontario, and thence passing through the midst of the Thousand Islands, and through successive rapids in the upper bed of the St Lawrence, they find their way by that river to the sea.

Those Lakes, as has been stated, cover an area of upwards of 84,000 square miles, which is nearly one-fourth of the entire area of Canada: Lake Superior alone having an area of 31,000 square miles.

The elevation of this lake is about 627 feet above the sea. The elevation of Lake Michigan, Lake Huron, and Lake Erie, is not much less; the difference of level between Lake Erie and Lake Ontario is considerable, and at the Falls of Niagara the waters are precipitated to a depth of 163 feet.

The upper Lakes are of considerable depth, but Lake Erie is shallow and it is slowly, but gradually, becoming shallower still.

In Finland—called by its inhabitants The Land of a Thousand Lakes, and The Lost Daughter of the Sea—two-fifths of the country is covered by lakes, a hundred of which may often be met with in the course of a day's journey, and beautiful and picturesque they are. They constitute some five distinct series or water systems, the lakes and lakelets of which flow one into another as do those of the lake district of America, and they thus pour their waters through successive basins into the sea. One of these, after passing through numerous lakes and gorges in the mountains, spreads itself out into the lake of which I have spoken as being nearly 30 miles long and 20 miles broad, from which the waters flowing onward in successive rapids some few miles further down precipitate themselves through the falls of Imatra into another lake below, and find their way to Lake Ladoga, the largest lake in Europe, having, as I have stated, an area of 6190 square miles, and being nearly as large as the whole principality of Wales. Into this lake flow also the waters of Lake Onega and the waters of Lake Ilmen, while the northern extremity of Lake Onega almost connects it with Lake Sigh and the White Sea. By the Neva, which flows through St Petersburg, the waters of these lakes empty themselves into the Gulph of Finland, and the Baltic, and the ocean beyond.

Both in America and in Finland are indications of the waters having formerly stood at a higher level than they do now. At the falls of Niagara may be witnessed the comparatively recent results of the operation of the waters in eating away retaining barriers.* And the cataract is said to have

* Of the fall of Table Rock the following graphic picture was given in the *Philadelphia Bulletin.* George Wilkes writes :—

"I said I had something to do with the fall of Table Rock, that broad shell on the Canada side, which in 1850 looked over the very cauldron of the seething waters, but which tumbled into it on a certain day in the month of June of that, by me, well remembered year. About noon on that day I accompanied a lady from the Clifton House to the Falls. Arriving at Table Rock, we left our carriage, and as we approached the projecting platform I pointed out to my companion a vast crack or fissure which traversed the entire base of the rock, remarking that it had never appeared to me before. The lady almost shuddered as she looked at it, and, shrinking back, declared that she did not care about going near the edge. 'Ah,' said I, taking her hand, 'you might as well come on, now that you are here. I hardly think the rock will take a notion to fall merely because we are on it.'

"The platform jutted from the main land some sixty feet ; but, to give the visitor a still more fearful projection over the raging waters, a wooden bridge, or staging, had been thrust beyond the extreme edge for some ten feet. This terminated in a small box for visitors to stand in, and was kept in its position, and enabled to bear its weight, by a ponderous load of stone heaped upon its inner ends. The day was very bright and hot, and, it being almost lunch time at the hotels, but very few visitors were out, so we occupied the dizzy perch alone. We gazed fearfully out upon the awful waters, we stretched our heads timidly over the frightful depth below, and we felt our natures quail in every fibre by the deafening roar that seemed to saturate us, as it were, with an indefiable dread.

"'This is a terrible place,' said I. 'Look under there, and see on what a mere shell we stand. For years and years the teeth of the torrent, in that jetting, angry stream, have been gnawing at that hollow, and some day this plane must fall.'

"My companion shuddered, and drew herself together in alarm. Our eyes swept the roaring circle of the waters once again ; we gazed about in fearful receded 50 yards since the commencement of the present century. Below the falls, the river flows in a channel upwards of 150 feet deep, and 160 yards wide, which has been thus formed. And at the Falls of Imatra, in Finland, may be seen the waters tearing along through a narrow gorge to reach a lower level.

Niagara has been often described—not so the Falls of Imatra. These I visited in company with a party of friends. We reached the Falls about three o'clock in the morning. It was the last day of July, and being near the summer solstice, it was light all night. We had travelled through a lovely country; there was hill and dale, woods and water; and we had good horses and excellent roads.

After a hurried look at the Falls, I went to bed, and by six o'clock I was again at the water side. The forenoon was given to botany, to entomology, and to rest, some of us gathering flowers, while one, with the occasional aid of others, was catching butterflies, and another was taking pencil sketches of the scenery around. In the afternoon we visited a waterfall about four miles lower down, where the river empties itself into a lake. After tea, we drove to a ferry some three miles above Imatra, where we crossed the stream caleche, and horses and all, and we drove along the other side of the river to see the Falls from that side, whence only a sight of the whole at once can be obtained.

The river is like the Niagara, a stream carrying the water from an upper to a lower lake, and these parts of a chain of lakes, the level of each of which is lower than the one immediately above it. Here the upper lake is the Zydersee, an immense inland lake, which, with its ramifications and connected lakelets, may be said to divide with the land and share between them

fascination, when suddenly turning our looks upon each other, each recognized a corresponding fear. ' I do not like this place! ' exclaimed I, quickly. 'The whole base of this rock is probably disintegrated, and perhaps sits poised in a succession of steps or notches, ready to fall out and topple down at any unusual perturbation. That fissure there seems to me unusually large to-day. I think we had better leave, for I do not fancy such a finish! and, besides, my paper must be published next week.'

"With these very words—the latter uttered jocosely, though not without alarm—I seized my companion's hand, and, in obsolute panic, we fled as fast as our feet could carry us towards what might be called the shore. We first burst into a laugh when we gained the land, and, jumping into our carriage, felt actually as if we had made a fortunate escape. We rolled back towards the Clifton, but, before we had proceeded two minutes on our way, a thundering report, like the explosion of an earthquake, burst upon us, and with a loud roar the ground trembled beneath our wheels. We turned to find that Table Rock had fallen. We were the last upon it, and it was doubtless the unusual perturbation caused by our flying footsteps that disturbed the exactitude of its equilibrium, and threw it from its final poise.

"In a minute more the road was filled with hurrying people, and during the following half-hour we were told a hundred times in advance of the next morning journals, that a lady and gentleman who were on the Table Rock had gone down the Falls. We are told that the trot of a dog would shake old London Bridge from end to end, when it would not be disturbed by the rolling wheels of heavily loaded trains. Table Rock had not been run upon in the way I have been describing for years—perhaps never—and therefore, whenever I hear it spoken of, I always shudder and feel as if I had something to do with its fall."

Leaving this to speak for itself, I may state that I have witnessed the effect produced by the fall of this rock, having visited the Falls in 1836, and again in 1873.

the whole extent of Finland. The lower, as has been intimated, is connected with Lake Ladoga, whence flows the Neva into the Gulf of Finland, which opens into the Baltic.

Like the Falls of Niagara, the Falls of Imatra present an appearance differing greatly from the conception generally formed of a waterfall; but this it does in a different way. In the Falls of Niagara the immense stretch of the fall in breadth, and the great excess of this above the height of it, occasions to many a feeling of disappointment on its first being seen, which continues until the spectator is enabled to realize what the height of the fall actually is, and then what the immensity of the flow must be, seeing that it is a fall of such a breadth and of such a height. In the Falls of Imatra, we have what the spectator is at first disposed to call a rapid, rather than a waterfall; but *such* a rapid! The falls reminded me of the Falls of Clyde; but while there is a similarity, *what a difference!* Here you have Corralinn, and Stonebyres Linn with its upper and its lower fall, and much more, all combined into one continuous plunging, dashing, foaming, pouring torrent, rushing through a rocky defile, apparently exceeding half-a-mile in length. There is on the eastern side a table-rock, whence the whole can be seen in one *coup d'oeil*—or rather, I should say, whence the whole can be traced with a continuous sweep of the eye—for this cannot take in the whole at one glance. But view it whence you may there it is, the torrent like a charge of cavalry, the cavalry rushing onward—broken—trying to re-form, all the while pushing on—failing to form—rushing and plunging, dashing, foaming, roaring on, on, still on. I have seen it in sunshine and rain, at sunrise and at sunset, by moonlight and in darkness, such darkness as there was when dawn and dusk constitute a single twilight, in clear light, and with an overcast sky, and I was filled with a growing and continually expanding idea which I received of the Falls.

The vegetation of the whole locality was luxuriant. Amongst its productions were many of my countrymen—plants with which I at once claimed acquaintance, as often do townsmen and even fellow-countrymen when they meet in a strange land, though, perhaps, had they met at their home they might have passed without even a look of recognition—and with these were many which told of a foreign land, and this gave a peculiar relish to the enjoyment experienced in recognising the former by the assurance they gave that we had met in what was really a land of strangers. Amongst the most luxuriant were wild Canterbury bells, and other species of campanula, agrimony, golden rod, shepherd's rod, willow herbs great and small, tormentil, silverweed, milfoil cranberries, blaeberries, goloobitza, broosnika, and sweinelange, in abundance. Ferns were not awanting, and mosses there were in plenty, and lichens—but *such* lichens!—in number, variety, magnitude, colouring, beauty of form, and height of growth far surpassing everything in that class of plants I could previously have imagined. There were rocks—and *rocks of such magnitude!*—enamelled with them as is a field in Britain with buttercups and daisies. I brought away a *Canina peltidea*, 12 inches in diameter. With the flowers named, there were very fine knapweeds, St John's Worts, chrysanthemums in considerable variety, and exquisitely formed blue corn flowers, and cow-wheat; but the campanules and lichens were what arrested the eye—the campanules on this side, the lichens on yonder.

The village in the vicinity of the Falls is a wretched ruckle of old houses, inhabited apparently by the poorest of the poor; but I have seen more

C

than one peasant—apparently, however, peasants from a distance and Russian—not Finnish—enjoying the scenery as much as did I; one peasant I still see, now launching trees into the torrent, witnessing their sudden disappearance, watching for their reappearance, tracing their progress with the rapidity of arrows, which told of the velocity with which they were carried down the stream, and of the desire of the observer to catch yet another sight of the Sea-Serpent-like body rushing on—now standing in silent amaze: I sympathized with his feelings, both in the one case and in the other.

Not the least exciting of the adventures of the day was the crossing of the ferry, in a smooth reach between two rapids, in a large boat with trees for oars—trees cut at one end into oar-like blades, and at the other cut so as to allow of their being held and plied. There, was the rapid above threatening to come down and engulf us; and there, was the rapid below, from which, had it caught us, there was no escape, and the Falls apparently but a little way, though really some two miles, below the ferry.

Next morning I was up by six o'clock as usual, and down to the Falls; at eleven we started for Willmann Strand, distant some forty versts, on our return to the coast by another route. The scenery was lovely; it was like that of the Trossacks and that of the Cumberland Lakes combined, with some resemblance to the Thousand Isles in Lake Ontario—hills wooded to the water-edge. Such land may be unproductive to the inhabitants, but to the tourist it is most delightful to see.

Such, it seemed to me, must have been the appearances presented by what is now the Colony in some bye-gone time. Friths and inland seas converted into lakes, from which water flowed from higher to lower levels, in some places in torrents like those of the Falls of Imatra, precipitating themselves through gorges like Tulbagh Kloof, Cogmans Kloof, Dunkel Kloof, and many more; and some eating away the restraining rock as do the Falls of Niagara—lowering thus the level of the lake above, while its basin was also being silted up by the deposit of earthy matter brought from a higher level.

There remain now only the lake basin and the torrent bed, but these have a tale to tell; and I would find it difficult to read off the physical geography of the Colony without seeing the hydrographic records with which in many places it is interlined, and which in places compose the text—the geography or contour of the country, telling what it is—these records telling what has been, and in some places telling how the *had been* had been transformed into the *is*.

But many, perhaps most—nor would I greatly err if I were to say all—of the mountain ranges by which these extensive valleys are surrounded are capped with sand in regular strata, or bear other indications that they themselves must have been under water, and that for long, a part it may have been of the ocean bed, from which the whole land has been upheaven, taking in the process the peculiar contour which Livingstone has suggested. And not a few of them show in the contour of their sides such lines of slope, surmounted by precipitous cliffs, as may be naturally supposed to be the effect of the retirement of the water and the consequent withdrawal of the lateral support it had supplied. This also demands our attention.

It may have been remarked that the slope at the base of some mountains and mountain ranges present an outline similar to that which earth rolling or falling from a height to the base of a precipitous cliff or of a wall would assume; while the country beyond presents the appearance of the comparative level assumed by the basin of a frith or bay of the sea, suggestive of the thought that the valley may have, at a period subsequent, and it may be long subsequent, to the deposit of the strata capping the mountain summits, and after these were exposed high and dry, remained filled, or have been again filled with water which was subsequently drained off by the outlet; and as it subsided, the mountain sides, being deprived of the support which it afforded, scaled off, and the debris not washed away, fell into the shape of these sloping masses, filling up the angle formed by the base of the precipice and the level ground beyond.

There rise before me as I write the appearances presented by the sides of the mountains extending from Table Mountain towards Kalk Bay as something similar to what I would fain describe.

In such slopes we seem to have indications of an earlier hydrographic condition of South Africa than was that when it was a land of lakes—that of a time when it was extensively covered by the sea. It requires no great effort of imagination to picture the Flats between False Bay and Table Bay so covered, and the Table Mountain range an island; and while it requires no great effort of imagination to picture this, nothing seems more natural when we look upon the scene from an elevation on either side than to conclude that at one time—and that a time perhaps not very remote—it must have been so. Something similar to this may have been, and apparently must have been, the case with some, if not with all of those plateaux or elongated plains to which reference has been made, they appearing as marine lochs, or friths, or elongated bays, if not as straits by the shores of which the mountain ranges appeared as islands separated thus from the mainland; and the strata of sand with which many of these mountains are capped tell that they also must have been at one time covered by the sea, more, it may be, than "twenty fathoms deep."

Such are some of the teachings of physical geography, and the testimony supplied by the general contour of South Africa in regard to the previous hydrographic condition of the country. It tells of the whole as having formed part of the ocean bed; it tells of a time when the mountains towered above the surface of the sea while the valleys were covered by its waters; it tells of a time when what is now so arid and dry was once a land of lakes and torrents, with all the aspects beautiful and sublime of a land which might be characterised as a land of mountain and of flood. But we have come to a point which seems to mark the transition from testimony supplied by the Physical Geography of South Africa to the previous hydrographic condition of the country, to that afforded by Geological discoveries. We are, however, still some way from the boundary line beyond which lie the domains of geology, and of geology—pure and simple geology—alone. Though we may have, in proceeding thus far, learned a good deal of the previous hydrographic condition of South Africa, we have not exhausted the testimony on this subject supplied by the physical geography of the country, or learned all that may be learned in the course of a leisurely tour, or even in the course of a rapid and somewhat hurried tour, through the Colony of the Cape of Good Hope. There, as elsewhere, there is much to be seen by those who have eyes to see it, which speaks of the past, and which may, if questioned, tell much more of primeval times than many dream of, adding to, if not extending, our information in regard to that past.

Before the voyager making for Table Bay has reached port and has landed from his ship, he has, it may be, looked with excited feelings at what have been called the twelve apostles, on the Lion's Head, on the Devil's Hill, and last of all, as he enters the Bay, on Table Mountain, with its precipitous front facing the ocean and sheltering the town, which nestles at its base.

Reference has already been made to similarity of strata, capping mountains widely separated by intervening plains, indicating that these strata were once continuous, and to correspondence of elevation, being indicative of the intervening plain having been scooped out by ocean currents. And thus does it appear to have been the case with the valley separating the Table Mountain range from the Hottentot Holland range of mountains beyond.

It may be new to some of my readers to read of mountains being remains of elevated plateaux, indebted for their mountainous character to the washing away of the ground once continuous with them in height, leaving them a mountain ridge lining a valley, or leaving a mountain standing by itself alone in the midst of a plain; and it may seem to them incredible that it can be true.

But I have found it impossible to look upon some of the mountain ranges of South Africa without seeing that it must have been so with them. Since this observation was made, I have been informed the Professor Geikie has shown that thus have been formed many of the mountain ranges in the Highlands of Scotland; and when a boy I have seen in the mud-banks of a tidal harbour the counterpart to the process in several of its stages.

The water draining off from the mass of mud and from little basins at a higher elevation made cuttings in the level mass—like to the deep and precipitous beds of many South African rivers. But as the sides were undermined they fell; a part of what had thus fallen was carried away, but part remain in the corner between the precipitous bank and the bed of the drain; —more fell in, and more, and yet more—raising and extending the sloping mass resting against the precipitous bank by which it was surmounted, the precipitous portion being ever diminished in height and removed to a greater distance from the opposite bank. And sometimes the process went on until all trace of the surmounting precipice had disappeared, and a rounded bank separated one vunnel from the next adjacent.

Often since this was observed, in the days of my childhood, have I looked from some little eminence and seen the exact counterpart on a larger scale at some parts of its course in the banks of the Tyne which flows through East Lothian, and in some of its tributaries; I see something similar in many a map which represents a chain of hills flanked by spurs; and while I have seen in the deep precipitous banks of many a river at the Cape what looks like the first stage of what is a comparatively recently commenced water-drainage, I have seen in many of the mountain ranges of South Africa what appear to me to be obviously the production of the latter stages of such a drainage on a stupendous scale.

The magnitude of the scale upon which this presupposes that the current must have flowed may itself suggest as an objection to the supposition that it is incredible; but this objection can easly be met.

First, as to the quantity of water required for currents such as are indicated. There are in round numbers about 50 millions of square miles of the earth's surface dry land, but about 150 millions of square miles are covered with water, and observations have been made which lead to the conclusion that the average depth of the sea must be between four and five miles. There are numerous instances of lines measuring 10, 20, 30, and even 40 thousand feet having failed to give distinct evidence of their having reached the bottom. Assuming then the average depth to be four miles, there must be in the ocean 788 or nearly 800 millions of cubic miles measurement of waters, and if these cover 150 millions of square miles of the earth's surface to an average depth of between four and five miles, they would suffice to cover the whole 200 millions of square miles to a depth of between three or four miles—a depth amply sufficient to meet the demands of all that is required by the observations which have been now advanced.

And again, while the average depth of the ocean now is between four and five miles, there are depths in the ocean bed, and these in connection with ocean currents, far in excess of the difference between the elevation of linear valleys and adjacent hills. The Commander of the United States steamer, "Tuscarora," engaged in deep-sea soundings in the Pacific, reported to the secretary of the navy at Washington, under date of June 26, 1874, that the difference between two of the soundings made by him, about 100 miles east by south from Kinghasan or Sendai Bay on the east coast of Japan, was 1594 fathoms! The height of Table Mountain above the Flats is short of 4000 feet; but the next cast showed a depth beyond that which I have mentioned of upwards of 1216 fathoms!

One sounding gave a depth of 1833 fathoms, the next a depth of 3427, and in the third, "the sinker carried the wire down 4,643 fathoms without reaching the bottom, and the report states that—

"On this occasion, when some 500 fathoms of wire had run out, the sinker was suddenly swept under the ship's bottom by the strong undercurrent, and all efforts to get the wire clear and keep it from tending underneath were unavailing, the difficulty being increased by a fresh breeze and a moderately heavy sea. Finally, when 4,643 fathoms of wire had run out, and only 150 fathoms of wire were left on the reel, it broke close to the surface, and about five miles of wire were lost.

"The strain on the reel was very great, and notwithstanding a weight of 130 lbs. on the pulley line, it took three men to check and hold the drum, and the wonder was that the wire had not parted sooner. This great strain must have been due to the action of the strong undercurrent upon the sinker, sweeping it with great force from the ship, as since that cast we have sounded repeatedly in depth of more than 4,000 fathoms, and had no trouble in reaching the bottom."

It must be mentioned that there was a distance of 30 miles between the first cast and the second, and of 45 miles between the second and the third; but these distances are not greater than the distance between the Bosjesveld and the Caledon valley, and the Flats between the Hottentot Holland range and Table Mountain. And it is not unreasonable to suppose that the strong current reported by Captain Belknap had had something to do with the scooping out of the ocean valley to the depth of upwards of 2,800 fathoms more than the depth of the sounding 75 miles distant; compared with such erosion—the erosion indicated by the low level of the Flats compared with the elevation of Table Mountain and that of the Hottentot Holland range beyond is little—but though comparatively little, it must have been effected by a current of tremendous force!

It may be new to some of my readers, I have said, to learn that there are mountain ranges which have not been thrown up in their existing form, but are only the remains of land of the elevation they have, much of which has been swept away by ocean currents, leaving them standing where they are—and that they owe their mountainous character, not to their elevation above the bounding valleys, but to the scooping out of these. But it is only in accordance with what is going on even now, both on a scale, which, compared with what must have occurred here, may be called infinitely less; and on a scale, which, compared with that, may be called infinitely greater.

The abrupt termination in Table Mountain of that southermost range of elevated ground, remains of ground not washed away by the ocean current which scooped out the portion between it and the Hottentot Holland range, leaving only the Flats and some little mounds, such as Blueberg, &c., on the valley, and to some extent lowered even this mountain range, tells its own tale in addition to what has already been learned; and in doing so it tells of a change in the ocean current, of a cessation, or of a new set of an old current which had left upon it and upon the land behind its mark; or it tells of either a subsidence of the sea or of an elevation of the land, which took place either while this current was in flow, or which itself occasioned the new current, and gave to this current a new set and direction, as well it might with the extent of ocean bed affected by it, or terminated the flow by raising the land above the ocean's surface. That you may be prepared to receive and enabled to understand and to appreciate testimony on these points which it has to give, look to any little tail of sand behind a shell or pebble on the beach, and study its direction and appearance. That you may do so the more thoroughly, study the formation of others even now under the waters of a receding wave; that wave as it advanced in its pomp and grandeur like a great sea-horse with flowing mane, with dappled neck of foam, and snorting spray, levelled and washed away a hundred such; but its strength exhausted, it returns to the ocean still strong in its weakness, and restores again, as it returns to the ocean whence it came, the little hills it had washed away in the moment of its fury and its pride, or it replaces them by others scarcely to be distinguished from those it destroyed, either in form, direction, or position. And mark how this is done.

Look to the little ridge. What is its form? a precipice in miniature, with a lengthened tapering prolonged declivity behind. Are the prolonged declivities in the same or in different directions in relation to this Lilliputian precipice? Generally the same, and those which are otherwise may be said to be also the same; but the same with a difference. And what is that direction in regard to the land, or the sea, or in regard to the flow of the receding wave by which they are formed? Always in the line of the flow of the receding wave, heading towards the land, tapering towards the sea. Mark, then, how it is formed. The current washes away and bears away all sand from the front, but leaves what is behind, and deposits there also in the long tapering line much that it has brought along. The shell or stone seems to break the current, the two halves of which, separated, meet again beyond, leaving still water immediately behind the obstruction, and in this still water the sand is left, or deposited; and it seems as if what takes place on either side of the obstacle takes place over its top, or say rather, all over it, leaving not a triangular but a rounded conical-shaped still water beyond, in which the tapering tail of diminishing height finds its resting place. And here I see where the shell has fallen; the current of the returning wave is washing away the mound, but it is doing it retaining the same fashion of the little mound, undermining the front, and as the superincumbent sand falls down washing it away, and in part depositing it, in a prolongation of the tail! Well, so it is; and if you go to any streamlet you may find many little eminences of similar formation always heading up stream or against the current, with the tail in the direction of the current's flow. And something similar may be seen upon a comparatively gigantic scale in the rocks and ridges surmounted by Stirling Castle, in Stirlingshire, and surmounted by Edinburgh Castle, in Mid Lothian. Some similar current—an ocean current—four thousand feet in depth, at the very least, must have formed this. A new current in the primeval ocean, or an old current, with a new direction given to it—a current diverted, it may be, by what is now called Riebecks Casteel—then another like thing than it is now—dashing direct on the face of what is now Table Mountain, or rather of what stood before, pouring along over it, on either side and above it, undermining, washing away the debris as it topples down, the divided current pouring over and washing into shape the irregular prolonged tail beyond into the original form of the outline which it now presents, a division of the current falling over the Kloof, and threatening to level down the whole ridge, as it did that,—the remains of which form Blueberg.

But it is stopped; a new direction is again given to the current. How, we need not now enquire; or the whole was elevated above the ocean surface; and *there* is the work left—left as it was when this occurred. I write from memory, and there may be points on which I am in error; but I doubt not my statement on the whole is correct.

Looking thus at the physical geography of South Africa, we learn not only of the existence of a primeval ocean covering deep the land, and what are now the highest mountains of the land, but we learn also of ocean currents in that primeval deep, scooping out valleys, reducing mountains to the level of the plain, and of these currents diverted into new directions, leaving traces of their effects, and in these traces of their effects records of their history, which he who is learned therein may be able to read, and understand, and explain.

But we have not yet done with the lessons to be read from Table Mountain as she stands there inscribed with records, crossing each other in different directions, which tell of what occurred in those old-world times. Look at her as she stands there magnificent and glorious, whether covered with fleecy cloud, or rejoicing in the sunshine which is ever bringing out new lights and shadows, every one of which is beautiful! Look at her! she exhibits in herself a section of the crust of the earth between 3000 and 4000 feet in thickness, such as it then and there was, placed in a light and in a position which reveals far more of its structure than could have been learned by sinking a shaft or pit to a corresponding depth from the surface. There it is the whole breadth of the ridge, with an outlying flank on either side, the whole exposed to the light of day—and what do we see? Layers or strata of sand at the top, with the stratification distinctly marked; underlying these well-defined strata a mountain mass of matter, with indications of its having been deposited from and under water, resting upon granite which presents indications of its having been projected from below in a state of fusion and of intense heat through the then existing crust. And resting on the sides of this upheaven granite, we see slaty matter with well-marked indications in its slate-like structure—it also having been deposited from water like the impalpable dust born by the wind far from the spot from which it had been brought, but deposited at last. But these strata could not have been deposited on the granite with such a dip or inclination as they have, which leads us to conclude that this must have constituted a portion of the solid crust through which the granite was protruded. The superincumbent mass seems to rest on the uptilted edge of these slaty strata, and the granite protruded throughout them suggests the conclusion that these strata were deposited from water before, and the overlying deposits after, the upheaval and protrusion of the granite.

We are thus introduced into acquaintance with another set of phenomena which have also their testimony to give in regard to the Hydrology of South Africa, and if we would make a precognition of all the testimony tendered in regard to this matter; to this also we must attend. To do this fully, it is necessary that we proceed from what is known as Physical Geography into the domains of Geology. Physical geography has to do with the surface, and the contour of the earth's surface; geology has to do with the structure of what has been called the crust of the earth, and with the operations by which it has become what it is; and we are trenching apparently upon this in advancing to the consideration of what is taught in regard to the former hydrographic condition of the land by what is seen of the structure of Table Mountain. But as the border land of separation may, without impropriety, be considered as in some measure common to both, there is no imperative necessity why we should not read off the lesson from the position we have reached, and return to the record, if necessary, after we have entered on the consideration of the testimony in regard to the former hydrographic condition of the country supplied by geological observations.

We scarcely need the geologist to tell us, while we look at Table Mountain as a monument of the past, that the underlying slate tells of a slow deposit of slaty matter in minute sub-division from water scarcely coloured by it, so small the quantity, so minute the particles, and so diffused; and of the water being there then still and motionless as it was limpid and transparent. Nor can the time have been short during which such a thickness of slate was so deposited. How long it was, we cannot now enquire.

The superincumbent mass of hardened mud, thousands of feet in thickness, tells another and a different tale: it tells of muddy waters and of mud borne by the water from a distance greater or less from the spot where it has been deposited and hardened into rock. And if, as we have been led to conclude, the bed of this deposit extended continuously to the mountain ranges beyond, the intervening Flats being the result only of the washing away of what had then been deposited, what a quantity must have been suspended in the waters, and what a length of time must have been occupied in the deposit of such a mass! Language fails—thought fails—we can only muse and be silent.

And the strata of sand capping Table Mountain and the Lion's Head have also their tale to tell. It has been observed, that as in motion communicated to a quantity of loose matter in sieve or in a vessel more confined, the larger pieces came to the surface, so is it also with the shingle put in motion by a stream or by waves on the shore, and that something similar occurs with a mixture of sand and mud when subjected to movements in a similar way.

Looking at the strata of sand in the light of these observations, and in view of the fact that the mass of the mountain is composed of a mixture of sand with some impalpable matter, the thought is suggested that the strength of the current which bore thither that mass of matter suspended in its waters may have become relaxed, with the result that the sand was dropped, and the bulk of the more impalpable matter carried further. Or, either through the silting up of the basin or some other means, the mud deposited there may have been brought so near to the surface of the water as to be subjected to such movements by its waves as led to a separation of the sand from the more impalpable matter with which it was co-mingled; a large portion of this being either washed away and deposited elsewhere, or allowed to fall through the interstices between the grains of sand allowing these to come to the surface. This seems to be the more plausible conjecture of the two, but in either case the production of sand tells of the depth of water being diminished, and so diminished that the bed of the ocean is moved by the movement of the waves.

Thus are we able to carry our study of the former hydrographic condition of what is now the southern extremity of South Africa back ages beyond those in which, by denuding currents, the plains which now separate mountain ranges were scooped out. We touch upon a time when the depth of water covering what is now Table Mountain was not so deep as it had been previously, but what was there the surface of the ocean basin was subjected to movement with the movement of its waves. We look through earlier ages during which, at a greater depth, was deposited the mass of underlying mud, to a period also, it may be, extending over ages, during which in perfect stillness was deposited from comparatively pellucid waters, the slaty matter underlying that mass of mud and resting on the sides of protruded granite, the protrusion of which may have been, and probably was, connected with what led to be the vast deposit of superincumbent mud.

Thus far have we gone, and thus much have we learned, without leaving the border land common to physical geography and geology. To go further and take up the question which has thus been mooted would take us into the domains of this latter science, which has also its tale to tell, and revelations to make, in regard to the distant past; and the question which here presents itself for consideration is, Shall we, or shall we not advance?

For myself, I may state I am not a geologist, nor do I make any pretensions to be such; but I have heard what geologists have to say. I have looked at what I have seen in South Africa as I have looked on what I have seen elsewhere, in the light of what they have said. I have found what I have seen to be in wonderful accordance with what they have said; and it seems to me, in this case, that the geological formations at the Cape, when viewed in connection with the conclusions to which geologists have come after careful observation, study, comparison and reasoning on phenomena brought under their consideration in the course of their investigations, supply important testimony to the primeval hydrographic condition of this part of the earth's surface, supplying indications of the following successive positions and conditions of the land :—

First. The whole under water at the bottom of the sea.

Next. An upheaval of it till portions rose above the ocean surface.

D

Then the submersion of the whole again for ages.

The subsequent upheaval of it again to a greater elevation, and for a time so protracted that for ages the projecting islands were covered with arborescent vegetation.

And the continued upheaval, until in the course of ages what was at first a thousand isles became a continent studded with lakes and inland seas; and the continued upheaval until these were drained, and the continent presented the appearance it has now assumed—but not so arid as it now is.

To the study of the geological formations which are indicative—or, if I must so limit my phraseology, which are alleged to be indicative—of all this, I would invite such of my readers as may be willing to place themselves under my guidance in the study of the same. Others may, if they be so disposed, cross the ridge by the mountain path while we are working our way through it, and await or meet us on our arrival at the other side, when we can proceed to what may form a more interesting subject of study than this would prove to them. In other words, let them pass the next chapter, and take up the study of the subject at the beginning of the chapter which follows.

To those who are willing to go with me I would say, Come along! Now for it! Hard work it may be; but hard work has its rewards.

> " Life is real! Life is earnest!
> Let us then be up and doing,
> With a heart for any fate;
> Still achieving, still pursuing,
> Learn to labour and to wait."

CHAPTER II.

TESTIMONY IN REGARD TO THE FORMER HYDROGRAPHIC CONDITION OF SOUTH AFRICA SUPPLIED BY GEOLOGICAL OBSERVATIONS.

The historical records of South Africa are all of them of modern date, and they do not embrace a very lengthened period; with the physical geography of the country it is otherwise, and the superficial aspect of the country, its mountains and its plains, with their arborescent productions, enable us to carry our study of the Hydrology of the country back to a period very remote from the present; if we wish to carry our enquiries still further back into the distant past the means are at command. The geologist is ready to read off for us, what we may not be able to read for ourselves, of the records of the rocks—either leaving us, if we so desire, to draw our own conclusions, or stating conclusions at which his fellow-students have arrived in regard to the length of the eras embraced by these records. This may perhaps make us feel as if the records of physical geography were but the records of what occurred yesterday, and we had got back to the times of which Wisdom spoke some 3000 years ago from the mountains of Palestine, the times "When there were no depths, . . . when there were no fountains abounding with water; before the mountains were settled, and before the hills : . . . while as yet he had not made the earth, nor the fields, nor the highest part of the dust of the world; when he prepared the heavens ; . . . when he set a compass upon the face of the depth : when he established the clouds above : when he strengthened the fountains of the deep : when he gave to the sea his decree, that the waters should not pass his commandment : when he appointed the foundations of the earth."—Prov. viii. 24–29.

My attention was given those matters from a bias in favour of such studies, and a feeling that he who would tender to others counsel which is not sought, ought to see to it that he has not wittingly overlooked any of the circumstances of the case in regard to which he desires to speak, but has studied it thoroughly it all its aspects. But, it may be, that to some this chapter on the testimony in regard to the former hydrographic condition of what is now known as South Africa, supplied by geological observations, and not a little of what has been stated in the chapter relating to that supplied by the physical geography of the country, may be uninteresting; and being uninteresting to them, it may be deemed by them to be unnecessary; and I have intimated that I do not consider that it is necessary to the formation of an intelligent judgment in regard to the adaptation of remedial means, which may suggest themselves, or may be proposed, as means of counteracting the desiccation which has taken place and the aridity of climate and of soil which in consequence exists, that the matters therein discussed should be clearly apprehended. But I consider them to be matters deserving the attention of any students of the subject who may desire to have it before them in its entirety.

In writing what I have written, or rather in determining and preparing to do so, I have been reminded of what is recorded of David having in the uprightness of his heart made every preparation for the building of the temple which it was in his power to make, though to him was denied the honour of laying so much as the corner-stone of the building. But there exists no necessity for anyone perusing all that has been written, and without detriment to the opinion to be formed in regard to the practical measures to be adopted in existing circumstances, any reader may pass over all and confine his reading to what is said in Part II. relative to the different causes of the aridity of South Africa, leaving others to read, if they will, what is written in the chapters preceding.

Chaucer has said to his readers in a prologue to one of his Canterbury Tales,—

> "And therefore whoso list it not to heere,
> Turne over the leef and cheese another tale,
> For he shall find enow bothe gret and small
> Of storial thing that toucheth gentillesse,
> And eke moralite, and holinesse—
> Blame ye not me, if that ye cheese amis."

So would I say to my reader here; and follow up what is said with the counsel with which it was followed up by the poet,

> "Avise, ye now, and put me out of blame."

Physical Geography I have used as a term applicable to the superficial aspect of the country. The term Geological Observations I employ as a term applicable to observations made upon the substance and structure of what gives to it its superficial aspect, and of what lies under, observations similar to those with which the latter portion of the preceding chapter was occupied, but prosecuted to a somewhat greater depth.

In places innumerable in which the structure of the superficial portion of the earth has been examined, there have been found a greater or less number of strata of homogeneous or heterogeneous, of the same or of different, kinds of matter, lying upon a kind of stratified granite, and this upon a granite in which no indication of stratification are observable, and through which we cannot penetrate to ascertain what is enclosed therein, or beneath it. Whatever that which it covers may be in its composition, it is conjectured by many that it must be in a state of fusion, and therefore is it that the name of crust has been given to that of which we have spoken.

None of these strata, it may be remarked, go completely round the earth as do the coats of an onion around the parts they enclose; through friction or abrasion many of them have become fragmentary, if ever they were more extensive than they now are. Neither are they of uniform thickness either throughout their extent or throughout their succession; some are comparatively thick, others are comparatively thin; while some are thick in one place and thin at another, and some thick throughout one portion of their extent diminish in thickness more or less gradually towards the edge of the mass. Neither is there any part of the earth's crust in which the **whole of them exist superimposed** one upon another; sometimes not more than one is to be found lying on the granite; nor is this always the same, but sometimes one and sometimes another, and sometimes when there are more, it is with a similar variation. This only has been observed, wherever they are found it is always in the same succession, which, excepting by those who in ignorance of the discoveries of modern science suppose the world was created so, is believed to have been the succession in which they were deposited on the spot from water by which it was covered, in which the matter had been suspended or by which it was borne along, with the exception of some strata-like beds of matter which appear to be solidified matter, which, expelled by some orifice in a state of fusion from below, had spread itself out as does the molten lava from a volcano, and some few similar beds.

So familiar is the experienced practical geologist with the appearance and composition of these strata, that he can often tell as easily to which of them a stone which he finds in the field belongs, as you, my reader, can distinguish the fruits of an apple tree or a pear tree, a quice or a pomegranate, an apricot or a peach, a fig or a grape.

But though the deposits are always, when found, found in the same succession, the first above and not below any of the others in connection with which it may be found: the sixth always below the first, second, third, fourth and fifth, if found in connection with any of these, and always above and not below the seventh, eighth, &c., with which it may be found, they are sometimes so contorted that one portion may seem to be otherwise situated, but even then the seeming exception is easily reduced to accordance with the rule. Thus:

Not unfrequently they are found not in a horizontal position, but in a position more or less inclined to the vertical or upright, through disturbances to which they have been subjected after deposit. The protrusion of matter from below, for instance, may bend them as one may with the thumb bend up the whole of the leaves of a book lying flat upon a table. By lateral compression some have been crushed up to such a degree as to form a loop, a section of which at some places may give us the strata so compressed in their regular order, then these in their reverse order, and then again the same strata in their natural order, while a horizontal section may show them in a vertical, or more or less inclined position.

Section I.—*Geological formations of Table Mountain.*

It matters little where we commence our examination of the geological formations of South Africa, everywhere they tell the same tale—a tale of deposit from waters of great depth—and they confirm all that is indicated by the physical geography, or general contour of the superficial aspect of the country. There exist what may seem to be exceptions to what I have stated; but even these, when examined, corroborate the general testimony. It happens that Table Mountain supplies in succession some of the earliest indications which are to be found of the primeval state of what is now the dry land of Southern Africa, corresponding with corresponding indications existing elsewhere, but existing here in such collocation as facilitates the investigation upon which we are about to enter; and with these we may commence.

The vertical section of the mountain range presented by Table Mountain as it faces Table Bay enables us without difficulty to examine its structure. At Sea Point we see granite upon which the mountain has been deposited; we find leaning upon this, as it were, a slate-like rock, to which I have had occasion to refer, presenting the appearance of having been uptilted, and having had the irregularities of edge, which might have been occasioned by any such process, planed down; and above we see a mountain of hardened mud and sand, which, in the Lion's Head and the upper portion of the face of Table Mountain, presents a very distinctly marked stratified structure. And we have to enquire what may be learned from what we thus see in regard to the particular subject of our inquiry.

In doing this we may commence with the granite. From the presence of this we learn first of all that we have reached the foundation of the continent, and we are thus enabled to commence our studies as far back as it is necessary to go.

There is reason to believe that everywhere, underlying all stratified formation, there is granite. It is too hard to be penetrated that we may see what lies beneath, or lines its under surface; but there is truth in the truism if we only penetrate all stratified formations to sufficient depth, we shall come at length to granite, or to gneiss which is something like it. We have thus, it would appear, reached the bottom—the foundation—the hard interior shell of the crust of the earth.

Besides the granite found at Sea Point and other places around the base of Table Mountain, and penetrating that mountain, granite is found at different places in the districts of the Cape—the Paarl, Malmesbury, and George, and in Namaqualand in abundance. And the conclusion to which we come is, that either no deposits of such stratified deposits as are found elsewhere have ever taken place on some spots, or, what is much more probable, that similar deposits have been deposited there, but these deposits have been planed down by such oceanic currents as by partial denudations have scooped out the valleys between the mountain ranges, and this to have been the case, whether the granite exposed on the surface at such places has retained there its original place, or has been protruded, as has been that at the base of Table Mountain, through a superincumbent deposit covering the shell of granite around.

In Namaqualand, in Bushmanland, in the Kalahari Desert, and in various parts throughout the interior of South Africa, is found a granite-like substance, varying in its composition, and in regular beds of more or less stratified layers,—rocks, known to geologists as granitic-gneiss, as gneiss, and as metamorphic schists, with some of which are found, and that very abundantly, in the Kalahari Desert, what is known as metamorphic limestone. And the mention of these renders necessary a description of granite, and also of these in so far as they resemble and in so far as they differ from this, that we may learn what they teach in regard to the hydrology of the district in which we are interested.

Granite sometimes consists of felspar and quartz and mica, sometimes of felspar and quartz and hornblende, sometimes of felspar and hornblende alone, and otherwise of various combinations of these several minerals.

It does not come within the scope of this treatise formally to teach geology, and I stop not minutely to describe the appearance and constitution of these different substances, as it is the constitution and appearance of the composite mass of granite which concerns us chiefly in our special enquiry; but I may mention briefly that quartz is a very hard crystaline substance —so hard that it cannot be scratched with a knife. Felspar is like quartz, but softer, and is easily scratched with a knife, and the other constituents of the granite are imbedded in this as the fruit of a plum-pudding is imbedded in the bread or dough of its composition. Hornblende is a black or dark-green mineral, which fractures like horn, from which circumstance it has received the name it bears. Mica is a glistening transparent or translucent substance, in scales apparently homogeneous in structure, very thin, or capable of being split up into very thin subdivisions.

Mica is sometimes found in sheets of considerable size and thickness. In Siberia such sheets are used as window panes. In England they have been used in place of glass or horn in the construction of lanterns, with the advantage that they are less liable to crack and break than is glass, and less likely to be burned than is horn. In America they are used in the construction of doors for Chamber stoves, allowing the cheering light of the fire to be seen while the door is kept closed. The thin laminæ of which they are composed being easily separated, scales of Mica have been employed in covering objects mounted for examination with a microscope, and sparkling shining sand often owes its sparkling shining metallic-like lustre to small fragments of Mica.*

There is much in the general appearance of the granite to suggest that felspar, the imbedding material, must have been fused, and from this state of fusion crystallized around unfused crystals and angular fragments of the imbedded material; but it is alleged that there are amongst these minerals some which fuse at a much lower temperature than does the imbedding felspar; and it is conjectured that had the felspar been in a state of fusion these also would have been fused, and the non-solidification of the felspar before them in the process of cooling would have prevented them from assuming the forms in which we find them. From this it is inferred that the felspar must not have been solidified from a state of fusion, but deposited from a state of solution. And in our ignorance of the existence at that time of other solvents, it is natural that it should be supposed that the solvent was water.

* Mr Barnabas Shaw, who was honoured to establish the first Wesleyan Mission in South Africa, tells of the commencement of his work at Wynberg, in the rear of Table Mountain:—

"On my first going thither, I met with a few soldiers who regularly assembled for religious worship. They had erected for themselves a small chapel in the midst of a forest, which was beautifully adorned with flowers, by the taste of corporals Tate and Kirby, and in this delightful spot I opened my commission among them. Previously to the erection of this chapel, they had built one in the village, which, by the order of the colonel of the regiment, had been burned to the ground. An officer, however, of the same regiment, Captain Proctor, then gave them liberty to build on his own private property, of which offer they willingly availed themselves. While digging for a foundation, they found a number of shining particles, both white and yellow, from which circumstance they conceived that they had discovered a silver or gold mine. Mrs Tate, the wife of one of the corporals alluded to, a pious and active woman, immediately filled her apron therewith and hastened to exhibit the treasure to Capt. P., saying, at the same time, 'Look here, Captain Proctor, the Lord is blessing you for allowing us to build upon your ground. We have found a mine!' As it had been reported that a silver mine was discovered during the time of the Dutch Government, and as there is a place not very far distant still called by that name, it was natural enough for the soldiers to suppose that they had hit upon a vein. The shining particles were well examined, and although better informed persons than the corporal's wife thought them valuable, after all, instead of gold or silver, they proved to be but pieces of common quartz and granite!"

It may be felt to be an objection to this supposition that granite does not appear do dissolve in water now; but neither does lime, or stucco, or roman cement after it has once set; it is alleged that even quartz is dissolved in minute quantities in water, that constituents of the constituents of granite may be fully soluble, that the solution in water of some other substance than the salt which gives to the water of the sea its present characteristic may have modified its solvent powers in primeval times, and that these solvent powers may have been modified by pressure and by heat, either, or both, apart, or combined, as is often done in the laboratory of the chemist, all which allegation, though not advanced as fact, theory, or conjecture as to what actually occurred when advanced thus, seems to me satisfactorily to meet the objection.

There are spots covered with material which has been protruded from beneath, but with the exception of these, wherever the superficial strata have been removed or penetrated to their lowest depth, there granite, or one or other of the modifications of granite which have been mentioned, or some corresponding composite rock, has been found. From which it seems to follow, if felspar be a crystallization from a state of solution, and not from one of fusion, that we have in this everywhere existing granite indications of the various parts of the world in which it exists, and South Africa amongst the rest, having been at the time—or the times of its formation—covered with water, though water, perhaps, of a temperature much higher than that at which water under the existing atmosphere is converted into vapour.

The structure of granite, it is remarked, is always massive and irregular; its texture is of various degrees of fineness from a hard and close-grained rock, to a coarse and loose aggregation of primary crystals.

Gneiss, like granite, consists of felspar, quartz, and mica, and sometimes hornblende and garnets enter into its composition. But in granite, the crystals of felspar, quartz, mica, and hornblende are entire and distinct, in gneiss their faces are broken as if water-worn. It is alleged that in granite there are no traces of a laminated or stratified structure; in gneiss this structure is evident, even when the strata are most indurated and contorted.

The metamorphic schists differ from gneiss chiefly in the degree of apparent attrition, to which the minerals of which they are respectively composed have been subjected and reduced; and the different names given to the schists indicate only this, and the characteristic constituent of each. *Mica schist* consists of mica and quartz, with hornblende and garnets imbedded in it. *Talcose schist* has talc instead of mica combined with the quartz, and differs only in this respect from the *mica schist*. *Hornblende schist* consists of hornblende and quartz, and is occasionally found with actynolite in it. *Chlorite schist* consists of chlorite and quartz.

The designation *metamorphic* is given to sedimentary deposits, which, subsequent to their deposition, have undergone a metamorphosis or change in their sedimentary appearance by fusion or otherwise, so that they manifest indications of igneous action. Talc, which gives its designation to talcose schist, is a transparent mineral like mica, but softer and not elastic as it is.

Actynolite is a crystalline body of a greenish-gray colour, which has obtained its name from the pointed thorn-like appearance of its crystals.

Chlorite is found sometimes of a crystallized and sometimes of a foliated or scaly structure; it is of a greenish-black colour, and from this it has got its name. It is this which gives colour to a greenish slate called chlorite slate.

Greenstone is what is known as whinstone, which is composed principally of felspar and hornblende, with a mixture frequently of a substance called hypersthéne. It is a rock of igneous formation.

Whatever other end may be subserved by these explanations, it is deemed necessary that the reader, wherever and however situated, may be able to carry with him a definite idea of the formation spoken of. The characteristic feature of these formations to which attention is specially called is the indications of attrition and of stratification, which seem to tell of the action and consequently of the presence of water, and, I may add, of the depth of water covering at the period of their formation the places where now they are. I do not deem it necessary to distract the attention of my readers by adducing other hypotheses which have been advanced in connection with the subject.

The strata of gneiss are sometimes so thick as to render it difficult for an unexperienced observer to determine whether the material be granite or gneiss, and the difficulty is increased if the constituent minerals have been but little abraded. Thus is it with what is spoken of as *granitic gneiss*; and connected with this or near to it is sometimes found what is called quartz rock, which consists chiefly of quartz, but has generally hornblende or mica irregularly imbedded in it.

It may be mentioned that it is in connection with quartz rock that gold has been found, in connection with gneiss that copper has been found in Namaqualand and in mountain ranges further inland, and in connection with schist that tin has been found in the neighbourhood of Swellendam.

The late Dr Rubidge, who at the instance of a mining company visited Namaqualand in 1854, to examine and report upon its metal-producing capabilities, states that at Namaqualand he found the gneiss assumed so granite-like an appearance that the dip and the strike were scarcely distinguishable. "I find it," says he, "a matter of great practical difficulty often to say whether a rock is granite or gneiss—therefore I call those rocks 'gneiss-like granite' or 'granite-like gneiss,' according to the appearance."

Elsewhere he writes:—"The centres of the axes are very frequently composed of granite, but this is not always the case; and I do not know any mine in which granite is not to be found in the works, though the gneiss may meet in well-defined character and with an opposite dip over it. In this country I have stood on granite with gneiss forming the sides of a ravine on either hand, with continuous dip. I have also seen hornblende schist (felspar and hornblende) passing, insensibly as it were, into syenite and greenstone of perfectly well marked characters near Pella. The ravine just noticed is between Pella missionary station and a detached station called Klein Pella."

Dr Rubidge found the veins of ores on what seemed axes of dislocation, though not on all such axes; and he found the axes numerous, often coinciding with the dip of the country, or nearly so, but occasionally at angles to it interrupting the main dip for from 5 to 50 or 100 paces, and in these axis were the metalliferous deposits. The surface of these metalliferous veins he found to be much fissured in the direction of the magnetic meridian, or near thereto, as well as in others. Some fine lumps of oxide, containing as much as 60 per cent. of copper, were found in the fissures or on the surface. When these were followed downwards they often widened at first into good-sized veins, which gave promise of a rich return of ore, but when a depth varying from 4 or 5 to 25 feet was reached they were generally found to contract, and sometimes they terminated abruptly. In either case they were rarely traced beyond that depth, though occasionally the dip of the rock carried them somewhat further. At a greater depth purple sulphurets are found, and these give way to pyrites which are contained either in fissures between masses of slightly decomposed felspathic granite or diffused in grains in the substance of the granite.

"In fact the formation of all these ores," he writes, "appears to be the result of a process of infiltration"—and thus do his observations become serviceable to us—"infiltration by which the original constituents of the rock are gradually removed, and their place occupied by silicates, oxides, or purple and yellow sulphurets, as the case may be—the silicates and oxides generally occurring on the surface, the sulphurets below. Masses of oxide of iron, in a state to be acted on by the magnet, are often found on the surface of these metallic axis. Sulphuret of molybdenum is found accumulated with copper pyrites at Concordia and at Kildunern; and tungstate of lime in a lump of about a pound weight was found enclosed in a mass of red oxide of copper in Springbok mine. Manganese, too, has been found in various parts of the country; and near Gams I found green oxide of chrome accumulated in small quantities between the layers of gneiss in an axis of disturbance."

This term he uses to designate axes which do not permanently change the dip of the gneiss, in contradistinction to those of dislocation, on either side of which the dip sometimes continues nearly the same for miles.

Some of the other terms employed in this statement may require explanation to make them perfectly intelligible to all.

Oxides are combinations of the substance named with oxygen, the constituent of the atmosphere by which life and combustion are sustained. Rust is an oxide of iron, or of some other metal, and such also are many of the ores.

Pyrites is a compound of sulphur and iron found often in cubic crystals in slates, of a bright yellow metallic colour. It occasionally produces spontaneous combustion, and from this it has obtained its name, which is derived from *pyr*, the Greek word for fire.

Sulphurets is the name given to combinations of sulphur with metals. Sulphuret of molybdenum is such a combination of sulphur with a metal of that name.

Silicates are combinations of what is called silicic acid with other substances, and silex may be considered the principal constituent of flint and of quartz.

Garnet is a reddish or iron-coloured mineral found in some mica slates and volcanic rocks.

Returning to the subject under consideration, it appears from observations cited, that in the metallic deposits in the copper districts—as there is in much besides connected with gneissic and schistose rocks—there are indications of their being composed of material supplied by the disintegration of granite or other primitive rocks, and indications of aqueous action in the deposit of the metalliferous ores, which fit in with the evidence otherwise obtained of the hornblende, quartz, and felspar, &c., having been deposited from water, movements occasioned by which caused the abrasion of angular projections, both of fragments and of entire crystals, by the friction of these upon one another. The suspension in the water, together with the movements of this, allowed the larger and heavier fragments first to find a resting-place, after which the lighter, together with material resulting from the further disintegration of these, would be deposited, and possibly raised again by a disturbance of the waters following such convulsions as produced those changes in the continent, and the dip of the granite gneiss and other rocks of which Dr Rubidge speaks.

We shall afterwards find that there occurred many such disturbances of the indurated crust, occurring, it may be, sometimes after protracted periods of repose, and sometimes in rapid succession. At present, it is the order in which these different formations occur here and elsewhere, and the indications thus supplied of the former hydrographic condition of the country with which we have to do.

"There is nothing like a regular order of succession among the primary strata," says Page in his Rudiments of Geology, published in Chambers' Educational Course, which I quote here, and shall have frequent occasion to quote again, as supplying the very information I wish to communicate. "It may be stated generally, however, that gneiss underlies mica schist; that mica and other crystalline schists are the lowest in the system, and that quartz rock, primitive limestone, and clay schist, make their appearance toward the upper part of the series;" and, otherwise than we find to be the case with higher lying strata of what are known as secondary rocks, in the primary system to which these belong, "the strata thicken, thin out, and disappear in a very capricious manner, and most of these rocks pass insensibly into each other, and thus many compounds are formed of which the student can only obtain a knowledge by the study of actual specimen." As to the origin of the gneiss and mica schist systems, he goes on to say,—

"*As to the origin of the gneiss and mica schist systems*, it is abundantly evident that the materials of which they are composed were derived from the underlying granite. It has been stated that this rock forms a solid and irregular basis, on which all the sedimentary strata rest; and if this be true, it is evident that its surface must have been partly under and partly above water, and subject to the degrading influence of atmospheric, aqueous, and chemical agencies. Moreover, if the granitic crust was formed by the cooling of an originally fused globe, the waters resting in the hollows must have been heated to a high degree, and the air must have been loaded with vapours. All this would further tend to hasten the degradation of the granite; the runnels and streams would carry down the loose particles, laying down the heavier first, and carrying out the lighter and smaller to deeper water. In process of time the loose matter would get consolidated by the pressure of its own mass; the high temperature then pervading the globe, together with chemical agency, would assist in producing the crystalline texture; and thus a variety of schistose rocks might be formed at one and the same time. That a high temperature existed during the formation of the primary rocks, we have ample evidence, not only in their hard and crystalline texture, and in the absence of all organic remains, but in the occurrence of certain minerals, such as garnet, whose presence denotes that the rocks in which it is found have experienced a degree of heat sufficiently high to form such a fusible mineral, but not enough to melt the other constituents of which they are composed."

There is a wide field for the exercise of the imagination in picturing what the effect of this heat on the water above may have been; but it is evidence of the previous existence of water above the land, now known as South Africa, which is alone at present under consideration. And it may be borne in mind that a different hypothesis than that of subterranean heat to account for the crystalline texture of the rocks has been proposed, and has commanded the attention of many geologists.

The mountain limestone of the Kalahari, associated with the metamorphic schists, has also its tale to tell; but the slate-like rock leaning upon the granite at Sea Point demands at this stage of our enquiry our first attention. Sea Point is not the only spot in the Colony in which such beds of slate-like flakes and other form of slates are found. In some places they are associated with grits or coarse sandstone, and both grits and slates are found, both of a greenish gray, and of a brown or brownish colour.

These have been identified by Mr Wylie, formerly Government Geologist at the Cape of Good Hope, with the so-called Silurian deposits of Europe and other lands—deposits which have received that designation from a district in England in which the same formation exists having been known in ancient times as the land of a people called the Silurii. They are found extending over regions of vast extent, and are much better known than ever the Silurii were in their day, and are more extensively known than but for this circumstance the Silurii ever would have been.

Subsequent to the deposit of the material constituting now the metamorphic rocks, and prior to the deposit of the silurian, there occurred in England the deposit of what has became known as the Grauwacke system. This is a term used by German miners, signifying Gray rock; but that to which it is applied in Germany is better known to English readers as the Cambrian system, so designated by English geologists from its covering a large portion of Wales—the ancient Cambria.

According to Mr Wylie, no trace of this is found at the Cape of Good Hope, but a reference to it is necessary as supplying an indication of the lapse of time which may have occurred between the deposit of the gneiss and schists, and the deposit of the slates and grits to which attention is now directed; in England the Cambrian rocks, including the Bala limestone, and the Festiniog and Bangor slates, show a verticle depth of some 26,000 feet, or about five miles! What time would be required for a series of deposits five miles in thickness, I must leave my readers to conjecture, only reminding them that this should be taken into account in all conjectures relative to the primeval hydrographic condition of the country. The deposits which have to be considered are records, not only of what materials have been deposited, and of how this was done, but also of the period in the world's history in which it occurred.

The succession of strata in the clay slate grauwacke or Cambrian, and the Silurian systems have not been very clearly ascertained. But an approximate classification of them may be formed, in doing which important assistance is given by fossil remains of vegetable and animal structures found imbedded in them.

We have no evidence that any organic structures—vegetable or animal or aught other, if aught other there have been or can be—did exist in the times of earlier formations; but neither have we evidence that they did not. And it is alleged, though perhaps prematurely, that we are not likely ever to obtain any evidence on the subject, as the fusion of which the granite and the gneiss and others of the metamorphic rocks give indications indicates a temperature which must have destroyed all traces of organic structures, if such had existed at the time of their deposit, whether from solution or suspension; or if this be disproved, the changes issuing in crystallization, whether effected by heat or by chemical action, by electric or magnetic, or any other form of these correlated forces, may have been fatal to their preservation.

In the clay state, which is the lowest lying formation of the older palaezoic rocks, or rocks in which are imbedded remains of primeval animated organic structures, and in the grauwacke, which is the next in succession, it is alleged that no trace of vegetable organisms have been found, but there have been found fossils of animal structures. And the existence of these may be considered indications of the contemporaneous existence of also the others, for animals require food, and if these animals, were constituted as are the animals with which we are acquainted, they could not find food in inorganic matter. If any of these were carnivorous, as are many now, the animals on which they preyed must have lived on something else, and if they also preyed on other animals, and these again on others, follow back the train of thought, and we are brought to the conclusion that the last, if not many besides, must have lived on vegetable diet, so that the existence of animal remains in the deposit from that waste of waters supplies evidence of the contemporaneous existence of vegetable structure, floating, it may be, in the same.

It is well known that wherever animal remains have existed, the fact, although not the least visible trace of them may remain, is cognizable to the chemist by the presence of phosphoric acid in the soil, and I find it stated that the late Dr Daubeny, Professor of Botany and of Chemistry in the University of Oxford, with a view to ascertain the prevalence of this in different beds, sowed a certain number of grains of barley in each, and compared the amount of phosphoric acid in the crop with that in the seed. As this substance does not exist in the atmosphere, it was supposed that any excess which might be found must have been taken up by the roots of the plant. When the experiment was tried with earth derived from any one of the fossiliferous strata, an excess appeared; but when with that supplied by the Cambrian formation, this was not the case; and it is alleged that nothing can be more conclusive than this ingenious experiment, as to the absence of animal life on the earth or in the ocean during the period in which the sedimentary deposits in question were formed; and it furnishes a striking instance of the way in which every branch of knowledge will sooner or later be brought to bear upon every other.

Against this, however, must be set the alleged fact that fossil remains have actually been found in such deposits. I accept both testimonies, and infer that organised beings, both vegetable and animal, did at the period of these deposits people the waters in certain localities at least, but that they may have been limited both in number and in their diffusion.

Mr Wylie describes the Silurian rocks of the Cape Colony as slates and grits, usually of a greenish-grey or brownish colour, in beds which as usually seen are vertical or at high angles, broken through and altered by granite. The designation grits employed in this description is one generally given to hard sandstones, in which the grains of quartz are sharp and angular, such as may be seen in what are designated millstone grit and grindstone grit, &c. Such particles must have been subjected to less abrasion by friction and long-continued movement in the water than those which are more rounded, and they thus seem to speak the strata in which they are to be found of a very early formation; and that they and the slates were formed by deposit from suspension in water no one who carefully examines them without prejudice in favour of the views formerly prevailing, that they were created so by God out of nothing, by the word of his power, can for a moment doubt. The evidence is unquestionable, and conflicting evidence of igneous agency there is none, excepting in circumstances in which, according to the popular use of a trite saying which has a very different import, the exception prove the rule.

And thus we are brought to feel in the study of these that we are almost if not altogether clean escaped from the difficulties connected with the study of what I have likened to the early fabulous history of nations, and entered upon the study of the records of that which, in contradistinction to the other, may be called the historic period, though in this we are studying formations deposited ages—and ages upon ages—anterior to the appearance of man upon the globe.

Occasionally we find—and may find at Sea Point, where granite in a state of fusion has been protruded through superincumbent stratified rocks—for some distance, an inch, six inches, or more from the protruded granite, the stratified rock shows evidence of having been there fused by the heat, while all beyond retains unchanged its stratified appearance of deposit, indicative of its aqueous origin.

Mrs Somerville, in her treatise on Physical Geography touching on this subject, wrote:—"According to a theory now generally adopted, which originated with Mr Lyell, the metamorphic rocks, which consist of gneiss, micaschist, statuary marble, &c., were formed of the sediment of water, in regular layers, differing in kind and colour; but, having been deposited near the places where plutonic rocks were generated, they have been changed by the heat transmitted from the fused matter; and in coming under heavy pressure, and at great depths, they have become as highly crystallized as the granite itself, without losing their stratified form. An earthy stratum has sometimes been changed into a highly crystallized rock to a distance of a quarter of a mile from the point of contact by transmitted heat, and there are instances of dark-coloured limestone, full of fossil shells, that has been changed into statuary marble from that cause; and similar alterations may frequently be seen to a small extent in rocks adjacent to a stream of lava."

The animal remains which have been found in the clay slate are corals and shells, and with them remains of crustacea, which are organically allied to the lobster, have been found in the Grauwacke. But in what is more strictly called the Silurian, with corals, shells, and crustacea, fish bones and teeth have been found; and it has been alleged that there have been found some fragments of sea-weeds, and also fragments of equisitaceæ and of ferns, belonging to the period of this formation; but on this point doubts exist.

I have spoken of equisitaceæ. The English designation of the different species of equisita, from which the order is named, is horse-tails. I hesitated to use this term, lest the expression "fragments of horse-tails" should have conveyed an erroneous idea whether that term were associated with the mare's-tail—a very different plant, *hippuris vulgaris*—or with the animals from which both botanic designations have been borrowed.

Whatever opinion may be adopted in regard to the terrestrial origin and the period of the formation of the fossils resembling the structure of the equisitaceæ and the ferns, it will be admitted that all the others speak of an ocean home.

Land there may have been somewhere or other above the surface of the ocean, but the rocks of the Colony all tell only of sea—if not of a sea without a shore—of a deep sea, at the bottom of which they found a resting-place after suspension and transport in its waters. This is indicated most distinctly—indicated in the lamination seen in the rocks of fine argillaceous composition, and in the stratification of the arenaceous or sandstone and the limestone formations.

Of the systems of rock now under consideration Page says,—

"*The clay-slate system* presents a vast thickness of fine-grained fissile argillaceous rock, of considerable hardness, varying in colour, and of glistening aspect. The prevalent colours of slate are black, green, bluish, purplish, and mottled; some varieties being hard and splintery, others soft and perishable. The character of any particular slate is, however, very persistent; the accidental or imbedded minerals are few—these being chiefly cubic-iron pyrites, and crystals of chiastolite and hornblende.

"*The composition of the grauwacke* is much more varied and irregular. As sandstone may be said to be consolidated sand, and conglomerate consolidated gravel, so may grauwacke be defined to be an aggregate of clay, grains of quartz, felspar, and mica, with fragments of jasper and other minerals. The cementing material is clay, which often constitutes the greater portion of the rock, and in such cases the texture differs little from that of clay-slate : but in many strata fragmentary ingredients prevail, so that the texture varies in fineness from that of a coarse slate to a conglomerate of pebbles more than an inch in diameter. Like clay-slate, grauwacke presents various degrees of hardness, though, generally speaking, it may be described as a highly indurate conglomerate—indicating most clearly its origin from the waste of earlier siliceous and argillaceous formations. Associated with the slates and grauwackes are occasional beds of concretionary limestone, which partake of the argillaceous character of the rocks with which they are associated.

"*In the silurian system* limestones occur more frequently, so that the calcareous type, or, at all events, an intimate blending of argillaceous and calcareous compounds, may be said to prevail. Until a recent period, this system was considered as a portion of the grauwacke group, and as marking its passage into the grey micaceous beds of the old red sandstone. Merely looking at cabinet specimens, it would be impossible to distinguish between many of the grauwacke and silurian rock, but taking them in the mass they are readily distinguishable. In the first place, their sedimentary character is very marked; they present more rapid alternations from one kind of strata to another; they have undergone fewer changes by heat; and are generally looser and more earthy in their texture. The limestones are less cyrstalline than those of the early grauwackes; the arenaceous beds are also less silicious, and more closely resembling ordinary sandstone, while the abundance of organic remains justifies their arrangement in a separate system."

In clay slates we find, besides the lamination, a cleavage, or tendency to cleavage, which facilitates or occasions its splitting up into thin plates ; but these, it may be observed, are generally at right angles, or nearly so, to the bed of stratification, and this is attributable to some change which has taken place in the matter of which it is composed subsequent to its deposit *in laminæ*, and which must not be confounded therewith.

The thickness of the deposits of the greenish-gray and brownish-coloured slates and grits at the Cape of Good Hope have not, so far as I am aware, been ascertained. In England they constitute an aggregate thickness measured by miles. I have already spoken of the Cambrian formation, including the Bala limestone, the Festiniog, and Bangor slates, &c., as estimated to be 26,000 feet in thickness. Above this in the series is the Lower Silurian, 1,500 feet; the Caradoc sandstone, 2,500 feet; the Upper Silurian, embracing the Ludlow and Wenlock rocks, the Woolhope limestone, &c., 5,000, or in all 9,000 feet deposited, apparently subsequent to the deposit of the 26,000 feet of the Cambrian deposit, and supplying in like manner an indication of the lengthened duration of the period of deposit brought under consideration, throughout the whole of which, it may be, what is now called South Africa was at the bottom of the sea, making its emergence as dry land but an event of yesterday when compared with its previous service as a part of the ocean bed.

And here I would meet a difficulty which may present itself to some entering upon such studies for the first time.

It may be asked, How can such measurements be determined? The answer is ready. It has been stated that in the Colony the beds under consideration are usually seen vertical, or at high angles, broken through and altered by granite. By measuring across the upturned edges, and noting the angle at which they are inclined, the actual thickness may be easily determined. The experiment may be made by attempting thus to determine the thickness of the upturned bed of slate reclining upon the base of the Lion's Head above low-water mark at Sea Point. I do not remember whether their aspect indicates lamination or cleavage; my recollection of the appearance presented by them inclines me to conclude the former; but the purpose now in view may be accomplished whatever may be the case in regard to the origin of the appearance referred to.

The slate-like layers in question have apparently yielded to the force by which the granite was protruded. They have thus been thrown into a position such as the leaves of a book are made to assume by running the thumb across them. In this position they may present a greater breadth of surface than they would of thickness if they had been completely tilted up into a vertical position, or had been allowed to retain their original horizontal position, which is their true thickness. But by determining the angle at which they are inclined, we are enabled, from the measurement of their breadth of surface, to calculate exactly their thickness; and thus it is that the thickness of some of the thicker layers have been determined.

At the high rocks on the sea shore at Sea Point these uptilted strata of laminated structure may be distinctly seen, and from them not a little may be learned. If my memory serves me right, they may be seen again in some of the roads skirting the base of the Lion's Rump. By the removal of a little soil they may probably be traced from the rocks at Sea Point to a considerable distance. It is the upturned edges of them which are seen, and the cause of the upturning appears to have been the protrusion of the granite on the sides of which the strata at Sea Point are seen to rest. If my recollection of the appearance they present be correct, it is natural to conclude from what is seen and from what is known that originally they must have lain in a horizontal position, and from this they have been thrust by the protrusion of the granite in question. If so, a vague idea may be obtained of the force with which that granite was protruded, and from the distance to which this effect of the protrusion may be traced. But we are thus supplied also with the means of ascertaining the thickness of the bed of strata thus disturbed. This is not the measurement of the distance from the granite at Sea Point to where they terminate. It would have been this had they been vertical. The thickness of the seam of the leaves of a book is the same whether the book lie upon the table or stand upon its edge; but when, by the thumb being passed over the edges of the leaves while they are held against the fingers near to the binding, they are spread out, and they measure across the edges double or triple what they do in an undisturbed horizontal position: so is it with the strata in question. But with the measurement of the extent of these, and of the angle of inclination, we have all the data required for a trigonometrical calculation of their original thickness. And thus are we supplied with an indication, if not with a measurement, of the lapse of time, and of the lapse of time during which there was here a continuous calm—unbroken, undisturbed.

During the protracted era of the deposit of the gneiss and schist formation there were probably numerous disturbances of the deposit. But during the deposit of the clay-slate there may have been—must have been—in this locality at least, a long-continued quiet.

It has been shown by geologists that though identity of strata indicates identity of circumstances, they do not necessarily indicate cotemporaneous formation or identity of time of deposit; for a deposit commencing near the locality of disintegration may be there abundant, while as yet it is only slowly extending, and that perhaps by the continuous re-transport of the deposited matter. Should these coloured slates be identified with the coloured clay-slate found elsewhere, immediately overlying the granite or the gneiss, it may be that the deposit of these clay-slates may have extended throughout a great portion, if not the entire period, of the time occupied in the deposit of the superior lying grauwacke or Cambrian formation, measuring in England 26,000 feet in thickness! It is only towards the close of the period required for this that we have any indication of the existence of dry land supplied by fossil plants of terrestrial production, and it has been questioned whether what have been deemed such in some of the upper strata should be so considered.

Let an estimate be formed of the length of time requisite for the deposit of such an accumulation of flaky strata in the calm depth of a deep, deep sea, and it will appear that for a long, long period indeed this land must have been covered with a waste of waters—a shipless, shoreless sea, countless fathoms deep—where in its depths, whatever storms agitated the surface, raising billows, all was calm and peaceful as the waters of a mountain lakelet on a summer's eve.

But long-continued as this calm had been—and how long none but a student of geology can imagine—it was not to continue for ever. These beds of greenish, gray, or brownish coloured grits and slates, it has been stated, are in the Colony usually seen in a vertical position, or at high angles broken through and altered by granite, as may be seen at Sea Point. This appears to have been effected from beneath by a protrusion of granite in a viscid semi-fluid state of fusion, as was the granite seen in connection with these slaty, flaky strata at Sea Point, where several

F

phenomena arising out of this protrusion of granite, which was probably of a high temperature, may be studied.

It is not necessary that I should stop to discuss at length how this upheaval and protrusion of granite came about. It may suffice to state in passing that it is not improbable it was effected by some such operation as in later times produced earthquakes and volcanoes, and that these have been attributed to the percolation of water through cracks in the basin of the earth, which, when it came into contact with the heated material at some depth below, was converted into vapour, and by its expansion heaved up the earth under which it passed towards a rent which already existed, or which it could make for itself, blowing up the viscid fused material before it. Or it may have been protruded by a more steady pressure on the somewhat elastic crust of the earth under the sea, occasioned by the accumulated deposit of matter measuring miles in depth. The phenomena is not peculiar to South Africa, and we have here only a representation in miniature of what about the same time was occurring on a scale of tremendous magnitude.

It is said—"There is scarcely a development of the clay-slate or grauwacke systems without associated granitic rocks; and the greater part of the silurian strata are thrown into inclined and contorted positions by the same agency, while effusions of trap make their appearance among the later strata.

"The Grampians, the Welsh range, the Pyrenees, Hartz mountains, Dofrafelds, Uralian, Himmaleh, Atlas range, Mountains of the Moon and other African ridges, the Andes, and Alleghanies all seem to have received their elevation at the close of the transition period"—the period now engaging our attention.

Captain Hall, in his Manual of South African Geography, commends the geological appearances on the flank of Table Mountain as supplying a good study for any one commencing the study of geology and desirous of extending his acquaintance with that science. "He will there," says he, "find the clay-slate rocks, once probably lying horizontally, violently upheaved, and standing, as it were, on edge against the mass of granite which appears to have been protruded in a state of fusion through the same, as will be seen in the line of junction on the beach near Sea Point, and above the gardens on the Kloof road—the clay-slate being intercepted by veins of the granite in every direction, and a band of rock alternately changing from clay-slate and granite into gneiss."

The gneiss, it is alleged, has been produced by the heat of the granite having sufficed to fuse portions of the material broken through and left reclining upon it. And the cleavage of the clay-slate has been attributed to the same cause.

"The peculiarities of this structure," says Page, "have given rise to many speculations and experiments. Mr R. W. Fox submitted a mass of moist clay, worked up with acidulated water, to a weak *electric* action for several months; and it was found at the end of that time to present traces of cleavage, the laminæ being at right angles to the electric forces. Others are of opinion that cleavage is superinduced, when considerable *chemical* action takes place in any finely pulverised substance as clay—cleavage being thus regarded as a species of rude crystallisation. Another class of theorists, from observing that slaty cleavage occurs among the shales of the coal measures, when these are in the neighbourhood of igneous rocks, attribute the structure to *heat*. It is not unlikely that all these causes may have been concerned in producing cleavage; for, when better understood, it is more than probable that heat, electricity, and chemical action, are only modifications of one universal agency."

The granite appears to have been here protruded to a considerable elevation. A continuation of that seen at Sea Point may be seen on the Wynberg side of Table Mountain; and it continues to appear along the beach on both sides of the peninsula to its termination at Cape Point. Perhaps this mountain range owes its preservation to resistance presented by the granite to the ocean current, by which the land along its sides was washed away. But the point to which I wish to call attention is, that while there are indications of this granite having been protruded through the clay slates, everything seen goes to show that the silurian deposit, of which the bulk of Table Mountain and the mountains beyond are formed, was deposited around and above the protruded granite, and consequently, after its protrusion, supplying us with a measurement of time elapsing after that protrusion, during which what is now a dry land was then the bed of an ocean a thousand fathoms deep.

Capping this deposit, thousands of feet in thickness, may be seen on Table Mountain and on the Lion's Head well defined horizontal strata, differing in substance as well as appearance from the mountain mass which they cover. This is characterised by abundance of clay, these by being composed in a great measure of sand, and all round the flanks of the mountain are beds of what is called ironstone gravel—indurated clay—the debris, it may be, of the sandstone cliffs which have been undermined, and of the schistose beds of clay slate by which they were sustained. It is said that many of the mountains both in Great and Little Namaqualand show horizontal beds of sandstone or quartzite, identical, seemingly, with that which overlies the clay slate and granite of Table Mountain; and it is probable that the extensive plateau of Bushmanland is practically composed of beds of the same rock, covered with deposits of tufaceous limestone; and it is alleged that similar deposits in patches of various size are found surmounting all of the rocks which have been previously described—in some cases with peculiarity of inclination which will call for subsequent remark,—and that they have few or no fossil remains, and that they are principally composed of silica, which is often stained with oxide of iron, corresponding with the descripting given by Wylie of strata examined by him.

Thus the sandstone of Table Mountain was identified by Mr Wylie, when he was Geological Surveyor to the Colony, with some of the lower strata of what is called the old red sandstone, which, having been found in Devonshire, has come from this circumstance to be known as the Devonian formation, though it is also found on extensive districts elsewhere; and such also are the sandstones of what he calls the fibular range of mountains. He describes these as "gray sandstones, conglomeritic at base, with reddish shaly sandstone below." He visited the Knysna, and though he mentions he had very little opportunity of seeing much of the geology, he says, "The hard, yellowish, iron-stained sandstone of the Heads appeared to me to belong to the Table Mountain sandstone, or Lower Devonian. In all probability it is a continuation of the sandstone of Cape St. Blaize and the Aasvogelberg, near Riversdale." And he subsequently says, "On going ashore for a few minutes at Mossel Bay, I could see that the sandstone there and at Cape St. Blaize was the same as that of Table Mountain."

In all of these observations we find indications of the extent, though not of the limits, of the deposit, and indications of all the spots named having been at the time of their deposit a portion of the ocean bed.

The question, Whence came all the material covering to such thickness areas of such extent? may press upon some who feel disposed to crave an answer before proceeding further. A question more pertinent to the subject under consideration is, How came the material to be deposited there? But this is no reason why a reply to the other should either be withheld or postponed.

In all the deposits which have been under consideration we have found no materials but what exist as constituents of granite; and this is suggestive of the alternate conclusions that either granite may have been formed from a solution or fusion of these and other deposits, or that these all are the products of the disintegration and decomposition of granite.

There are those who are inclined to adopt the former of these hypotheses—the latter has commanded more general attention.

The various schists present us with constituents of granite in various degrees of disintegration; quartzite, or quartzose sand, appears to be quartz in a state of greater or less comminution; clay is an abundant product of the decomposition of felspar, &c.; and gneiss appears to be only another form of granite itself.

The opinion has been advanced that the gneiss seen at Sea Point has been produced by the effects of heat on the stratified rocks, through which the granite in a state of fusion was protruded; and a friend of my own, a German Professor of Physical Science, whose scientific attainments I highly respect, maintains that all granite is the product of the fusion or solution of materials which at one time composed stratified rocks, similar in every respect to those of what are now superincumbent strata. Such are not my views. But be the case as it may in regard to the formation of granite, there is much in the general appearance of the superincumbent strata to favour the supposition that gneiss is composed of disintegrated granite; schists, of the same, with the process of disintegration carried somewhat further; sandstone formations, something of the same; and clay, one of the products of the decomposition of felspar, or of some of the other primary minerals in the composition in which it takes part.

The appearance of the gneiss and of the schists is indicative of the possibility and to some extent probability of the material of which they are composed having previously existed in the same locality. But it is not so with the superincumbent stratified rocks. The material composing these may have been conveyed to the spot in which they are found from a considerable distance, and there are not awanting indications of the deposit of some having followed an arrest, sudden or gradual, of the velocity in the ocean current by which they were being suspended and borne along; and it is at this point of the history of these deposits that they become more particularly interesting to the student of Hydrology.

It has been observed—the observation has been tested and illustrated by experiment, and the fact has been turned to practical account in washing for gold and in many other operations besides—that a current of force sufficient to carry with it heterogeneous matter, when weakened, allows the heavier materials to drop, and bears along only the lighter to a greater distance. And from the size and weight of stones which have apparently been thus deposited, some idea may be formed of the force of ocean currents which existed in the locality at the time of their deposit.

The strata of sandstone capping Table Mountain and the Lion's Head have been identified with the so called Devonian or Old red sandstone deposits in Britain; amongst these are beds of conglomerates in which stones of considerable bulk are found. I use with reluctance a phrase so vague, but I have not the means of ascertaining their magnitude. Stones of a corresponding magnitude have been found in conglomerates at the Cape of Good Hope, and these supply indications of what must have been the rapidity of the current by which they were borne along.

Deposits of conglomerate speak of the rapidity and consequent force of the ocean currents, and they tell at the same time in some cases of the depth of the ocean at the time of their deposit, and of the length of time throughout which that deposit was going on; they leave however much to be imagined. Let the reader imagine the depth of an ocean in which a deposit could go on until it had attained a thickness of 4000 feet, which is the thickness of some of these deposits, and the length of time which must have been required for such a deposit !

Such may have been the time represented by these stratified Old red sandstone deposits capping the Silurian deposits, some 3000 feet in thickness, previously deposited. But that sand has also another tale to tell. Allusion has already been made to its tale of diminished depth of ocean.

Of this shallowing of the water, in whatever way it may have been brought about, we have also other indications—indications as instructive as was to Noah the indication afforded by the olive leaf in the mouth of the dove—that the waters were abated.

Besides these mountain-capping strata, there are in the district over which they extend strata which have been identified with strata of the same system in other lands, and these of an aggregate thickness of 1100 feet. These are described by Mr Wylie as consisting of "dark-gray and brownish shades, with fossils abundant—of a Devonian or carboniferous limestone type,—and of beds of brown rippled sandstone with long winged sperifers."

These are of a later formation than the strata on Table Mountain, but they confirm their testimony—they tell of shallow water, if not also of adjacent land. We are approaching the time of which it is written, "And God said, Let the waters under the heaven be gathered together into one place, and let the dryland appear, and it was so."

The ripple mark so common on the surface of sandstones of all ages, and which is so often seen on the sea-shore at low-tide, seems to originate in the drifting of materials along the bottom of the water. But it is by no means confined to the beach between high and low water; it is also produced on sands which are constantly covered with water. Similar undulatory ridges and furrows may also be sometimes seen on the surface of drift-snow and of loose sand. Sir Charles Lyal informs us he had once an opportunity of observing how the wind produced this effect on a large extent of level beach exposed at low-tide near Calais. The following is the account which he has given :—

"Clouds of fine white sand were blown from the neighbouring downs, so as to cover the shore, and whiten a dark level surface of sandy mud; and this fresh covering of sand was beautifully rippled. On levelling all the small ridges and furrows of this ripple over an area several yards square, I saw them perfectly restored in about ten minutes, the general direction of the ridges being always at right angles to that of the wind. The restoration began by the appearance here and there of small detached heaps of sand, which soon lengthened and joined together, so as to form long sinuous ridges, with intervening furrows. Each ridge had one side slightly inclined and the other steep, the lee-side being always steep and the windward a gentle slope.

"When a gust of wind blew with sufficient force to drive along a cloud of sand, all the ridges were seen to be in motion at once, each encroaching on the furrow before it, and in the course of a few minutes filling the place which the furrow had occupied. The mode of their advance was by the continual drifting of grains of sand up the slopes—many of which, on reaching the summit, fell over the scarps, and were under shelter from the wind, so that they remained stationary, resting, according to their shape and momentum, in different parts of the descent, and a few only rolling to the bottom.

"Occasionally part of a ridge, advancing more rapidly than the rest, overtook the ridge immediately before it, thus causing those bifurcations and branches which are so common. We see this configuration in sandstones of all ages; and in them also, as now on the sea-coast, we may often detect two systems of ripples interfering with each other—one more ancient and half effaced, and a newer one, in which the grooves and ridges are more distinct and in a different direction. This crossing of two sets of ripples arises from a change of wind and the new direction in which the waves are thrown on the shore."

Thus is the ripple mark produced, and in the ocean-bed it tells in general of a rising beach, though it may be below low-water mark. At the Cape such indications of a shore are found, and if of a shore then of dry land behind. We are now in sight of land—not that cloud-land or bank by which a landsman might be deceived, but firm land, and no mistake.

"*Beds of brown rippled sandstone?*" Yes! these ripples on the sandstone tell of ripples on the wave, and tell of a shore on which the waves rolled playfully—as they may be seen now to roll in seeming sport and play on the beach half-way between Sea Point and Camp Bay beyond.

If the "beds of brown rippled sandstone" have been covered with other matter conformed to their shape, this shows that they may have been at some later time again submerged, and, it may be, submerged to a considerable depth; but these ripples show that they have been near, or at, or above the level of the sea, on a gently inclined, almost horizontal, shore.

We are then brought to land at last!

Thus by the study of the granite, such as is seen at Sea Point, and the gneiss and the schists which elsewhere are associated with it, we are carried back to a time when "the earth was without form and void"—no earth, no sea, as these designations are generally understood—a lurid, incandescent mass—viscid and plastic—cooling down till the incandescence disappeared, "and darkness was upon the face of the deep." What now exists as water, if existent then, existed as vapour and cloud—thick clouds and dense, impervious to the solar ray. "And the Spirit of God moved upon the face of the waters"—the breath of God, a mighty wind—which might be described in the language of the psalmist David as raining snares, or as it reads in the margin, quick-burning coals, fire and brimstone, and an horrible or burning tempest—thunder, and lightning, and storm. "Then," to quote again from the sweet singer of Israel, "the earth shook and trembled; the foundations also of the hills moved and were shaken, . . There went up a smoke out of his nostrils, and fire out of his mouth devoured: coals were kindled by it. He bowed the heavens also, and came down: and darkness was under his feet. And he rode upon a cherub, and did fly; yea, he did fly upon the wings of the wind. He made darkness his secret place; his pavilion round about him were dark waters and thick clouds of the skies. At the brightness that was before him his thick clouds passed; hailstones and coals of fire. The Lord also thundered in the heavens, and the Highest gave his voice; hailstones and coals of fire."

Such are the phenomena suggested by what is learned of the primitive condition of the earth from the appearance of the granite.

As the world cools down the violence of the tempest, the duration of which, it may be, far transcends our wildest dreams of duration and time is allayed; the clouds condensed into rain become translucent, "And God said Let there be light, and there was light." The process proceeds, and much of the moisture is precipitated while the clouds float aloft. "And God said, Let there be a firmament," or, as is stated in the margin it reads in the Hebrew, "Let there be an expansion in the midst of the waters, and let it divide the waters from the waters." And God made the [expansion or] firmament, and divided the waters which were under the firmament from the waters which were above the firmament, and it was so." And this is the era of the world's history to which we are led back by the study of the gneiss and the schists, and other so called primary rocks.

The hydrologic records of the granite and the so-called metamorphic rocks are, as has been said, in some respects like unto the fabulous chapters of the early history of many nations, in which fragments of pure history are, in minute fragmentary portions, imbedded, and conglomerated by much which is other than history pure and simple, but in which again there are often more minutely comminuted portions of fact. Even from such fabulous history the true may, by careful study, be eliminated, and even from these metamorphic rocks generally considered to be manifestly igneous formations, may be produced evidence of a cotemporary or prior state and condition of things in which they were in their structure the consequences of aqueous action.

The gneiss and the schists are apparently composed of disintegrated granite, and it may be the disintegration took place ere water was precipitated from the atmosphere; it may be that the materials of which they are composed were deposited where we find them by the mighty rushing winds, which it is possible may have been what was spoken of as the Ruach of the Hebrew, and the Pneuma of the Septuagent, which moved upon the face of the deep; it may be that the water-worn appearance of their constituents was produced by trituration and friction occasioned by the wind; but the preponderating evidence is in favour of the supposition that the materials in question were deposited where we find them by the agency of water. But while the solvent power of water, pure, or in combination with other matter, at a higher temperature than that at which water now becomes vapourous and boils, and which might be the case if the pressure under which it lay were greater than is that of the atmosphere at present—while the solvent power of the water in such circumstances might be such as to hold felspar in solution, the preponderating evidence seems to be considered in favour of the supposition that these metamorphic rocks must have been subsequent to their deposit in an incandescent state; and by much which is seen in these rocks we are led, whatever may have been the facts of the case in regard to these particulars, to think of the primeval ocean as differing in temperature, if not in other respects, from the ocean of the present, and to conclude, that possibly there may have have been local if not universal conversions of the water of the ocean into vapour, to be again deposited from the atmosphere; and that that may have occurred oftener than once.

It seems to be generally accepted as indicated by the appearances of these so-called metamorphic rocks—the gneiss and the schists—that the places in which they are found must have been at the time of their formation covered, and covered deeply, by the primeval ocean. If the crystallization of these rocks was a crystallization from a state of fusion, this fusion seems to indicate incandescence, and consequently a temperature sufficient to convert the ocean, if subjected only to such pressure as that of the atmosphere now, into vapour, and that a vapour in quantity sufficient, when condensed in the atmosphere into cloud, to cause darkness again to cover the face of the deep, until again, after a lapse of time for which I have no measurement, the cooling of the molten mass—effected, it may be, by the continuous influx and evaporation of surrounding water (if the incandescence were only local)—allowed of the condensation and deposit of the watery vapour; and there, as elsewhere, the waters under the firmament were again divided from the waters which were above. But even then the temperature of the ocean, as at first, may have been, and probably was, far above the temperature of the present sea—approximating at first the temperature of the boiling point of water—if not rising above even this, and far above it.

It was shown at the meeting of the British Association for the promotion of Science, held at Brighton in 1872, that while a red-hot ball of iron introduced into a vessel of pure water was quickly quenched, a similar red-hot ball of iron introduced into a vessel of water holding soap in solution continued incandescent for a length of time, and was seen through the water to be so. The rationale is, a film of vapour formed around the ball was retained there through the stronger cohesion of the saponaceous water, and prevented for a time the closer approach of the water around to be, as in the case of the pure water, converted into steam, though after a time this failed, and an explosion followed.

Dismissing all thoughts about this, but that of the phenomenon of an incandescent mass surrounded by water, I avail myself of this to suggest the possibility of what may be considered a wild dream having been actually the case, though I do not consider this to be probable. It is conceivable that the pressure of the then existing atmosphere, and of the waters of the sea, and the mechanical constitution of these, might possibly have been such as to prevent the evaporation and escape of water heated by the fused mass; and that, had there been eye to see it, there might have been seen through the depths of the ocean the glowing incandescent ocean-bed imparting a lurid hue to the thick cloud above impervious to solar ray; while tempestuous storms swept the face of the deep as the Spirit of the Lord moved upon the face of the waters!

This weird dream I give as one which possibly might be descriptive of what occurred; but the views I entertain are more in accordance with what is previously stated.

So much for the testimony in regard to the early or primordial hydrographic condition of what is now known as South Africa, supplied by the granite, the gneiss, and the schists there found.

In the Kaleghari there is found what is called mountain limestone, associated with metamorphic schists such as we have had under consideration.

The designation mountain limestone is given to limestone strata, which are generally found flanking or crowning trap hills, intermediate in age between the Old Red Sandstone and the so-called coal measures, and presenting bold escarpments. Sometimes it consists of two, four, or six beds divided by portions of clayey matter; at other times the beds are separated by layers of calcarious sandstone and shale; while not unfrequently it occurs in one mass of vast thickness, flanking some trap hills precisely after the manner in which a coral reef skirts the island around which it is forming.

The organic remains in the mountain limestone are evidently marine. The occurrence in some strata of seams of coal attest the presence of terrestrial plants which must have drifted into the sea of deposit. There is some doubt among geologists as to the origin of certain limestones in the lower strata; but laying these aside, the whole character of the group is as decidedly oceanic as is that of the living coral reefs of the Pacific.

The zoophites, by which the limestone was produced there, may have lived subsequent to the deposit of the sandy strata capping Table Mountain and the Lion's Head; and if so, if the metamorphic character of the rock and of the schists with which it is associated be the result of fusion, we are led to conclude that the phenomenon of fusion must have occurred, in the places in which they are found at a period subsequent to the deposit of the whole of the material of which Table Mountain is composed.

These strata belong to what is known as the Old Red Sandstone formation. There is no one whose name is so intimately and extensively associated with the name of this formation as is the name of the honoured and lamented Hugh Miller. Amongst writers who have attempted reproductive descriptions of former aspects of the earth, few have approached him, and I know of no one who has excelled him in the combination of graphic description with scientific truth.

He thus writes of the phenomena of the earlier eras of which we have hydrographic records at the Cape of Good Hope—the eras during which were deposited or formed the granite, the gneiss, the mica and talc schists, the clay slates, and other so-called primary rocks:—

"At this time," says he, "the temperature of the earth's crust seems to have been so high that the strata, deposited at first in water, passed into a semi-fluid state, became strangely waved and contorted, and assumed in its composition a highly crystalline structure. Such is peculiarly the case with the fundamental or gneiss deposits of the period. In the overlying mica schist there is still much of contortion and disturbance, whereas the clay-slate which lies over all gives evidence, in its more mechanical texture and the regularity of its strata, that a gradual refrigeration of the general mass had taken place, and that the close of this period was comparatively quiet and cool.

"Let us suppose that during the earlier part of this period of excessive heat the waters of the ocean had stood at the boiling point, even at the surface, and much higher at the profounder depths; and further, that the half-molten crust of the earth, stretched out over a molten abyss, was so thin that it could not support, save for a short time after some convulsion, very small islands above the sea-level. What, in such circumstances, would be the aspect of the scene optically exhibited from some point in space elevated a few hundred yards over the sea? It would be simply a blank, in which the intensest glow of fire would fail to be seen at a few yards distance.

G

"An inconsiderable escape of steam from the safety-valve of a railway engine forms so thick a screen, that, as it lingers for a moment in the passing opposite the carriage windows, the passengers fail to discern through it the landscape beyond. A continuous stratum of steam then, that attained to the height of our present atmosphere, would wrap up the earth in darkness, gross and palpable as that of Egypt of old—a darkness through which even a single ray of light would fail to penetrate. Beneath this thick canopy the unseen deep would literally 'boil as a pot,' wildly tempested from below; while from time to time more deeply seated convulsions would upheave sudden to the surface vast tracks of semi-molten rock, soon again to disappear,—from which waves, of bulk enormous, would roll outwards to meet in wild conflict with the giant waves of other convulsions, or return to hiss and sputter against the intensely heated and fast foundering mass whose violent upheaval had first elevated and then sent them abroad.

"Such would be the probable state of things during the times of the earlier gneiss and mica schist deposits—times buried deep in that chaotic night which must have continued to exist for mayhap many ages after that beginning of things in which God created the heavens and the earth.

"To a human eye stationed within the cloud all, as I have said, must have been thick darkness. To eyes divine, that could have looked through the inveiling haze, the appearance would have been that described by Milton as seen by angel and archangel at the beginning of creation, when from the gates of heaven they looked down upon chaos:—

> "'On heavenly ground they stood, and from the shore
> They viewed the vast immeasurable abyss,
> Outrageous as a sea, dark, wasteful, wild,—
> Up from the bottom turned by furious heat,
> And surging waves as mountains to attack
> Heaven's height, and with the centre mix the pole.'" *

The Scripture record is, "In the beginning God created the heaven and the earth. And the earth was without form, and void; and darkness was upon the face of the deep."

It is added to this description of the then chaotic condition of the earth, "And the Spirit of God moved upon the face of the waters." I have indicated my opinion to be, that in this there is a reference to mighty rushing winds which then prevailed.

A statement made by Ruskin, another master in the art of word-painting, enables me to give some idea of what I suppose to have been then the state of the atmosphere in proximity to the waste of waters covering the earth whilst such commotions and darkness prevailed. It occurs in a work on a very different subject from that of Hugh Miller, but it is not the less suitable for my purpose. It is given in illustration of the power of representation manifested by painters:—

"There are comparatively few people," says he "who have seen the effect produced on the sea by a powerful gale, continued without intermission for three or four days and nights, and to those who have not it must be unimaginable, not from the mere size or force of surge, but from the complete annihilation of the limit between sea and air. The water from its prolonged agitation is beaten, not into mere creaming foam, but into masses of accumulated yeast, which hang in ropes and wreathes from wave to wave, and when one curls over to break, they form a festoon like a drapery from its edge; these are taken up by the wind, not in dissipating dust, but bodily, in wreathing, hanging, coiling masses, which make the air white and thick as with snow, only the flakes are a foot or two long each; the surges themselves are full of foam in their very bodies underneath,

---

* Testimony of the Rocks, Pages 176-177.

making them all white through, as the water is under a great cataract; and their masses being thus half water and half air, are torn to pieces by the wind whenever they rise, and carried away in roaring smoke, which chokes and strangles like actual water. It seems also as if the spray of the sea were caught by air and covered the surface of the sea, not merely with the smoke of finely divided water, but with boiling mist; and the low rain clouds brought down to the very level of the sea may be seen whirling and flying in rags from wave to wave. And finally, the surges themselves are to be seen in their utmost pitch of power, velocity, vastness, and madness, lifting themselves through all this chaos in precipices and peaks, furrowed with their whirl of ascent.

"Realize all this, and you will understand that in such a scene there is no visible distinction left between the sea and the air, that no object, nor horizon, nor any landmark or material evidence of position is left, that the heaven is all spray, and the ocean all cloud, and that you can see no further in any direction than you could see through a cataract.

"Few people have had an opportunity of seeing the sea at such a time, and few when they have can face it. To hold by a mast or a rock and watch it is a prolonged endurance of drowning which few people have courage to go through. To those who have, it is one of the noblest lessons of nature.

"The following passage from Fennimore Cooper describes such a scene, and it may be depended upon as entirely free from exaggeration:—

"'For the first time I now witnessed a tempest at sea. Gales and pretty hard ones I had often seen, but the force of the wind on this occasion as much exceeded that in ordinary gales of wind as the force of these had exceeded a wholesale breeze. The sea seemed crushed; the pressure of the swooping atmosphere, as the currents of the air went howling over the surface of the ocean, fairly preventing them from rising; or, when a mound of water did appear, it was scooped up and borne off in spray, as the axe dubs inequalities from the log. When the day returned, a species of lurid sombre light was diffused over the watery waste, though nothing was visible but the ocean and the ship. Even the sea birds seemed to have taken refuge in the caverns of the adjacent coast, none reappearing with the dawn. The air was full of spray, and it was with difficulty that the eye could penetrate as far as half-a-mile into the humid atmosphere.'—*Miles Wallingford.* Half-a-mile is an over estimate in coast.

"Turner has attempted to represent the ocean, after such a storm, in the *Slave Ship*:—It is sunset on the Atlantic, after prolonged storm; but the storm is partially lulled, and the torn and streamy rain-clouds are moving in scarlet lines to lose themselves in the hollow of the night. The whole surface of the sea included in the picture is divided into two ridges of enormous swell, not high nor local, but a low broad heaving of the whole ocean, like the lifting of its bosom by a deep drawn breath after the torture of the storm; between these two ridges the sunset falls along the trough of the sea, dyeing it with an awful but a glorious light, the intense and lurid splendour which burns like gold and bathes like blood. Along this fiery path and valley the tossing waves, by which the swell of the sea is restlessly divided, lift themselves in dark, indefinite, fantastic forms, each casting a faint and ghastly shadow behind it along the illumined foam. They do not rise everywhere, but three or four together in wild groups, fitfully and furiously as the under strength of the swell compels or permits them; leaving between them treacherous spaces of loose and writhing water, now lighted with green and lamp-like fire; now flashing back the gold of the declining sun; now fearfully dyed from above with the indistinguishable images of the burning clouds, which fall upon them in flakes of crimson and scarlet, and giving to the reckless waves the added motion of their own fiery flying. Purple and blue the lurid shadows of the hollow breakers are cast upon the mist of the night, which gathers cold and low, advancing like the shadow of death upon the guilty ship as it labours amidst the lightnings of the sea—its thin masts written upon the sky in lines of blood, girded with condemnation in that fearful hue, which signs the sky with horror, and mixes its flaming flood with the sunlight, and casting this far along the desolate heave of the sepulchral waves, incarnadines the multitudinous sea."

To any one who can divest his mind of the anachronisms of a sunset while as yet no sun had been seen, and a slave ship while as yet man was not, the triple picture supplied by what is said by Turner, Cooper, and Ruskin, may suggest some idea of what may have been the state of the atmostphere while darkness was upon the face of the waters, and the granite and the gneiss were being formed below.

Again I betake myself to Hugh Miller's *Testimony of the Rocks*. At the place at which I broke off my quotation he goes on to say :—

"At length, however, as the earth's surface gradually cooled down, and the enveloping waters sank to a lower temperature, let us suppose, during the later times of the mica schists and the earlier times of the clay slate, the steam atmosphere would become less dense and thick ; and at length the rays of the sun would struggle through, at first doubtfully and confused, forming a faint twilight, and gradually strengthening, as the later age of the slate formation passed away, until at the close of the great primary period *day and night*—the one still dim and gray, the other wrapt in a pall of thickest darkness—would succeed each other as now, as the earth revolved on its axis, and the unseen luminary rose high over the cloud in the east, or sank in the west beneath the undefined and murky horizon."

Turning to the Bible we read, "And God said, Let there be light : and there was light. And God saw the light, that it was good : and God divided the light from the darkness. And God called the light Day, and the darkness he called Night. . . . And God divided the waters which were under the firnament from the waters which were above the firnament : and it was so."

Then followed the deposit of the Cambrian, the Silurian, and Devonian systems, the grauwackes and sandy slates, the Silurian limestone, and the Old Red Sandstone : the first of which has been found 26,000 feet in thickness, and each of the others upwards of 8,000 feet : the first equivalent to about five miles, and each of the latter to about a mile and a half in measurement,—of which some idea may be formed from seeing in the face of Table Mountain a Silurian deposit upwards of half a mile in thickness.

To prevent misapprehension, I may mention that the masses presenting such measurement represent local accumulations and not the thickness of deposits the whole world round ; and that they are referred to now, only as supplying rough measurements of the lapse of time.

In all of these we find organic remains. Those found in the first mentioned stand low in the order of organic structures, those in the second stand somewhat higher in the order of classification generally adopted, and those in the third stand higher still. In the first, remains of mollusks—invertebrate animals—and fishes are found ; in the second appear remains of land animals ; and in the later deposited strata of the last are found remains of ferns—lepidodendra—and coniferous trees, and of amphibious animals which lived in the water but breathed air ; of none of which organic structures are remains found in the earlier deposits. Of what occurred in the course of the long vista of ages through which we thus look back to the periods of the deposit of gneiss, and schists, and slates, Hugh Miller writes :—

"The invertebrate life of the Silurian period, or even the ichthyic life of the earlier Old Red Sandstone period, must have been comparatively inconspicuous from any sub-ærial point of view, elevated but a few hundred feet over the sea level. Even the few islets of the later ages of the period, with their ferns, lepidodendra, and coniferous trees, forming as they did an exceptional feature in this age of vast oceans, and of organisms all but exclusively marine, may have well been excluded from a representative diorama that exhibited optically the grand characteristics of the time.

"Further, it seems equally probable that the introduction of organised existences on our planet was preceded by changes in the atmospheric condition which had obtained during the previous period in which the earth had been a desert and empty void.

"We know that just before the close of the Silurian ages terrestrial plants had appeared, and that before the close of the Old Red Sandstone age air-breathing animals had been produced, and we infer that the atmosphere in which both could have existed must have been considerably different from that which lay dark and heavy over the bare hot rocks and tenantless steam-emitting seas of the previous time.

"Under a gray opaque sky in which neither sun nor moon appear, we are not unfrequently presented with a varied drapery of clouds—a drapery varied in form though not in colour—a bank often seems placed over a bank, shaded beneath and lighter above; or the whole breaks into dappled cloudlets which bear, to borrow from the poetic description of Bloomfield, the

"Beauteous semblance of a flock at rest."

And if such aerial draperies appeared at this early period, with the clear space between them and the earth, which we so often see in gray sunless days, the optical effect must have been widely different from that of the previous time in which a dense vapourous fog lay heavy upon earth and sea, and extended from the earth's surface to the upper heights of the atmosphere."

He expresses the opinion—"It is certainly possible that in a vision of creation the atmospheric phenomena of the second great act of the creation drama might have stood out with much greater prominence . . . than any of its other appearances." And likening the record of ancient cosmogony in the beginning of Genesis to a vision in which, "as in the vision of St John in Patmos, voices were mingled with scenes, and the ear as certainly addressed as the eye," he goes on to say :—

"A 'great darkness' first falls upon the prophet, like that which in an earlier age fell upon Abraham, but without the 'horror;' and, as the Divine Spirit moves on the face of the wildly-troubled waters, a visible aurora enveloped by the pitchy cloud, the great doctrine is orally enunciated, that 'In the beginning God created the heavens and the earth.' Unreckoned ages, condensed in the vision into a few brief moments, pass away; the creative voice is again heard, 'Let there be light,' and straightway a gray diffused light springs up in the east, and, casting its sickly gleam over a cloud-limited expanse of steaming vaporous sea, journeys through the heavens towards the west. One heavy, sunless day is made the representative of myriads; the faint light waxes fainter,—it sinks beneath the dim undefined horizon; the first scene of the drama closes upon the seer; and he sits awhile on his hill-top in darkness, solitary but not sad, in what seems to be a calm and starless night.

"The light again brightens,—it is day; and over an expanse of ocean without visible bound the horizon has become wider and sharper of outline than before. There is life in that great sea,—invertebrate, mayhap also ichthyic life; but, from the comparative distance of the point of view occupied by the prophet, only the slow roll of its waves can be discerned, as they rise and fall in long undulations before a gentle gale; and what most strongly impresses the eye is the change which has taken place in the atmospheric scenery. That lower stratum of the heavens occupied in the previous vision by seething steam, or gray, smoke-like fog, is clear and transparent; and only in an upper region, where the previously invisible vapour of the tepid sea has thickened in the cold, do the clouds appear. But there, in the higher strata of the atmosphere, they lie, thick and manifold,— an upper sea of great waves, separated from those beneath by the transparent firmament, and, like them too, impelled in rolling masses by the wind. A mighty advance has taken place in creation; but its most conspicuous optical sign is the existence of a transparent atmosphere,—of a firmament stretched out over the earth, that separates the waters above from the waters below. But darkness descends for the third time upon the seer; for the evening and the morning have completed the second day."

Thus are we brought on to the period of the formation of the Old Red Sandstone, during which was deposited the strata capping Table Mountain and the Lion's Head,—designated old in contradistinction to a later stratification of red sandstone, designated new.

SECTION II.—*Geologic Formations less ancient than those of Table Mountain.*

The gneiss and schistose deposits, associated with granite such as is seen at Sea Point, and the slate and clay and sandstone deposits, of which Table Mountain and other mountains once connected with it are formed, tell of the whole district having been for ages—for untold ages—covered by a deep, deep sea—with, it may be, an occasional temporary elevation of it, or of some portion of the ocean bed near it, above the surface of the waste of waters only to be again submerged—but to establish this the evidence is defective. But the later formed deposits, with others of apparently a similar character and of the same age, seem to bring us within sight of what we may call dry land; and that dry land studded, if not clothed and covered, with vegetation appearing above what erewhile may have been a shoreless ocean. And of this elevation of the land, "standing," according to the statement of the apostle Peter, "out of the water and in the water," we find in later formed deposits, the remains of which exist in other parts of the Colony, additional and abounding indications.

In the Witteberg, in the Zuurberg at Winterhoek, and in the neighbourhood of Graham's Town, are sandstones of a white or yellowish colour, and a few beds of red or yellow shales, or clayey deposits, more or less impregnated with bituminous matter like petroleum, or mineral oil as it is called, the product of the decomposition, probably, of vegetable matter or of fat.

The aggregate deposits of dark-gray and brownish shales give a thickness of 1100 feet. Those in the Witteberg, the Zuurberg, and in the vicinity of Graham's Town, give a thickness of about 1000 feet. At Piennaar's Kloof and the Zuurberg are dark coloured shales, usually contorted like the sandstone below them, which must, therefore, have been deposited after them and contorted with them, possibly by the unequal contraction of these and of underlying strata. These shales, though of small thickness, give an aggregate thickness of 800 feet. These are known as the lower Karroo shales.

Subsequent to the deposit of these must have been projected from beneath, through clifts in the ground, what is called trap-rock—a conglomerate of this material and "numerous rounded and angular fragments of the older rocks, from the smallest grain to two feet in diameter, conformable as a mass to the beds above and below, showing a rude cleavage nearly at right angles to the general bedding." This, measuring from 500 to 800 feet in thickness, may be conjectured to be the product of submarine volcanoes.

After this, apparently, were deposited dark-gray shales and beds of sandstone about 1200 feet, or about a quarter of a mile, in thickness—seen in **the Karroo plain and at Fort Brown Flats**—and known as the upper **Karroo** shale, that below the trap being known, as I have stated, as the lower Karroo shales.

Both in the upper Karroo shale, in the lower Karroo shale, and in the underlying sandstone are found remains and impressions of land plants; and in the second of these are marine shells, from which it may be inferred that while land had by this time raised its head above the ocean surface, these were still a part of the ocean bed.

In the Kleine Roggeveldt, the Fish River, and at Fort Brown are brown sandstone, brown shales, and greenish shales of an aggregate thickness of 1500 feet, or about a third of a mile. In these the remains of plants are pretty common.

This supplies an indication that land upon which these had grown must have existed, and could not have been very remote from the place where they are found, though that place—the place of their deposit, may have been under deep water and long continued to be so—if it were not then being slowly lowered to a lower level throughout or in the course of a protracted period, for the deposits are of a thickness estimated at 1000 feet.

Thus are we brought to that part of the world's history of which we read, "And God said, Let the waters under the heaven be gathered together unto one place, and let the dry land appear: and it was so. And God called the dry land Earth; and the gathering together of the waters called he Seas: and God saw that it was good. And God said, Let the earth bring forth grass, the herb yielding seed, and the fruit-tree yielding fruit after his kind, whose seed is in itself upon the earth: and it was so. And the earth brought forth grass, and herb yielding seed after his kind, and the tree yielding fruit, whose seed was in itself, after his kind: and God saw that it was good." Remains of what appears to have been a species of grasswrack, *zostera*, or alva marina, which grows on sand or mud banks on the sea shore, and in creeks and salt water pools, have been found in Devonian or Old Red Sandstone deposits in Scotland, which were deposited long anterior to these; and it is only in strata deposited long subsequent to these that we find remains of what are known generally as trees yielding fruit; we are, however, supplied with indications of a luxuriant vegetation of some kind having now appeared on the dry land.

In these strata we find remains of plants, and amongst these have been identified remains of the *lepidodendron*, a plant the remains of which are frequently found in coal. In the best preserved specimens the inner portion of the plant has been petrified or decomposed and removed, and replaced by a deposit of soft quartzose sandstone, and the bark or skin has been converted into coal. This portion presents the appearance of overlapping scales, which is the characteristic of the species referred to, and from this it has received its designation, one from the Greek composed of *lepis*, a scale, and *dendron*, a tree.

It may be a help to some of my readers in enabling them to carry with them a definite idea of the ages of these formations, if I mention that some of the strata which come now to be noticed belong to what are known as the coal measures, immediately underlying which is the mountain limestone of which mention has been made, and which surmounts the Devonian or Old Red Stone. With this in mind let us study these strata more in detail.

While the superficial aspect of the earth was at this period such as has been indicated, there were then, as there had been before, and have been since, internal commotions protruding matter in a state of fusion from beneath, which in a viscid state spread out extensively from the rent by which it was ejected, crushed out by pressure on the elastic crust by increased deposits on some limited locality in the ocean bed, or blown out by steam produced from water which had percolated or sunk through some rent in the rocks by which it was separated from the molten mass of the globe.

As has been stated, in the Karroo are found what have been designated the *lower* Karroo shales, usually contorted like the sandstones below them.

They are themselves of small thickness, but the aggregate thickness of the whole is estimated at 800 feet. They may be seen both at Piennaar's Kloof and on the Zuurberg.

These must have been deposited after the beds of sand upon which they lie were deposited, but there are found in them marine shells, which show that, though there may have been islands or more extensive expanses of dry land above the ocean surface, upon which lepidodendra and other land plants grew more or less remote, this district at least was then a portion of the ocean-bed.

But overlying these shales, and underlying the other shales, which from this circumstance have been designated the *upper* Karroo shales, we find a kind of rock altogether different from all those which have come under our consideration hitherto. It is called trap conglomerate.

The designation trap has been given from the Swedish word *trappa*, a stair,—many hills formed of a kind of stone entering largely into the composition of this formation, presenting step-like terraced sides, having suggested the designation. It is applied to basalt, greenstone or whinstone, clinkstone, and several other similar rocks.

And the designation trap conglomerate is given to this formation because imbedded in the trap rock of which it is composed are numerous rounded and angular fragments of the older rocks, varying in magnitude from that of the smallest grain to two feet in diameter.

This mass of trap conglomerate, it is estimated, is from 500 to 800 feet in thickness.

It shows a rude cleavage nearly at right angles to the general bedding. It is in its lower surface conformable as a mass to the beds upon which it lies, and the overlying beds are conformable to its upper surface.

These circumstances, and together with these everything connected with it, indicates its having been formed by the protrusion from below of the material of which it is composed in a viscid semi-fluid state, allowing either of its spreading out in beds of this thickness under the ocean, or of its subsiding, after a sudden eruption in a more limited space, to the varying level which it now exhibits over its more extended bed. Thus does it appear that we have come upon strata not deposited by precipitation, but of volcanic origin, and thrown up from below.

Volcanoes in the form of burning mountains, as they are called by school-boys, may be confined apparently to dry-land, but in some cases it is only dry-land cast out by themselves, and the term is not so limited in its application by geologists and by students of physical geography. By them the term volcano, or some such term as *volcanic*, derived from it, is applied to other eruptions besides those of flame, including all discharges, through rents in the earth's crust, of cinders, ashes, stones, and rocky matter in a state of fusion.

Many islands of the Pacific and Atlantic oceans are accumulations of volcanic matter thrown up, it may be, through rents at the bottom of the sea, and the magnitude of some of these is very great. "Owhyhee," to quote from De la Beche, "is a magnificent example of such an island: the whole mass, estimated as exposing a surface of 4,000 square miles, is composed of lava or other volcanic matter, which rises in the peaks of Mouna Roa and Mouna Koa to the height of between 15,000 and 16,000 feet above the level of the sea."

Similar, apparently, has been the origin of this trap conglomerate. Whether it rose above the surface of the sea or not does not appear, but cases have not been unknown in our own day of islands of volcanic ashes having been thrown up, and again in a short time washed down and strewn upon the ocean basin. And thus may this trap conglomerate have found a resting-place, and after the temporary disturbance—if it did rise above the waves—the deposit of debris appears to have gone on as before; but in this debris are imbedded indications that there was land not far off, for above this trap conglomerate, and conformed thereto, we find dark-gray shales and a few beds of sandstone, in which impressions of land plants are found. These strata, as has been intimated, are what are called the upper Karroo shales, being so designated in contradistinction to the *lower Karroo* shales, or those underlying this mass of trap conglomerate.

These upper Karroo shales may be seen in the Karroo plain, and on the Fort Beaufort Flats, and with them have been identified the Ecca shales. They are of an aggregate thickness of about 1200 feet, which speaks of a long duration of the then existing state of things.

With regard to the numerous rounded or angular fragments of the older rock imbedded in the trap, it is alleged, in accordance with phenomena observed in our own day, that a volcano in action throws up often red-hot stones, torn off, by the force of the current of molten matter, from the rocks through which it passes towards the natural orifice.

I find it more satisfactory to attribute the severance of the fragments to the heat of the lava than to the force of the current, and to the impinging force of fragments thus borne along by the current. In illustration of what may be effected by heat, I may state that Dr Livingstone, writing of the highlands in the districts of Gova, says, "Several of the mountain sides in this country are remarkably steep, and the loose blocks on them sharp and angular, without a trace of weathering. For a time we considered this angularity of the loose fragments as evidence that the continent was of comparatively recent formation, but we afterwards heard the operation actually going on by which the boulders are split into these sharp fragments. The rocks are heated by the torrid sun during the day to such an extent that one is sometimes startled, on sitting down on them after dusk, to find them quite too hot for the flesh, protected only by the trousers, to bear. The thermometer placed on them rises to 137° in the sun. These heated surfaces, cooling from without by the evening air, contract more externally than within, and the unyielding interior forces off the outer parts to a distance of one or two feet. Let any one in a rocky place observe the fragments that have been thus shot off, and he will find in the vicinity pieces, from a few ounces to one or two hundred pounds in weight, which exactly fit the new surface of the original block; and he may hear in the evening among the hills, where sound travels readily, the ringing echo of the reports which the natives ascribe to Mchesi, or evil spirits, and the more enlightened to these natural causes."

Fragments severed thus from the solid rock by the heat of the traps in a state of fusion, borne along with force, may, in such an eruption as produced this trap's formation, have broken off other fragments to be borne along in a similar way and with similar effect.

It may seem to some that the rounded form of some of the stones imbedded in the trap speaks of water action, but I do not feel myself shut up to adopt this conclusion. In an active volcano may be seen stones thrown up to a great height, which fall again and again into the crater, knocking against each other, and knocking the corners from each other more quickly than is done by the friction of shingle on the beach, and thus may these stones have been rounded. While this is not proven, it should be borne in mind that the rounded form of the pebble, attributed to water action, has been produced by the fluidity and not by the constituents of the water, and by the fluidity acting as a means of occasioning the friction of one hard substance on another, and thus leaving them to do the work; and this might be accomplished by a current of trap as well as by a current of water.

The Geysers in Iceland, fountains of hot-water rising to a height of 200 feet, which are intermitting in their action, have been brought to play at other times than they naturally would by throwing quantities of stones into the orifice whence issues the jet. Dr Henderson, in his Journal of a Residence in Iceland during the years 1814 and 1815, in narrating what occurred in connection with one of these induced eruptions, writes, "Having made a speedy retreat, I now took my station on the windward side, and was astonished to observe the elevation of the jets, some of them rising higher than two hundred feet; many of the fragments of stones were thrown much higher, and some of considerable size were raised to an invisible height. For some time every succeeding jet seemed to surpass the preceding, till the quantity of water in the subterranean caverns being spent, they gave place to the columns of steam, which continued to rush up with a deafening roar for upwards of half-an-hour."

Next day he repeated the experiment. He writes, " Being anxious to ascertain the reality of my supposed discovery, I got my servant to assist me about eight o'clock in casting all the loose stones we could find into the spring. We had not ceased five minutes when the wished-for phenomena recommenced, and the jets were carried to a height little inferior to what they had gained the preceding evening. At half-past nine I was obliged to set out on my journey, but often looked back on the thundering column of steam, and reflected with amazement at my having given such an impulse to a body which no power on earth could control."

In writing of a natural eruption, he mentions, " The large stones which we had previously thrown into the pipe were ejaculated to a great height, especially one which was thrown much higher than the water;" and in writing of another he says, " The jets of water now subsided; but their place was occupied by the spray and steam, which, having free room to play, rushed with a deafening roar to a height little inferior to that of the water. On throwing the largest stones which we could find into the pipe, they were instantly propelled to an amazing height; and some of them that were cast up more perpendicularly than the others remained for the space of four or five minutes within the influence of the steam, being successively ejected, and falling again in a very amusing manner."

In these the transparency and tenuity of the water let the stones be seen. It is not unnatural to suppose that in the eruption of the trap in a state of fusion something similar may have occurred to the stones borne along by it, and such collisions as they had might suffice to give them something at least of the rounded form which many of them present.

Superimposed on this trap conglomerate lie the upper Karroo shales.

In the upper part of the scarp of Kleine Roggeveldt at Fort Brown, and at other parts of the Fish River valley, we find brown sandstone and shales, and greenish-coloured sandstone and shales, which appear to be of a still later deposit than the upper Karroo shales. In these the impressions and remains of plants are pretty common, which shows that though these parts were still under water there was land not far off, and this land probably gaining upon the sea in that region, for no such abundance of evidence of the existence of land plants is found in the lower-lying strata.

The period over which this subsidence of the sea—or elevation of the land—extended must have been a very protracted one, for the aggregate thickness of these beds is estimated at 1,500 feet, those of the upper Karroo shales is estimated at 1,200, and those of the lower Karroo shales at 800, or 3,500 feet in all; and though some of these deposits may have been going on in different places at the same time, the time required for the abrasion, suspension, conveyance, and deposit of the whole must have been long; and at a corresponding slow progress periods of still greater changes were approaching.

Towards the north of the Colony, and in regions beyond, we find deposited above those already described, and consequently of a later formation, beds of purple, gray, and greenish shales, intermixed with fewer sandstone beds, giving in the aggregate a thickness of 1,700 feet, or very nearly a third of a mile; and in these are found remains of plants, fish teeth, and reptilian bones,—indicative of the existence of inland lakes separated from the ocean by intervening land, which may have allowed of an outlet to the vast reservoir, but no entrance, or this only at times far separated, and even then only a partial one, to the waters of the sea. Islands rising above the level of the sea is all of which we have had indications hitherto; now we have indications of the lower-lying lands between these rising above the waters, and with them forming a continent, with a vast extent of it covered with the waters of an inland lake, and that for such a length of time that the silt is of the thickness stated.

The strata now under consideration have been called the Dicynodon strata, from the fossil remains of a reptile so named being found in them. They will afterwards come under consideration.

In the Stormberg, the Sneewberg, Nieuveldt, Roggeveldt, &c., are found distinct tiers of sandstone, separated by shales containing abundance of land plants and beds of coal and of graphite or black-lead, which is apparently altered coal, together with remains of reptiles, but these in diminished numbers. The aggregate thickness of these beds is about 1,800 feet, or upwards of a third of a mile. All these tell still of water under which the deposits have been made, but they tell also of the great increase of dry-land. If the coal be formed from wood which had grown on the spot where it is found, they tell of alternations of periods of lengthened duration, during which the same land was above and below the water surface. But if of this there be no indication, it may be conjectured that the wood was carried thither by water currents.

These later deposits have been identified with those of the coal measures of other lands, and they introduce us to indications which give us a glimpse of another and that a very different hydrographic condition of the land, from that of a deep and shoreless ocean, such as was indicated by the primary beds of gneiss, of schists, and of slate; and the superimposed Cambrian, Silurian, and Devonian deposits. To quote again from the historian of the Old Red Sandstone, "Yet again the light rises under a canopy of cloud; but the scene has changed, and there is no longer an unbroken expanse of sea. The white surf breaks at the distant horizon, on an insulated reef, formed mayhap by the Silurian or Old Red coral zoophytes ages before, during the bygone yesterday; and beats in long lines of foam, nearer at hand, against a low, winding shore, the seaward barrier of a widely spread country. For at the Divine command the land has arisen from the deep,—not inconspicuously and in scattered islets, as at an earlier time, but in extensive though flat and marshy continents, little raised over the sea level, and a yet further flat has covered them with the deep carboniferous flora. The scene is one of mighty forests of cone-bearing trees,—of palms, and tree-ferns, of gigantic club-mosses, on the opener slopes, and of great rocks clustering by the sides of quiet lakes and dark rolling rivers. There is deep gloom in the recesses of the thicker woods, and low thick mists creep along the dank marsh or sluggish swamps. But there is a general lightening of the sky over-head: as day declines, a redder flush than had hitherto lighted the prospect falls athwart fern-covered bank and long withering glade."

And elsewhere he writes, "For seven formations together—from the lower Silurian to the upper Old Red Sandstone—our course has been over oceans without a visible shore, though, like Columbus on his voyage of discovery, we have now and then found a little floating weed to indicate the approaching land. The water seems fast shallowing,—we are passing into new scenes. Yonder passes a broken branch with the leaves still unwithered, and there floats a tuft of fern,—and now, there is land! Land! A low shore thickly covered with vegetation as we approach it.

"Huge trees of wonderful form stand out far in the water. There seems no intervening beach. A thick hedge of reeds tall as masts of pinnaces run along the deeper bays, like water flags at the edge of a lake. A river of vast volume comes rolling from the interior, darkening the water for leagues with its slime and mud, and bearing with it to the open sea reeds. and ferns, and cones of the pine, and immense floats of leaves, and now and then some bulky tree undermined and uprooted by the current. Entering the opening of the stream, we find a scarcely penetrable phalanx of reeds, that attain to the height and well nigh the bulk of forest trees, ranged on either side. The bright and glossy stems seem rodded like Gothic columns; the pointed leaves stand out green at every joint, tier above tier, each tier resembling a coronal wreath or an ancient crown, with the rays turned outwards; and we see a top that may be either large spikes or catkins.

"Strange forms of vegetable life appear in the forests behind! Can that be a club-moss which raises its slender height far more than 50 feet from the soil? Or can these tall palm-like trees be actual ferns, and these spreading branches mere fronds? And these gigantic reeds!—are they not mere varieties of the common horse-tails of our bogs and morasses, magnified some sixty or a hundred times?

"Have we arrived at some such country as the continent visited by Gulliver, in which he found thickets of weeds and grass tall as woods of twenty years growth, and lost himself amidst a field of corn fifty feet in height?

"The lesser vegetation of our own country—its reeds, mosses, and ferns —seem here as if viewed through a microscope. The dwarfs have sprung up into giants, and yet there appears to be no proportionate increase in size among what are unequivocally its trees!

"Yonder is a group of what seem to be pines—tall and bulky, 'tis true, but neither taller nor bulkier than the pines of America or Norway; and the club-moss behind shoots up its green hairy arms, loaded with what seem catkins, above their topmost cones. But what monster of the vegetable world comes floating across the stream—now circling round in the eddies, now dancing on the ripple, now shooting down the rapid? It resembles a gigantic star-fish, or an immense coach-wheel divested of the rim. There is a green, dome-like mass in the centre, that corresponds to the nave of the wheel or the body of the star-fish, and the boughs shoot out horizontally on every side, like spokes from the nave or rays from the central body. The diameter considerably exceeds 40 feet; the branches, originally of a deep green, are assuming the golden tinge of decay; the cylindrical and hollow leaves stand out on every side, like prickles of the wild-rose on the red, fleshy, lance-like shoots of a year's growth, that will be covered two seasons hence with flowers and fruit. That strangely-formed organism finds no existing type among all the numerous families of the vegetable kingdom.

"There is an amazing luxuriance of growth all around us. Scarce can the currents make way through the thicket of aquatic plants that rise thick from the muddy bottom; and though the sun shines bright on the upper boughs of the tangled forest beyond, not a ray penetrates the more than twilight gloom which broods over the marshy platform below.

"The rank steam of decaying vegetation forms a dense, thick haze, that partially obscures the underwood; deadly lakes of carbonic acid gas have accumulated in the hollows; there is silence all around, uninterrupted save by the sudden plunge and splash of some reptile fish that has risen to the surface in pursuit of its prey, or when a sudden breeze stirs the hot air and shakes the fronds of the giant ferns or the catkins of the reeds. The wide continent before us is a continent devoid of animal life, save that its pools and its rivers abound in fish and mollusca, and that millions and tens of millions of the infusorial tribes swarm in the bogs and marshes. Here and there, too, an insect of strange form flutters among the leaves. It is more than probable that no creature furnished with lungs of the more perfect kind could have breathed the atmosphere of this early period and have lived."

"At the close of the Old Red Sandstone period," says Page, "the earth seems to have undergone an almost total change in its geological conditions. The red sandstones and gravelly conglomerates which had been formed along the shores and bottom of the sea were upheaved into dry land; thus adding to the extent of land previously existing, and gradually circumscribing the limits of the ocean in which subsequent deposits were to take place As disintegrated granite furnished the felspar, quartz, and mica of the gneiss and mica schist, and as from these, again, were obtained the materials of the clay-slate, grauwacke, and silurian rocks, so from all these, together with the newly upheaved red sandstone, were derived the material of the succeeding formation. These successive attritions would reduce quartz to sand of various fineness, felspar to loose impalpable clay, mica from large plates to minute scales, and crystalline limestone to a dully powdery consistence. The rocks formed of these ingredients would necessarily present a less compact texture; and thus it is in the Carboniferous System that the sandstones are more arenaceous, the shales soft and earthy, and the limestones non-crystalline and often impure. Besides the sandstone, clay, and limestone, two new rock substances make their appearance among the strata of this system, namely, *coal* and *ironstone*—the former being the result of compressed and altered vegetation, and the latter a chemical aggregation of the metallic particles around some earthy basis. The iron of the Old Red Sandstone was disseminated through the mass as mere colouring matter; in the carboniferous formation it is principally collected in layers, or in nodules. The vegetation of previous periods was so scanty, as to leave only a few dubious impressions among the strata. During this era it was so abundant as to form numerous beds of coal, ranging in thickness from a few inches to twenty or even thirty feet."

Writing of the organic remains found in the so-called coal measures, he remarks that,—" The abundance of terrestrial vegetation is by far the most distinguishing feature, though, as might be expected from the nature of the deposit, marine shells, fishes, and other aquatic exuviæ, are not unfrequent."

Having previously stated that coal is in its mass composed of plants, altered by compression and conversion into bitumen, he goes on to say,— " On account of this change, it is often impossible, at first sight, to detect any trace of vegetable structure; but on closer inspection, the woody fibre may be seen in many specimens; while it is possible in almost all to make visible the cells and fibre by exposing thin slices to the transmission of a powerful light. In this way Mr Witham observed the various vegetable tissues in coal, thereby adding another testimony to the numerous evidences of its organic origin. In most of the bituminous beds, however, the external form is obliterated, and it is to detached fossils in the sandstones and lighter shales that the geologist is indebted for his knowledge respecting the Flora of the carboniferous era. About four hundred species have been already determined, chiefly gigantic equisetums, ferns, clubmosses, cactuses, pines, and plants allied to the bulrush, cane, and bamboo. Most of these resemble existing plants merely in their generic distinctions, having belonged to species which flourished during the coal-forming period, and became extinct with the peculiar conditions of the globe which gave them birth. Some of the most characteristic of the vegetable fossils belonging to this formation are—1. *Sigillaria*, so called from the graven appearance of its stem; 2. *Calamites*, from the reed-like jointings of its stalk; 3. *Stigmaria*, from its stigmata, or punctures; 4. *Lepidodendron* (Gr., *lepis*, a scale, and *dendron*, a tree), from the scaly appearance of its bark. These fossils occur in all the members, from the lowest white sandstone beneath the mountain limestone, up to the commencement of the new red sandstone, at which stage they disappear, and do not seem to have flourished during the deposition of any subsequent formation. The best preserved specimens are found in the shales and sandstones; the interior structure of the plant being converted into soft quartzose sandstone, and the bark, or cuticle, into a glistening bituminous coal. In the coal, the vegetable structure is always more or less obliterated, though sometimes a solitary trunk occurs of the same quartzose material as those imbedded in the shales and sandstones. Of these fossil trees, many have been found of gigantic dimensions; as, for example a lepidodendron in the Jarrow coal-field, 13½ feet wide at the base, and 39 feet high, exclusive of the branches at the top, which were also entire; and a conifera of the genus *auracaria* in Craigleith quarry, 3 feet in diameter, and 20 feet long. Besides the sigillaria, &c., above described, there are numerous species of tree-ferns, club-mosses, equisetums, and other cryptogamic plants preserved in the shales; their dark carbonaceous leaves and branches being often beautifully displayed upon the light-coloured ground of the material in which they are imbedded; namely, *Asterophyllites* (Gr., *aster*, a star, and *phyllon*, a leaf); *Sphenopteris* (*sphen*, a wedge, and *pteron*, a wing); *Pecopteris* (*pecos*, a comb, and *pteron*, a wing); all so named from the shape of their respective leaves.

"*Of the conditions of the world during the deposition of the carboniferous system*, we have more obvious evidence than of those under which any of the earlier systems were formed. The extent of the seas in which the deposit took place is very clearly indicated by the course of the mountain limestone, which must have been formed at no great depths from the shore, as its corallines, corals, shells, and other exuviæ, prove it to be of littoral origin. All the members of the system, with the exception perhaps of the limestones, are eminently sedimentary; and the numerous alternations of these strata evince frequent changes in the depositing agents. At one time the rivers seem to have carried down sand to form sandstones, at another clay and mud to form shale, and at a third period vegetable drift to form coal; for strata of these material often directly overlie each other. It must be borne in mind, however, that sand, clay, and plants, might be carried down at the same time, and that they would arrange themselves according to their gravity—the sand depositing itself along the shores, the mud farther seaward, and the vegetables in any still bay where currents of wind or water might drift them. Such an arrangement would take place under the ordinary operations of water; but during violent inundations, there would be a confused intermingling of sand, mud, and plants, and this we often discover; so that, taking all things into account, we learn that the same agencies of rivers, waves, and tides, existed during the deposition of the carboniferous rocks as exist at the present day, only on a more gigantic and uniform scale. Looking at the abundance of marine life which must have thronged the waters during the formation of the mountain limestone, and at the vast amount of vegetation which the earth must have sustained while the deposition of the coal measures took place, we are led to infer that the earth then enjoyed a much higher and more uniform temperature than it has ever since experienced. At present, we find a faint analogy in the Fauna of the tropical seas, and in the Flora of the tropical jungles, to those of the carboniferous era; but so faint, that we can scarcely institute a comparison between the results produced. The coral-reefs of the Pacific are insignificant compared with the thickness and extent of the mountain limestone; and the vegetable drift of the Mississipi and Ganges combined would scarcely produce carbonaceous matter sufficient to colour one stratum of shale. Notwithstanding this there is a resemblance between the coral productions of the Pacific and those of the mountain limestone; and between the palms, tree-ferns, canes, and cactaceæ of the tropies, and the fossil plants of the coal measures. The heat of the tropics is directly derived from the sun, and the torrid zone occupies but a narrow belt of the earth's surface; whereas the coal measures are to be found in almost every region of the globe. The sun could not, therefore, have yielded that temperature which nourished the plants and animals of this period; for though the sun's heat had been greater than at present, it could not have been universally diffused. The conclusion, therefore, to which most geologists have come is, that the earth, originally an incandescent mass, was gradually cooled down —hot enough to render gneiss and mica schists crystalline; cool enough during the grauwacke and silurian eras to permit of marine corals, shell-fish, and crustacea; cooler still during the life of the plated fishes of the old red sandstone; and only sufficiently genial throughout the deposition of the carboniferous period to foster a growth of terrestrial vegetation all over its surface, to which the existing jungles of the tropics are mere barrenness in comparison. This high and uniform temperature, combined (as suggested by Brogniart) with a greater proportion of carbonic acid gas in the atmosphere, would not only sustain a gigantic and prolific Flora, but would also create denser vapours, showers, and rains; and, these, again, gigantic rivers, periodical inundations, and deltas. Thus all the conditions for the extensive estuary deposits would arise from this high temperature; and every circumstance connected with the coal measures points to such conditions.

"*With regard to the formation of coal*, geologists are not yet fully agreed. On examining sandstone or shale, it is easy to perceive from their structure, texture, and composition, that they must at one time have been respectively loose sand and mud, borne down and deposited by water; but the case is somewhat different with beds of coal. This mineral, being chiefly composed of carbon, hydrogen, and oxygen—the same elements which enter into the composition of plants—and revealing in its mass evidence of vegetable structure, no doubt is entertained of its organic origin. But whether the plants of which it is composed were drifted down by rivers, and deposited along with layers of mud and sand in estuaries, or whether dense forests and peat mosses were submerged, and then overlaid by deposits of sand and mud, are the questions at issue. According to the latter hypothesis, the vegetable matter must have grown in dense jungles for many years; then the land must have sunk, and become the basin of a lake or estuary, in which situation rivers would wash into it mud and sand, and these would cover the vegetable mass, and form beds of shale and sandstone. This being done, it is supposed that the area of deposit was again elevated, so as to become the scene of luxuriant vegetation; again submerged, and overlaid by new deposits of sandstone and shale; once more elevated, and covered with plants, and then submerged: and this alternating process of submergence and elevation is contended to have taken place as often as there are beds of coal in any particular coal-field. The other theory is, that while partial elevations and submersions might take place as at the present day, the great mass of the coal measures was deposited in lakes and estuaries; that the vegetable matter of which coal is formed was drifted into these estuaries by rivers and inundations; and that various rivers might discharge themselves into one estuary, some chiefly carrying down sand, while others transported plants, mud, and heterogeneous debris. This theory also supposes that the transporting rivers were subject to periodical inundations, and that, during the intervals of overflow, the deltas were choked with a rank vegetation, which, in conjunction with the vegetable drift from inland, went to the formation of beds of coal.

"*Both theories are at present beset with many difficulties;* but the latter is the generally received, as accounting for most of the phenomena connected with our coal-fields. According to the former theory, a submergence and elevation must have taken place for every seam of coal; and as in some districts from thirty to forty seams occur, varying in thickness from a few inches to many feet, it is impossible to conceive how the earth, in this unstable condition, could have nourished such a prolific Flora as the coal measures clearly demonstrate. It is also justly objected against this theory, that some thick beds of coal are subdivided by thin layers of sandstone, or ferruginous shale, a fact which would imply that many elevations and submergences took place even during the formation of a single coal bed; whereas by the latter theory, those layers of sandstone, &c., present no difficulty, as the river, while it bore down vegetable drift, would carry at the same time sand and other debris. Further, shells and fishes are sometimes found imbedded in coal; and it is difficult to conceive how these could have got there, unless in the ordinary way of deposit and sediment. Forests of coniferæ, palms, and tree-ferns, could not have been submerged and covered up with sand and mud, without the trunks being abundantly found in an upright position; now, this upright position of fossil trees is rarely or ever met with. Again, had coal resulted from submerged peat mosses, instead of from growing forests, there is no means by which we can account for the occurrence of shells, fishes, and thin layers of sandstone in its mass. By the latter theory all these can be readily accounted for. Over vast deltas, such as those in which it supposes the coal measures to have been deposited, there would not only occur growing stems of palms, ferns, reeds, and the like, to be silted up perpendicularly, but there would also occur morasses choked up with a rank growth of grasses, while in the creeks and lagoons, shell-fish, fishes, and other aquatic life would abound. In the deltas of existing rivers, the latter theory meets with a perfect analogy; and when the student is told of the rafts of the Mississipi, the mangrove jungle of the Niger, and the sand and mud-banks of the Ganges, he can have little difficulty in forming a conception of the estuaries in which the sandstones, shells, shell-limestones, and coal of the carboniferous era were deposited."

The vegetation of the coal period seems to have resembled, in some measure, that of islands in the middle of vast oceans; and the prevalence of ferns indicates a climate similar to that of New Zealand at the present day.

In speaking of the island vegetation of the coal epoch, Professor Ansted remarks—" The whole interior of the islands may have been crowned with thicks forests, the dark mauve of which would only be interrupted by the bright green of the swamps in the hollows, or the brown tint of the ferns covering some district near the coasts.

"The forests may have been formed by a mixture of different trees. We would see then, *e.g.* the lofty and wide-spreading lepidodendron, its delicate, feathery, and moss-like fronds, clothing in rich luxuriance branches and stems which are built up, like the stem of the tree-fern, by successive leafstalks that have, one after another, dropt away, giving by their decay additional height to the stem, which might at length be mistaken for that of a gigantic pine.

"There also should we find the sigillaria, its tapering and elegant form sustained on a large and firm basis, enormous matted roots, almost as long as the trunk itself, being given off in every direction, and shooting their fibres far into the sand and clay in search of moisture. The stem of this tree would appear like a fluted column, rising simply and gracefully, without branches, to a great height, and then spreading out a magnificent head of leaves, like a noble palm tree.

"Other trees more or less resembling palms, and others like existing firs also abounded, giving a richness and variety to the scene; while one gigantic species, strikingly resembling the Norfolk Island pine, might be seen towering a hundred feet or more above the rest of the forest, and exhibiting teir after tier of branches richly clothed with its peculiar pointed spear-like leaves, the branches gradually diminishing in size as they approached the apex of a lofty pyramid of vegetation.

"Tree-ferns, also in abundance, might there be recognised occupying a prominent place in the physiognomy of vegetation, and dotted at intervals over the distant plains and valleys, the intermediate space being clothed with low vegetation of more humble plants of the same kind. These we may imagine exhibiting their rich crests of numerous fronds, each many feet in length, and produced in such quantities as to rival even the palm trees in beauty.

"Besides all these, other trees of that day, whose stems and branches are now called *calamites*, existed chiefly in the midst of swamps, and bore their singular branches and leaves aloft with strange and monotonous uniformity. All these trees, and many others that might be associated with them, were perhaps girt round with innumerable creepers and parasitic plants climbing to the top-most branches of the most lofty amongst them, and enlivening, by the bright and vivid colour of their flowers, the dark and gloomy character of the great masses of vegetation."

The condition of the country, indicated by the strata and the fossils of the coal measures of the Colony, must have extended far to the north of districts of the Colony in which they are found. The coal mines of Natal promises to be more productive than those of the Cape of Good Hope, and hundreds of miles to the north of Natal their are similiar indications of a similar state of things having, in the same era, prevailed also there.

Speaking of the Moio hills, which are hills close to or intersecting the Zambesi below the Victoria Falls, Dr Livingstone says—"They are generally of igneous or metamorphic rocks—clay-slate or trap—with porcellanite and zoolite. The principal rock in the central part of the country, where no syenite or gneiss had been upheaved, seems to be a gray, coarse sandstone, known to us by the name of Tette sandstone. Large masses of it still lie horizontally or only slightly inclined. When much disturbed, it has been tilted up by the eruption of igneous rocks, and near the point of contact it has either been hardened or melted, and the coal which elsewhere still lies under the undisturbed stratum is crystallized or entirely burned. The igneous rocks often form dykes, as that called Nakabele, which stretches like a dam across the western entrance to the Kariba gorge. In the vicinity of the erupted rocks we usually meet soft, calcareous tufa, as if after the igneous action many hot fountains flowing had deposited lime from their water. Previous, however, to this period of eruption and upheaval, it is probable that the sandstone formed the bed of prodigious inland seas, along the low shores of which the plants of the coal flourished, succeeded, as the land was gradually elevated, by the trees we now find silicified on the surface; these may perhaps have been submerged, as the land again sank under some igneous agency, and became subject to the action of water, at a high temperature holding silica in solution. However that may have been, it is certain that a coal-field of unknown extent exists, for coal is found cropping out near to the lava or basalt, which is the principal rock of the Victoria Falls, and, with the 'faults' alluded to, it extends to the east of Tette. Then again we saw it in the Bovum, with the same characteristic of fossil-wood lying in the gray sandstone. With abundance of fine iron ore, the existence of this prodigious coal-field leads to the belief that an important future is in store for Africa."

Writing again of the Zungive, a little nearer the Falls, he says—" As in many other streams from Chicova to Sinamane, shale and coal crop out of the bank; and here the large roots of stigmaria, or its allied plants, were found."

The beds of coal found in the Stormberg and elsewhere have been identified with the coal measures of Europe and America. The aggregate thickness of those found in the Cape Colony is about 1,800 feet, but these represent deposits which in Wales measure 15,000 feet in thickness. And in the one country as in the other there are indications of many successive elevations and submergences of land having occurred in the course of the protracted period of their formation.

Knowing that Dr George Grey, of Cradock, Fellow of the Geological Society of Edinburgh, had given much attention to the geology of the district in which he dwelt, I took occasion to write to him, requesting information in regard to fossil-vegetable remains which had come under his notice, and the condition in which they were found. I received in reply the following letter:—

"CRADOCK, *November* 30, 1865.

"MY DEAR SIR,—I duly received your note of the 16th inst., in which you ask me to send you any printed notices relative to the Botanic Geology of the district, and would have answered it by first post, but I have been since its receipt a good deal engaged with country work at considerable distances, which has prevented me till now. It would give me great pleasure to be of any service to you in such a way. Unfortunately, all *printed* letters or notices on geological subjects, which might be considered as of any interest, have had reference chiefly to the trap and other igneous rocks, greenstone dykes, quartz rocks and their connections, and sometimes general remarks on the Dicynodonts—written in a popular style, being designed for perusal by ordinary readers.

"The only letter on carboniferous deposits was published in our local paper about two years since, when I alluded to some mineral carbonaceous substances belonging to the northern part of our district, and located on the southern edge of the Stormberg carboniferous series. These substances seemed to approach in nature to a mineral, discovered a short time previously, named 'Dysodile.' Dysodile of itself is not quite a combustible matter; the largest part of it is inorganic, the following being its analysis in 100 pts.:—

Combustible matter,	36·51
Water, &c.,	2·30
Mineral matter (containing Silica, Alumina, Iron, &c.),	61·19
	100.00

"In the same letter I stated the carbonaceous substances in question to be mingled with the shales of the upper coal measures, presenting the appearance of a brownish-gray slate, rather than that of any kind of fuel, burning freely though with an offensive smell. The odour evidently results from the impregnation of sulphurets, which obtain extensively throughout our igneous chains of hills, whether the latter are clothed with carboniferous formations, as in the Stormberg, or with the calciferous marls and sandstone of the secondary deposits of the mountain masses in our more immediate neighbourhood.

"The fossil coal plants of the Stormberg series (a goodly number of specimens of which I lately sent to the Geological Society of Edinburgh) consist chiefly, as far as I have seen, of well-marked specimens of calamites, lepidodendra, zamites, sigillaria, and various ferns of the order neuropteris, pecopteris, sphenopteris, &c. A friend who lived for some time in the locality of the Stormberg tells me that 'Calamite reticulations (called "rootlets" in the Graham's Town museum) are observable in all the sandstones of the Stormberg, from the base to the recurring sandstones of the upper Stormberg overlying the coal-beds.' Graphite has frequently been found in the black shales, which contain also impressions of ferns. Doubtless, coal seams may be found to prevail in all the series of the Stormberg shales and sandstone, say 1000 feet or so beneath the present coal-beds. From the base of the Stormberg range, the district of Queenstown extends away towards the south, and as viewed from the Stormberg presents the appearance of a great plain studded all over with mountains of every variety of shape.

"The deposits of the upper coal measures of the Stormberg series are shalsy and thin, alternating with softish dark sandstone and marly clay admixtures. It is very doubtful whether the expenses of transport will admit of the coal being made use of for economic purposes.

"Mr W. Baillie, of Andries Nek, was good enough, a short time since, to send me a large sack of his 'best' coal. It contained a good deal of lignite. Some specimens were hard, approaching to anthracite. It burned pretty fairly, giving out a moderate amount of heat which, however, was of rather limited duration. Andries Nek is about three hours ride from Queenstown. I should suppose its coal affords a fair illustration of what may occur in the whole Stormberg seams. Igneous causes beneath had probably rendered the coal in many parts semi-anthracitic. Various kinds of mineral pyrites, and other sulphurites abound thereabouts, probably in considerable quantities.

"The fossil-wood deposits near here are distinct from the upper coal measures which stop at the southern edge of the Stormberg. These wood deposits are to be found in combination with the Dicynodon beds, and would appear to have been disintegrated from below by eruptive force. In the Dicynodon beds the matrix of the animals is in juxtaposition to these broken up and triturated materials, which are doubtless disintegrated from older carboniferous formations; whilst other particles of various kinds now lying in the same beds may have been detached from metamorphic and crystalline compounds, according to their composition, as noticed *in situ*. It is therefore not to be wondered at that the matrix and bones of the animals are quite commonly found to have precipitated on their surface deposits of silica, mica schist, &c.

"The carboniferous fossil fragments of these beds are confined to the secondary rocks, and have nothing in common with the tertiary sandstones or the argillaceous beds conjoining them. These fragments can be occasionally picked up in small detached pieces, and not unfrequently present the appearance of having belonged to trunks of a goodly size; but, having been subjected to action of a decidedly convulsive nature, they are, as a rule, of an indeterminate class. They have in all probability been broken up and propelled by eruptive forces identical with those which have probably worked the beds themselves into their present position.

"Igneous agency below and aqueous agency around must have in the course of time effected curious transformations in the deposits of these beds in olden days; and this is shown in the fact of many of the sandstones of these beds forming conglomerates with all sorts of foreign deposits, as igneous rock fragments, forming, to the present view, nuclei for clays and sandstones, chalybeate oxides. The above-mentioned fossil-woods, &c., &c., in fact almost every imaginable kind of petrified material, inclusive of the Saurian organisms, may there be found.

"The Dicynodon beds, with their deposits, are visible only where they have been propelled through superincumbent sandstone, by means of the eruptive forces I have just alluded to. Denudation by action of water has worked out for them a comparatively recent bed of a blue argillaceous nature; and these beds are only to be found on the slopes of the igneous hills, or where cracks or fissures have occurred in the superincumbent sandstones.

"That the true coal formations stop short at the southern edge of the Stormberg is evident on inspection. The upper coal measures are, as I think I have already stated, shaley and thin, alternating with dark shales of softish sandstones. Although they are pretty prolific in fossil monocotyledonous plants and ferns, yet the 'carboniferous or mountain limestone' on which they rest, and which as a formation seems pretty extensive, contains very few organic remains. The 'Millstone Grit,' I should suppose, may be pronounced, in these parts, as incorporated with the carboniferous limestone.

"Fossil facoid impressions may occasionally be noticed on the sandstone connected with the coal measures. Perhaps you may recollect my subjecting a small specimen to your notice on your visit here, on which at the time you expressed doubt as to whether it might have belonged to marine or fresh-water algæ. Is it not possible that in these ancient days there may have been, as in other continents, here and there a line of transition between marine and fresh water deposits, and characters according to the deposit be now found consequently common to both? Again, in some places, previous to eruptive disturbances, decidedly marine deposits have existed below, and fresh-water deposits have been found located above. It is possible, in such lengthened periods, there may have been gradations or alternations from one to the other.

"Wylie seems inclined to think that the surfaces of the later deposits may have been subjected to marine action. I will not venture to offer an opinion to you at present on this subject, but I may state that no salt water shells or other organic marine remains have ever been found beyond a distance of about 50 miles from the coast."

The Dicynodon strata lie generally on Devonian rocks. "They are generally," says Hall, "little disturbed, and then locally assume the horizontal position, and are intersected in all directions by dykes of igneous rocks, which, when large, form the central axis of mountain chains. They abound in fossil remains, bones, shells, and vegetables." And he goes on to say—"There seems, according to Professor Owen, to be good reason for referring them to the age of the New Red Sandstone, nearly. They also abound in lime and salt, and are probably of lacustrine origin. Mr Bain considers these beds as the bottom of an ancient lake or sea, which extended north as far as the Zambesi, which was probably one of the outlets by which its waters escaped. The Nieuweveld, Roggeveld, Sneewbergen, Winterbergen, Stormbergen, and Quathlamba mountains are all composed of these rocks, more or less capped with greenstones."

The greenstone spoken of is elsewhere known as whinstone. It is a species of trap which, with clinkstone and basalt, appears to have been protruded extensively about the period of the earth's history to which we have now been brought.

The greenstone capping the mountain ranges must have been protruded prior to the elevation of the district above the surface of the water, and not only prior to the silting up of the valley by lacustrine and other deposits, but prior to the scooping out of the valley by ocean currents.

Towards the close of the period, during which these limestone deposits of 1700 feet in thickness were silting up their mediterranean sea, or inland lake, there must have been going on other changes of which indications have been left in what are now mountain ranges, but which were at the period referred to still under water, either fresh water of the lake or salt water of the sea.

The mention of the reptilian Dicynodon indicates our having entered upon the times of which we read, "And God said, Let the waters bring forth abundantly the moving creatures that hath life, and fowl that may fly above the earth in the open firmament of heaven." And again, "God said, Let the earth bring forth the living creature after his kind, cattle, and creeping thing, and beast of the earth after his kind: and it was so."

"After the deposition and upheaval of the carboniferous system," says Page, "a new era occurs in the history of the globe. Overlying the coal measures in some places conformably, and in others not, there appears a set of *red* sandstones, variegated (yellow, purple, and greenish) shales, thick-bedded magnesian limestones of a cream colour—all of which present an aspect not to be mistaken for any previous system of strata. As to their organic remains: there are a few species of marine zoophytes, shells, and fishes, but scarcely a trace of vegetation, showing that the conditions which gave birth to the exuberance of terrestrial plants during the coal era had undergone an extensive and peculiar change. To these red sandstones, magnesian limestones, and mottled shales, the term *New Red Sandstone System* has been applied, in contradistinction to the Old Red which underlie the carboniferous strata.

"The extent of country over which this system is spread is not well ascertained. Slight traces of it occur on the western coast and islands of Scotland, and on the Fife shores of the Forth; it occupies a wider area in the basin of the Solway and its tributaries; spreads largely over the central districts of England from the Tyne southwards; and is found in the north of Ireland. Extensive areas are covered by it in the continent of Europe—in France, Germany, Poland, along the flanks of the Alps, in Austria, and between the Volga and the Ural mountains; and, according to Professor Hitchcock, it is spread over considerable spaces in some of the river valleys of the United States.

"The physical aspect of New Red Sandstone districts, as may be conjectured from the limited force of the igneous rocks, is rather flat and gentle. There are no picturesque craigs, mountain ranges, or deep ravines to diversify the scenery; which consits of rounded terraces of magnesian limestone, and level expanses of Red Sandstone and shales, here and there dotted with a gentle eminence of limestone or gravel. Over the limestone the sward is thick and verdant, and the soil above the red sandstone is of average fertility; but where the retentive shales spread out in flat hollows, they form the basis of extensive morasses—as, for example, those of south Lancashire, in England."

At Enon, and at Bushman's River, and at the Knysna are beds of conglomerate which have been identified with the New Red Stone formations, and which must have been deposited long after the formation of the coal measures. The thickness of these is unknown, but Mr Wylie conjectured that they might be in the aggregate about 300 feet—a measurement trifling compared with the 1000, 1800, and 4000 of which we have previously had occasion to speak,—but requiring for the deposition of their constituents a length of time of which it is difficult for us to form a conception.

During the period of the deposit of this formation the districts in which it occurs appear to have been covered, and covered deep, with still waters. What few fossils have been found in the strata tell of progress. With calamites, like those of the coal formation, are mingled cycas-like plants, —plants of the same order as the *zamia*, or *encephalartos*, the *kafferbrod* of the Eastern province. But like the vegetation of the coal era the plants of the New Red Stone are chiefly vascular cryptogamia, with traces of marine plants.

The most important minerals of this formation which have commercial value are magnesia and rock-salt. Of this Page writes:—

"The formation of rock-salt is a subject, in connection with this system, which has much engaged the attention of speculative geologists. The sandstone and marls with which it is associated are evidently derived from deposition in water; but the irregularity of the salt beds, the fact of their occurring in masses of vast thickness, and the soluble nature of the compound, all point to a somewhat different origin. At present, salt lakes and superficial accumulations of salt occur in various parts of the world, and these have furnished data for reasoning as to the saliferous deposits of earlier eras. Salt lakes are chiefly derived from salt springs, and being subjected to the vaporising influence of the sun, which carries off only *fresh* vapour, their waters become in time saturated with saline matter. But water can hold only a fixed amount of salt in solution; and so soon as this amount is attained, the salt begins to fall to the bottom by its own gravity. In the course of ages, these layers will form a thick bed, interstratified, it may be, with mud, or other earthy sediment; and if the lake should be ultimately dried up, the salt will constitute a deposit something analogous to the rock-salt of the New Red Sandstone. Such is the process which some geologists have advanced to account for the formation of rock-salt—supposing that portions of the seas of deposit were occasionally cut off from connection with the main ocean, and subjected to a rapid evaporating power, without receiving fresh accessions of water. The limited extent of rock-salt basins seems to favour such a theory; but when we consider the frequency of disturbance by volcanic forces in earlier ages, and the fact of many of these deposits occurring near to, or in connection with, mountain elevations, it is more than probable that igneous action, as well as a high atmospheric temperature, had to do with their formation. If such were the origin of rock-salt, it must have been formed during the deposition of other systems than the New Red Sandstone; and this geological research has confirmed; for, although the most extensive accumulations do occur amid the sandstones and shales of the system under review, still, deposits of considerable thickness are found in connection with oolite, green-sand, and tertiary rocks, while numerous salt springs issue from the carboniferous strata.

"The formation of magnesian limestone has also given rise to several theories. Minute quantities of magnesia occur variously combined in the crust of the earth; but only in the limestones of this system is it sufficiently developed to constitute a peculiar and distinguishing feature. The most prevalent hypotheses advanced to account for this peculiarity are—first, that the carbonate of magnesia was deposited at the same time as the carbonate of lime; and, second, that it was subsequently injected in the form of gaseous vapour. Neither hypothesis seems to account for all the phenomena presented; although the former is that which admits of most extensive application."

Another peculiarity of these strata is the occurrence in them of what are called Ichnites.

"Ichnites, or fossil footsteps, present a curious example of the means by which geologists are enabled to decipher the history of the earth. Most people must have observed how distinct the impressions of the feet of birds and other animals are often left on the mud or sand of ebbing rivers. If this mud should remain exposed to the sun and air till sufficiently dried, and then be overlaid by some new sediment, the impression of the foot will form a mould into which the new matter will be deposited. Should the two layers ever be consolidated into stone, on being separated the one would present a *mould*, and the other a *cast* of the footsteps; and this is precisely what takes place among the strata of the earth's crust. Fossil footsteps have been discovered in the New Red Sandstone of Cocklemuir in Dumfriesshire, and in that of Hildburghausen in Saxony, supposed to be those of reptiles; hence termed *sauroidichnites*. Others have been detected in the sandstones of Connecticut, United States, and ascribed to gigantic birds allied to the ostrich family; consequently called *ornithichnites*, from the Greek words *ornis*, a bird, and *ichnon*, a trace or footprint. To these Professor Hitchcock adds a third class, *tetrapodichnites*, or the footsteps of some unknown *four-footed* animal."

In regard to South Africa, to quote from a letter appended to my Report as Colonial Botanist in 1863 :—

" In several parts I have found a salt efflorescence on the soil; but in other parts there are saltpans, from which there is obtained, and may be obtained continuously, an unlimited supply of salt for sale.

" I visited the saltpan at Bethelsdrop, and I found the salt for more than a mile covering the dry portion of the valley like snow. The salt which is solid is raked from the water like the half-melted snow with which occasionally rivers and pools in Britain are filled. It requires no further preparation if it has been washed from sand, and it is sent off in waggon loads to Port Elizabeth, which is not ten miles distant.

" The production of this salt cannot be accounted for on the supposition that it is brought thither by streams from the surface. Within the memory of inhabitants of Bethelsdrop the saltpan was a fresh-water pool.

" I can best account for what I have seen by supposing that the water communicates by cracks in the bed of the lake with a bed of rock-salt not far from the surface, and a saturated solution being made when the water is most abundant, the evaporation during the dry seasons occasions the deposit of salt. Not many miles distant are two more pans, one larger, the other smaller. Upon these I look as indications that the bed of salt is of considerable extent; the correctness of my surmise can easily be tested by boring; and should there be found not far from the surface a bed of salt of considerable thickness, I have no doubt it would be found highly remunerative to work it."

Among other ichnites preserved in this formation are footprints of birds of the existence of which we have now no earlier indications. And thus does, Hugh Miller tell of the changes which have meanwhile passed upon the world :—" While the fourth evening has fallen on the prophet, he becomes sensible, as it wears on, and the fourth dawn approaches, that yet another change has taken place. The Creator has spoken, and the stars look out from openings of deep unclouded blue; and as day rises, and the planet of morning pales in the east, the broken cloudlets are transmuted from bronze into gold, and anon the gold becomes fire, and at length the glorious sun arises out of the sea, and enters on his course rejoicing. It is a brilliant day; the waves, of a deeper and softer blue than before, dance and sparkle in the light; the earth, with little else to attract the gaze, has assumed a garb of brighter green; and as the sun declines amid even richer glories than those which had encircled his rising, the moon appears full-orbed in the east,—to the human eye the second great luminary of the heavens,—and climbs slowly to the zenith as night advances, shedding its mild radiance on land and sea.

" Again the day breaks; the prospect consists, as before, of land and ocean. There are great pine woods, reed-covered swamps, wide plains, winding rivers, and broad lakes; and a bright sun shines over all. But the landscape derives its interest and novelty from a feature unmarked before. Gigantic birds stalk along the sands, or wade far into the water in quest of their ichthyic food; while birds of lesser size float upon the lakes, or scream discordant in hovering flocks, thick as insects in the calm of a summer evening, over the narrow seas, or brighten with the sunlight gleam of their wings the thick woods. And ocean has its monsters: great '*tanninum*' tempest the deep, as they heave their huge bulk over the surface, to inhale the life-sustaining air; and out of their nostrils goeth smoke, as out of a 'seething pot and cauldron.' Monstrous creatures, armed in massive scales, haunt the rivers, or scour the flat rank meadows; earth, air, and water are charged with animal life; and the sun sets on a busy scene, in which unerring instinct pursues unremittingly its few simple ends,—the support and preservation of the individual, the propagation of the species, and the protection and maintenance of the young."

"After the deposition of the New Red Sandstone," says Page, "a further change was effected upon the general conditions of the globe, so as to produce not only an entirely different set of strata, but also different races of plants and animals. In most districts, the red sandstones and magnesian limestone were upheaved, to form new land, while portions of the former dry land were submerged beneath the ocean. By this process of elevation and depression the courses of previous rivers would be altered, former seas circumscribed and rendered more shallow, plants and animals subjected to a new distribution, and thus a different set of deposits would necessarily ensue. Instead of magnesian rocks, we have dark argillaceous and oolitic limestones; for variegated saliferous marls, we have blue pyritous clays; and instead of red and mottled sandstones, yellow calcareous grits. All this points to a new epoch in the terrestrial conditions of the world; and to the system of strata thus deposited geologists apply the term *oolitic* (Gr., *oon*, an egg, and *lithos*, a stone), from the resemblance which the texture of many of the beds bear to the roe or eggs of a fish. Oolite, or *roestone*, is an aggregate of rounded calcareous particles, varying from the size of a millet-seed to that of a marble—the smaller being almost perfectly spherical, the larger irregular, and having their interstices filled with calcareous matter or broken shells."

These also find their representatives in South Africa. At Sunday's river, Bushman's river, the Koega, and Swartzkop, are beds of an aggregate thickness of 400 feet, which have been identified with the jurassic, which is an oolitic, formation.

"The extent of country occupied by the oolite is by no means extensive, though partial deposits are very generally disseminated over the globe. It is most fully developed in England, occupying the eastern sea-board from Yorkshire to Dorset; it occurs in a small patch at Brora in Sutherland, in Skye, and other of the Hebrides, and partially in Ireland and Wales. Portions of the system are also found in France and Germany; skirting the Alps; in Spain and the Balearic islands; flanking the Apennines and Atlas range; on the southern slope of the Himmalehs;·but no true equivalents to the European oolite have hitherto been detected in America."

The beds at Sunday's river contain, together with marine shells, fossil-wood and land plants, which shows that it was a marine and not a lacustrine or alluvial deposit, and that though found in the depths of the sea there was dry land not far off. And thus are we brought to the close

K

of another protracted period of the world's history—that known as the period of the secondary formation, separated from the so-called primary formations—the gneiss, the schists, and the slates—by the so-called transition series, the Cambrian, the Silurian, and the Devonian or Old Red Sandstone formations,—and including the mountain limestone, the coal measures, the New Red Sandstone, the saliferous marls, the oolite limestones and grits, covered by green sandstone and chalk beds, seen in the chalk cliffs which have given to England the name of Albion.

All this must have occurred very long anterior to the creation of man. But we are not without indications of what occurred in the interval.

Near Oliphant's Hoek are beds of marine clay and limestone, and at the Cape Flats are beds of lignite and clay; all of which, together with the Tygervley sandstone, have been identified with the formations of the Tertiary period.

According to the statement of Page:—" The tertiary system comprises all the *regular strata* of limestone, marl, clay, sand, and gravel which occur above the chalk. Before the labours of the celebrated Cuvier and M. Brogniart, these beds were regarded as mere superficial accumulations, not referrible to any definite period. Now, however, they are recognised as constituting a distinct formation—differing from the cretaceous not only in its mineral composition, but in the higher order of organisms which it contains, and from the superficial sands and clays, in being regularly stratified, and in imbedding the remains of animals distinct from existing races. In general the strata are loosely aggregated, are of no great thickness, and present appearances which indicate frequent alternations of marine and fresh-water agencies. Thus, marine remains are found in some beds, while others contain exclusively land animals and plants, and fresh-water shells. The whole suit being less consolidated than any of the secondary systems, and containing plants and animals approaching to existing forms, it presents a freshness of aspect which serves to distinguish it from older deposits; at the same time the regularity of its deposition prevents it from being mistaken for any mere alluvial accumulation. In general it occupies very limited and detached areas, as if it had been formed in shallow inland seas and estuaries, to which the waters of the ocean at times had access, and where at other periods fresh-water inundations prevailed. Another essential difference between the tertiary and the more ancient formations consists in the fact, that the latter maintain a wonderful uniformity in their composition and character all over the globe; whereas the former present almost as many distinctions in composition as there are areas of deposit. For this reason it is impossible to give a description applicable to all tertiary strata; those of England and France, however, may be taken as types sufficiently characteristic.

" Respecting the composition of the system, arenaceous and argillaceous beds may be said to prevail, with interstratified limestone, calcareous grits, and marls. The *arenaceous* members are either pebbly conglomerate of a rusty yellow, or sands little indurated and variously tinted by the oxide and silicate of iron. The sands are seldom sufficiently consolidated to form sandstone; and the conglomerates are often mere layers of rolled pebbles, without any cementing matrix. The *argillaceous* beds also present many varieties; some being almost pure laminated clay of a dull blue colour, others of a brownish tint, with a slight admixture of sand, while many pass into marls more or less calcareous. None of these clays are so compact as to form shales; indeed lamination is more frequently absent than otherwise, there being nothing except their fossils and associated beds to distinguish them from the clays of subsequent alluvial valleys. The *calcareous* layers are still more varied in their composition and aspect, and bear no resemblance to the indurated half-crystalline limestones of older formations. The marine limestone of the Paris basin is of a coarse sandy texture; that of Austria a rough corraline rock: the fresh-water beds near Weimar are hard and compact; those of other districts are soft, marly, and full of shells. In some localities marls are so calcareous as to be used as limestone, while in others they pass into soft friable clays. From this extreme diversity of composition, it is evident that many agencies have been concerned in the deposition of the tertiary system, and that most of them have been of a local character, producing results not differing widely from those of the present day. . . .

"As to the extent of country occupied by tertiary deposits, there is yet no very accurate knowledge, inasmuch as many sands and clays, now regarded as the alluvium of existing valleys, may hereafter be referred to this system; and several areas of gravel, now looked upon as tertiary, be classed with more recent accumulations. As developed in Europe, the system spreads over wide areas, all remarkable for their conformation and connection with the outline of existing seas. Indeed, were the islands and continent of Europe to be submerged to the depth of 600 or 800 feet, the waters of the German, Baltic, English Channel, and Mediterranean seas, would cover most of the tertiary strata, showing that, with the exception of the general elevation which raised them into dry land, there has been comparatively little subterranean disturbance since the time they were deposited. In Britain the formation is exhibited in Hampshire, Isle of Wight, in the basin of London, and from the Thames northwards along the coast to the mouth of the Yare; but has not been detected either in Ireland or Scotland, though several gravel and clay deposits in the latter country may yet be discovered to belong to the same era. It occurs interestingly developed near Paris; trends along the north coast of France, Belgium, Westphalia, Holstein, and Jutland, in apparent connection with the German Ocean; spreads over the level tract lying between the Baltic and Northern Ocean in Russia; and occupies the greater portion of the central flats which lie between the Baltic and Black seas. Besides these expanses, there are many secluded patches along the valleys of the Rhone and Danube, the Swiss lakes, and the Italian shores of the Mediterranean. The system has also been detected along the southern basis of the Himmalehs, and in several of the North American valleys; and when geological research has been further extended, there is little doubt of its being discovered in other quarters of the world. In speaking of the extent of country occupied by deposits of incoherent sands, marls, and clays, like those of the tertiary epoch, it must be borne in mind how much more waste they would suffer by denudation than the older and more consolidated strata. No doubt every rock system, on its being elevated into dry land, must have suffered diminution by denuding causes; but most of all those whose materials are loosely aggregated like the strata now under review."

Of this period Hugh Miller writes:—"The curtain drops over this ancient Flora of the Oolite in Scotland; and when, long after, there is a corner of the thick enveloping screen withdrawn, and we catch a partial glimpse of one of the old Tertiary forests of our country, all is new. Trees of the high dicotyledonous class, allied to the plane and the buckhorn, prevail in the landscape, intermingling, however, with dingy funereal yews; and the ferns and equiseta that rise in the darker openings of the wood approach to the existing type. And yet, though *eons* of the past eternity have elapsed since we looked out upon Cycas and Zamia, and the last of the calamites, the time is still early, and long ages must elapse ere man shall arise out of the dust, to keep and to dress fields waving with the productions of yet another and different Flora, and to busy himself with all the labour which he taketh under the sun. Our country, in this Tertiary time, has still its great outbursts of molten matter, that bury in fiery deluges, many feet in depth and many square miles in extent, the debris of wide tracts of wood-land and marsh; and the basaltic column still forms in its great lava bed; and ever and anon as the volcanic agencies awake, clouds of ashes darken the heavens, and cover up the landscape as if with the accumulated drifts of a protracted snow-storm. Who shall declare what, throughout these long ages, the history of creation has been? We see at wide intervals the mere fragments of successive Floras; but know not how what seem the blank interspaces were filled, or how, as extinction overtook in succession one tribe of existences after another, and species, like individuals, yielded to the great law of death, yet other species were brought to the birth, and ushered upon the scene, and the chain of being was maintained unbroken. We see only detached bits of that green web which has covered our earth ever since the dry land first appeared; but the web itself seems to have been continuous throughout all time; though ever, as breadth after breadth issued from the creative loom, the pattern has altered, and the sculpturesque and graceful forms that illustrated its first beginnings and its middle spaces have yielded to flowers of richer colour and blow, and fruits of fairer shade and outline; and for gigantic club-mosses stretching forth their hirsute arms, goodly trees of the Lord have expanded their great boughs; and for the barren fern and the calamite clustering in thickets beside the waters, or spreading on flowerless hill-slopes, luxuriant orchards have yielded their ruddy flush, and rich harvests their golden gleam."

All the fossil remains of these deposits, those of vegetable and animal structures alike, are much more like to the corresponding structures of the present than were those of earlier ages.

According to Unger, what is called the Eocine fossil flora resembles much that of Australia at the present day, and the Tertiary flora has a marked resemblance to that of North America.

Page writes, "Of the conditions of the world during the deposition of the tertiary strata, we are enabled to form some estimate from the nature of their fossils, and from the peculiar composition and aggregation of their rocky materials. So far as Europe is concerned, part of the existing land must have been then elevated above the waters, forming a series of insular ranges, with flat valleys and shallow seas between. From these islands, and from continents now submerged, rivers of considerable extent seem to have borne sand, clay, and vegetable debris, and to have deposited them in the seas and estuaries, while gravel, flint pebbles, broken corals, and shells, were strewn along the shore by ordinary littoral influences. Such materials would give rise to beds of sand, clay, gravel, lignite, and calcareous conglomerate, enclosing marine remains, with others of fresh-water and terrestrial origin brought down by the rivers. But several tertiary basins exhibit strata of decided fresh-water origin, alternating with others as decidedly marine; and to account for this phenomenon, we must have recourse to another set of agents. In the deltas of many modern rivers, like that of the Niger, lagoons of fresh-water are frequently cut off from connection either with the branches of the river or with the ocean, and in these myriads of shell-fish, aquatic plants, crocodiles, hippopotami, and other fresh-water and amphibious races abound. At some subsequent period the connection with the ocean is renewed—there being in general only a slight eminence of mud or sand to separate them—and thus the succeeding deposits assume a character decidedly marine. By these means it is easy to conceive how alternations of marine and fresh-water strata would occur; and particularly when we know that the south of Europe (central France and the Alps) was during the tertiary era subjected to extensive volcano disturbances, which would give rise to frequent submergences and elevations. We are thus enabled to account for the composition and aggregation of the tertiary strata; and when we reflect on their comparatively recent origin, and the fact that they are in many places not overlaid by other material, there is no difficulty in perceiving how they should be so loose and incoherent in their texture. Again, when we look at the nature of their fossils, we are led to associate with them ideas of a warm and genial climate. The lands which furnished the cycadeæ, palms, cocoa nuts, and monkeys of the English tertiaries, and the mastodons, elephants, rhinoceroses, hippopotami, crocodiles, and turtles of the Paris basin, must have enjoyed a temperature similar to that of the present tropics. The beds of lignite bear evidence of a luxuriant vegetation for the support of so many huge graminivora; while the presence of birds, insects, and the higher orders of mammalia, point to atmospheric and other vital conditions little different from those now existing. In fact, we find in the deltas of the Ganges and Niger—in their jungles, lagoons, and swamps—in their elephants, hippopotami, and crocodiles—almost perfect analogies to those estuaries and shallow seas in which the tertiary strata of Europe were deposited. . . . .

"After the deposition of the Tertiary Strata, a great change took place in the relative distribution of land and ocean. Most parts of Europe, America, and the other continents were elevated above the waters; other regions seem to have been submerged, and an arrangement of physical conditions established not differing widely from those now existing. But these new conditions did not for an instant arrest the degrading and transporting power of water, the wasting effects of the atmosphere, the disturbing efforts of volcanoes, or the progressive development of organic life; the same agents which had exerted themselves, from the beginning of time, in modifying the physical features of the world, continued their career, only differing in power and degree according to this new arrangement. Thus, accumulations of sand, gravel, clay, vegetable and animal matter, took place above the previously deposited strata—every river, lake, sea-shore, shell-bed, coral-reef, and peat-moss, contributing its peculiar quota."

One of the deposits of this period is that of blocks of stone, far from the mountains whence they had been borne, and dark tenaceous clays. Of this Page writes,—"The terms 'erratic block group,' 'boulder formation,' 'diluvium,' and 'diluvial drift,' are indiscriminately given by geologists to a thick mass of dark tenaceous clay which overlies extensive districts, intermingled with numerous boulders having a rounded and water-worn appearance. There is nothing like regularity of deposit in this formation, unless it may be said that it attains the greatest thickness and uniformity of composition on extensive plateaus like those of the coal measures, at the eastern extremity of certain valleys, and on the south-eastern flank of hills belonging to the secondary period. The clay is generally of a dark blue colour, though in some localities it assumes a reddish hue. There are no lines of lamination in the mass, and no appearances of stratification, unless in some districts where there is a sort of natural division into 'upper and lower clays'—the lower being dark and more compact, the upper lighter in the hue, and separated from the other by a thin reddish streak. Waiving these minutiæ, the whole may be described as a covering of compact dark clay, from 10 to 120 feet in thickness, full of boulders and rolled stones from the size of an egg to many tons in weight; these blocks occupying the bottom, middle, or surface of the mass, without regard to gravity or any other law of arrangement. The boulders are of granite, syenite, primitive greenstone, gneiss, mica schist, and other crystalline rocks of a hard and durable texture. Limestone blocks are of very rare occurrence, and the more friable rocks of the upper formations are seldom or ever to be met with. This clay, with its intermingled boulders, generally rests upon the denuded outcrops or edges of the rock formations; is sometimes underlaid by masses of gravel; and not unfrequently contains 'nests,' or irregular patches of rounded pebbles.

"Besides these patches which are interwoven with the clay, there are independent accumulations of gravel, and rubbly masses of rock-fragments, which seem to have been formed contemporaneously with the boulder-clay, and by the same agency. In Britain such accumulations generally occupy the eastern proximity of longitudinal valleys, where they form curious ranges of flat-topped hillocks; abut against the base of some mountain; or gather, without regard to any order of arrangement, along the eastern flank of those trap hills which present a bold front or 'crag' to the westward. They are found for the most part in more open situations than the clay, as if they had been arrested in their progress eastward by prominences and shallows, while the clays were borne to deeper and more sheltered recesses. Like the dark clays, they are destitute of organic remains, their larger pebbles are derived from primitive rocks, interspersed with fragments of sandstone, shale, and coal from the secondary formations.

"To account for the origin of the group thus described, many theories have from time to time been advanced, of which only two deserve notice, as being at all adequate to the purpose intended. The *first* is that which supposes a set of powerful currents to have passed over Britain and the adjoining continent; these currents taking a course from the north and north-west towards the south and south-east, and sweeping before them clay, sand, gravel, and loose blocks, which were deposited, as the force of the waters abated, without any order or arrangement. How long the currents continued, theorists do not aver; but from the water-worn aspect of the boulders and gravel, an indefinite period is allowed. With respect to the direction of the drifting force, little doubt is entertained, for many reasons: —1. Blocks of granite, gneiss, &c. which must have been derived from the Grampians, are found scattered along the eastern lowlands of Scotland; primitive rocks from the Lammermuir and Cheviot ranges are detected in the vale of the Tweed and in Northumberland; others from the Cumberland mountains are widely dispersed over Durham and the east of Yorkshire; boulders from the Welsh range are found in the midland counties of England; while the erratic blocks of Friesland and Germany point to the Scandinavian ridge as the source from which they were derived. 2. Those hills which range east and west have, without exception, their western brows swept bare, while their eastern flanks are thickly strewed with gravel and boulders. 3. Many accumulations of gravel bear evidence of their having been piled up by a force from the north-west. 4. Blocks evidently derived from the outcrops of certain strata are often found among the debris a few yards to the south-east, showing clearly that the transporting power passed over them from the north-west. 5. The supposed currents have been modified in their direction by ranges of hills, so as to set the volume of water with greater rapidity down the valleys which lie between them, as the greatest accumulations of drift and boulders are found at the eastern extremities of such gorges and valleys. But while no doubt is entertained either as to the agency of water in the formation of these accumulations, or as to the direction in which the waters flowed, great difficulty is felt in conceiving any current sufficiently powerful to sweep before it blocks of several tons weight, and that over heights and hollows for many hundreds of miles. Indeed it seems impossible to reconcile the theory of violent currents with the phenomena presented; for, granting the occurrence of some extraordinary cataclysm, during which the waters of the ocean were thrown over the land, the currents must have abated in velocity as they drew to a close, leaving the detritus to arrange itself more in accordance with the laws of gravity than what is exhibited in a mass of clay and boulders.

" The *second* theory supposes that those portions of Europe now covered with erratic blocks were submerged after the deposition of the stratified formations; that this submergence was caused by some extraordinary revolution in the planetary relations of our earth; that it was accompanied by a change of climate, and other terrestrial conditions; that while in this state, icebergs and avalanches formed around the earlier mountains which were still left above water; and that these icebergs, as they were loosened from the shore by the heat of summer, and floated southward by the currents of the ocean, dropped their burden of boulders and gravel precisely as Captain Scoresby found modern icebergs dropping their debris in the nothern seas, and as the officers of the recent Antarctic expedition observed similar phenomena in the Southern Polar Ocean. It is further supposed, that while icebergs distributed the erratic blocks and other debris in deep waters, avalanches and glaziers were forming *moraines* of gravel in the valleys of the then existing land analogous to what is observed in the alpine glens of Switzerland. Again, one cannot read Mr Simpson's account of the shores of the Polar Seas, and learn that the ice formed during winter over whole leagues of gravel, breaks up during the summer, and is blown on the beach by winds, or piled up by the tides, where, melting, it leaves long flat-topped ridges, without perceiving a wonderful resemblance between these effects and the long singularly-shapen ridges of 'deluvial' gravel. According to this theory, it is easy to account for the south-eastward direction of the drift, for the Polar Ocean still maintains its great southward current to the equatorial seas, modified, undoubtedly, in its course, by the inequalities of the bottom over which it passes. The chief difficulty to be obviated is the temporary diminution of temperature which the north of Europe must have then experienced; and this can only be accounted for by some derangement in the planetary relations of our globe.

"Both theories are beset with many difficulties, and though the latter accounts more satisfactorily for most of the phenomena of the erratic block group, still there are many points respecting the distribution and extent of the deposit to be investigated before either can be finally adopted. All that can be affirmed in the present state of the science is the composition and nature of the clay, gravel, and boulders, as above described—the course of the currents concerned in their deposition—the fact of the land having a configuration of hill and valley not differing much from what now exists—and the peculiar scantiness, if not total absence, of organic remains. If the latter theory be adopted, it is easy to perceive how the soft bottom of the ocean, as it was elevated into dry land, would be furrowed and channeled by the receding waters—here being swept bare of its mud, but retaining the boulders; there being covered by accumulations of transportable clay and gravel; while the deeper hollows, being left undrained, would form lakes and morasses, which were in turn to be silted up by subsequent material."

We have what may look like memorials of the drift period in South Africa in the bed of tenacious pit-clay, underlying a thin covering of soil, throughout extensive districts of the colony of the Cape of Good Hope, and in the boulders found on the Paarl and on the sides of Table Mountain and of the Lion's Head, at Wynberg, and at other places in the locality. But what is of more interest to us, in the study of the hydrology of the country, is the circumstance that it has been conjectured that the drift period was synchronous with the conversion of the Great Sahara from being a sheet of water of immense extent—well entitled, whether its waters were salt or fresh, to be called an inland sea—into a sandy desert; and an attempt has been made to account for the cold of that glacial period by the existence of that sea.

The Rev. Mr Ward, of Bridgenorth, in a paper which appeared in a number of the *Journal of Science* for April 1861, says—"A large number of our most eminent geologists appear to have given in their adherence to the theory that the glacial epoch was coincident with the period during which the Sahara of North Africa formed the bed of an ocean or vast inland sea. Many, I believe, consider further that these physical conditions, so different from existing ones, were not merely coincident but were closely connected as cause and effect—that is to say, that the phenomena of the glacial epoch may (to a certain extent) be accounted for by the fact of the existence, during that epoch, of an expanse of water where now is to be found only one of sand." He goes on to say—"It would be needless for me to dwell on the facts and reasonings by which this theory is supported, for by this time they must be tolerably familiar to the readers of this periodical; but so far as I am acquainted with what has been written on the subject, only the *immediate* and *direct* influence which the former of these states exerted on the climate and temperature of Southern, Western, and Central Europe has been touched upon, whereas it appears to me that the indirect influences must have been far greater and more widely felt."

In illustration of his views he submits for consideration the following argument—"Everyone now-a-days is aware that the warm climate of Western and North Western Europe is owing to the gulf-stream." Of this gulf-stream he says—"Subsidiary causes there may be, but undoubtedly the main one is the north-east trade wind, blowing incessantly and with considerable force in the Atlantic, from a few degrees north of the equator to about the 27th or 28th parallel. The effect of this steady pressure all in one direction, over so enormous an expanse of water, . . . is an abnormal elevation of the water on the north-east coast of South America to the height of about 30 feet. . . . This enormous accumulation of water streams off northwards until, released from the pressure of the trade winds, but still retaining its northern impetus, it trends to the north-east, towards our own shores [Britain], Iceland, and even Spitzbergen."

Enquiring then, "What causes the N. E. trade wind?" he says, "Most geographers I believe will reply, without hesitation, mainly the Sahara." And he proceeds to account for its action by the general heat of the tropics. "The air throughout the whole of the tropics being heated, and thus rarified, ascends into the higher regions, and its place is supplied by the colder air streaming in from the north and the south. This simple statement, however, requires of course many modifications. I must confine myself to two immediately connected with our subject :—the first is this, as the air streams in from the arctic regions, where the velocity of the earth on its axis is small, to the tropical regions, where it is considerable, it is obvious that the motion of the earth from west to east being only partially communicated to the air, the latter will be left behind as it were—*i.e.*, there will be an apparent motion in it from east to west on those parts of the earth's surface towards the equator. *North* of the line, then, this westerly direction of the wind continued, with the southerly direction spoken of before, gives (by the well known mathematical parallelogram of forces) as a resultant a direction of the wind from the north-east—this is the trade wind of the North Atlantic."

So far all is intelligible, and commands assent, but not so is it with what follows. "But next," says he, " let it be observed, this wind owes almost all its force to the fact of the enormous radiation of heat from the surface of the Sahara, causing a prodigious rarification in the atmosphere above it —hence a vehement impetus is given to the current of air traversing it from the north-east—that is to say to the wind, which, as we have seen by its action on the waters of the Atlantic, is the main cause of the Gulf Stream."

It appears to me that Mr Ward over-estimates the effect of the Sahara in the production of the trade winds, which both in the northern and the southern hemispheres are produced by the ascending body of air over the whole longitudinal extent of the tropics. That that upward flow is likely to be much more marked over an expanse of sand than over an equal expanse of ocean is more than probable; but the hypothesis seems to assume that it bears a much greater proportion in its effects to the effects of that upward flow over the whole superficial extent of the tropics than I know facts sufficient to warrant me to believe.

Further, I do not see how a vehement onward impulse can be given to a north-east wind advancing to the tropics by its traversing the Sahara, extending from 15° to 30° north latitude, while the ecliptic passes from $23\frac{1}{2}$° N. to $23\frac{1}{2}$° S. latitude. Toward the Sahara, extending from say 15° W. to 15° E. long., there may be an influx of air from all sides to follow the ascending column, or fill the vacuum occasioned by it; this may be most powerful on the north-east side; but the effect may be appreciable, even if not perceptible, on all other sides beside. With these observations I resume the thread of the argument as laid down by Mr Ward :—

"Suppose then the Sahara to be an expanse, not of *sand* as now, but as formerly, of *water*, what would be the results? The trade wind would cease,

L

or be so reduced in strength as to exert but slight pressure on the surface of the Atlantic; then, as a consequence the Gulf Stream would either cease or sink into insignificant dimensions; the icebergs from Greenland, instead of being melted by the heated waters flowing towards the north, would encroach more and more southwards; the seas around our own island (Britain) and a portion of those more to the south would again present the character of an arctic or subarctic climate, at least as severe as that of Labrador in the same latitude, in short,—

'Grave rediret sæculum,'—

the phenomena of the glacial epoch would be renewed over the greater part of temperate Europe."

The subject was taken up in a subsequent number of the same journal (p. 565), but I have not access to what was then written.

In connection with the Hydrology of South Africa, I may mention that the project of converting the Sahara into an inland sea by a cutting through the mountain range which keeps from it the waters of the Mediterranean, which fill a basin at a higher level, has been submitted to men of science, to practical engineers, and to statesmen in Europe, by M. Leseep, the engineer to whom the world is indebted for the formation of the canal across the Isthmus of Suez; and it was one of the subjects discussed at an international conference of geographers, hydrographers, and scientific travellers, held in Antwerp in the autumn of 1871.

It is mentioned by Marsh, in his treatise on *The Earth as Modified by Human Action*, that some interesting observations on the secular desiccation of the Sahara and of Persia are given in the *L' Année Geographique* for 1873 (pp. 72 and 176).

In regard to the project of converting it again into an inland sea, he writes:—"It is now established by the observations of Rohlf and others that Strabo was right in asserting that a considerable part of the Libyan desert, or Sahara, lay below the level of the Mediterranean. At some points the depression exceeds 325 feet, and at Siwah, in the Oasis of Jupiter Ammon, it is not less than 130 feet. It has been proposed to cut a canal through the coast dunes, on the shore south of the Syrtis Major, or Dshun el Kebrit of the Arabs; and another project is to re-open the communication which appears to have once existed between the Palus Fritonis. or Sebcha el Nandid, and the Syrtis Parva." And he states in an appendix:—" The subject has been, at least, partially studied, has been entertained by the French Chambers, and has become a subject of much discussion. The most careful estimates I have seen allow to the new internal sea a length of 350 kilometres, a width of 60, and a depth of from 40 to 60 metres [or about 200 miles long, 30 miles broad, and 150 feet deep].

"There has been much wild conjecture in regard both to the ameliorating effects of such an expanse of water on the climate of Northern Africa, and the injurious consequences to Europe of the large addition of moisture to the atmospheric currents, which it is argued might increase the rain and snow on the Alps to a very prejudicial extent. The possibility of the scheme is by no means yet established, and the doubt whether it would be practicable to keep open, through the sandy isthmus, a channel wide enough to furnish a sufficient supply of water to counterbalance the evaporation deserves consideration." In the text he mentions:—" The rapid evaporation would require a constant influx of water from the Mediterranean, which might, perhaps, perceptibly influence the current through the Straits of Gibraltar."

Such are the far-reaching consequences reckoned on; and from such consequences being contemplated as possible consequences of the refilling the basin, there may be conjectured how great and far-reaching may have been the hydrological consequences of the drying up of that former sea.

With a view to impressing these more deeply on the mind of any of my readers who may now, for the first time, have his thoughts directed to such subjects, I may bring under consideration consequences contemplated as possible should another basin in the vicinity of the Mediterranean be converted into an inland sea.

In 1855 were published two volumes, entitled "The Dead Sea a new route to India." The project of the author, Captain Allan, was to connect the Mediterranean with the Red Sea, by a canal between the Mediterranean and the Dead Sea, and a canal between the Dead Sea and the Red Sea. The watershed between the latter is not less than 300 feet, but the summit level between the Mediterranean and the Jordan, near Jezreel, is believed to be little, if at all, more than 100 feet, above the sea; and writing on the question raised Mr Marsh says:—

"Although, therefore, we have no reason to believe it possible to open a navigable channel to India by way of the Dead Sea, there is not much doubt that the basin of the latter might be made accessible from the Mediterranean.

"The level of the Dead Sea lies 1316·7 feet below that of the ocean. It is bounded east and west by mountain ridges rising to the height of from 2000 to 4000 feet above the ocean. From its southern end a depression, called the Wadi-el-Araba, extends to the Gulf of Akaba, the eastern arm of the Red Sea. The Jordan empties into the northern extremity of the Red Sea, after having passed through the Lake of Tiberias, at an elevation of 663·4 feet above the Dead Sea—or 653·3 below the Mediterranean—and drains a considerable valley north of the lake, as well as the plain of Jericho which lies between the lake and the sea. If the waters of the Mediterranean were admitted freely into the basin of the Dead Sea, they would raise its surface to the ground level of the ocean, and consequently flood all the dry land below that level within the basin.

"I do not know that accurate levels have been taken in the valley of the Jordan above the Lake of Tiberias, and our information is very vague as to the hypsometry of the northern part of the Wadi-el-Araba. As little do we know where a contour line, carried around the basin at the level of the Mediterranean, would strike its eastern and western borders. We cannot, therefore, accurately compute the extent of the now dry land which would be covered by the admission of the waters of the Mediterranean, or the area of the inland sea which would be thus created. Its length, however, would certainly exceed an hundred and fifty miles, and its main breadth, including its gulfs and bays, could scarcely be less than fifteen, perhaps even twenty. It would cover very little ground now occupied by civilized or even uncivilized man, though some of the soil which would be submerged—for instance, that watered by the Fountain of Elisha and other neighbouring sources—is of great fertility, and, under a wiser government and better civil institutions, might rise to importance, because, from its depression, it possesses a very warm climate, and might supply south-eastern Europe with tropical products more readily than they can be obtained from any other source. Such a canal and sea would be of no present commercial importance, because they would give access to no new markets or sources of supply; but when the fertile valleys and the deserted plains east of the Jordan shall be reclaimed to agriculture and civilization, these waters would furnish a channel of communication which might become the medium of a very extensive trade.

"Whatever might be the economical results of the opening and filling of the Dead Sea basin, the creation of a new evaporable area, adding not less than 2000 or perhaps 3000 square miles to the present fluid surface of Syria, could not fail to produce important meteorological effects. The climate of Syria would probable be tempered, its precipitation and fertility increased, the courses of its winds and the electrical condition of its atmosphere modified. The present organic life of the valley would be extinguished, and many tribes of plants and animals would emigrate from the Mediterranean to the new home which human art had prepared for them. It is possible, too, that the addition of 1300 feet, or forty atmosphers of hydrostatic pressure upon the bottom of the basin, might disturb the equilibrium between the internal and the external forces of the crust of the earth at this point of abnormal configuration, and thus produce geological convulsions, the intensity of which cannot be even conjectured."

This may show that there is much, very much, connected with hydrology involved in the remoter consequences which may have followed the drying up of the Sahara, and in the consequences which might follow the filling that basin with water from the Mediterranean.

The drying up of the Sahara it has been attempted to identify with what is known to geologists as the Drift Period; and with the consideration of this we are brought to the close of another epoch. To quote again from Hugh Miller—"Again the night descends, for the fifth day has closed; and morning breaks on the sixth and last day of creation. Cattle and beasts of the field graze on the plains; the thick-skinned rhinoceros wallows in the marshes; the squat hippopotamus rustles among the reeds, or plunges sullenly into the river; great herds of elephants seek their food amid the young herbage of the woods; while animals of fiercer nature,—the lion, the leopard, and the bear,—harbour in deep caves till the evening, or lie in wait for their prey amid tangled thickets, or beneath some broken bank. At length, as the day wanes and the shadows lengthen, man, the responsible lord of creation, formed in God's own image, is introduced upon the scene, and the work of creation ceases for ever upon the earth. The night falls once more upon the prospect, and there dawns yet another morrow,—the morrow of God's rest,—that Divine Sabbath in which there is no more creative labour, and which 'blessed and sanctified' beyond all the days that had gone before, has as its special object the moral elevation and final redemption of man. And over *it* no evening is represented in the record as falling, for its special work is not yet complete. Such seems to have been the sublime panorama of creation exhibited in vision of old to

'The shepherd who first taught the chosen seed,
In the beginning how the heavens and earth
Rose out of chaos;'

and, rightly understood, I know not a single scientific truth that militates against even the minutest or least prominent of its details."

CHAPTER III.

INDICATIONS OF THE FORMER HYDROGRAPHIC CONDITION OF THE COUNTRY, SUPPLIED BY ARBORESCENT PRODUCTIONS FOUND IN THE INTERIOR OF SOUTH AFRICA.

It was the branch of an olive tree which told Noah of the assuaging of the waters of the deluge, and it happens to be clumps of olive trees to which I shall first have occasion to refer, as supplying indications of such subsidence of the waters as this chapter treats of. But let us, ere we leave the geological observations cited, take a retrospective glance at what has been revealed by them.

Far back as are carried our thoughts by physical geography when it is made to discourse of the former hydrographic condition of South Africa, to a period so much more remote are they carried back by the geological phenomena which there present themselves when these are made to speak of the past, that it seems as if it were but yesterday that the dry land appeared; and we are brought, both by the one and by the others, to hear of eras, and periods, and times, for the representation of the duration of which we have no numbers, and to form a definite conception of which we have no power—our conception of this is as vague as is our conception of eternity, in regard to which we speak of a past eternity, and an eternity to come, and an eternal Now.

But *there* are the voiceless, mute records looking as if they would compel us to read and think. And though "There is no speech nor language; their voice is not heard; yet their line is gone out through all the earth, and their words to the end of the world."

Passing without remark the gneiss and schists, while with dumb eloquence they solicit our attention, What a tale of duration of time is told by the strata of clay lying at the foot of Table Mountain, resting on the flanks of the protruding projected granite, by which it was upheaved and torn ! And what a tale of duration of time is told by that Mountain of Silurian deposit surmounting it, well-nigh a mile in thickness !

In the prevalence of sand in the strata with which this is capped, we find an indication of these having been covered by shallower water than that from suspension in which was deposited the clay, slate, and Silurian mud; and in accordance with this we find in upper beds of this formation, seen elsewhere in the Colony, a rippled sandstone, like to what may be seen on the sea-shore of the present day. But the aggregate upper and lower Devonian deposits are 5100 feet or nearly a mile in thickness, and the time required for the deposit of this is what is represented by those few cliff-like strata seen capping Table Mountain and the Lion's Head.

But this is not all. There is an interval indicated by the composition of these strata which must not be overlooked if we would read the details of the record. They may be conformable in their under surface to the upper **surface of the Silurian deposit, but it follows not that the process of deposit** was continuous. We have found it stated that the Dicynodon strata lie upon the Old Red Sandstone or Devonian formation, but we have seen enough to satisfy us that untold ages separated the eras of their deposit—and so was it here, or so at least it may have been. The mass of the mountain is Silurian, the capping strata belong to the Devonian or Old Red Sandstone formation; and the difference of the fossils found in the one and found in the other of these formations tell of the lapse of ages of the duration of which we can form no conception, but of which no other indication is here given; and during this period the upper surface of the Silurian may have been above the water's surface, or may have received accessions which were subsequently washed away by the water's flow.

Surmounting these, and of a deposit subsequent to them, we have the mountain limestone, 1000 feet in thickness, the lower Karroo shale, 800 feet in thickness, and the coal measures and upper Karroo shale, which together give an aggregate thickness of 6200 feet—together 8000 feet—or strata a mile and a third in thickness, deposited after dry land had appeared, before we come to the formation of the Dicynodon beds; and how long these took to silt up, who can tell?

But only South African deposits have thus been brought forward. Elsewhere, as has been stated, the Devonian or Old Red Sandstone strata are 8000 feet in thickness, surmounted by strata of carboniferous slates and yellow sandstone 2000 feet thick; while the coal measures—consisting of shale, and sandstones, and grit, with intervening seams of coal—measure in Wales 15,000 feet in thickness, in all 25,000 feet, or well-nigh six miles in thickness; and the Permian system, so named from its being widely developed in the Kingdom of Permia, which extends for several hundred miles along the western flanks of the Uralian chain, and thence westward to the River Volga, and which seem to have been deposited cotemporaneously with the New Red Sandstone, is reckoned to be 1000 feet in thickness.

All of these deposits tell of the lapse of time between the deposit of the strata capping Table Mountain and the Lion's Head and the deposits of the Dicynodon beds, supposed to have been the bottom of an ancient lake or inland sea, extending from the district of Cradock, if not farther to the south, to the district of the Zambesi, if not beyond it to the north. Of this I have mentioned that, according to Professor Owen, there are good reasons for referring this formation to the age of the New Red Sandstone. The draining off of the waters must have taken place a very long time after the first formation of the lake, the thickness of the deposit being so great as it is. This may have been effected by the Zambesi, as was conjectured by Dr Livingstone. I have no means of determining the time, as indicated by geological observations made elsewhere, at which the waters were dried up; but an attempt has been made to identify the disappearance of an inland sea supposed to have covered the Sahara with the close of the drift or glacial period; and coming nearer to our own times, we have, I think it not unlikely, a means of determining the time at which lakes and lakelets, the boundaries of which in some cases are well defined, had subsided or sunk to levels not less well defined.

From travellers in the interior of South Africa I have, in the prosecution of other researches, heard of groups of trees growing on low knolls in extensive plains, and on slightly elevated ground surrounding or lining such plains, which groups of trees present an appearance suggestive of their sites having been formerly islands and banks of lakes. All the trees in each group are said to approximate a uniform magnitude, but the magnitude of the trees in different groups varies much; and these facts collectively have suggested to me the probability of the different groups of trees being the produce of seed which germinated after the waters had subsided to a level a little below the elevation at which they severally are situated.

Much remains to be done for the verification of what is thus advanced, and of what is implied in the application proposed, but it appears not unreasonable to hope that, should such verification be obtained, we may, by determining the ages of the trees in the different groups, possibly obtain a series of measurements of the gradual subsidence of the waters once covering the land, and of the progressive desiccation of the country.

With this caution or protest against premature reliance on results which may be obtained by the application of the supposed standard, I proceed to show the application of it which may be made.

I was informed by the Rev. Chas. Murray that in travelling from the Cape Colony to Porcherfstrom, or Mooi-Rivers-dorp, he observed many trees of Olivienhout (*Olea verrucosa* Link), growing in remarkable quadrangular patches on the eastern slopes of hills, and on rising grounds. The trees in some of these he estimated to be of about 12 feet in girth. They were large and old trees. He remarked that in general the trees of each patch were apparently of uniform magnitude, but that the magnitude of the trees in different patches varied considerably. The statement may appear vague; I give it as I received it; it was the statement of an intelligent traveller through the district, observing what he saw, unbiased by any foregone conclusion; and it was these observations, communicated to me by Mr Murray, which first suggested to me the views I have just advanced. These views subsequently received confirmation from my learning that numerous observations, similar to those mentioned to me by Mr Murray, had been made by the late Mr James Chapman, in journeys made by him far beyond the Colony, and noted by him, though he found nothing significant in the fact until we had together talked over the matter; so that he also was unbiased in the observations made by him.

My conjecture is that the trees observed by Mr Murray commenced their growth when the slopes and rising grounds on which they stand were a little above the level of the waters covering the ground below—the seed having germinated before the land on which they grow had become anything like so arid as it now is. And supposing such a position and condition of soil to have been characteristic of the land on which patches differing in magnitude are found, at different periods, separated it may be by centuries, it seems to follow that the time which has elapsed between these different periods and the present might be ascertained, or determined approximately, by counting the number of concentric rings in the trunks of the trees in different patches; while the comparative thickness of rings in the same, or in trees felled in different patches, and the order in which these appear, might supply data for the solution of other questions connected with the progress of desiccation; and this, even though it should turn out that these trees are only remains, and at the same time the only remains, of more extensive forests of which the other trees have perished by fire or otherwise.

Mr Chapman had travelled extensively in the interior of the country beyond the Colony: he had travelled from Natal to the Zambesi, from the

Zambesi to Walvisch Bay, and hither and thither in many directions in the country between. From him I received much information on subjects embraced by Natural History which was afterwards verified by the observations of others; while I never had information communicated by him subsequently disproved.

By him I was informed that to the west of Lake Gnami are beds of limestone, on which grow a great many Motjcharra *(Combretum?)* and Omboroomboongo *(Acacia)* trees, the former in clumps, and the latter around vleies or other spots where there is a moist soil. On intermediate ground is found in abundance the Haakdorn *(Acacia detinens)* of a comparatively later growth. On elevations which appear to have been at one time islands are clumps of eight or ten baobab trees *(Adansonia digitata)* with trunks averaging 60 feet in circumference, with bark nearly a foot in thickness, as is seen when, in accordance with the usuage of the nation, from time to time immemorial, vertical stripes have been cut off for fibres to be employed in the manufacture of bags and baskets; and over the whole district are scattered thickly trees of the Sweet Gum Acacia.

To the westward of Twass is a sandy wilderness covered with trees of no great height, but amongst these appear here and there fine groups or small forests of Kameel doorn *(Acacia giraffaea)*. Near Elephant's Fountain these forests of Kameel doorn are very extensive, and the trees are of considerable age. And the Karroo doorn *(Acacia horida)* is conspicuous in the valleys and in the vicinity of vleies. To the west of Elephant's Fountain are here and there large trees of the same kind, and forests of smaller ones varying greatly in bulk and apparently in age; but most or all of the trees in each clump, or patch, or forest are apparently all of the same age, suggestive of either a succession of periods of drainage, in accordance with the views now advanced, or the recurrence at lengthened intervals of seasons favourable to the germination of seed—there being neither young trees nor solitary trees of intermediate ages.

In the course of his journey Mr Chapman travelled some way up the banks of the Shua, a large periodic stream flowing westward from the country of Moselekatsi. In the country through which that river flows he found large baobabs *(Adansonia digitata)* growing in the vicinity of springs and limestone rocks, and Mopani *(Bauhinia)* forests growing on level ground which looked like hardened mud containing a good deal of limestone, but near the river were only grassy plains, intersected by what appeared to have been river beds, and these were covered with an efflorescence of salt.

It is conjectured that these baobabs grew on islands of limestone rocks rising above the waters of the lake, while these as yet filled the basin; and that at a later period the mopani trees sprung up and grew while the waters were receding, and covered only the space now appearing as grassy plains; and that these stood above the level of the waters while they still filled, and afterwards only partially filled, the river beds; and that at a later period still did the waters left in them by the disturbance of level, evaporate and leave the efflorescence of salt.

By sections of these baobabs and mopane trees interesting chronological data might be obtained. Nor is it the times of the more marked eras alone which might thus be determined; for, according to Mr Chapman's observations, "The mopane trees are small in the lower portion of the Shua valley,"—which is that part which would be longest under water—"but they are longer and stronger the higher that valley is ascended,"—in proportion, that is, as the soil has been longer free from the covering of water—"and very much longer in the vicinity of the River Naté, which comes in a direction from the town of Moselekatzi, where they have attained a considerable magnitude;" and sections of trees at different elevations might reveal approximately the respective periods at which the spot became fitted, by the draining off of the waters, for the production of these trees.

Of the Madénisana and Kaleghari deserts, he said—"There are, here continuous forests, but more frequently the trees are in clumps or patches, consisting sometimes of one kind of tree and sometimes of several different kinds of these, with occasionally solitary trees of gigantic growth towering above the others or standing in solitary grandeur. Some kinds are found covering mountain slopes, others are found on sandy plains, others near to rivers or river beds, and others in the neighbourhood of leeghties of greater or less extent; some in all of these situations, *but decreasing in number or in magnitude, and perhaps increasing in one of these particulars while decreasing in another, according as they grow more near to one or other of the situations referred to.*" These may supply in a similiar way chronological data which might prove important in such an investigation.

"To the south of Tsamasechie," he said, "there are found springs and fountains in the sand, and in some places immense ripple-like parallel elevations 30 or 40 feet high. On the tops of these are generally large trees growing, the most prevalent being the Kushé *(Milletia Caffra)* and the Shashanga, while in the level plateau of sand between them, measuring three, four, or five miles in breadth, are forests of the Magonane *(Grewia cana?)* and in the valleys and depressions, in the soil of which water is found near the surface, grows the Makow.

"At Mottomoganyani, to the west of this, are beds of limestone like consolidated mud. To the east is Moselekatzi's country. It is very level, and abounds in salt-pans and salt vleies, especially to the south, where they seem to represent the beds of ancient lakes. In the north are forests of mopane trees, but the most characteristic arborescent feature of the country is baobabs growing on islands in these salt-pans, and around the fountains, at a distance of about 200 feet, and slightly above the water's level."

And in connection with the same thing he mentioned, "That to the north-eastward of this are incipient forests of very young mopane trees. No large trees, however, are there to be found."

These Mopane trees in other districts are found of a great magnitude. The youth of the forests found here I attribute to the comparatively recent time at which the ground had become suitable for the germination of the seed and the growth of the trees; and in the drying up of the vley, within the memory of the inhabitants of the district, I see an indication of the natural operation whereby this preparation of the soil was effected. A section of the trunk of one of these mopane trees would reveal, by the number of concentric rings in its substance, how long it has been growing there; and from similar data much might be collected in regard to the hydrography of the district.

If this be admitted, as I doubt not it will, and that at once, a ponderous volume of hydrologic records is at our command.

In illustration of the fact that information bearing on the hydrology of South Africa, additional to and different from what has been referred to, may be obtained by the study of the arborescent productions of the country, I may mention I was told by Dr Fritsch, that in travelling in the district lying between Sicklagole and the Morizane, and between these rivers and the Molapo, he found a great many Kameel Doorns *(Acacia giraffœa)*, the typical form of which was a double-dome-shaped growth of branches, widely separated by a comparatively naked stretch of trunk, the upper crown far overspreading the lower dome, the branches of which sometimes showed signs of decay, while those of the crown did not. Many branches were frequently seen strewn around the trees; these were apparently branches which had fallen by their own weight after decay had commenced; and the fall of these, it may be, had left the tree with its upper dome-shaped umbrella-like crown supported by a naked trunk rising through the lower dome.

Something similar to this has been seen elsewhere by Dr Moffat and others, but the form was not the same, and it was exceptional, while this was characteristic of those found in the district marked out by the rivers I have named; and it was suggestive to me of a possibility that a lengthened period of ordinary growth on a dry soil and in an arid atmosphere, during which the lower dome of branches was produced, had been succeeded by a period of abnormal growth, arising, it may be, out of an abundant or superabundant supply of moisture, during which the general growth of branches was more rapid—more rapid but less dense—the products of which were less durable; but the trunk or ascending axis, carried throughout this period of rapid growth to a higher and still a higher elevation, gave permanent support to the larger and upper dome, produced during a subsequent period of comparative aridity extending to the present time, in accordance with the normal growth of the tree, being enabled to do so by the strength imparted by the exogenous layers of wood produced in it by the leaves, and twigs, and branches which it sustained, while the branches of intermediate growth, being liable to decay, and lacking these, fell.

The correctness of this supposition might possibly be determined by inspection of a section of the trunk of one of these trees, and an examination of the concentric rings of which it is composed; and if thus confirmed, we may find that we have in these data by which not a little might be learned in regard to the hydrographic condition of the country throughout the period of the growth of its trees.

While this is stated, it is admitted freely that there is much connected with the conjecture which has been advanced—namely, that a section of the trunk of trees growing in such clumps as have been referred to, by revealing the number of concentric rings of which it is composed, and thus revealing its age, might be made to reveal the period at which the waters had subsided to a level a little lower than that on which it stands,—which requires to be verified before aught worthy of the designation scientific use can be made of it for this purpose. It may be admitted that proof may thus be obtained that for the time indicated by the number of concentric rings the ground has been above the level of the waters, but that this comes far short of proof of what is desiderated. It may be alleged that in the conjecture—that sections of the trunks of trees such as are referred to might be made to yield information in regard to the whole time that the land on which they are growing has been above the surface of the subsiding waters approximately correct—it is implied that these trees are of a growth so protracted as to carry us back, by thoughts of them as seedlings and saplings, to a period so remote as that spoken of.

It is; and that so obviously so that it may seem like a truism to say it; but it is said that it may be shown, first, that this has not been overlooked, and secondly, that there are amongst the trees referred to trees of dimensions so great, and by inference of a growth so protracted, that it is not unreasonable, on this account, to entertain the conjecture if it be not on other grounds found to be untenable.

Amongst these trees is the baobab; and elsewhere there are baobabs reckoned by savants to be of an age measured not by centuries only but by thousands of years,—and there are olive trees belonging to the same genus, if not the same species, as those of Gethsemane, where, it is alleged, still grow trees which must have been old trees in the days of our Lord.

Moffat says—" In the course of my journeys I have met with trunks of enormous size, which, if the time were calculated necessary for their growth, as well as their decay, one might be led to conclude that they sprang up immediately after the flood, if not before it." And there are facts known in regard to the baobab which are in accordance with the opinion he expresses. I have been informed that both Dr Livingstone and Dr Kirk have entertained and expressed the opinion that the baobab is a tree of quick growth, and that those which they saw and examined, some of which were of great size, were probably of an age not exceeding 300 years, or 500 years at most; and I am prepared to accept their statements without hesitation, but I accept also the statements which have been made by others.

According to Sprengel, who was Professor of Botany in Halle, the earliest account we have of the baobab occurs in the travels of Cadmosto, who visited the Cape de Verds and the western coast of Africa in 1456, and who mentions having seen a tree of this kind 17 ells, or 30 English feet, in diameter.

The baobab was afterwards described by Thevit, who saw it in 1555.

Adanson, who subsequently studied the natural history and botanic characteristics of the tree, and after whom it has been named by Willdenow and other botanists, *Adansonia digitata*, entered into some curious calculations in regard to the age of some of the specimens which he saw. He was an eccentric but a learned man—certainly very learned for his time. He was born in 1725, and published various works. Of these the most remarkable are the account given of his voyage to the Senegal, and his *Familles des Plants*. It is in the latter work that the calculations are given.

One of the calculations made by Adanson was founded on the supposition that he had remarked on one of the trees letters which indicated their having been cut in the thirteenth century—five hundred years before !

But another, and that a more satisfactory calculation, was founded on the measurement made of a tree, which he ascertained to be a tree which had been observed by Thevit in 1555—two hundred years before. He considered that this tree when seen by Thevit must have been from three to four feet in diameter. In his time it was six feet—showing an increase in diameter of from two to three feet in two hundred years.

From data thence obtained—for it is not a question of simple arithmetical progression—he calculated that a tree of this species would acquire a diameter of 10 feet in 550 years; of 14 feet in 1080 years; of 20 feet in 2800 years; of 30 feet in 5150 years.

Many trees of this species are met with from 25 to 27 feet in diameter. Adanson saw some which were from 75 to 78 feet in circumference. Barrow saw a specimen in St Jago 56 feet in circumference, and 80 feet high.

Baobabs, to the west of Lake Gnami, have been found measuring 60 feet in circumference, indicating, according to Adanson, a growth of 2800 years; and baobabs found to the east of the Lake are of much greater magnitude: I possess a photograph of a baobab growing near Lake Gnami, called after some native chieftainess *Mama Kahuwe*, which measured 70 feet in circumference; but they are frequently found measuring 90 feet in circumference, indicating, according to Adanson, a growth of 5150 years. And Mr Chapman, to whom I was indebted for the photograph mentioned, states that in the course of his travels he found one measuring 154 round the trunk.* On an application to this tree of data furnished by Adanson, the results are such as to stagger belief. The tree seen by Thivet in 1555, conjectured to be from 3 to 4 feet in diameter, took to attain 6 feet 200 years, whence it is calculated a diameter of 10 feet requires a growth of 550 years; increase from 10 to 14 feet, 530 years more; increase from 14 to 20 feet, 1720 years more; increase from 20 to 30 feet, 2350 years more; increase from 30 to 50 feet—we fear to advance! It seems a *reductio ad absurdum*; but there stand the figures still.

A more satisfactory mode of estimating ages of trees than was at the command of Adanson is one now followed—namely, that referred to above —counting the numbers of concentric rings in a trunk, and reckoning each as the product of a year: and this could be applied to such trees as are referred to. The rule cannot be considered absolute; but it supplies an approximation upon which reliance may be placed. I have been told that Dr Livingstone applied it to baobabs, and never found one with a trunk consisting of more than 300 concentric rings; but I have failed to obtain an explicit statement of his observations, and therefore I cannot use them otherwise than as a ground of caution against relying with perfect confidence on bulk as an indication of a growth of thousands of years, according to the calculations of Adanson. But this is not essential to the argument embraced in the conjecture; the argument is the same be the ages of the trees what they may; it is the age we wish to ascertain; and by ascertaining the ages of baobabs, growing in different localities—whatever these ages may be—we may learn that for a period, equal at least to that of the age of the tree, that spot, and all in the vicinity of it of a higher level, has been dry land.

Mr L. A. Tollemache reports of Babbage :—" It seemed to him possible to obtain an exact record of the succession of hot and cold years for long periods in bygone ages. His plan was as follows :—Among the stumps of trees in some ancient forests, he proposed to select one in which both the number and the size of the rings that have been annually produced were clearly marked. He would write down the succession of hot and cool summers as marked in this tree, assuming that the larger the ring in each case the hotter has been the summer. He then proposed to examine other trees of about the same date, until he found some which recorded a series of hot and cold seasons exactly similiar to that which he had already noted down, and until the series extended far enough for him to be sure that the resemblance was not accidental, but that he had before him a natural register of the same seasons which had been recorded in the first tree. As

---

* The baobab, though presenting such a bulk of trunk, is not a tree of great height. Specimens of the tree may be seen at Sierra Leone; but there the tree does not grow, or has not grown, larger than an orchard apple tree. I have seen a similar specimen in the *Jardin des Plants* in Paris.

some of these trees would be somewhat older than the first tree, while others would have survived it, he considered that it would be possible, so to say, to piece out the information obtained from one tree by means of the others; and that, after examining a great number of trees, his record of warm and cold seasons might be extended at both ends almost indefinitely."

From this it may be seen that it has been considered probable, and that the conjecture is not without plausibility, that there are in the histology and structure of trees valuable records of the past, which may add to our knowledge of what has occurred in that past if we could decipher and translate them.

All that has been referred to as implied in the assumption that by these trees we may determine at what time the waters had subsided to a little below the level of the ground on which they are growing is, first, that they are of an age sufficient to do so, and second, that their age can be ascertained; in the conjecture that sections of the trunks of the trees referred to might be made to yield the information desired, it is implied, third, that they are the produce of seeds which germinated shortly after the subsidance of the waters to a little below the level of the ground on which they grow. But how is this to be proved?

Proof positive we have not and cannot obtain. We have only circumstantial evidence; we can obtain no other; and the circumstantial evidence is such as has been obtained accidentally, a circumstance which may add to its value but leave it less full, complete, and satisfactory than may be desired.

Observations made by students of botany have led to the conclusion that for the germination of seeds a certain degree of moisture, varying, it may be, with different kinds of seeds, but confined in the case of many within a limited range, is requisite, deficiency and excess being both prejudicial to the process; the clumps of trees are found growing upon what appear, by their slight elevation above the adjacent ground, to have been the banks of lakes or islands in large sheets of water; such banks and islands would offer hydrometic conditions favourable to the germination of seeds; and the combined circumstances, that the trees in such clumps, though differing in size from those in other clumps, have been observed to be of a uniform size themselves, and that the trees are, to a considerable extent, found on these eminences and not on the level ground around, are favourable to the supposition that the seeds from which they sprung germinated there at a time when the ground was a little, and only a little, above the level of the waters of a lake or river of which they are the banks, or islands which they enclosed, when the soil was, and probably had only shortly before become, adapted to promote the germination of such seeds, and to sustain their subsequent growth; and if this be in accordance with the facts of the case, we are supplied thus with indications of the progress of the drainage and desiccation of the country, in the greater age, indicated by the larger growth of the trees on the more elevated ground, and in the lesser age, indicated by the lesser magnitude of these in lower situations in the same locality; and thus we may be supplied with means of determining at what distance from the present time it was that the waters had sunk to different levels, or an approximation thereto, by ascertaining the ages of the trees growing on such different levels.

CHAPTER IV.

HYDROGRAPHIC CONDITION OF THE COUNTRY WITHIN THE HISTORIC PERIOD.

The hydrographic picture of the land suggested by the supposed testimony of the baobab, and other trees of corresponding age, is such as the physical geography in many districts also suggests—extensive sheets of shallow water, the remains, it may be, of larger, deeper lakes, lowered in their surface level by the lowering of the outlets as these have worn away, or shallowed by the silting up of the basin. The trees on slight elevations add little to our data beyond supplying an indication of the time at which things were so, and enabling us to fill up the outline pictured, with groups of trees and the reflection of their trunks and foliage in the waters beneath them. And something of the same thing may be said even of the baobab and mopane trees growing on the banks of the Shua and the Naté.

We cannot say we are thus in our chronological review brought up to the historic era, but we are apparently brought within sight of it, for within this we find notices of the drying up of such sheets of water as these appear to have been in the testimony of natives in regard to what has occurred within the memory of man, and in the testimony of European travellers of our own day. The historic period goes further back, and may be said to embrace four centuries; but the earlier centuries supply little information beyond what we have obtained, and in so far as the hydrography of the country is concerned the historic period of its hydrology may be said to embrace little more than the last fifty years.

It is customary to speak of the Cape of Good Hope as having been discovered by Bartholomew Diaz, the Portuguese navigator. Of him it is said that, "After having traced nearly a thousand miles of new country, and endured innumerable hardships, he at length came in sight of the Cape which terminates South Africa; but he proceeded no further, fancying that he had arrived at the boundary of the earth; and being intimidated with the darkness and tempests with which he was surrounded, on account of the heavy gales which he experienced he gave it the name of '*Cabo des totos Tormentos*,' or the Cape of Storms; which was subsequently exchanged by John II. of Portugal for '*Cabo du Buonne Esperance*,' or Cape of Good Hope, from the prospect which it afforded him of opening a maritime path to India." It may be that at that time the country was in a condition such as we have pictured!

But there are much earlier records of South Africa than is thus supplied. According to Herodotus, the Phœnicians circumnavigated the continent of Africa in the time of Pharaoh Necho, or about 600 B.C. Fourteen hundred years thereafter, A.D. 800, we find the coast of South Africa known to the Arabs, as far south as Delagoa Bay, in latitude 28°, which bay was by them called Dugutha. In 1480 Sofala was visited by a Portuguese from Abyssinia—Pedrao Cavalliao—and in 1484 Diego Cam, a Portuguese captain, and Behem of Nuremburg reached 22° south latitude, and erected a cross on Cape Padrone, or Cape Cross, near Walvisch Bay.

In 1486 Bartholomew Diaz planted a cross on Sierra Parda, in 24° south latitude, a few miles south of the present Sandwich harbour; landed at Cape Voltas, to the south of the Orange River, now Alexander Bay; rounded the Cape without seeing it, and landed in Angra des Vaqueino. On 14th September of that year he landed and planted a cross on St Croix Island, in Algoa Bay, and he penetrated as far east as the Great Fish River—which he calls after one of his captains Rio del Infante—and it was on his return voyage homewards that he sighted the Cape.

After the discovery of the Cape by Bartholomew Diaz it was next visited by Vasco de Gama on a subsequent voyage of discovery. He too had his troubles. "It was on the 8th July 1497 that Gama left the Tagus, and his voyage was extremely tempestuous. During any gloomy interval of the storm the sailors, wearied out with fatigue, surrounded their commander and implored him to return homewards. But Gama's resolution was unalterable; and having suppressed a formidable conspiracy against himself, in which all the pilots were ringleaders, he, with his brother and a steady band of adherents, stood night and day at the helm. And on the twentieth of November hope was turned to fruition Vasco de Gama rounded the Cape which had long been the boundary of navigation. Soon after this event the King of Portugal despatched ships with orders to touch there, which they did; but, fearful of approaching the mainland, they anchored near Robben Island, which is at the entrance to Table Bay, and proceeded from thence with their boat to see the natives."

In 1497, on November 7, Vasco de Gama landed in St Helena Bay, where he was wounded in the leg by the natives while he was taking the altitude of the sun; on the 19th he doubled the Cape on his way to India; on December 25 he discovered the coast of Natal, to which that name was given in consideration of its having been discovered on the natal day of our Saviour; and he explored the east coast as far as Melinda,—including Delagoa Bay, Quillimane, and Mozambique. The first-named place was by him called *Aguaido de Boa Pax*.

In the same year the Portuguese Rio del Infante, then an Admiral, landed in Table Bay.

In 1499 Vasco de Gama, on his return voyage, landed at Mossel Bay, called then Angra San Blas; and in that year Bartholomew Diaz perished off the Cape in a ship of a fleet under Pedro Alvarez.

In 1500 the Portuguese began to form settlements on the west coast of Angola, and Pedro Alvarez Cabral landed at Mossel Bay.

Equally numerous are the notices of the landing of European navigators on different parts of the coast of South Africa in subsequent years. Fain would I learn in what state they found the country in regard to lakes and forests! I cannot; but this I have learned, that in some of the earliest notices we have of the eastern coast it is spoken of as "a veritable *Terra del Fuego*"; and from this I draw inferences which I shall afterwards state.

It was not till upwards of a hundred and fifty years after this—viz., in 1652—that possession of the country was taken by the Dutch East India Company, and a fort was erected under the direction of Jan van Riebeck, who had previously visited the country, and to whom was entrusted the government of the infant settlement; and it was not until about a hundred and fifty years later that it came into the hands of the British. In 1796 it came into their possession by capitulation; in 1801 it was restored to the Batavian Government; and in January 1806 it again became British by capitulation. Since this time well nigh three-quarters of a century have passed away, and it is only of late years that we have learned anything of the drying up of lakes. From all of the records of these events to which I have had access we learn nothing of the former hydrographic condition of the country, and it is not until we come to our own day that we find this matter of observation and testimony. What we have learned may be little, but it is significant and suggestive.

Dr Moffat has graphically described the effects of aridity of soil and atmosphere, witnessed and experienced by him on his coming to Africa, as Mr Campbell and others had done before him; and he mentions that "on his settlement some years later at Latakoo, in 1821, the natives were wont to tell of the floods of ancient times, the incessant showers which clothed the very rocks with verdure, and the giant trees and forests which once studded the brows of the Hamhan hills and neighbouring plains. They boasted of the Kuriman and other rivers with their impassable torrents, in which the hippopotami played, while the lowing herds walked to their necks in grass filling their *makukas* (milk sacks) with milk, making every heart to sing for joy." And he incidentally, again and again, supplies testimony confirmatory of their testimony that such had been the case; while he also supplies testimony of the progress of the desiccation extending over the fifty years of his residence and labours in the country, and so diminishing the flow of rivers that the country was more arid when he left it than when he came.

Mr Chapman, in narrating to me what he saw on the journey he made from Natal to the Victoria Falls, describing the country through which he passed before reaching the Botletlie River, stated that to the eastward of the route by which he crossed the eastern extremity of the Kalihara desert the country is covered with open grassy plains, in which are extensive salt-pans, from which, in many cases, the water has dried up, leaving only a thick encrustation of salt on the surface of the ground, and in other cases, though containing water, presenting the appearance of thousands of tons of beautiful salt on and towards the margin. One discovered by him in 1853, and marked in accordance with his discription in Hall's Mass of the district, it took him several days to travel round. Yet within the memory of men then living in the district this was a pool of water connected with the Botletlie river. As it dried, thousands of fish, from time to time, were left to perish, and for months the vultures hovered about unable to devour all that had died.

Livingstone, by graphic sketches of what he saw on his expedition to the Zambesi, and of what he inferred from what he saw must have been the former level of the waters through extensive regions of that district, has enabled us to feel as if we were looking upon the scene—both as it now is, as it must have been; and references made by him to baobabs of gigantic size tell that that past must have been anterior to the present by a period equal at least to the age of the baobabs, if not greater, for these baobabs could not have grown in the bottom of a lake.

The supposition of Dr Livingstone, was that these lakes were drained of in a great measure by the Zambesi.

To the south of the high-land, constituting the water shed south of the Zambesi, in the longtitude of the falls, is a portion of the Madenisana desert, which was described to me by Mr Chapman as characterised by springs and fountains found at some little depth in the sand, and presenting an appearance suggestive of the waters from the upper country having at one time drained off through this level as well as through the valley of the Zambesi, and left lines of vleies in which, under the surface of the sand now filling them, water is obtained, but all the water which filled, while flowing over, the district is now only a thing of the past.

In the account given by Dr Livingstone of his second voyage up the Shire, in 1859, he says,—" As we ascended we passed a deep stream about thirty yards wide, flowing in from a body of open water several miles broad. Numbers of men were busy at different parts of it filling their canoes with the lotus root, called *Nyika*, which, when boiled or roasted, resembles our chestnuts, and is extensively used in Africans' food. Out of this lagoon, and by this stream, the chief part of the duckweed of the Shire flows. The lagoon itself is called Nyanja ea Motope (Lake of Mud). It is also named Nyanja Pangono (Little Lake), while the elephant marsh goes by the name of Nyanja Mukulu (Great Lake). It is evident from the shore-line still to be observed on the adjacent hills that in ancient times these were really lakes; and the traditional names thus preserved are only another evidence of the general desiccation which Africa has undergone; which is even now going on there, and has already been accomplished in other parts of the district."

Dr Livingstone describes a salt-pan to the west of Ngami, called Ntetwe, the width of which he estimated at ten miles, and its probable length at a hundred; and south of it is the still larger pan discovered by Mr J. Chapman.

The whole of these large surfaces, says Hall, are generally perfectly dry, and covered with reeds.

Within the Colony is a salt-pan, in Bushmanland, known as the Commissioners' Pan, described by Hall as a shallow basin with a circuit of eighteen or twenty miles, its surface generally dry and covered with a crust of salt.

" Many of the rivers and fountains in Great Namaqualand, Bushmanland, and the Kalihari country, permanent in the recollections of many now living, have," says Hall in his *Manual of South African Geography*, " been dry for years. Livingstone tells us that the water supply of the Lake Gnami takes place in channels prepared for a far more copious flow. It resembles a deserted eastern garden, where all the embankments and canals for irrigation can be traced; but where the main dam and sluices being allowed to get out of repair, only a small portion can be got under water. When Sebituane the Makololo chief passed through the Kalihari desert, about the year 1820, the Sarotli fountain was a large pan of water; the burnt up and gaping Makoko, in the remembrance of many living, was a flowing stream; and the fountain at Kurumangve, when Mr Moffat settled there, gave a much more copious supply than it does at present. Many deep pools formerly existed in the Kuruman and Malapo rivers, now long dried up; and it would also appear that in general the fountains of the Nieuwe-Veld, Winter Veld, and Midden Veld, or the country forming the northern slope of the great mountain range, have been getting for years weaker."

The passage in which Dr Livingstone speaks of the appearance of the vicinity of the Gnami in the manner cited is the account given by him of his visit to the lake with Messrs Oswell and Murray, on the first of August

N

1849. The account given by him is as follows :—" Twelve days after our departure from the waggons at Ngabisane, we came to the northeast end of Lake Gnami; and on the first of August 1849 we went down together to the broad part, and, for the first time, this fine looking sheet of water was beheld by Europeans. The direction of the lake seems to be N.N.E. and S.S.W. by compass. The southern portion is said to bend round to the west, and to receive the Teoughe from the north at its northeast extremity We could detect no horizon where we stood looking S.S.W., nor could we form any idea of the extent of the lake, except from the reports of the inhabitants of the district; and as they profess to go round it in three days, allowing twenty-five miles a-day, this would make it seventy-five, or less than seventy geographical miles in circumference. Other guesses have been made since as to its circumference, ranging between seventy and one hundred miles. It is shallow, for I subsequently saw a native punting his canoe over seven or eight miles of the northeast end; it can never, therefore, be of much value as a commercial highway. In fact, during the months preceding the annual supply of water from the north, the lake is so shallow that it is with difficulty cattle can approach the water through the boggy, reedy banks. These are low on all sides, but on the west there is a space devoid of trees, showing that the waters have retired thence at no very ancient date. This is another of the proofs of desiccation met with so abundantly throughout the whole country. A number of dead trees lie on this space, some of them imbedded in the mud, right in the water. We were informed by the Bayeiye, who live on the lake, that when the annual inundation begins, not only trees of great size, but antelopes, as the springbock and tsessebe *(acronotus lunata)*, are swept down by its rushing waters. The trees are gradually driven by the wind to the opposite side, and become imbedded in mud.

" The water of the lake is perfectly fresh when full, but brackish when low; and that coming down the Tanunak'le we found to be so clear, cold, and soft, the higher we ascended, that the idea of melting snow was suggested to our minds. We found this region, with regard to that from which we had come, to be clearly a hollow, the lowest point being lake Kumadau; the point of the ebullition of water, as shown by one of Newman's barometric thermometers, was only between $207\frac{1}{2}°$ and $206°$, giving an elevation of not much more than 2000 feet above the level of the sea. We had descended above 2000 feet in coming to it from Kolobeng. It is the southern and lowest part of the great river system beyond, in which large tracts of country are inundated annually by tropical rains, hereafter to be described. A little of that water which in the countries further north produces inundation comes as far south as $20°\ 20'$, the latitude of the upper end of the lake, and instead of flooding the country falls into the lake as into a reservoir. It begins to flow down the Embarrah, which divides into the rivers Tzō and Teoughe. The Tzō divides into the Tamunak'le and Mababe; the Tamunak'le discharges itself into the Zouga; and the Teoughe into the lake. The flow begins either in March or April, and the descending waters find the channels of all these rivers dried out, except in certain pools in their beds, which have long dry spaces between them. The lake itself is very low. The Zonga is but a prolongation of the Tamunak'le, and an arm of the lake reaches up to the point where the one ends and the other begins. This last is narrow and shallow, while the Zonga is broad and deep. The narrow arm of the lake, which on the map looks like a continuation of the Zonga, has never been observed to flow either way. It is as stagnant as the lake itself.

"The Teoughe and the Tamunak'le being essentially the same river, and receiving their supplies from the same source (the Embarrah or Varra), can never outrun each other. If either could, or if the Teoughe could fill the lake—a thing which has never happened in modern times—then this little arm would prove a convenient escapement to prevent inundation. If the lake ever becomes lower than the bed of the Zonga, a little of the water of the Tamunak'le might flow into it, instead of down the Zonga. We should then have the phenomenon of a river flowing two ways; but this has never been observed to take place here, and it is doubtful if it ever can occur in this locality. The Zonga is broad and deep where it leaves the Tamunak'le, but becomes gradually narrower as you descend about 200 miles; there it flows into the Kumadau, a small lake about three or four miles broad and twelve long. The water which, higher up, begins to flow in April, does not make much progress in filling this lake till the end of June. In September the rivers cease to flow. When the supply has been more than usually abundant, a little water flows beyond Kumadau, in the bed first seen by us on the 4th of July; if the quantity were larger it might go further in the dry rocky bed of the Zonga, since seen still further to the east. The water supply of this part of the river system, . . . takes place in channels for a much more copious flow. It resembles a deserted eastern garden, where all the embankments and canals for irrigation can be traced, but where—the main dam and sluices having been allowed to get out of repair—only a small portion can be laid under water. In the case of the Zonga the channel is perfect, but water enough to fill the whole channel never comes down; and before it finds its way much beyond Kumadau the upper supply ceases to run, and the rest becomes evaporated. The higher parts of its bed even are much broader and more capacious than the lower towards Kumadau. The water is not absorbed so much as lost in filling up an empty channel, from which it is to be removed by the air and sun. There is, I am convinced, no such thing in the country as a river running into sand and becoming lost. This phenomenon, so convenient for geographers, haunted my fancy for years; but I have failed in discovering anything except a most insignificant approach to it."

According to the statements of others, the situation of the lake Gnami, determined of course by the part at which the observation was made, is given as lat. 20° 40', and long. 23° east. It is said to be at an elevation, above the level of the sea, of 3713 feet; to be about fifty miles long; and of an average breadth of eight or ten miles. It was visited by Mr F. Green, who found the depth of the centre to be only six feet, and with difficulty could he push a boat of light draught through its shoals; and now its depth seems to be still less.

I first heard of the lake in 1845, and what I heard was of natives from a distance having visited it and been confounded on seeing men of the locality fleeing from them, disappear in its waters, and afterwards reappear on the shore beyond; a fact, if a fact it was, suggestive of its having been a lake of depth sufficient to allow of a man swimming in its waters, if not, of a depth so great as to prevent him wading across, which is in accordance with the statement of Mr Green. By Mr Chapman I was told of its having been visited by him in 1864, and that then nowhere was it of a depth which would bring its waters above the knee of a wader.

Dr Livingstone tells of the indications of its greater extent at a former day than its extent when visited by him and his fellow travellers. In accordance with this I have been told that at a considerable distance from its present shores there are what by a little stretch of language may be called mines of ivory and bones, the remains of animals which, coming there to drink, have there perished, probably killed by beasts of prey. The earth covering these appears to have been deposited over these remains from suspension in water, and this indicates that so far at least the lake then extended.

Thus are we enabled to connect the distant past with the present, and trace the dessication from pre-adamic times to the present, and to see going on in remote regions what had occurred, in the land now colonised by Europeans, ages before.

In a paper read before more than one of the Scientific Societies of Britain, amongst others, before a meeting of the Royal Geographical Society, on the 15th March 1865, which the author has placed at my service, there occur the following statements on this subject:—"A very noticeable physical fact, which has of late years attracted considerable attention from residents in South Africa, is the gradual drying-up of large tracts of country in the Trans-'Gariep. That great expanse of wilderness, called the Káláhári, remarkable for few inhabitants, little water, and considerable vegetation, seems to be gaining in extent, gradually swallowing up large portions of the habitable country on its confines, and slowly, but surely, assimilating their fertile character to its own sterile one. It has become matter of notoriety that springs, which a few years ago supplied a sufficient quantity of fluid to irrigate considerable breadths of garden and field, have diminished in their flow and dwindled away, causing the migration of the inhabitants to a more favourable dwelling-place; while desert sucking-places and well-filled pools, such as that of Serotli, described by Livingstone, are at present either completely dry, or afford only a small quantity of liquid after much digging, where formerly existed a large piece of water.

"At Lopépe and other places on the road to Lake 'Ngami this is the case, as well as at Tunobis in Damaraland, and elsewhere; but it is most conspicuous in the territory of the Bakwain tribes, in which, as one of the many evidences of the growing desiccation of the country, streams, *e.g.* the Mahalapi River, that at Lopelóle and at Porapora Pass, are pointed out where thousands and thousands of cattle formerly drank, but in which water never now flows, and where a single herd could not find fluid for its support.

"When Mr Moffat first attempted a settlement at the Kúrúman forty years ago, he made a dam six or seven miles below the present one, and led out the stream for irrigation, where not a drop of the fountain water ever now flows; and other parts, fourteen miles below the Kúrúman gardens, are pointed out as having contained, within the memory of people now living, hippopotami and pools sufficient to drown both men and cattle.

"The fountain at Griqua Town, which a few years ago yielded a sufficiency of water to irrigate four square miles of corn and garden ground, has of late years and in the most marked manner diminished its supplies, almost ceasing to flow, and occasioning the emigration of many of the Dutch-speaking inhabitants to other and more fertile localities not subject to the absence of moisture.

"As this diminution of water has been coincident with the failure of fountains over a wide extent of territory in Buchuanaland, it is evident that from some cause, more or less obscure, *a great change in the external physical characteristics of the entire region between the Orange and the 'Ngami Lake has taken place since the country was first explored by Europeans.*

" This great change has not, however, been confined to the comparatively short space of time during which missionaries have been in the country. On the contrary, the traditions of the natives point to more remote periods, when the country was far more fertile and much better watered than at present—when the Kúrúman and other rivers, with their impassable torrents, were something to boast of. Moffat says that accounts of floods of ancient times, of incessant showers which clothed the very rocks with verdure, and of the existence of giant trees and forests which once covered the brows of the Hamhana Hills, are wont to be related by garrulous elders to the utter astonishment of their younger listeners. In those ancient days the lowing herds walked up to their necks in grass, and filling their owners' milk-sacks with rich milk, made every heart to sing for joy.

" But, independent of this oral and traditional testimony, travellers have before their eyes, in the immense number of stumps and roots of enormous trunks of the Acacia giraffæa, where now scarcely a single living specimen is to be seen raising its stately head above the shrubs, and in the ancient beds of the dried-up rivers Matlaurin, Mashaua, Molapo, and others, positive demonstration of the departed former fertility of the lands of the Bechuana nation. In fact the whole country north of the Orange River, and lying east of the Káláhári Desert, presents to the eye of a European, to use the words of the missionary just quoted, ' something like an old neglected garden or field.' "

The statement is made preparatory to a statement of the conclusions to which the writer (Mr J. F. Wilson) has come in regard to the cause of this desiccation of the land: these conclusions will afterwards be cited ; but at present we have under consideration the state of the country. Having made the remark that we must seek reasons for the continued spread of drought in the physical characteristics of the Gariēpine Basin itself, and in some of the customs of its inhabitants, he goes on to say, " In the first place, *the countries drained by the Great River are naturally arid*, both from their interior position and from the interposition of the Quathlamba Mountains between them and the Indian Ocean, whence the chief supplies of rain are evaporated. It will be necessary, therefore, to speak here of the three meteorological zones into which South Africa may be divided, and at the same time give a description of the different sections into which the 'Gariepine territories are apportioned by recent writers. The meteorological divisions may be regarded as three zones of climate *(Livingstone)*: the eastern, comprehending Zulu-land, Natal, Independent and British Kaffraria ; the central, comprising a portion of the elevated Central Basin of the continent, and divided from the eastern by the Drakensberg, Malutis, and other ranges ; and the western, including the Káláhári Proper, the wastes of Namaqualand, and the wilds of Bushmanland—the latter situated to the south of the Orange River.

" The first of these, which may be called the zone of the Kaffirs, is pronounced by travellers to be decidedly fertile. It is covered with evergreen succulent trees, occasional extensive forests, and gigantic timber. The zone is comparatively well watered by numerous streams, and has a considerable annual rainfall.

"The second, or zone of the Bechuana, consists for the most part of rolling plains or arid prairies, with but few fountains, fewer permanent rivers, and forests *(if such they may be called)* gradually diminishing to a final destruction, which from present appearances cannot long be delayed. Rain here, as a rule, is far from abundant; irrigation is absolutely necessary to raise European grain, and droughts are of frequent occurrence.

"The third, or zone of the Namaquas and Bushmen, sterile and barren in the extreme, is dependent upon thunderstorms alone for the rain, which rushes down its periodical rivers or supplies the vegetation of its deserts.

"The prevailing winds of most of the country thus divided are from the northeast. Heavily laden with vapour from the Indian Ocean, the clouds, under the influence of these easterly currents, are driven over the Zulu territory, Natal, and Kaffirland, watering those lands luxuriantly; but when the moisture-bearing nimbi arrive at the peaks of the mountain ranges, not only have they parted with a large proportion of their water, but they are then on the edge of the more arid central basin, and begin to meet with the influences of the heated and naked plains, under the radiation from the surface of which, and in an increasing degree as the Bechuana tribes are past and the Kálahári is reached, the clouds rise higher above the earth, the moisture evaporates in a thinner vapour, and as a consequence fewer showers fall upon the hot thirsty soil beneath.

"The further we journey from the Drakensberg eastwards, the greater becomes this diminution of water.

"Leaving the mountains, the Lesuto or Basuto land, as it is frequently called, is, without doubt, the best-watered portion of the central meteorological district, mainly, it is presumed, on account of its being intersected by the Malutis range. Towards this important section of country, from November to April, the northeast winds blow from the shores of Mozambique and the delta of the Zambesi immense masses of cloud, which sweep heavily over the earth, darkening the sky, and preceded in their course by dreadful peals of thunder. On reaching the high land, the aërial lake is shut in by the huge table-headed mountains; as a consequence, a rapid condensation takes place, and then a veritable deluge ensues. In a few moments cataracts rush from the mountain heights, the smallest and most thread-like rivulets are transformed into torrents, and the rivers, overflowing their banks, cover the plains: this sometimes lasts for days together *(Casalis).* It is from the accumulation of these waters that the Lekoa, the Caledon, and many other tributaries of the great Orange River, which with slow and majestic course flow to the westward across the vast plains of the centre of South Africa, take their rise. As the mountains, however, merge into the plains, and these again into the Kálahári, we are reminded by the gradually diminishing rivers of the continual aridity of the soil, till we reach Great Namaqualand, where the occurrence of periodically filled watercourses again testifies to the descent of rain.

"In this latter district, however, as well as in the desert, rain falls only from thunder-clouds. These rise from the northeast, and are always hailed with delight by the inhabitants of those parched and burning regions; but they are partial in the distribution of their precious treasure, the storms frequently passing over with tremendous voilence, striking both European and native with awe at their terrific grandeur, while not a particle of rain descends to cool and fructify the barren waste. There is something terribly sublime in a real Namaqualand or Kálahári thunder-storm. The air becomes sultry and oppressive to an unusual degree; the whole animated creation is silent as death; not a breath of wind is perceptible. Low down the horizon a dense black cloud emits a faint rumbling, which momentarily becomes louder and louder, while the threatening mass, ever increasing, gradually rises, lighted up with the quick flashes of forked lightning. At length a cloud of dust approaches, a storm of wind rushes over the plain, overturning trees, uprooting bushes, and sweeping everything before it in its tumultuous course; a few large spattering drops are heard, and then, with the almost simultaneous blinding glare of lightning and deafening crash of thunder, torrents of mingled hail and rain descend. In a few minutes the country is flooded; currents of turbid water, half-a-mile wide, roar through a ravine which has not shown a drop of water for years previously, rivulets flow where one would think water had never run before, and the ear is charmed with the sweet strains of a long-silent music. Perhaps in less than an hour the cloud has passed over, and may be seen speeding onwards to pour out its treasures over many a sunburnt plain and parched mountain.

"Barren, burnt up, and roasted by the sun as are the desolate territories in the western meteorological zone, there are few spots, nevertheless, even in the Káláhári Proper, which are covered with shifting sands, or are wholly destitute of vegetation. Even large trees are occasionally to be met with; and some of the periodical rivers of Namaqualand and the Cis-'Gariepine plateaux, in which water seldom flows, may be traced in their winding courses by the mimosa and camel-thorn trees that thinly line their banks. The parched and arid plains of a large portion of the northern division of the British Colony support sheep on the thin sprinkling of grass and ice-plants which covers them; and undoubtedly the alpaca and the camel might here be introduced with advantage both to commerce and the highest interests of the native tribes. In fact, however barren and quasi-desert the different sections of the 'Gariepine Basin may be, there are none which do not support countless hosts of wild animals fitted by Providence for dwelling in droughty countries; and the presence, wherever water can be found, of the wandering Bushman and Molala (poor Mochuana), the lean Mokáláhári, the stupid Koranna, and avaricious Namaqua, who make up the sum of the desert's human inhabitants, testifies that the great market of the world must derive *some* commodities even from its least inviting districts. Water, however, in the shape of a fountain (sometimes hot in Namaqualand), a sucking-place or subterraneous expanse of wet sand, generally in the bed of a periodical or dried-up river, or a shallow desert pool *(vley)*, is an absolute necessity to the small communities which war, poverty, or choice, has led to the wilderness.

"In those countries, generally remote from the sea, where the average rainfall is but a few inches in the course of a year, the diminution of an inch or two is felt with very much greater intensity than in those favoured lands where the rainfall is more abundant. In arid countries similar to the lands now under consideration, the revolution of the weather in cycles of years is also much more marked than elsewhere. It follows, therefore, that meteorologists find in such countries a sphere for their observations of the greatest interest and importance as connected with the phenomena of drought. In Britain, happily, a dry season conveys only an inadequate idea of drought; but in South Africa extreme droughts sometimes continue for whole years together, reducing the natives to the direst misery, depriving them of their scanty harvests, destroying their herds, and driving them from their homes to wander in search of subsistence.

"During the year 1862, an unexampled and very widely-extended drought prevailed throughout the Cape Colony, and made itself felt far into the tropical regions in the neighb.... .. .. s. It was very severely felt in the Lesuto, which is a territory generally blessed with abundant rains at stated periods. In this portion of the country, by the month of November, no traces of vegetation remained, the vast grass plains becoming mere sandy deserts from the excessive heat that prevailed. The clouds which overcast the heavens, apparently laden with fertilising treasure, if they would but part with it, seemed to mock at the hopes of the inhabitants. They passed away with the wind which bore on its wings thousands of tons of dry dust, gathered in its sweep over the parched ground for miles and miles; and which went on gathering and still gathering over mountains and plains, until it reached the South Atlantic and Indian Oceans, blasting and destroying vegetation on its way. The largest streams, too, ceased to flow. The cattle died by thousands, and famine began to appear throughout the land. Scarcely any crops could be got into the ground. The sun scorched the earth with its fire, and the rain-makers, whose assumed power over the elements had been nearly overthrown by the advance of Christianity and civilisation into these regions, again attempted to re-establish their waning authority. The mighty Orange River could be stepped across by a child, and in its upper part at last ran dry, exposing in its bed, near Hope Town, the remains of a waggon which had been lost in a sudden flood while crossing the river some thirty years before. At last, when articles of food had risen to extremely high figures, breadstuffs being higher in price than during the Kaffir war, and cabbages selling at the rate of a penny the leaf at Colesberg, the heavens, whose inexorable serenity had lasted more than a year, were covered with clouds, and drops of rain were heard to fall upon the parched ground, soon to be saturated with delightful showers. Although late in the season, the people were enabled to sow a little corn, and by degrees the visitation passed away, leaving behind it the remembrance of a dark dismal dispensation during the continuance of which men's hearts failed them for fear, thousands losing more than half their substance, and multitudes looking forward to absolute ruin and starvation."

It was at this time I returned to the Colony, after an absence of fifteen years, and I found everywhere lamentations being made over the consequences of the severe and long-continued drought, from which the community was then suffering, though reviving hope was beginning to cheer the drooping spirits of many. And several of the facts mentioned by Mr Wilson were stated to me also in the localities in which they occurred, connecting the geological record of the past with its experiences and observations of the actual present.

By a study of the physical geography of South Africa much may be learned in regard to its former hydrographic condition; by the consideration of deductions which may be drawn from geological observations which many have made within the limits of the portions colonised by Europeans, much may be learned in regard to the hydrographic condition of what is now so named in the earlier ages of the world's history; by observations made by these European colonists, and the comparison of these with what they have learned from the aboriginal, or at least earlier, inhabitants of the land, it appears that the desiccation, which seems to be extreme, is a process which has been going on from earlier times until now, and which is still going on.

We have indications of the whole land having lain long covered deep by what may have been a shoreless sea, but experiencing, it may be, changes of temperature, causing it to hiss, and bubble, and boil, and rise in vapour, —as does the drop of water falling on the stove,—covering the heavens above with blackness, and darkness, and cloud ; a sea, for ages limpid as the waters of the ocean rising with a waveless tide ; for ages charged with mud, dense as that of the waters of the Yellow river ; for ages placid and motionless in its depths as the mirror-like lake in the mountain recess by which it is sheltered and shielded from every wind that blows ; for ages disturbed by ocean currents which cut deep into the ocean bed, making valleys where erewhile it was a plain, and leaving mounds intact a mile in height, to show to what a depth they have cut and planed away the ground around. We have indications of portions rising or being raised above the surface of the waste of waters, sometimes to be again submerged, and again raised to be again submerged, but only to be raised again. We have indications of land thus raised having appeared, and it may have been for ages as it slowly rose, as the land of a thousand isles, and passing by degrees, as changes are effected in dissolving views, from a land of a thousand isles into a land of a thousand lakes, and these, as time rolls on, emptied and dried up, and converted into arid valleys and arid plains, and the whole converted in extensive districts into a land in which there is no water.

And we can trace the latter progress of the desiccation subsequent to the drainage and evaporation up to the present day from a period extending as far back as that vaguely, but frequently, described as embraced by the memory of man.

PART II.—CAUSE OR OCCASION OF THE DESICCATION AND ARIDITY OF SOUTH AFRICA.

THE desiccation and consequent aridity of South Africa is attributable, primarily and principally, to the draining off of the water, in consequence of the elevation of the land above the level of the sea; and secondarily, to the evaporation of water and its subsequent dissipation in the atmosphere, which evaporation has been promoted by the clearing away by man of arborescent and herbaceous vegetation which otherwise might have retarded the process.

CHAPTER I.

PRIMARY AND PRINCIPAL CAUSE OF THE DESICCATION AND CONSEQUENT ARIDITY OF SOUTH AFRICA.

In the hydrographic records which we have had under consideration, we have found indications of the whole land having been, at one time, lying deep in the bottom of the ocean, to which, like the fabled goddess of beauty, it may trace its birth; indications of its rising or having been raised, before emergence, to near the level of the ocean's surface; of portions of it rising above that surface and looking out upon the waste of waters around; of either these portions, or other islands adjacent or not far distant, having become clothed with vegetation—marine vegetation at a little below the water's edge, and terrestrial vegetation of primitive forms on the land beyond; of extensive districts long after this remaining still under cover of the ocean, or if they, too, had risen above that covering, of their having been again submerged, and having remained submerged for ages; of extensive districts rising above the ocean to a greater elevation, and some of these either carrying with them in natural depressions portions of the ocean, or retaining in similiar depressions water collected in them from the rising ground around, and that for ages, till at length finding or making a way of escape they returned to the mother Sea, leaving debris accumulated in their basins as records of what had occurred during the continuance of their existence as lakes or inland seas. And combined with these indications we have met with indications of the recession of the waters having, from a very remote period, been the consequence of the land which was under the ocean bed having been raised above the ocean level, the waters, in accordance with the law of gravity, flowing off to that lower level.

To this relative elevation of the land we may attribute, primarily and principally, the desiccation and consequent aridity of the land: this elevation I attribute to an upheaval of the land: and this upheaval I attribute to a depression of the ocean bed elsewhere. In the cause or occasion of this depression may be found the original cause or occasion of all that has followed; but the desiccation commenced only with the elevation above the ocean's surface of the upheaved land, and therefore do I speak of that elevation as the primary cause or occasion of the aridity, and I speak of it as the primary and principal cause of this in reference to the evaporation which has been going on ever since that elevation occurred, and which is going on still, and to which may be attributed the completion of the work, in carrying on the evaporation to the stage which has resulted in the degree of aridity which now prevails.

To the consideration of this elevation of the land: its cause and its effects, is this chapter confined.

I. The fact that the land is above the level of the sea is apparent—it is unquestioned and unquestionable. That it has been elevated or upheaven is not less a fact, but it is not so apparent. It is a fact, the elucidation of which is pertinent to the subject of this treatise; but it is one which might be discussed apart without detriment to the practical object of the treatise. There are, however, advantages to be secured by its being discussed in connection therewith; and therefore is this done.

To whatever it may be attributable, the fact is demonstrable that there is going on still, as heretofore, depressions and elevations of the earth's crust throughout extensive regions of the earth's surface.

Maps, representative of the regions thus affected, may be found in Atlases illustrative of physical geography. On reference to a map illustrative of areas of subsidence and elevations in the southern oceans, engraved and apparently prepared by Messrs A. W. & A. K. Johnston, of Edinburgh, as an accompaniment to the late Professor Nicol's work, entitled *Thoughts on some Important Points relating to the System of the World*, the only map bearing on the subject to which I have access while writing this, I find that in the Indian Ocean throughout a region extending from 15° S. to over 15° N., and over about 20° of long., is a district of depression; while along the corresponding east coast of Africa—with the exception of a small portion about 10° N. lat. where the elevation is stationary, and a small portion about 20° N., or half-way up the Red Sea, where it is being depressed—the coast and adjacent sea basin from the Mediterranean to beyond the southern point of Madagascar is represented as an area of elevation; as is also that portion of India to the east of the area of subsidence, the Gulf of Bengal and islands beyond, the elevation of which may be considered correlated to the depression of the western portion of the Pacific and Australia, and connected with the elevation of the eastern portion of the Pacific and a large portion of the continent of America.

It is difficult to lift a full bowl without its overflowing; and the hypothesis offered almost necessitates with the supposition of one portion being elevated to a greater height in a certain time than another the supposition that an outflowing and draining off of a portion of the water would be the consequence. A glance at Hall's map of South-Eastern Africa shows, from the Kei northward to Delagoa Bay, a river system exactly accordant to what may be seen in the runnels along an exposed mud bank of a tidal river from which the ebb has withdrawn the life-like stream; and this is seen not only in the depicted courses of the rivers on the map, but in the relative depths of the different river-beds, at the mouths of the rivers, and also at points nearer to their source; and corresponding indications of the declivity or rapid slope of many of the water-courses of the Colony of the Cape of Good Hope are supplied by the rapidity or velocity of their currents.

When a river comes down there is a torrent where before there was, it may be, a dry river-bed. Quickly does the water flow away, and in a day or two, it may be, the stream is as it was before A measurement of the altitude, above the level of the sea, of the upper part of the course, and a measurement of the length of the river-bed, might have given the fall per foot; but not so impressive would a knowledge of the numbers be as is a sight of the torrent in its might. In the appearance of the country we see indications everywhere that the interior is far above the level of the coast, and in the directness of the flow of the rivers referred to indications that the upheaval must have occurred in what, compared with what is seen in other countries, may be called comparatively recent times, or with comparative rapidity.

The river-courses on the eastern coast, as represented on the map, seem to indicate a rapid slope from the foot of the mountains to the sea. We see not the same thing in the rivers of the Cape Colony, and in the rivers further to the north, but characteristic of all of these are these torrents which in some cases are the only thing about them which entitles them to the name of river. To anyone acquainted with the Colony this needs only to be mentioned to remind them of numerous cases. South Africa is not the only Colony of which it is alleged that the rivers are, without water, the flowers without fragrance, and the birds without song; but such are its privations, and travellers in the interior of the country tell of going miles, it may be, up or down a water-course in quest of some pool or damp soil which may encourage them to dig in hope of finding water a little way below the surface. And there are water-courses within the Colony almost equally dry, it may be for months, perhaps for years, which at times are found filled from bank to bank with a torrent tearing along. All which speaks the greatness of the declivity towards the sea.

In Europe rivers are said to rise: the body of water flowing along gradually increases in bulk till it flows a swollen torrent. In South Africa the rivers are not said to rise: they do not swell: the terms are inapplicable to what is seen in them, and they are not employed. There the rivers are said to come down—and the rivers do indeed do so,—coming down a body of water, it may be, breast high; and in a short time, in the dry channel, or channel of a stream a few inches deep, may be seen a torrent twelve, twenty, thirty feet in depth, tearing along as if for life—racing as if seeking to flee from ten thousand foes in hot pursuit. Seldom does a year pass without notices appearing in the colonial journals of some unfortunate party, who had encamped for the night in the river bed, being swept away, or if they escaped, escaped with their waggons and all its contents swept away to the deep; and accounts of what seemed like hair-breadth escapes are numerous.

The directness of the river course may be less apparent in the river system of the colony of the Cape of Good Hope than in the Transkie territory; but here we may see better how, on the assumption of such gradual upheaval, throughout what appears an older country, though composed of strata of perhaps an earlier formation, the upheaval operates. Here it is less a slope than an intricate system of valleys—independent, or connected, or inter-penetrating each other—but often showing by their contour where, and there indicating how, the waters were drained off.

In some cases it would seem as if overflowing, it may be gently, the lower portion of the basin, they had gradually fretted this away, until now only traces of it can be found.

Thus does it appear to have been the case with the basin to a large sheet of water at Colesberg; and thus may it have been with the outlet by which was drained off the waters of the Dicynodon, or reptilian, basin in the Orange River free state, examined by Dr Rubidge, in consequence of gold having been found there. An extensive district in the vicinity of Graaffreinet may also have been drained in a similar way. Of this Dr Rubidge remarks in a paper on irrigation and tree-planting, which appeared in the volume entitled *The Cape and its People*, that a wall just above Graaffreinet, 200 yards long and 500 feet high, would form a lake nearly as large as Derwentwater; and the river (the Sunday) might be led over a neck, deprived of its load of silt and shorn of its destructive and unmanageable impetus, to fertilise the great plain bounded by the Camdebo and Tantjesberg mountains.

In the geological observations which have come under consideration in a previous chapter, not only have we had indications of successive depressions and upheavals of land, but mention has been made of dykes, cracks, or rents in the strata, filled with material different from that of which the strata were composed. These cracks or rents tell of breakages in the crust of the earth, occurring, most probably, in connection with these changes of level. And in some places in the Cape Colony, and in places beyond it, it almost seems as if some rent, occasioned by the breakage of the sheet of land in its more rapid upheaval at one place than its weight or attachment at another would allow, had allowed a speedy escape of retained waters.

Thus may it have been with the emptying of a lake covering the site and adjacent district of Montague, by Cogman's Kloof, while the rent extended towards the warm spring about a mile further inland. It would require careful consideration of all the appearances presented by the fissure, or at least of many of these, and of much besides, to justify a declaration either that it was, or that it was not so; but enough is known by me of these to warrant a reference to these kloofs in illustration of what is alleged.

In some cases an opening so produced may have extended but a little way below the surface of the stream; but by some such process as that by which the Niagara has made for itself a bed from Lake Ontario to the Falls, may the river-bed have been lowered and levelled at a period so remote in the past that the weathering of the confining rocks—after, by the undermining and removal of lower-lying portions, they had fallen into the angle of repose—has given them the appearance of a hoar antiquity. Thus may it have been with the Tulbagh Kloof and the Dunkel Kloof, referred to again only for illustration.

More illustrations, and these perhaps more striking illustrations of the same things—the emptying of lakes or of inland seas, the pouring of water into rents or cracks, and the creating of courses for themselves there, all connected with the upheaval of the land and illustrative of the dessication thus carried on—are supplied by the narratives of travel in lands further to the north, given to us by Livingstone and others. Some of these I shall quote *in extenso*, as I wish to give to my readers definite ideas of the resulting phenomena.

The observations made by Dr Livingstone and his associates, in the district of the Zambesi, have made us acquainted with terrestrial operations going on even now, and, within a period not very remote from the present, similar to what are indicated by appearances, presented in many districts within the colony of the Cape of Good Hape, as having occurred there at a time, it is impossible to say how long before.

One of the rivers ascended, and that oftener than once, by that intrepid traveller on his expedition to the Zambesi was the Shire.

The upper Shire is apparently less a river than a prolongation of the Nyassa—a lake 200 miles .long, at places 50 or 60 miles broad, and of unfathomed depth, for a line of 35 fathoms did not reach to the bottom.

The lower Shire, for 200 miles above its confluence with the Zambesi, follows in peaceful tranquility what appear to be interminable windings. But these two portions of the Shire are separated by tremendous cataracts.

Of these cataracts of the Shire, Dr Livingstone writes :—" They begin in 15° 20' S., and end in lat. 15° 55' S. The difference in latitude is, therefore, 35'. The river runs in this space nearly north and south till we pass Malango ; so the entire distance is under forty miles. The principal cataracts are five in number ; and are called Pamofunda or Pamozima, Morewa, Panoreba or Tetzane, Pampatamanga, and Pape Kira. Besides these, three or four smaller ones might be mentioned. While these lesser cataracts descend at an angle of scarcely 20°, the greater fall 100 feet in 100 yards at an angle of about 45°, and one at an angle of 70°. One part of Pamozima is perpendicular, and when the river is in flood causes a cloud of vapour to ascend, which, in our journey to Lake Shirwa, we saw at a distance of a least eighty miles. The entire descent from the upper to the lower Shire is 1200 feet. Only on one spot in all that distance is the current moderate—viz., above Tedzane. The rest is all rapid ; and much of it being only fifty or eighty yards wide, and rushing like a mill-race, it gives the impression of water power, sufficient to drive all the mills in Manchester, running to waste. Pamofunda, or Pamozima, has a deep, shady grove on its right bank. When we were walking alone through its dark shade, we were startled by a shocking smell like that of a dissecting room ; and on looking up saw dead bodies in mats suspended from branches of the trees—a mode of burial somewhat similar to that which we subsequently saw practised by the Parsees, in the Towers of Silence at Poonah, near Bombay. The name Pamozima means ' The departed spirits or gods,' a fit name for a place over which, according to the popular belief, the disembodied souls continually hover.

" The rock lowest down in the series is dark reddish-grey syenite. This seems to have been an upheaving agent, for the mica schists above it are much disturbed. Dark trappean rocks, full of hornblende, have in many places burst through these schists, and appear in nodules on the surface. The highest rock seen is a fine sandstone of closer grain than that of Tetle, and quite metamorphosed where it comes into contact with the igneous rocks below it. It sometimes gives place to quartz and reddish clay schists, much baked by heat. This is the usual geological condition of the right bank of the cataracts. On the other side we pass over masses of porphyritic trap in contact with the same mica schists ; and these probably give to the soil the great fertility we observed. The great body of the mountain is syenite. So much mica is washed into the river that on looking attentively on the stream one sees myriads of particles floating and glancing in the sun, and this too when at low water."

These floating particles of mica tell of the eating away of the rock—

slowly, but surely—and the continuance of the cataract is only a question of time ; and in the Kebrabasa rapids of the Zambesi we have a later stage of the same process.

What is going on at the Murchison cataracts of the Shire is a process through which the Kebrabasa rapids of the Zambesi have apparently passed through long ago.

"The name as pronounced by the natives is Kaora-basa, 'finish or break the service.' The Portuguese word Kebra (Quebra) means the same thing, and refers to the break which occurs in the labour of toiling up thus far in heavy canoes, and then carrying the luggage thence overland to Chicova. These rapids, like the Murchison cataracts of the Shire, seem to debar the upper portion of the river from navigation by ships from the coast."

From the Portuguese Dr Livingstone and his friends had learned "that some three or four detached rocks jutted out of the river in Kebrabasa, which though dangerous to the cumbersome native canoes could be easily passed by a steamer, and that if one or two of these obstructions were blasted away with gunpowder no difficulty would hereafter be experienced in the navigation of the river at that place."

But this did not satisfy the enterprising traveller. He writes—" Our curiosity had been so much excited by the reports we had heard of the Kebrabasa rapids that we resolved to make a short examination of them, and seized the opportunity of the Zambesi being unusually low to endeavour to ascertain their character while uncovered by the water. We reached them on the 9th of November. The country between Tetle and Panda Mokua, where navigation ends, is well wooded and hilly on both banks. Panda Mokua is a hill two miles below the rapids, capped with dolemite containing copper ore.

"Conspicuous among the trees for its gigantic size and bark, coloured exactly like Egyptian syenite, is the burly baobab. It often makes the other trees of the forest look like mere bushes in comparison.

"The lofty range of Kebrabasa, consisting chiefly of conical hills covered with scraggy trees, crosses the Zambesi, and confines it within a narrow, rough, and rocky dell of about a quarter of a mile in breadth ; over this, which may be called the flood-bed of the river, large masses of rocks are huddled in indescribable confusion. The drawing, for the use of which, and of others, our thanks are due to Lord Russell, conveys but a faint idea of the scene, inasmuch as the hills which confine the river do not appear in the sketch. The chief rock is syenite, some portions of which have a beautiful blue tinge like *lapis lazuli* diffused through them ; others are grey. Blocks of granite also abound of a pinkish tinge, and these with metamorphic rocks, contorted, twisted, and thrown into every conceivable position, afford a picture of dislocation or inconformability which would gladden a geological lecturer's heart ; but at high flood this rough channel is all smoothed over, and it then conforms well with the river below it, which is half-a-mile wide. In the dry season the stream runs at the bottom of a narrow and deep groove, whose sides are polished and fluted by the boiling action of the waters in flood, like the rims of ancient Eastern wells by the draw-ropes. The breadth of the groove is often not more than from forty to sixty yards, and it has some sharp turnings, double channels, and little cataracts in it. As we steamed up, the masts of the 'Ma Robert,' though some thirty feet high, did not reach the level of the flood-channel above, and the man in the chains sung out, 'No bottom at ten fathoms.' Huge pot-holes, as large as draw-wells, had been worn in the sides, and were so deep that in some instances, when protected from the sun by overhanging boulders, the water in them was quite cool. Some of these holes had been worn right through and through, and only the side next the rock remained, while the sides of the groove of the flood-channel were polished as smooth as if they had gone through the granite-mills of Aberdeen. The pressure of the water must be enormous to produce this polish. It had wedged round pebbles into chinks and crannies of the rocks so firmly that, though they looked quite loose, they could not be moved except with a hammer. The mighty power of the water here seen gave us an idea of what is going on in thousands of cataracts in the world. . . . .

"After we had painfully explored seven or eight miles of the rapid we returned to the vessel, satisfied that much greater labour was requisite for the mere examination of the cataracts than our friends supposed necessary to remove them; we therefore went down the river for fresh supplies, and made preparations for a more serious survey of this region.

"The steamer having returned from the bar, we set out, on the 22nd of Nov., to examine the rapids of Kebrabasa. We reached the foot of the hills again late in the afternoon of the 24th, and anchored in the stream.

"Leaving the steamer next morning, we proceeded on foot, accompanied by a native Portuguese and his men, and a dozen Makololos, who carried our baggage. The morning was pleasant, the hills on our right furnished for a time a delightful shade; but, before long, the path grew frightfully rough, and the hills no longer shielded us from the blazing sun. Scarcely a vestige of a track was now visible, and, indeed, had not our guides assured us to the contrary, we should have been innocent of even the suspicion of a way along the patches of soft yielding sand, and on the great rocks over which we so painfully clambered. These rocks have a singular appearance, from being dislocated and twisted in every direction, and covered with a thin black glaze, as if highly polished, and coated with lamp-black varnish. This seems to have been deposited when the river was in flood, for it covers only those rocks which lie between the highest watermark and a line about four feet above the lowest. Travellers who have visited the rapids of the Orinoco, and the Congo, say that the rocks there have a similar appearance, and it was attributed to some deposit from the water formed only when the current is strong. This may account for it in part here, as it prevails only where the narrow river is confined between masses of rock, backed by high hills, and where the current in floods is known to be the strongest; and it does not exist where the rocks are only on one side, with a scanty beach opposite, and a broad expanse of river between. The hot rocks burnt the thick soles of our men's feet, and sorely fatigued ourselves. Our first day's march did not exceed four miles in a straight line, and that we found more than enough to be pleasant."

They waded across the rapid Lina, which took them up to the waist, and is about forty yards wide, and at length they reached Chiperiziwa. "When we reached the foot of the mountain named Chiperiziwa, whose perpendicular rocky sides are clothed with many coloured lichens, our Portuguese companion informed us that there were no more obstructions to navigation, the rivers being all smooth above; he had hunted there and knew it well. Supposing that the object of our trip was accomplished we turned back; but two natives, who came to our camp at night, assured us that a cataract, called Morumbwa, did still exist in front, Drs Livingstone and Kirk then decided to go forward with three Makololos and settle the question for themselves. It was as tough a bit of travel as they ever had in Africa, and after some painful marching the Badèma guides refused to go further, 'the Banya,' they said, 'would be angry if they showed white men the country; and there was, besides, no practicable approach to the spot, neither elephant, hippopotamus, nor even a crocodile, could reach the cataract.' The slopes of the mountains on each side of the river, now not 300 yards wide and without the flattish flood-channel and groove, were more than 3000 feet from the sky line down, and were covered either with dense thornbush or huge black boulders; this deep trough-like shape caused the sun's rays to converge as into a focus, making the surface so hot that the soles of the feet of the Makololo became blistered. Around, and up, and down, the party clambered among these heated blocks, at a pace not exceeding a mile an hour; the strain upon the muscles in jumping from crag to boulder, and wriggling round projections, took an enormous deal out of them; and they were often glad to cower in the shadow formed by one rock overhanging and resting on another; the shelter induced the peculiarly strong and overpowering inclination to sleep, which too much sun sometimes causes. This sleep is curative of what may be incipient sun-stroke in its first gentle touches, it caused the dream to flit over the boiling brain that they had become lunatics, and had been sworn in members of the Alpine Club; and then it became so heavy that it made them feel as if a portion of existence had been cut out of their lives. The sun is excessively hot, and feels sharp in Africa; but, probably from the greater dryness of the atmosphere, we never heard of a single case of sun-stroke, so common in India. The Makololo told Dr Livingstone they 'always thought he had a heart, but now they believed he had none,' and tried to persuade Dr Kirk to return, on the ground that it must be evident that, in attempting to go where no living foot could tread, his leader had given unmistakeable signs of having gone mad. All their efforts of persuasion, however, were lost upon Dr Kirk, as he had not yet learned their language, and his leader knowing him to be equally anxious with himself to solve the navigableness of the Kebrabasa, was not at pains to enlighten him. At one part a bare mountain spur barred the way, and had to be surmounted by a perilous and circuitous route, along which the crags were so hot that it was scarcely possible for the hand to hold on long enough to ensure safety in the passage; and had the foremost of the party lost his hold, he would have hurled all behind him into the river at the foot of the promontory; yet in this wild region, as they descended again to the river, they met a fisherman casting his hand-net into the boiling eddies, and he pointed out the cataract of Morumbwa; within an hour they were trying to measure it from an overhanging rock, at a height of about one hundred feet. When you stand facing the cataract, on the north bank, you see that it is situated in a sudden bend of the river, which is flowing in a short curve; the river above it is jammed between two mountains in a channel with perpendicular sides, and less than fifty yards wide; one or two masses of rock jut out, and then there is a sloping fall of perhaps twenty feet in a distance of thirty yards. It would stop all navigation except during the lighest floods; the rocks showed that the water then rises upwards of eighty feet perpendicularly.

"Still keeping the position facing the cataract, on its right side rises Mount Morumbwa, from 2000 to 3000 feet high, which gives the name to the spot. On the left of the cataract stands a noticeable mountain which

P

may be called onion-shaped, for it is partly conical, and a large concave flake has peeled off, as granite often does, and left a broad, smooth convex face as if it were an enormous bulb. These two mountains extend their bases northwards about half-a-mile, and the river in that distance, still very narrow, is smooth, with a few detached rocks standing out from its bed. They climbed as high up the base of Mount Morumbwa, which touches the cataract, as they required. The rocks were all water-worn and smooth, with huge pot-holes, even at 100 feet above low-water. When at a later period they climbed up the north-western base of this same mountain, the familiar face of the onion-shaped one opposite was at once recognised; one point of view on the talus of Mount Morumbwa was not more than 700 or 800 yards distant from the others, and they then completed the survey of Kebrabasa from end to end."

To such a rapid may the falls of the Shire yet be reduced, if it be not from such a rapid that they originated; for this also is possible though more improbable.

These rapids are dependent on the difference of the level above and below the part of the river at which they are found. They are always eating their way upward, as do and have done the waters at the falls of Niagara; and as they do so they drain off more and more of the upper waters. In the district of the Zambesi this has not been completely effected. There are still in that region lakes like inland seas. I have refered to one of these, the Nyassa, of which the upper Shire is a prolongation, as the upper Niagara is a prolongation of Lake Erie, and more manifestly so.

Dr Livingstone writes of the Nyassa, in giving a narration of his second visit to it,—"Looking back to the southern end of Lake Nyassa, the river from which the Shire flows was found to be about thirty miles long, and from ten to twelve broad. Rounding Cape Maclear and looking to the southeast we have another arm, which stretches some eighteen miles southward, and from six to twelve miles in breadth. These arms give the southern end a forked appearance, and with the help of a little imagination it may be likened to the 'boot-shape' of Italy. The narrowest part is about the ankle—eighteen or twenty miles. From this it widens to the north, and in the upper third or fourth it is 50 or 60 miles broad. The length is over 200 miles. The direction in which it lies is as near as possible due north and south."

Of the depth of Lake Nyassa, he writes,—"This is indicated by the colour of the water, which, on a belt along the shore, varying from a quarter to half-a-mile in breadth, is light green, and this is met by the deep blue or indigo tint of the Indian Ocean, which is the colour of the great body of Nyassa. We found the upper Shire from nine to fifteen feet in depth; but skirting the western side of the lake, about a mile from the shore, the water deepened from nine to fifteen fathoms; then, as we rounded the grand mountainous promontory, which we named Cape Maclear, after our excellent friend the Astronomer Royal at the Cape of Good Hope, we could get no bottom with our lead-line of thirty-five fathoms."

But even there the depth of the water has apparently been diminished from what it was at an earlier time, for near to it there is what, but for the difference of level, I would suppose must have been connected with the Shirwa; nor is the difference of level fatal to this supposition, it may only affect the element of time.

Further up the Zambesi and near, though below, the **Victoria Falls**, the

Zambesi receives the waters of the Longkwe, or as the Makololo call it, the river of Quai or Tobacco, which comes in from the southeast. A little below this, a mass of mountain called Govangue or Golongwe, is said to cross the river, and the rent through which the river passes is by native report fearful to behold. This Golongwe, it is conjectured by Dr Livingstone, was probably the dam which before the rent was made kept the whole Linyanti valley a lake.

"The Longkwe, or, as the Makololo call it, the river of Quai or Tobacco, comes in from the southeast and joins the Zambesi above Golongwe. This fact may corroborate what is said by Mr Thomas, that all the rivers rising on the one side of Moselekatsi's country runs easterly, and into the Shashe, to join the Limpopo, while all the others runs westerly, and then northerly to the Zambesi. Golongwe was probably the dam which before the rent was made converted the whole Linyanti valley into a lake; but we could not on the path we came observe any difference of level by the barometer.

"From the falls to Sinamani's the country sloped, and was all lower than Sesheke; still, a considerable difference of level must have taken place since the deep undisturbed mass of soft tufa was deposited on the great flats of Sesheke and Linyanti.

"The courses of the rivers in the country of Moselekatsi, and on the Batoka Highlands west of the Kalomo, show that, in reference to the countries east of it, the great Makololo valley is still a hollow."

In writing later of his journey northwards to the Lekone, having mentioned that the existence of the tsetse in the district, and stated that the fear of this insect, the wounds occasioned by which are so fatal to cattle, obliged them to travel the first few stages by night, he goes on to say,—
"We could not well detect the nature of the country in the dim moonlight; the path, however, seemed to lead along the high bank of what may have been the ancient head of the Zambesi, before the fissure was made. The Lekone now winds in it in an opposite direction to that in which the ancient river must have flowed. Both the Lekone and Unguesi flow back towards the centre of the country, and in an opposite direction to that of the main stream. It was plain, then, that we were ascending the further we went eastward. The level of the lower portion of the Lekone is about 200 feet above that of the Zambesi at the falls, and considerably more than the altitude of Linyanti; consequently, when the river flowed along this ancient bed instead of through the rent, the whole country between this and the ridge beyond Libebe westwards; Lake 'Ngami and the Zouga eastwards; and eastwards beyond Nehokotsa, was one large fresh water lake. There is abundant evidence of the existence and extent of this vast lake in the longitudes indicated, and stretching from 17° to 21° S. latitude. The whole of this space is paved with a bed of tufa, more or less soft, according as it is covered with soil, or left exposed to atmospheric influences. Wherever cataracts make deep holes in this ancient bottom, fresh water shells are thrown out, identical with those now existing in the lake 'Ngami and the Zambesi.

"The Barotse valley was another lake of a similar nature, and one existed beyond Masiko, and a fourth near the Orange River. The whole of these lakes were let out by means of cracks or fissures made in the subtending sides by the upheaval of the country. The fissure made at the Victoria Falls let out the water of this great valley, and left a small patch in what was probably its deepest portion, and is now called Lake 'Ngami. The

Falls of Gonge furnished an outlet to the lake of the Barotse valley, and so of the other great lakes of remote times. The Congo also finds its way to the sea through a narrow fissure, and so does the Orange River in the west, while other rents made in the eastern ridge, as the Victoria Falls and those to the east of Tanganyenka, allowed the central waters to drain eastward. All the African lakes hitherto discovered are shallow, in consequence of being the mere residue of very much larger ancient bodies of water. There can be no doubt that this continent was, in former times, very much more copiously supplied with water than at present; but a natural process of drainage has been going on for ages. Deep fissures are made probably by the elevation of the land, proofs of which are seen in modern shells imbedded in marly tufa all round the coast line. Whether this process of desiccation is as rapid throughout the continent as in a letter to the late Dean Buckland, in 1843, I showed to have been the case in the Bechuana country, it is not for me to say; but though there is a slight tradition of the waters having burst through the low hills south of the Barotse, there is none of a sudden upheaval accompanied by an earthquake."

" If we take a glance back at the great valley, the form the rivers have taken imparts the idea of a lake slowly drained out, for they have cut out for themselves beds exactly like what we may see in the soft mud of a shallow pool of rain water, when that is let off by a furrow. This idea would, probably, not strike a person on coming first into the country, but more extensive acquaintance with the river system, certainly, would convey the impression. None of the rivers in the valley of the Leeambye have slopes down to their beds. Indeed, many parts are much like the Thames at the Isle of Dogs, only the Leeambye has to rise 20 or 30 feet before it can overflow some of its meadows. The rivers have each a bed of low-water, a simple furrow cut out of the calcareous tufa, which lined the channel of the ancient lake; and another of inundation. When the beds of inundation are filled, they assume the appearance of chains of lakes. When the Clyde fills the holms (haughs) above Bothwell Bridge and retires again into its channel, it resembles the river we are speaking of—only here, there are no high lands sloping down towards the bed of inundation, for the greater part of the region is not elevated fifty feet above them. Even the rocky banks of the Leeambye, below Gonge, and the ridges bounding the Barotse valley, are not more than two or three hundred feet in altitude over the general dead level. Many of the rivers are very tortuous in their course, the Chobe and Shirwa particularly so; and if we may receive the testimony of the natives, they form what anatomists call 'anastamose,' or a net-work of rivers. Thus, for instance, they assured me that if they go up the Sirwah in a canoe, they can enter the Chobe and descend that river to the Leeambye; or they may go up the Kama and come down the Sirwah. And so is the case of the Kafue. It is reported to be connected in this way with the Leeambye in the north, and to part with the Loungwa; and the Makololo went from the one into the other in canoes. And even though the interlacing may not be quite to the extent believed by the natives, the country is so level, and the rivers so tortuous, that I see no improbability in the conclusion—and here is a net-work of waters of a very peculiar nature. The reason why I am disposed to place a certain amount of confidence in the native reports is this, when Mr Oswell and I discovered the Zambesi in the centre of the continent in 1851, being unable to ascend it at the time ourselves, we employed the natives to draw a map embodying their ideas of that river. We then sent the native map home, with the same view that I now mention their ideas of the river system—namely, in order to be an aid to others in farther investigations. When I was able to ascend the Leeambye to 14° south, and subsequently descend it, I found, after all the care I could bestow, that the alterations I was able to make in the original plan were very trifling."

The circumstance that such were the views formed by Dr Livingstone in the midst of the scenes by which they were suggested entitles them to some consideration. At present they are adduced as embodying evidence that there has been—and that apparently oftener than once—a great disturbance in the level of the land—a disturbance indicative of upheaval of the land, and of a consequent rush of water to the lower level of the sea —corroborative of the supposition that to such upheaval of the land is attributable, primarily and principally, the desiccation of the country farther to the south.

By the cutting down of some such dam may the waters have been drained away from the lacustrine valley near Smithfield, referred to as a valley in which gold has been found, if this was not effected in the way previously spoken of—overflowing water gradually eating down or sawing down the barriers.

Thus, in a time more near to the present, may have been drained off waters from behind the Gates of the Oomzimvoobo; and in a time more remote, the waters from behind the Heads at the Knysna,—whether these, either or both, have originated in a rent or otherwise; and at a period still more remote may what is now the entrance to the Knysna from the sea have allowed a large body of water to have escaped.

In the Victoria Falls we have a rent more like that of the Kogman Kloof at Montague, but differing from it in extent, in fissure, and in direction, in regard to the river current.

Of these Falls Dr Livingstone writes,—" The entire Falls are simply a crack made in a hard basaltic rock from the right to the left bank of the Zambesi, and then prolonged from the left bank away through thirty or forty miles of hills. If one imagines the Thames filled with low tree-covered hills immediately beyond the tunnel, extending as far as Gravesend; the bed of black basaltic rock instead of London mud; and a fissure made therein from one end of the tunnel to the other, down through the keystones of the arch, and prolonged from the left end of the tunnel through thirty miles of hills; the pathway being a hundred feet down from the bed of the river instead of what it is, with the lips of the fissure from eighty to a hundred feet apart; then fancy the Thames leaping bodily into the gulf; and forced then to change its direction, and flow from the right to the left bank; and then rush boiling and roaring through the hills,—he may have some idea of what takes place at this, the most wonderful sight I had witnessed in Africa."

Of his visit to these Falls he thus writes:—

" After twenty minutes' sail from Kalai, we came in sight, for the first time, of the columns of vapour, appropriately called 'smoke,' rising at a distance of five or six miles, exactly as when large tracts of grass are burned in Africa. Five columns now rose, and bending in the direction of the wind, they seemed placed against a low ridge covered with trees; the tops of the columns at this distance appeared to mingle with the clouds. They were white below, and higher up became dark, so as to simulate smoke very closely. The whole scene was extremely beautiful; the banks and islands dotted over the river are adorned with sylvan vegetation of great variety of colour and form. At the period of our visit several trees were spangled over with blossoms. Trees have each their own physiognomy. There, towering over all, stands the great burly baobab, each of whose enormous arms would form the trunk of a large tree, beside groups of graceful palms, which, with their feathery-shaped leaves, depicted on the sky, lend their beauty to the scene. As a hieroglyphic they always mean 'far from home,' for one can never get over their foreign air in a picture or landscape. The silvery mohonono, which in the tropics is in form like the cedar of Lebanon, stands in pleasing contrast with the dark colour of the motsouri, whose cypress-form is dotted over at present with its pleasant scarlet fruit. Some trees resemble the great spreading oak, others assume the character of our own elms and chesnuts; but no one can imagine the beauty of the view from anything witnessed in England. It had never been seen before by European eyes; but scenes so lovely must have been gazed upon by angels in their flight. The only want felt is that of mountains in the background. The falls are bounded on three sides by ridges 300 or 400 feet in height, which are covered with forest, with the red soil appearing among the trees. When about half a mile from the falls, I left the canoe by which we had come down thus far, and embarked in a lighter one, with men well acquainted with the rapids, who, by passing down the centre of the stream in the eddies and still places caused by many jutting rocks, brought me to an island situated in the middle of the river, and on the edge of the lip over which the water rolls. In coming hither there was danger of being swept down by the streams which rushed along on each side of the island; but the river was now low, and we sailed where it is totally impossible to go when the water is high. But though we had reached the island, and were within a few yards of the spot, a view from which would solve the whole problem, I believe that no one could perceive where the vast body of water went; it seemed to lose itself in the earth, the opposite lip of the fissure into which it disappeared being only 80 feet distant. At least I did not comprehend it until, creeping with awe to the verge, I peered down into a large rent which had been made from bank to bank of the broad Zambesi, and saw that a stream of a thousand yards broad leaped down a hundred feet, and then became suddenly compressed into a space of fifteen or twenty yards.

"In looking down into the fissure on the right of the island, one sees nothing but a dense white cloud, which, at the time we visited the spot, had two bright rainbows on it. (The sun was on the meridan, and the declination about equal to the latitude of the place:) From this cloud rushed up a great jet of vapour exactly like steam, and it mounted 200 or 300 feet high; there condensing, it changed its hue to that of dark smoke, and came back in a constant shower, which soon wetted us to the skin. This shower falls chiefly on the opposite side of the fissure, and a few yards back from the lip there stands a straight hedge of evergreen trees, whose leaves are always wet. From their roots a number of little rills run back into the gulf; but as they flow down the steep wall there, the column of vapour, in its ascent, licks them up clean off the rock, and away they mount again. They are constantly running down, but never reach the bottom.

"On the left of the island we see the water at the bottom, a white rolling mass moving away to the prolongation of the fissure, which branches off near the left bank of the river. A piece of the rock has fallen off a spot on the left of the island, and juts out from the water below, and from it I judged the distance which the water falls to be about 100 feet. The walls of this gigantic crack are perpendicular, and composed of one homogeneous mass of rock. The edge of that side over which the water falls is worn off two or three feet and pieces have fallen away, so as to give it somewhat of a serrated appearance. That over which the water does not fall is quite straight, except at the left corner, where a rent appears, and a piece seems inclined to fall off. Upon the whole, it is nearly in the state in which it was left at the period of its formation. The rock is dark brown in colour, except about ten feet from the bottom, which is discoloured by the annual rise of the water to that or a greater height. On the left side of the island we have a good view of the mass of water which causes one of the columns of vapour to ascend, as it leaps quite clear of the rock, and forms a thick unbroken fleece all the way to the bottom. Its whiteness gave the idea of snow, a sight I had not seen for many a day. As it broke into (if I may use the term) pieces of water all rushing on in the same direction, each gave off several rays of foam, exactly as bits of steel when burnt in oxygen gas give off rays of sparks. The snow-white sheet seemed like myriads of small comets rushing on in one direction, each of which left behind its nucleus rays of foam. I never saw the appearance referred to noticed elsewhere. It seemed to be the effect of the mass of water leaping at once clear of the rock, and but slowly breaking up into spray.

"I have mentioned that we saw five columns of vapour ascending from this strange abyss. They are evidently formed, by the compression suffered by the force of the water's own fall, into an unyielding wedge-shaped space. Of the five columns, two on the right, and one the left, of the island were the largest, and the streams which formed them seemed each to exceed in size the falls of the Clyde at Stonebyres, when that river is in flood. This was the period of low water in the Leeambye, but as far as I could guess, there was a flow of five or six hundred yards of water, which, at the edge of the fall, seemed at least three feet deep. I write in the hope that others more capable of judging distances than myself will visit this scene, and I state simply the impressions made on my mind at the time. I thought, and do still think, the river above the falls to be one thousand yards broad; but I am a poor judge of distances on water, for I showed a naval friend what I supposed to be four hundred yards in the bay of Loanda, and, to my surprise, he pronounced it to be nine hundred. I tried to measure the Leeambye with a strong thread, the only line I had in my possession, but when the men had gone two or three hundred yards, they got into conversation, and did not hear us shouting that the line had become entangled. By still going on they broke it, and being carried away down the stream, it was lost on a snag. In vain I tried to bring to my recollection the way I had been taught to measure a river, by taking an angle with the sextant. That I once knew it, and that it was easy, were all the lost ideas I could recall, and they only increased my vexation. However, I measured the river farther down by another plan, and then I discovered that the Portuguese had measured it at Tete, and found it a little over one thousand yards. At the falls it is as broad as at Tete, if not more so. Whoever may come after me will not, I trust, find reason to say I have indulged in exaggeration. With respect to the drawing, it must be borne in mind that it was composed from a rude sketch as viewed from the island, which exhibited the columns of vapour only, and a ground plan. The artist has given a good idea of the scene, but, by way of explanation, he has shown more of the depth of the fissure than is visible, except by going close to the edge. The left-hand column, and that farthest off, are the smallest, and all ought to have been a little more tapering at the tops.

"The fissure is said by the Makololo to be very much deeper farther to the eastward; there is one part at which the walls are so sloping, that people accustomed to it can go down by descending in a sitting position. The Makololo on one occasion, pursuing some fugitive Batoko, saw them, unable to stop the impetus of their flight at the edge, literally dashed to pieces at the bottom. They beheld the stream like a 'white cord' at the bottom, and so far down (probably 300 feet) that they became giddy, and were fain to go away, holding on to the ground.

"Now, though the edge of the rock over which the river falls does not show wearing more than three feet, and there is no appearance of the opposite wall being worn out at the bottom in the parts exposed to view, yet it is probable that, where it has flowed beyond the falls, the sides of the fissure may have given way, and the parts out of sight may be broader than the 'white cord' on the surface. There may even be some ramifications of the fissure, which take a portion of the stream quite beneath the rocks; but this I did not learn.

"If we take the want of much wear on the lip of hard basaltic rock as of any value, the period when this rock was riven is not geologically very remote. I regretted the want of proper means of measuring and marking its width at the falls, in order that at some future time the question whether it is progressive or not might be tested. It seemed as if a palm-tree could be laid across it from the island. And if it is progressive, as it would mark a great natural drainage being effected, it might furnish a hope that Africa will one day become a healthy continent. It is at any rate very much changed in respect to its lakes within a comparatively recent period.

"At three spots near these falls, one of them the island in the middle on which we were, three Batoka chiefs offered up prayers and sacrifices to the Barimo. They chose their places of prayers within the sound of the roar of the cataract, and in sight of the bright bows in the cloud. They must have looked upon the scene with awe. Fear may have induced the selection. The river itself is, to them, mysterious. The words of the canoe-song are—

"'The Leeambye! Nobody knows
Whence it comes and whither it goes.'

The play of colours of the double iris on the cloud, seen by them elsewhere only as the rainbow, may have led them to the idea that this was the abode of Deity. Some of the Makololo who went with me near to the Gonge looked upon the same sign with awe. When seen in the heavens it is named 'motsé oa barimo'—the pestle of the gods. Here they could approach the emblem, and see it stand steadily above the blustering uproar below—a type of Him who sits supreme—alone unchangeable, though ruling over all changing things. But not aware of His true character, they had no admiration of the beautiful and good in their bosoms. They did not imitate His benevolence, for they were a bloody, imperious crew, and Sebituane performed a noble service in the expulsion from their fastnesses of these cruel 'Lords of the Isles.'

"Having feasted my eyes upon the beautiful sight, I returned to my friends at Kalai, and, saying to Sekeletu that he had nothing else worth showing in his country, his curiosity was excited to visit it the next day. I returned with the intention of taking a lunar observation from the island itself, but the clouds were unfavourable, consequently all my determinations of position refer to Kalai. (Lat. 70° 51′ 54″ S., long. 25° 41′ E.) Sekeletu acknowledged to feeling a little nervous at the probability of being sucked into the gulf before reaching the island. His companions amused themselves by throwing stones down, and wondered to see them diminishing in size, and even disappearing, before they reached the water at the bottom.

"I had another object in view in my return to the island. I observed that it was covered with trees, the seeds of which had probably come down with the stream from the distant north, and several of which I had seen nowhere else, and every now and then the wind wafted a little of the condensed vapour over it, and kept the soil in a state of moisture, which caused a sward of grass, growing as green as an English lawn. I selected a spot—not too near the chasm, for there the constant deposition of the moisture nourished numbers of polypi of a mushroom shape and fleshy consistence—but somewhat back, and made a little garden. I there planted about a hundred peach and apricot stones, and a quantity of coffee-seeds. I had attempted fruit trees before, but, when left in charge of my Makololo friend, they were always allowed to wither, after having vegetated, by being forgotten. I bargained for a hedge with one of the Makololo, and if he is faithful, I have great hopes of Mosioatunya's abilities as a nurseryman. My only source of fear is the hippopotami, whose footprints I saw on the island. When the garden was prepared, I cut my initials on a tree, and the date 1855. This was the only instance in which I indulged in this piece of vanity. The garden stands in front, and were there no hippopotami, I would have no doubt but this will be the parent of all the gardens which may yet be in this new country."

Of another visit paid by him to the Falls he wrote, under date of Sesheke, September 10, 1860, to Sir Roderick Murchison,—" When within 20 miles of Victoria Falls we could see the columns of vapour with the naked eye, and there I could not resist the temptation of acting the showman to my companions, Dr Kirk and Mr C. Livingstone, though by diverging from our straight course to Sesheke we added some forty miles to our tramp. The hippopotami had eaten all my trees, so henceforth we shall have war with them to the knife. They are good food, half beef and half pork, and lots of fat, that serves as butter. This is part of the 'casus belli.' By the way, our good friend, Professor Owen, and the gastronomic committee, will stand very much in their own light if the she-giraffes die a natural death. If they praised the eland so, which we consider but so-so, a dinner of she-giraffe will leave them all lying on their backs."

And again,—" Tette, November 26, 1860.—My dear Sir Roderick,—We unfortunately missed the opportunity of sending overland by the elephant-hunters, so I open the letter written at Sesheke to insert some further particulars. The river was so low we could easily see the bottom of one half of the fissure which forms Victoria Falls; and, indeed, people could wade from the north bank to my Garden Island, to form a stockade for fresh seeds. The depth is not 100 feet, but 310 feet—probably a few feet more, as the weight attached to the line rested on a slope near the bottom. The breadth from bank to bank is not 1000 yards, as I conjectured in 1855, but between one statute and one geographical mile—we say 1860 yards to assist the memory, but it is a little more, yet not quite 2000 yards. The lips of the crack at Garden Island may be more than 80 feet, as we could not throw a stone across, but the sextant gave that. Now come to the other, or south-eastern, side of the crack, and the fissure, which from the upper bed looks like the letter L, is prolonged in a most remarkable zigzag manner. The water, after leaping sheer down 310 feet, is collected from both ends to the upright part of the letter as the escape, and then flows away on the zigzag part. The promontories formed thereby are flat at the top, and of the same level as the bed of the river above the Falls. The base of the first on the right is only 400 paces from the Fall fissure, and that on the left about 150. Their sides are as perpendicular as the Fall, and you can walk along among the trees, and by a few steps see the river some 300 or 400 feet below, jammed in a space of some 20 or 30 yards, and of a deep green colour. As a whole, the Victoria Falls are the most wonderful in the world. Even now, at extreme low water, or when it is two feet lower than we ever saw it, there are 800 feet of water falling on the right of Garden Island. And the two columns of vapour, with the glorious rainbows, are a sight worth seeing. A fall called Momba, or Moamba, below this, is interesting, chiefly because you look down it from a height of some 500 feet. It is really nothing like Mosioatunya. We visited the river twice on our way down to Sinamani's, and found it in a very deep crack. The standing point gives 1600 of descent from the Falls to Sinamani's."

In this wonderful rent we see what, had it extended to the mass of matter in a state of fusion below, might have become a dyke filled and overtopped with igneous rock; or, had it been in position favourable to the influx from above of clay and sand and gravel, as perhaps it is, it might have been, as perhaps it may yet become, a dyke of such debris as may be seen in not a few of the dykes in the diamond fields. But it is cited here as a rent, indicative of such a disturbance of level as might be occasioned by an upheaval of land having occurred—and as a rent which, had it extended over any part of a mountain range, confined a lake, or might have drained off the mass of waters and converted the lake into a plain; and as it is it may have had some effect in draining off the waters from that higher level.

II. I have used freely the word upheaval as descriptive of the cause of the elevation of the land above the level of the ocean into which the water flows. Two demurrers may suggest themselves, one to one class of readers, and the other to another. To some the idea of upheaval—the upheaval of a whole continent—may be a new idea, and if new, startling, so startling as to awaken scepticism not only in regard to that having taken place, but scepticism in regard to that which may extend to much besides which has been advanced. And to others it may appear that if upheaval has been the cause of the elevation, which is the cause or occasion of the water flow, —to the cause of that upheaval, or the cause of the cause of this cause of desiccation, should be applied the designation primary and principal cause of the desiccation and consequent aridity of South Africa. I have the necessary leisure, and have no objection to provide for half-an-hour's consideration of the questions raised, giving notice thus to any to skip this and the following sections of the chapter, and pass on to the perusal of what follows, if so disposed.

I proceed first to adduce evidence of the upheavals of land being a phenomenon fully established as one of which there are indications in various countries; and then to state how it appears to have been effected.

1. Directing attention to the well-defined strata capping Table Mountain, the Lion's Head, and the other mountain ranges in South Africa, as indications of these mountains having been at one time a portion of the sea basin, in accordance with what is admitted by all students of geology, I would ask, How does it come to pass that they now occupy the elevated position which they do, thousands of feet above the ocean's bed? There seems to be but two suppositions possible: the sea must have subsided, or the land must have been raised. These two suppositions may be so maintained that they will be seen to resolve themselves into one—being so correlated that what caused a subsidence of the sea might and must at the same time have caused the elevation of the land; and such is the hypothesis as will be afterwards explained.

Before proceeding to the exposition of the hypothesis, I may revert to the fact already mentioned, that such a correlated elevation of land and subsidence of the sea basin is going on at present over extensive areas of the world, and state that in Britain and elsewhere there exist satisfactory indications of such elevations having occurred also in ages which may be considered remote from the present.

Hugh Miller, in a lecture which he delivered in Exeter Hall to the Young Men's Christian Association, some years before his death, speaking of one of these indications, said,—" There runs around the shores of Great Britain and Ireland a flat terrace of unequal breadth, backed by an escarpment of varied height and character, which is known to geologists as the Old Coast line. On this flat terrace most of the seaport towns of the empire are built. The subsoil, which underlies its covering of vegetable mould, consists usually of stratified sands and gravels, arranged after the same fashion as on the neighbouring beach, and interspersed in the same manner with sea-shells. The escarpment behind, when formed of materials of no great coherency, such as gravel or clay, exists as a sloping, grass-covered bank,—at one place running out into promontories that encroach upon the terrace beneath,— at another receding into picturesque, bay-like recesses; but where composed, as in many localities, of rock of an enduring quality, we find it worn, as if by the action of the surf,—in some parts relieved into insulated stacks, in others hollowed into deep caverns,—in short, presenting all the appearances of a precipitous coast line, subjected to the action of the waves. Now, no geologist can, or does, doubt that this escarpment was at one time the coast line of the island,—the line against which the waves broke at high-water in some distant age, when either the sea stood from 20 to 30 feet higher along our shores than it does now, or the land sat from 20 to 30 feet lower. Nor can geologist doubt that along the flat terrace beneath, with its stratified beds of sand or gravel, and its accumulations of sea-shells, the tides must have risen and fallen twice every day, as they now rise and fall along the beach that girdles our country. But, in reference to at least human history, the age of the old coast line and terrace must be a very remote one. Though geologically recent, it lies far beyond the reach of any written record. It has been shown by Mr Smith of Jordanhill, one of our highest authorities on the subject, that the wall of Antoninus, erected by the Romans as a protection against the northern Caledonians, was made to terminate at the Friths of Forth and Clyde, with relation, not to the level of the old coast line, but to that of the existing one; and so we must infer that, ere the year A.D. 140 (the year during which, according to our antiquaries, the greater part of the wall was erected), the old coast line had attained to its present elevation over the sea. But we know, historically, that for at least twenty centuries the sea has been toiling in these modern caves; and who shall dare affirm that it has not been toiling in them for at least ten centuries more? But if the sea has stood for but even two thousand six hundred years against the present coast line (and no geologist would dare fix his estimate lower), then must it have stood against the old line, ere it could have excavated caves one-third deeper, three thousand nine hundred years. And both periods united (six thousand five hundred years) more than exhaust the Hebrew chronology. Yet what a mere beginning of geologic history does not the epoch of the old coast line form! It is but a mere starting-point from the recent period. Not a single shell seems to have become extinct during the last six thousand five hundred years. The shells which lie embedded in the subsoils beneath the old coast line are exactly those which still live in our seas. Above this ancient line of coast, we find at various heights beds of shells of vastly older date than those of the low-lying terrace, and many of which are no longer to be found living around our shores. I spent some time last autumn in exploring one of these beds,—once a sea-bottom, but now raised 230 feet above the sea,—in which there occurred great numbers of shells now not British, though found in many parts of Britain at heights varying from 200 to nearly 1400 feet over the existing sea-level. But though no longer British shells, they are shells that still continue to live in high northern latitudes, as on the shores of Iceland und Spitzbergen; and the abundance in which they were developed on the submerged plains and hill sides of what are now England and Scotland, during what is termed the Pleistocene period, shows of itself what a very protracted period that was. But in a still earlier period, of which there exists unequivocal evidence in the buried forests of Happisburg and Cromer, the country had not only its head above water, as now, but seems to have possessed even more than its present breadth of surface."

And there are other shores on which the same thing can be seen. In the Morea there are no less than three, or perhaps four, ranges of what were once sea-cliffs—well preserved—rising one above the other, at different distances from the shore, the summit of the highest and oldest occasionally exceeding 1000 feet in elevation; and at the base of each there is usually a terrace which is in some places a few yards, in others above a hundred yards, wide—the ocean shore of a former time.

I have before me notes of an excursion, made some years ago by the members of the Geological Society of Edinburgh, along the coast from Portobello to Newhaven. Near Seafield they examined an ancient oyster scalp, which is situated about two feet above ordinary high water mark, and extends for about 118 yards along the coast. This oyster bed lies beneath a stratified deposit of sand and gravel of from four to five feet in depth, and it has been traced inland to a height of more than forty feet above the level of the sea, and nearly a quarter of a mile from the shore. Mr Smyth, by whom the company were conducted, stated that, as the habitat of oysters in the Firth of Forth was from four to seven fathoms deep, this ancient oyster scalp showed that there must have been an upheaval of about thirty feet since it was formed. No storm wave, he said, could have transported those shells for such a long distance inland, and to a height of forty feet. It had been ascertained from actual measurement, he added, that the highest storm-wave along a level coast never exceeded, even in the greatest hurricane, an altitude of 28 feet above the usual level of the sea. Mr Smyth then pointed out a boulder on the shore, which must have been embedded there for ages, and from which parties forty years ago were in the habit, when about to bathe, of stepping into the sea at ordinary high tides. At the present day the same parties would have to walk over sixty-six yards of a sandy beach before they could touch the water at those tides, and, vertically, the boulder is 2 feet 1 inch above the present level of ordinary high tides. The same difference of level has been observed on the solid rock near Cockburnspath, Tantallon, South Queensferry, and elsewhere, and from the examination of several old maps, the testimony of many witnesses still alive, and Mr Smyth stated that, from the comparison of the records of various tide-gauges along the coast, he had arrived at the conclusion that the whole of the southern shore of the Firth of Forth, and that part of the east coast of Scotland between North Berwick and St Abb's Head, are at present rising at the rate of about five feet per century. And what is supposed to be going on there is going on also elsewhere.

By Page it is stated,—"As in Scotland, so in England, evidences of a former sea-beach have been detected along the coasts of Lancashire, Yorkshire, and Durham, in the valley of the Mersey, and in the Bristol Channel. The same terraced appearances, with the remains of existing sea-shells, are found on the coasts of France, Portugal, Sicily, Greece, Norway, Sweden, and other parts of the European sea-board. In the Mediterranean, one terrace, nearly 50 feet above the sea, and full of shells, is discernible at many distant parts of the shore; on the coast of Norway, accumulations of marine shells are found nearly 200 feet above the existing beach; and along the borders of the Baltic, well-defined plateaux of marine detritus occur at elevations varying from 50 to 100 feet. All these examples, with many others which might be adduced from the coasts of South and North America, point to successive elevations of the land, analogous to those by which the stratified formations were raised from their seas of deposit into open day. The remains found in the gravel and sand of these beaches are chiefly shells belonging to *species* now inhabiting the ocean, though a careful examination detects *varieties* apparently extinct. The more elevated terraces, like those of Scotland and Scandinavia, are evidently of great antiquity."

The Rhone, it is said, has gained from four to six miles on the Mediterranean within the last thousand years. Notre Dame de Port was a harbour in A.D. 898, but it is now a league from the shore. Psalmodi was an island in A.D. 815, but it is now two leagues from the sea. The town of Tignaux, on the shore in A.D. 1737, is now a French mile distant from it.

I have slept in a Chateau, separated from the Gulf of Finland by a belt of fir trees half-a-mile broad, but which, within the memory of the older inhabitants of the district, stood within a hundred yards of the waves on the beach. In returning thence to St Petersburg I saw a fortress miles distant from the gulf, which in the last century was approached by boat. In some cases the encroachment of land upon the sea near the mouths of rivers may be attributable to the lodging there of detritus brought down by the river from its upper course, but we cannot thus account for raised beaches such as have been seen in various parts of the world.

Sometimes the process is sudden—almost instantaneous—and the phenomenon of submergence is not unknown. In 1596 several towns in Japan were covered by the sea; in 1638 St Euphemia became a lake; in 1692 Port Royal, in Jamaica, was submerged; in 1775 the great earthquake of Lisbon sank many parts of the Portuguese and African shores 100 fathoms under water; in 1819, at the mouth of the Indus, a large tract of country, with villages, was submerged, while a new tract was elevated, called the "Ullah Bund;" in 1822 about 100 miles of the Chili coast was elevated to the height of four or six feet.

The late Professor Nicol gave the following beautiful illustration of the fact of depression and upheaval of land going on over extensive areas of the world's surface, in his work entitled *The System of the World* :—

" The vast expanses of the Southern ocean are peopled near the surface by inconceivable throngs of creatures of extreme minuteness, whose continual, incessant, and inexplicable activities, are nevertheless, efficient towards building up the Coral rocks. The chemistry by which the Nautilus elaborates its gorgeous shell, apprehended by the instinct of these living molecules, enables them, as they work in myriads, now to erect a fabric solid and extensive as a bed of limestone, now regular and convoluted like the human brain, and again so delicate in fibre and of whiteness so snowy that it equals some cherished plant in fragility and beauty. Now when traversing the Pacific, the Naturalist meets with a display of this architecture of most peculiar arrangement, and which by its magnitude, and immense diffusion—for its separate instances are strewn along many thousand miles—has never failed to fill him with a just astonishment. It is an island—if island it may be called—which consists simply of a circular coral reef, of the average width of a quarter of a mile, enclosing an area varying from a mile to fifty or sixty in diameter. The features even of one such object are sufficiently singular. The insects, for instance, that formed it cannot live beneath a certain depth, and the coral fabric often arises in the midst of waters so deep that we can nowise fancy it to have been built up from the bottom of the ocean. The difficulty was at first apparently overcome by the supposition that the creatures had reared their stupendous walls on the rim of the crater of a submarine volcano long probably extinct; but, overlooking the improbability of craters existing there of a size that rather likened them to the prodigious formations in the Moon than to any exemplar upon Earth, the explanation failed in regard of the two most important and characteristic facts of the case. In the first place, the existence of the coral reef has been recognised at depths quite beyond the limit at which any insect can now carry on its work: but, inasmuch as this phenomenon might be supposed only to point to a disappearance, in the course of the world's history, of *species* of creatures fitted to live at such profundities, I insist the most on another argument, which seems to admit of no reply. The proposed solution takes no account whatever of the countless number of those islands which stud the Pacific, along a line of upwards of four thousand miles. The question as to the various depths at which corals, living or extinct, could possibly have elaborated these rocks, is doubtful only in regard to a number of feet wholly insignificant in respect of any large elevation; so that the foregoing hypothesis would imply the existence over that immense extension of ranges or groups of submarine volcanos, or other mountains *differing by no appreciable amount in altitude* ; and this also without regard to the absolute depths of the ocean on whose floor they rest. It were, in fact, as if over some wide continent—irrespective of valley, low land, or table-land—groups and ridges arose, across whose peaks a plane might be stretched so as nearly to touch them all ; and surely nothing can be conceived more opposite to what is visible—nothing less analogous to the jagged and varying outline of the most regular masses of existing mountains. That these coral reefs must rest on the tops of submarine elevations, is manifest; but some new feature or element is thus clearly wanting to render the theory inclusive of all the phenomena. Now this element is supplied, if, as suggested by the sagacity of our admirable Darwin, we suppose these mountains placed on an *area of subsidence*. Picture, for instance, some island, whose coasts are now encircled by a fringe of coral, gradually sinking, first beneath the surface of the waters, and by continuation of the same mysterious workings of Nature, afterwards deeper and deeper in the sea. The process, as usual with mighty operations, being eminently slow and gradual, contains nothing to disturb the labours of the tiny architects who had, in the shape of a fringe, laid the foundation of their wall. Ever as the island sank, their edifice would rise to the surface ; on the disappearance of dry land in its interior, it would first assume the aspect of a circle of coral ; and this, ever added to with perseverance the most marvellous, might, through all future ages, preserve its crest on a level with the waves, although the solid land that constitutes its base had long disappeared among the profoundest depths of the ocean. But the explanation, which thus meets every difficulty in the case of a single atoll, can account for their diffusion over any extent, or in whatever numbers. Suppose, for instance, that these islands of ours had, in the course of the mutability of Nature, passed through their epoch of stability, and were now slowly subsiding. In the course of centuries—their mainland having sunk under the confluence of the Atlantic and German Oceans—there would remain, of their present greatness, only a number of islets, constituted by our mountains, around which we may fancy coral fringes to begin to grow. Now—subsidence continuing—the lowest peaks would first disappear, bequeathing only an atoll as their memorial, and although Ben Nevis might remain for centuries longer, with its crest above the waters, it, too, would be submerged, and we should have no other trace of its existence. The area of Great Britain would thus be changed into a sea of circles of coral, presenting, in miniature, what exists at present over an immense expanse of the Pacific. The conclusion, however strange, seems irresistible. Occupying that mighty area,—in length, according to Darwin, 4500 miles, and now filled only by these atolls and a few groups of islets (summits of mountains not yet wholly submerged)—a majestic continent must have existed, and taken part in the history of the Earth's evolutions, during epochs comparatively recent ; and, of all the gorgeous life and lofty activities which must have thronged it, there remains but the incessant working of those infinitesimal creatures, whose structures so emphatically indicate the place of its tomb.

"But other features of those seas are equally pregnant ; and we must peruse them ere the picture can be complete. Whilst immense and uninterrupted tracts are characterized by the exclusive presence of these atolls, many in their neighbourhood exhibit a totally different character. They are occupied, also, by islands ; but, among them the coral rocks abound *in the interior*, often rising in terraces as we proceed inward, until we follow them almost to the tops of the highest interior elevations. Now, it cannot for a moment be doubted that these corals were formed under the only condition in which coral can be formed, viz., below the surface of the waves ;

and knowing of energies manifested in the volcanoes, which can rend the solid earth, and force large mountains through its crevices, the inference is easy, that these islands must have been *elevated*, and, as indicated by the *terraces*, perhaps *gradually*, from a former inferior level. But this inference is rather sustained and its significance extended by two important facts: First, as in the previous case, the symptoms of elevation *exclusively* characterize large isolated tracts, being, for the most part, unmixed except at their margin, by symptoms of depression, so that we cannot refer them to partial elevating movements, but to an action including *great areas within its range;* and this is confirmed by the circumstances, that to these areas our clearest evidence of the energy of a protruding or upheaving force from below, viz., the volcano, is at present confined. How extraordinary the scene we have here unfolded! Through all the wide solitude of the Pacific, from which no tidings were wont to come, except of scattered tribes of savage people, or of new and rich aromas, we are now summoned to discern the manifest progress of the most stupendous changes to which our world can be subject; mighty movements of its solid crust, here subsiding and carrying for ever from human sight the marvels of great continents, and, elsewhere, promising the birth of new ones, amidst the deepest silences of the ocean."

And he goes on to say,—" That there is no portion of these continents which has not been subject to such memorable revolutions. That the whole land now protruded above the waves, had long lain at the bottom of oceans, appears from the character and contents of all the sedimentary rocks; for while these demonstrate, by their structure, that they must have been deposited by the agency of superincumbent waters, they envelope, now turned into stone, the remains of the sea-creatures that lived on the floor of the ocean, when the stratum of mud, or sand, or lime, was there spread out, which through the course of ages has become hardened into a corresponding rock. To dwell on a consideration, at the present time so generally understood and accepted, does not appear needful; but a careful analysis of the rocks of these continents has revealed another feature in the history of the changes which have affected the Earth by far too remarkable to be passed slightly by. Not only have our existing masses of land been subjected to a process of *emersion*, such as these tracts in the Pacific are undergoing, by whose gradual rise novel forms and combinations are visibly preparing, but it is certain that they have experienced many and signal *oscillations*, now sinking beneath the sea, now reappearing, so that those grand metamorphoses of the surface of our Planet seem almost without limit or end. Look in illustration to the south-eastern counties of England. We discern there, as characteristic of extensive localities, three singular formations of considerable thickness.

"The lower and upper formations are *marine*, that is, they contain solely the relics of creatures that lived in the sea; while the middle one, consisting of three distinct beds, is entirely, or very nearly, of *fresh-water* origin. Now observe the significance of this curious intermixture. When the stratum No. 1 was deposited, it is indubitable that the whole wide surface over which it is diffused must have been the floor of the ocean. On the deposition of No. 2, which required the agency of a lake or river, the first bed must have arisen from its previous depths, and constituted part of the dry land. Ages then had passed,—the beds of No. 2 being meanwhile formed, in quiet and perfect order; and, at the close of this period, the land must again have sunk, and received from the ocean the superincumbent chalk of No. 3, which by one more of those stupendous revolutions has since been heaved up, so as now to constitute the bright cliffs of that portion of our island. Two grand movements of upheaval, and one at least of subsidence, are thus demanded for the explanation of this mere leaf in the annals of the earth; and a minuter inquiry would only add to the variety, and the better impress the majesty of these changes. The intermediate fresh-water formation, for instance (the Wealden), was the estuary of a river rivalling the Ganges, which there delivered its volume of water into the ocean. Now that river must have drained some continent of magnitude corresponding,—a continent (as we learn from the scattered bones buried in the mud of its estuary) filled with life in some of its strangest and most gigantic developments; and that has wholly disappeared; carried downwards, either entirely or in parts, by the subsidence which prepared the Wealden to receive the chalk."

As has been already intimated, in many atlases published in illustration of physical geography, there may be found maps representing the results of observations carefully made by scientific men of similar changes in various parts of the world, horizontal lines being employed to indicate areas of subsidence, while those of elevation are marked by vertical lines, and intermediate districts of indecision are pointed out by crossings of the two sets of lines.

By a representation of these already spoken of, it appears, as has been intimated, that throughout the region of the West Indies and the western coast of Mexico and South America, and throughout a triangular space included by a line through these places, subtending an angle at and including the Sandwich Islands, a right angled triangle, measuring upwards of 100° of longitude and 75° of latitude, the land and ocean bed are rising; that, throughout an irregularly formed figure, including Australia and the islands of the South Pacific, 145° of longitude and 75° of latitude, the land and ocean bed are being depressed; that, throughout the gulf of Bengal, the China Sea, and east to the Carolina's, including Sumatra, Borneo, and the Phillipine Islands, the land is being elevated, which is also the case in the Mauritius, Madagascar, and along the east coast of Africa, while that portion of the Indian Ocean which lies between these and the west coast of India is being depressed.

In regard to these statements this general remark must be made,—the measure of the elevation or of the depression, and the evidence of the fact, varies greatly in different localities in the regions specified; but, with every allowance which may legitimately be demanded on this account, enough will remain to show that we have evidence of the process of change of elevation going on now on the coast, and of its having been going on long, and that to an extent corresponding to the elevation of the continent in its present form and contour—not of South Africa alone, the Cape of Goood Hope and lands adjacent, but of the whole of the vast continent of which this is the southern extremity.

2. This may prove more credible if, pausing here, information be given in regard to the process or operation by which the depression and upheaval is supposed to be effected.

There is scarcely a river in the world that is not carrying down in its waters the debris of mountains and of the lands through which it flows.

Few are limped and transparent, and the discolouration of these which are not is owing to solid matter suspended in these waters. Analysis will show that many which are limpid, are stealing, concealing, and bearing away other matter in solution; and if any there be which can pass such a trial and come forth with a full acquittal, watch them closely and you will see them, it may be stealthily, rolling down golden sand or other material from the upper country, too heavy to be suspended in their waters. The quantity of solid matter thus conveyed and transported is immense.

Look at any runnel after rain; look at any river in the colony coming down in torrents where shortly before there were only shingle and pools; look to rivers and river-beds in other lands, and the ocean or ocean-beds beyond. Of the Mississippi, it is stated that the whole valley of the river-bed, measuring from thirty to fifty miles in breadth, and at its mouth 120 miles or more, is filled with debris, which has been thus brought down from the higher lying country. And, according to Captain Hall, deposits are formed of rafts of drift trees matted together into networks many yards in thickness, and stretching over a hundred of square leagues, or a thousand square miles.

The sediment of the Amazon discolours the waters of the ocean for three hundred miles off from the shore.

The Delta of the Ganges occupies no less than 44,000 square miles, and the sea does only recover its transparency sixty miles from the coast.

Sir George Staunton inferred from certain experiments that the Hoango-ho contains one part of sediment in every two hundred parts of its water, and estimating its average depth at 120 feet, he calculates that this river by itself is capable of converting an English square mile of the coast at its mouth into solid land in seventy days.

At the head of the Adriatic, the Po and other streams have brought down so much sediment, that from the northernmost point of the Gulf of Trieste, round and down to the south of Ravenna, there is an uninterrupted series of recent accessions of land more than 100 miles in length, which within the last 2000 years have increased from ten to twenty miles in breadth.

All the solid matter brought down by these and other rivers is borne away by them from higher lying lands. But the material thus transported is not only removed from the place where it was, it is deposited elsewhere. Much of it is deposited in the basin of the sea; and from this important consequences must follow.

One of the first lessons of children, over extensive districts of Britain, some fifty years ago, told of a thirsty raven or crow coming to a jug containing a little water, but this in the bottom of the vessel beyond the reach of its bill, and of its gathering and dropping into the jar pebble after pebble, looking at the result and hopping off to get another and again to get another until at length the water was raised to the neck of the jug, when it was enabled to quench its thirst. Even in an infant-school may be found many who can tell that if into a basin full of water you pour sand or mud it will overflow. And what seem to be effects something similar may be seen in the ocean-bed.

Under the clear waters of the Mediterranean, it is said, may be seen in some places buildings which at one time must have stood on dry land, on or above and beyond the level of the beach; and on other shores may be seen trunks of trees, not as in a growing position, but deep under the surface of the water.

But these are only a part of the phenomena of the present time; and it would be rash, in ignorance of all, to conclude that in this effect of material brought down by the rivers of all lands, and deposited in seas connected with the whole ocean waters of the world, we have learned all that may be learned in regard to the process whereby, in some quarters, the land gains upon the sea, and in others the sea gains upon the land. We must examine more fully the facts of the case.

Water always finds its level; but we do not see everywhere along all shores indications of the rising of the water. In some places the rising of the waves of ocean, rolling in upon the land in their pride, has apparently been stopped at the same point for ages, and in other places they never reach the high-water mark of a former day. We see indications of accessions of land having been gained by alluvial deposits on the shore; but there are other phenomena, similar in character to these, which cannot be thus accounted for, and to these also we must attend.

The ocean-bed must, throughout very lengthened periods, be within a very limited range of variations, always the same; and we are thus led to the conclusion that the encroachment of the ocean in some portion of its many-bayed and tortuous shore, and the subsidence of it in others, must be the counterparts of each other. And assuming that the level of the whole remains nearly the same, that these correlated phenomena must have been occasioned by the depression of some portion of the ocean-bed together, it may be, with adjacent land, as in some parts of the Mediterranean, and by the elevation of some portion of the sea-bed and adjacent land, or of some portion of the ocean-bed alone, at a distance from all dry land—island and continent alike—a power or force adequate to the production of this we have in the solid matter carried down by rivers and deposited in the depths of the sea.

According to a generally-received opinion, the earth is a hollow globe of solid crust, enclosing a mass of material in a state of fusion. The crust, though solid, is to some extent elastic. The weight of matter deposited from rivers causing a depression—slight, it may be, but appreciable—a corresponding elevation must take place elsewhere; and thus regions of the earth's surface of immense extent may be elevated and depressed, producing such encroachments of the sea upon the dry land, and of the dry land upon the sea, as those to which I have referred as seen in the present time. To some such operation as this may be attributed the elevation of the vast continent of Africa, and the elevation of it in a mass; and it happens that we have what may be considered by some a corroborative testimony to the correctness of the supposition in evidence supplied by the outlying island of St Helena of the depression of the ocean-bed beyond from what was once its level. But it would be premature to do more here than allude to that circumstance as an intimation that, while advancing what it is deemed proper to advance, there is more to follow. The subject I shall treat in sections.

SECTION I.—*Objections to the Hypothesis.*

It may be objected, that the alleged fact of this upheaval is a mere conjecture, and by some it may be contemptuously spoken of as a mere theory.

It is more of a theory than a conjecture, but I do not yet claim for it even this title; all that I allege at present is, that it is a hypothesis which is in accordance with the general contour and the geological formations of Southern Africa—a hypothesis which much that I have seen, and much that I have read of the country, supports—while nothing has come under my own observation, or been reported to me of the observations of others, which is inconsistent with its truth—and I find it to be a hypothesis which enables us to account satisfactorily to a great extent for the desiccation of the land.

The general contour of the country I have already described. A succession of mountain ranges, separating plains or level valleys, at higher and yet higher elevations as they recede from the sea, until, in the interior, is reached a vast basin-shaped expanse, finding outlet—if outlet it have—far away from the southern promontory of the Cape. It has been conjectured that one outlet is by the Congo, and that another is the Nile; while the Zambesi drains a portion intermediate between the valley of the Orange River and the extensive basin of Central Africa.

Some idea of the superficial aspect of the continent as thus depicted may be suggested by the accumulation of ice sometimes seen on the banks of a river, on which the continuous sheet has successively given way at different places in consequence of the rising of the water under the continuous sheet, and has subsequently collapsed when the river had again subsided within its usual limits, or, escaping by the rents, had overflowed the dislocated ice. The overlapping sheets of ice, and even some which are not overlapping, are somewhat precipitous at the edge of the rent looking towards the bank, but slope more gently from the summit of that precipice towards the river beyond. While the unbroken sheet of ice beyond that, though not throughout its extent lower than the ice at the edge, is much lower than the uptilted edges of sheets of ice between, and in some places depressed below even the ice at the edge, and is overflowed with water, as was at one time the Great Sahara.

It is the contour of the continent of Africa alone which I seek thus to illustrate. But I proceed to remark that such a contour of the continent is in accordance with the supposition that the whole has been upheaven in a mass, excepting where it may have given way, and, by rents and fissures, allowed of one portion being elevated, while another remained for a time at the elevation it had attained, or temporarily sunk back again beneath it.

The contour of the continent speaks not of a sudden upheaval but of an elevation of the land, effected by a slow and lengthened process, in the course of which the comparatively thin crust of solid matter supposed to cover the molten mass of the globe, though yielding to the pressure from below, being unable to maintain itself unbroken, has given way in long rents, which, though now appearing as dykes, while empty, or filled only with the matter they now contain in a state of solution or fusion, allowed the portion raised highest to raise also the portion on the other side of the rent by the tenacious consistence of the crust, and its continuous hold at one or both of the extremities of the rent.

And the hypothesis is not otherwise than in accordance with the geological observations brought forward in a preceding chapter.

Of some of the mountain ranges I have given an account which may be thought to be different and somewhat at variance with what is now advanced;

but it is not so. The mountains and mountain ranges referred to are not overlapping edges of continuous sheets terminated there by a rent or dyke, but, as has been intimated, portions of the elevated land left standing, while the portion on one side or other, or all round, was washed away by ocean currents. And here lies the only ground on which I anticipate that an objection to the hypothesis is likely to be raised, a hypothesis which I scarcely need say is not one which I have had the honour of originating, but is one generally received, and is only adduced by me to show its applicability to South Africa, and the extent to which it enables us to account satisfactorily for the desiccation of the country. The difficulty in the way of its acceptance by others, which I anticipate, is one arising from the consideration of the extent of the country which must have been elevated in a mass, if the hypothesis be applied to the phenomenon—the immensity of the force which would be required for the production of this. It is not the mountain range alone, nor even at successive times one mountain range with the tableau beyond, but the whole of Southern Africa, nor yet the whole of Southern Africa alone, but the whole vast continent of what it is but the southern extremity, which it is alleged has been raised; and great is the elevation to which the whole continent, throughout its vast extent, must have been raised, if this hypothesis be correct.

Even on this southern extremity projecting into the ocean, and continuous with its unfathomable depths, there are not only mountains but extensive plateaux, thousands of feet above the level of the ocean. The plains of the Free State are 5000 feet, the plateaux of Damaraland are 6,000 feet, above the level of the sea; and besides these plateaux there are mountains, connected therewith, or apart, of still greater height. There is the Stormberg range, near Queenstown, the average height of which is 7,000 feet; the great Winterberg, near Fort Beaufort, 7,800 feet in height; Komsberg, in the Roggeveld mountains, estimated to be upwards of 8,000; the Mont aux Sources, in Basuto land, estimated by the French missionaries by whom it was first visited at 10,000 feet above the level of the sea; and Lievenberg, Omhotozu, and the Omatko mountains, in Damaraland, reported by Messrs Galton and Anderson as respectively 7,200, 7,300, and 8,800 feet in height: the lowest of them more than double the height of Table Mountain above the sea, this being only 3582 feet.

Nor is it mountains and mountain ranges alone which force themselves upon our thoughts, but along with these the observations previously referred to that several of them owe their elevations above the height of circumjacent land, not to an upheaval of themselves above that level, but to some accidental occurrence determining their conservation, while the kloofs and valleys on their flanks, and the valleys or the plains beyond, were scooped away by a process of denudation occasioned by ocean currents, or terrestrial torrents of resistless force, leaving them as intimations of the elevation from which the intervening earth had been cut down to form these kloofs, and valleys, and plains, and their summits leaving indications that they, too, had been subjected, for times more ar less protracted—it may have been ages—to the same denuding operation, whereby they were reduced to mere stumps compared with what otherwise they had been.

And the mention of this sends the thoughts onward to the mountains and mountain ranges of the interior, towering to a height above the level of the sea of——Who shall say what?

We have not the evidence necessary to prove that the whole continent at any one time exhibited the form of an extensive bulging, of which these mountains remain the measurement of the height of the arc above the level of the sea or of the sea-basin, but something of the kind is suggested; and the question or doubt raised by the consideration of the whole case is, How is it possible that any upheaval at all corresponding to this could be effected? And it may be felt by some that this question must be met before the hypothesis can be entertained, even for consideration. It does not seem to me to be unreasonable that such an objection should be started, but neither does it appear to me to be unreasonable to meet it, not in argument for victory but in the quest after the truth, with the question in reply—There it is, once under the sea, now far above its level; and if not by upheaval of the whole land how has this come to be the case?

To escape from the necessity of connecting all that has been remarked with some supposed upheaval, and that an upheaval of the whole continent to such an elevation as any reading of the phenomena would demand, it may be asked—Could not the whole be accounted for satisfactorily by the supposition of a falling in or depression of the basin of the sea when the waters were gathered together into one place? If it were, again my answer, if given, would be in Scottish fashion—answering one question by asking another,—How, when, or where did any such depression ever occur? And if it be admitted to be only a supposition I would ask, Would it not be as difficult, or perhaps more so, to account for such a depression as to account for the upheaval if taken by itself alone? And yet again—How would the supposition account for the indications of portions of this land, at least, having been submerged subsequently to their first emergence, and having again emerged, and this, it may be, oftener than once?

This much, however, may be admitted: the hypothesis in question embodies the supposition of some such depression as being the cause or occasion of the upheaval, or prior con-sequence with the upheaval of a common cause; and to this correlated depression is attributed one-half of the elevation of the mountain summit above the lowest ocean depth, as one-half of the apparent height of the wave on lake, river, or sea may be attributed to the corresponding depression which precedes or follows it. But it must be borne in mind that the sea level taken generally as a standard of measurement corresponds to the medial line which that measurement of the wave supposes; and it is only an approximation to the truth that even that illustration supplies. Assuming that in both cases the elevation and depression are correlated—the one depressed as much below as the other is elevated above the true level—if it be the case that at one time the waters covered the whole earth, the cubic contents of the depression below the water line must necessarily be greater than the cubic bulk of the elevations above,—containing, as they must do in such a case, not only all the water displaced by the upheaval of the land, but in addition to this all the waters covering at a prior time their own surface.

At the present day the proportion of land to sea is reckoned as one to three in superficial extent—one-fourth of the earth's surface being land, and three-fourths covered with sea—and while Chimborazo in America towers 21,450 feet above the level of the sea, and Jamatri and Dhawalagiri, in the Himialaya range of mountains, rise respectively 25,500 feet and 26,862 feet above that level, it is estimated that the extreme depths of the Atlantic are about 50,000 feet, or more than nine miles, below the surface of the ocean.

Such are the elevations and depressions with which we have to do in such investigations as those upon which we have entered, and while it may surprise, it may also prepare for the further prosecution of the investigation to state, that, great as such measurements may seem, compared with the littleness of man, they are actually as nothing compared with the bulk of the globe. A mile more or less in height of a mountain, or a mile more or less in the depth of an ocean bed, is only 1-8000th part of the earth's diameter, and has been compared to a single grain of sand, more or less bulky, or a scratch with a pin, more or less deep, on a globe a foot or more in circumference.

And with regard to the extent of the surface supposed to have been affected, we have evidence that within certain limits such changes of elevation and depression are even now going on in extensive regions of the earth's surface. Facts have been stated showing that such is the case, from the East Indies and eastern coast of America, round by the Pacific and the Indian Ocean, to the eastern coast of this continent, where upheaval is still going on.

These are facts or phenomena with which scientific men are well acquainted; they lie at the very threshold of the cognate sciences of Physical Geography and Geology; the means by which they are brought about have been to some extent determined, and that thus, as has already been intimated, it is by many scientific observers held, that the earth is a mass of matter in a state of fusion inclosed within a crust consolidated by the cooling of its external surface, which crust, though reckoned thick when measured by measurements with which we are familiar, is really thin when compared with the bulk of the earth. Objections have been raised against this view of the constitution of the earth, and other views have been offered, but this view is held by many.

It is not impossible that irregular contractions of this crust, as it cooled and became consolidated at different depths, may have caused blisters, contortions, eruptions, and irregularities of surface, or inequalities in elevation of superficial portions, and these irregularities of surface may have been still further magnified and increased by volcanic action, of the occurrence of which, while, or when, the earth was still covered deep with the primeval ocean, we have innumerable indications in many lands.

Even there and then there may have been levelling and transporting influences at work, and that with similar effects to those which we see upon dry land; and as these we have it in our power to study, to these we must give for a little our attention.

It may have been remarked in the course of ordinary observations of what is taking place around us, that, whatever is raised in elevation upon the earth's surface tends by gravitation to descend to a lower level, as if the object were, as the tendency is, to reduce the surface of the earth to a smooth and perfect spheroid: undermine what constitutes its support, and down it rolls to the lowest level it can reach. And thus has the undermining of rocks by the lashing of the waves allowed mountain masses to find a resting-place in the ocean-bed.

What has been effected thus is probably trifling compared with what has been effected by the continous action of the rain and the dew, which, compared with that, may seem scarcely deserving of a thought.

Besides the masses which were thus buried in the sea, there were many fragments of rock, fragments some of them small as the dust of the street, left behind, and similar fragments are to be found in numerous plains beside. They too would follow the mountain mass, but supports, which under these would have been crushed, sustain them far above the ocean-bed, and there they must abide their time. All that they require is a little water to partially float them over the barrier, and that water put in motion to promote their downward movement, and they too are off and away for the deep deep sea. This, it may be the dew or the mist-cloud, or failing these the first shower of rain, may supply, and accordingly we find that not a shower falls but some of them seize their opportunity and run.

The water which forms the dew-drop, or falls in the form of rain, is pure and limped as is the air of heaven; but in the runnel or the streamlet it is discoloured with mud, which mud is composed of such fragments of earth as it is aiding to escape. It is the feeder of a river. By the streamlet to the river, by the river to the sea, is aided on the mud—and at length it also finds its resting-place in the ocean-bed. The quantity of debris thus borne downward is almost incredible.

The power of water to tear away and transport earthy matter has been made the subject of calculation and experiment. Water moving with the velocity of 3 inches per second will tear up fine clay; moving with double that velocity, or 6 inches per second, it will lift fine sand; with a velocity of 8 inches it will raise sand as coarse as linseed; and of 12 inches, fine gravel; with a velocity of 24 inches it will roll along rounded pebbles an inch in diameter; and with a velocity of 36 inches per second it will sweep away angular stones of the size of a hen's egg. Rivers in flood often acquire a much greater velocity than this, and stones of considerable weight are then borne down by their current, while the ocean in a storm has moved stones tons in weight.

Water in motion can not only bear away, but it can tear away, the solid matter over which it flows. Loose soil, clay, and sand yield readily to its impulse—granite or basalt offer more resistance; but all rivers carry down sand and gravel, and these rubbing and striking against rocks, with the momentum given to them by the velocity of the stream, they rasp, or file, or hammer away the hardest of these. "The Nerbuddah, a river of India, has thus scooped out a channel in basaltic rock 100 feet deep. Messrs Sedgwick and Murchison give an account of gorges scooped out in beds of the rock called conglomerate, in the valleys of the eastern Alps, 600 and 700 feet deep. A stream of lava, which was vomited from Ætna in 1630, happened to flow across the channel of the river Simeto. Since that time, the stream has cut a passage through the compact rock to the depth of between 40 and 50 feet, and to the breadth of between 50 and several hundred feet. Allusions have already been made to the Niagara, the Ganges, and the Amazon. The cataract of Niagara, in North America, has, as has already been intimated, receded nearly 50 yards during the last 40 years. Below the falls the river flows in a channel upwards of 150 feet deep and 160 yards wide, for a distance of seven miles; and this channel has evidently been produced by the river."

To the presence of material thus being removed from a higher to a lower level do turbid rivers owe their turpidity. And it is alleged that the transference of the pressure from the land whence the material is brought to the basin of the sea is sufficient, in the elastic condition of the earth's crust, to deepen the depression of the ocean-bed, and to allow of compensation being obtained, by the incompressible matter in a state of fusion, for the space when it is displaced, by pressing up to a corresponding extent some portion of the crust elsewhere. And thus may objections taken *in limente* to the hypothesis be met.

SECTION II.—*Application of the hypothesis to the Geological Phenomena and Physical Geography of South Africa.*

If a hypothesis be complete and true it should fit in with all the facts and phenomena observed, as does a key with the wards of a lock for which it was made; then, and not till then, may it be legitimately employed as a working hypothesis in directing inquiries designed to elicit information in regard to the unknown. I know of no test which can be supplied by the geological phenomena or physical geography of South Africa with which this hypothesis does not fit in exactly; of this I shall give a single illustration.

In Europe miners meet often with what are called dykes and faults— dykes and faults which occasion to them no little expense and trouble. Dykes, in accordance with the Scottish use of the term, is the designation applied by geologists and miners to interruptions to the continuity of strata, which seem like a wall to terminate, or bound, or separate one portion from a continuation of it which lies beyond. Sometimes these dykes are a few feet in thickness, sometimes they are as many yards; sometimes they are composed of igneous rock ejected from below, sometimes of clay and gravel washed in from above; in every case they appear to have been cracks or rents occasioned by a disturbance of level, extending, in the case of those filled with igneous rock, to the matter in a state of fusion below, but in the case of the others, extending only a comparatively little way below the surface, and indicating thus their relative position in regard to the upheaval by which they were occasioned—the one, it may be, being made nearer to the centre of depression, the other nearer to the centre of upheaval. In some cases, when the dyke is cut through it is found that the strata beyond are not the same as those by which the dyke has been reached, but strata corresponding to strata far above or far beneath—indicating in the latter case that the portion wrought had been wrenched away and upheaven, in the former that the portion reached had been thus upheaven. Sometimes it is found, also, that the inclination of the strata has been changed, through variations in the direction of the upheaval. It is to such disturbances that the designation *fault* has been given; and there may be a fault where there is no dyke, no vacant space having been left between the masses on the sides of the rent.

This mode of fracture is one with which the working of coal-fields has made geologists and miners well acquainted, and they tell of the irregularities in the upheavings or depressions which have taken place as illustrating, in a striking manner, the nature of the agitations which have taken place. Something like to them may sometimes be seen in accumulations of ice thrown upon a river's bank when the sheet of ice covering the river has broken up.

"In the vale of the Esk, in Mid-Lothian, which does not measure more than 10 miles each way, the coal-field shows 120 ascertained dislocations; one of which at Sheriffhall throws down the strata [or upheaves them] 500 feet. In the Newcastle coal-field there is a famous slip, called the *ninety fathom hitch*, the deviation from the line of stratification being no less than 450 feet. The coal-fields of Fife and Clackmannan abound in such dislocations, several of them throwing the strata from 400 to 1200 feet up or down, as the case may be, from the general position."

All of these speak of upheaval; and such dykes are not awanting in South Africa, in accordance with the hypothesis in question.

Dr Rubidge, in a paper written shortly before his death, maintains that "The elevated lands, whether mountains, hills, or chains of hummocks (locally called 'Koppies'), have generally dykes of igneous rock for their axes, and these run in straight lines through the country for miles, some of them, perhaps, for hundreds of miles;" and I may remark, in passing, such igneous rocks manifest much greater power of resisting the erosive action of water currents than do Silurian and Devonian deposits; and thus may they, when they projected above or beyond masses of these, have diverted the flow, and thus to some extent determined the direction and the contour of the valley created by the process of denudation.

The rents in the rocks into which flows the Zambesi at the Victoria Falls, and which extends for thirty or forty miles beyond, is suggestive of the back-bone of a mountain range, or elevated table-land, having broken, through the disturbance of level. The *dicynodon* valley is seamed with *dykes*; and Dr Rubidge's observations in the Copper Mines show that *faults* exist as well as *dykes;* so that thus far the key fits the ward of the lock. So is it also with all the geological phenomena reported in preceding chapters, and in the preceding sections of this. And a similar accordance may be remarked all along, as we proceed to make the application of it to these phenomena and others, in illustration of the effect of the upheaval of the land on its desiccation, and the production of the aridity by which it is now characterized.

In Table Mountain we have a mass of deposit well-nigh 4000 feet in thickness overlying the granite, and evidently deposited from water in which it had been suspended, floating not on the surface but in the water. The weight of such a deposit, whencesoever it may have come, may have been sufficient to occasion some depression, more or less extensive, throughout the locality in which it was formed. And thus may it have been in the district in which Table Mountain stands.

Overlying sandstone, which was apparently a continuation of that with which Table Mountain and the Lion's Head are capped, there is in some places a deposit of dark-gray and brownish shales, of an aggregate thickness of 1100 feet; and there are not awanting indications that this proved sufficient, notwithstanding the increased thickness of the earth's crust, to produce a local depression where it was deposited, for, from observations made by Mr Wylie when Geological Surveyor to the Colony, and from memoranda furnished to him by Captain Bayley of the trigonometrical survey, the Table Mountain sandstone, identified by the former in the Lower Devonian, dips southward at about an angle of 70°; and from the same memoranda, says Mr Wylie, "It would appear that the Potteberg sandstone dips the opposite way, or northward, thus indicating a basin in the Devonian rocks extending from the Drakenstein eastward to the sea, in the hollow of which it is that the Upper Devonian or fossiliferous shales probably occur all along from the Bosjesveldt to Cape Barracouta and the Kafirkuils River."

All the strata which have been brought under our notice are the results of denudation, being formed of deposits of the debris of older deposits, or of primitive rocks, and the changes thus produced by the removal of the superincumbent weight from one locality to another may have been followed by local changes of elevation, leading to yet other changes in the course of the ages, the eras—or by whatsoever name may be indicated the lapse of time during the transformation of the globe into its existing condition—which followed.

Passing other deposits of 500, 800, 1000, 1200, and 1500 feet in thickness, we find—higher, and, it may be, much higher in the series of deposits than these, though probably not overlying even portions of the whole of them—the Reptilian or Dicynodon beds of purple, greenish, and gray shales, a lacustrine deposit 1800 feet in thickness. Even this may have sufficed to produce the lacustrine basin, or at least to deepen the depression in which it was formed.

But notwithstanding, and over and above all this, there appears to have been produced contemporaneously or subsequently a depression of the ocean-bed beyond, but continuous with the immense mud-banks, sand-banks, and rocky islands of the nascent continent, a depression of the ocean-bed correlated thereto,—the continuous, or oft-renewed, increased, and extended depression of which may have caused an elevation of the whole mass, not only in its entire thickness, but throughout its vast extent to its present elevation above the sea. This could not be effected without a far greater extent of the surface being raised with it; but it is with this portion of the continent alone I have at present to do.

It may be asked, Can any indications of such depression be adduced? And the demand implied in such an enquiry is not unreasonable. It is easily met.

We have both indications of such depression having occurred in the remote past, and indications of a similar depression going on at the present time having apparently gone on for ages.

The former is that which bears primarily upon the subject now under discussion; the bearing of the latter is adventitious, only illustrating upon a smaller scale by what is going on in the present what the hypothesis assumes has gone on in the same land on an extensive scale in the past.

Much that has been said in regard to the Baltic and the Mediterranean and the South Seas might be cited in illustration of such depressions and such upheavals as these imply having gone on elsewhere. What is called for are indications of such depressions having occurred in the vicinity of Southern Africa, and these are supplied by the island of St Helena. In regard to this I find amongst my memoranda the following:—

"The island of St Helena is composed of basaltic streams of a gentle inclination. Taking a section of the coast cliffs and bottom of the sea, we find that from the foot of High Knoll to the edge of Ladder Hill they slope from an elevation of 1600 feet to one of 510 feet above the level of the sea. Were this line produced it would extend at least to a point now covered by the sea to a depth of 30 fathoms, and it is probable much farther, for the inclination of the streams is less near the coast than further inland. And other sections of the coast would have given still more striking results if the exact data had been at command. Thus, on the windward side the cliffs are about 2000 feet in height and the cut-off lava streams very gently inclined, and the bottom of the sea has nearly a similar slope all round the island.

"Everything thus leads to the conclusion that this is a mountain of volcanic origin—composed, in its external covering at least, of matter which had been thrown up in a molten state, which found emission somewhere near the centre of the mass, and which, running over on all sides—a viscid mass—moving onwards till it reached the more level ground at the base of its nucleus, if nucleus it have of other matter than the basalt of which it is composed, and if it have not, the more level ground of the ocean-bed.

"If so, the question is raised,—How has all the hard basaltic rock, which once extended beneath the surface of the sea, been worn away? According to Captain Austin, by whom the coast was surveyed, the bottom is uneven and rocky only to that very small distance from the beach within which the depth is from 5 to 6 fathoms; outside this line, to a depth of about 100 fathoms, the bottom is smooth, gently inclined, and formed of mud and sand; outside the 100 fathoms it plunges suddenly into unfathomable depths, as is very commonly the case on all coasts where sediment is accumulating. At greater depths than the 5 fathoms it seems impossible, under existing circumstances, that the sea can both have worn away hard rock, in parts to a thickness of at least 150 feet, and have deposited a smooth bed of fine sediment.

"But now, if we had any reason to suppose that St Helena had, during a long period, gone on slowly subsiding, every difficulty would be removed; for, looking at the diagram and imagining a fresh amount of subsidence, we can see that the waves would then act on the coast cliffs with fresh and unimpaired vigour, whilst the rock ledge near the beach would be carried down to that depth at which sand and mud would be deposited on its bare and uneven surface; after the formation, near the shore, of a new rocky shoal, fresh subsidence would carry it down and allow it to be smoothly covered up." And thus does this island appear to supply evidence of the gentle subsidence of the bottom of the ocean.

For this illustration I am indebted, if I mistake not, to the late Dr Daubeny, Professor of Botany and Chemistry in the University of Oxford. And the argument founded on the outline of the island, illustrative of the probable chronological history of the reduction of the volcanic rock, I understand to be this,—

The lava stream of which the superficial rocks are composed, extended originally far—very far—beyond the present outline of the rock. The ledge, now extending a short distance beyond the present beach, and upon which the water is from five to six fathoms in depth, has been formed by the action of the waves on rock, which formerly covered that space, to a height corresponding to the height of the mountains on the face of the island rising from that shore. The ocean and the atmosphere, the water and the air, through, it may be, a long succession of ages, disintegrating these solid rocks, the debris was deposited, it may be in part, in a gently inclining plain; while a part may have fallen from the edge into the depth beyond, and there found a resting place 100 fathoms deep.

But that this resting place is only a ledge, is shown by the circumstance that beyond it the plumet plunges into an unfathomable deep; from which it may be inferred that that ledge was formed in the same way in which that now used as a roadstead was formed,—for there, too, "the bottom is smooth, gently inclined, and formed of mud and sand." But the action of the waves being limited to a depth of five fathoms, we seem to be shut up to the adoption of the inference that that ledge, and probably all intermediate points above it, must have been in earlier times level with the ocean surface. And it is more reasonable to suppose that the ocean-bed has been depressed, carrying this island with it, than to suppose that the ocean has otherwise increased, throughout its extent, in a corresponding volume of its waters, or that the island has sunk in altitude through a displacement of its base, or its interpenetration of underlying rocks. And the thought is suggested—May not the precipitous frontage of these rocks on all sides be the result of the continuous, or occasionally interrupted, operation of the disintegrating process by which these two ledges have been formed, the diversity of vertical outline on this side of the island being attributable to some difference in the density, friability, or facility of decomposition of rocks found at or about the levels at which these ledges occur?

Be this as it may, the island seems to stand like a measuring-rod indication of depression to which the ocean-bed then has been subjected by the deposit of earthy debris, supplying another illustration of the hypothesis fitting in with the phenomena.

That island is surrounded by unfathomable depths, and such depths apparently have at one time covered the land of South Africa; but it should be borne in mind that we are not shut up to the conclusion that the depths were such as, without change, to receive in succession all the successive deposits found upon it.

The science of geology has made us acquainted with numerous indications of repeated alternations of elevations, and of subsidence beneath the sea level of extensive areas of the earth's surface; there may have been accompanying alternations of elevation and depression elsewhere at a lower level; and there may have been either continuous or intermitted depression brought about by the same means. But it is the general question of upheaval in connection with the Hydrology of South Africa with which we have at present chiefly to do, and in connection with this I proceed to remark that, as has been already stated, there may be seen at Sea Point, and along the beach towards Table Bay, and even on the streets of Cape-Town—as at a street at the back of the Custom-House at North Wharf—strata of these slate-like flakes, which look not less like successive deposits from water than do any strata of sand, and much more so than do many strata attributed to such deposition; but these, instead of lying horizontally, as layers of deposit of solid matter from water in which it had been deposited generally do, are inclined, and in some places, almost perpendicular to the horizon—a line of deposit of solid matter from water in which it has been suspended which is almost impossible.

These thin flakes or strata have the usual appearance of thin flakes or strata of slate deposited from water, but their position gives them very much the appearance of having been subsequently uptilted. Looking at them as they crop up, and examining them with attention and care, there seems to be nothing unreasonable in supposing that they were originally deposited in a position almost horizontal, but that, at a time while they were yet elastic, if not plastic, a little of the land adjacent had been upheaved by the protrusion of a quantity of granite in a state of fusion, which, bursting through them, bent upward the edges of the fissure, so that they assumed the position of reclining against the base of the protruded mass—a position which they may still be seen retaining at the base of the Lion's Head.

The hypothesis enables us to account for this by supposing the pressure at some part of the ocean-bed on which debris had accumulated to have been greater than the cohesion of these strata could resist when it was bearing upon them from below, in accordance with the hydraulic paradox of a few ounces of water in a long tube of small bore raising a greater weight on a wider upturned tube with which it is connected, and in accordance with the practical application of such pressure in the hydraulic press; and the cohesion which held them together on an extended level giving way, relief from the pressure was obtained by the protrusion of what is now solid granite, but what was then this material in a state of fusion.

But if the strata had not given way, and the pressure had been the same, and if no rent had been obtained for the pressure elsewhere, the crust being elastic, there must have been raised what would look like a blister, and according to the tenacity of the cohesion this would have been more or less extensive. This, according to the hypothesis, is what subsequently occurred, extensive regions being more or less elevated according as the cohesion of their substance was more or less tenacious; and the result of the process came to be the slow steady elevation of the whole by a force from beneath, as steady in its operation as the force of the hydraulic press, which slowly, but apparently with a force irresistible by the material to which it is applied, elevates the board on which this rests.

With the view thus obtained of the comparatively puny application of force in the hydraulic press, to which tons are as ounces to the unaided powers of man, we can look upon the whole continent of Africa as a blister thus raised by the pressure of the fused material below, in consequence of the pressure to which it is subjected by the deposit, on the equally elastic crust of the ocean, of the material carried down by runnels and rivers from this and other lands which have been so upheaven from the ocean's depth to the elevation they have reached above the ocean's surface.

There may be mountain ranges—whole ranges of mountains—formed of material protruded ages and ages ago through lengthened rents in the earlier formed strata, as was the granite protruded through the slaty deposit, prior to the deposit of the Silurian and Old Red Sandstone, with which both now are covered. But most of the mountains which have come under our consideration are apparently indebted for their mountainous character to the removal of material, by ocean currents, from the district around them, leaving them as indications of the elevation to which the whole district had been raised.

Thus may be obtained some idea of the pressure which the deposit, formed here must have exerted when it was a portion of the ocean-bed; and thus may be obtained some idea of the pressure to which portions of what is now the ocean-bed may be being subjected.

Excavators, to facilitate the measurement of work done by them, often leave, in the excavated plot, pillars of the soil and underlying material, by the height of which may be determined how much and what have been removed. I look, as I have formerly intimated, upon the mountain ranges to which I have referred as the counterpart to these.

I have had occasion to speak of the Gates of the Oomzimvooboo, or St. John's River, in Kaffraria, and I have spoken of these as upwards of 1200 feet in height, with the land behind varying in height from 800 to 1000 feet. At a distance of about 25 miles is Thaba 'Nkooloo, a remarkable mountain, which, from its outline, its formation, and its composition, appears to have been at one time continuous with the so-called Gates of the Oomzimvooboo. This is a mountain which may be considered a counterpart of the excavator's pillars to which I have referred. And the description given to me by Mr A. S. White of Oomzimvooboo, who had been long resident in the district, was that this, with the Gates and the Ingweli mountains, indicated clearly what must have been at one time the level of the whole of the intermediate country.

So does it appear to have been the case with the land intermediate between Table Mountain and the mountains beyond. If an unexperienced observer would form for himself some idea of what the thickness of this deposit must have been, let him pace on a straight road three-quarters of a mile; thus will he learn something of what the statement that a mountain is 4000 feet in height means; or let him, if he care to do so, take his stand on the exposed granite at Sea Point, and with his eye measure the elevation of the Lion's Head; let him then, with the data thus obtained, walk round this by the Kloof road, and compare with the height of the Lion's Head the height of Table Mountain, and estimate then the elevation of Table Mountain above the level of the sea, and bear in mind that this is 3582 feet.

With the data thus obtained let him next endeavour to form a definite idea of the mountains and elevated lands beyond. The summit of Riebeck's Casteel is 3109 feet. The summit of Sneewkop, in the Hottentot Holland Mountains, bounding the flats connecting Table Bay and False Bay, and bounded on the nearer side by the Table Mountain range, is 5066 feet. Let him then estimate, if he can, what must have been the pressure of a continuous sheet of deposit, of such a thickness, over the whole district and far beyond.

When he has done this, or perhaps before it is accomplished, incredulity will steal over him, and he will be ready to say, No—It is impossible—or at least incredible, that any ocean-current can have so deeply furrowed the earth's crust!

But, there, are the strata capping Table Mountain and the Lion's Head distinctly seen by whoever looks upon them; and, there, is the testimony of a geologist that what must have been a continuation of them remains on the mountains far beyond; there, are the uptilted strata of clay slate resting on the protruded granite exposed at the base of the Lion's Hill, the exposed extremities of which exhibit not any of the forms usually seen in a mass uptilted from a horizontal position, the curves of a plastic and ductile mass, or the sharp corners of a mass more solid and unyielding, but it is comparatively level, as if all projections had been planed down, an appearance with which geologists are familiar, and which they attribute to a process of denudation affected by water in movement bearing along suspended in it stones, sand, or mud, whereby is effected what the friction occasioned by a flow of pure water might have done, but would have done more slowly.

The force of a wave, or of a torrent, or even of a douche bath may be more than a man can withstand, and before such force mud, sand, and stones may be borne away like chaff before the wind. Sand driven before wind will polish hard rock over which it passes. I have seen fossils beautifully polished by being exposed to such a current of sand blown over a beach by a westerly wind; and figures are now beautifully traced on glass by simply exposing to a current of sand the portion requiring to be ground down. The flow of water alone might suffice to have effected the denudation; but the flow of water suspending stones and sand and mud would effect it more rapidly;

nor are there awanting deposits of stones and sands and mud which may have been thus borne along.

Mention has been made of conglomerate. In this we have rounded stones imbeded fast in ironstone or clay or other cement, and there are whole mountains composed of such material, the stones in which are not angular but rounded, as would be the shape of stones subjected to mutual attrition in being rolled about together and striking one upon another as they might have done in the rapid of a river, or on a shingly beach, or in an ocean current, till every angular projection of a rough fracture was worn down. Much more would require to be known about them than is here stated before we would be warranted in affirming that the last stated was the occasion of their collision, but they cannot have been rounded in the place in which they are: the mud which now hardened around them cements them into a conglomerated mass would when soft have prevented attrition. The mountain masses of conglomerate must then have been transported from some other spot, and must have been deposited after these stones had acquired their somewhat rounded form.

The current by which these were borne along, whencesoever it may be they were brought, must have been a current of great force and of great depth; and such a current may have sufficed to sweep away the four thousand feet thickness of material formerly covering the Flats and plains beyond. The submarine valley connected with an ocean current which Commander Belknap, of the American Navy, attempted to fathom in his surveying voyage in the east coast of Japan, was one of much greater depth than those with which we are conversant at the Cape; and by Geikie it has been shown, as I have formerly intimated. that both the longitudinal outline of mountain ranges in the Highlands of Scotland, but also intersecting and connecting valleys, may be the result of a process of denudation; it is not less manifestly the case that thus also it may have been here.

Imagine then the pressure which must have been exercised by such a mass of material collected here before relief was afforded by these ocean-currents relieving it by scooping out the plains, and carrying away the material to deposit it elsewhere; and mark a consequence, the ocean-bed has been deeply depressed in the locality in which St Helena stands, and there has been a corresponding bulging upward here. The plateau of the Great Karroo is 3000 feet above the level of the sea; the plateau of Bushmanland 3500 feet; the plateau of Damaraland is 6000 feet; the town of Colesberg is about 4000 feet; and the plains of the Orange River Free State are about 5000 feet above the ocean level.

As the land rose the water would recede, drain off, leaving lateral valleys, as lakes; as it rose these would tilt up and drain off; by the same courses rain which subsequently fell would follow their waters to the sea, and the dry channels would become open drains by which the land, to at least the depth of these channels, would be drained dry; and by rents and cracks which occurred in connection with the disturbance of the level in the upheaval of the land, other channels were opened up for the draining off of the rainfall, and that, perhaps, to an extent of which few of the inhabitants of the land have any conception. It is in view of all this that I have spoken of the upheaval of the land as the primary and principal cause of the desiccation and consequent aridity of South Africa.

It may be alleged this that is only saying of South Africa what may be said of any land under heaven. It is—and something is accomplished if it have been made apparent that so far there is nothing exceptional in the primary cause of the aridity which it is desired to counteract—and something more may be effected if it can be made apparent how the effect, such as it is, has been brought about.

In connection with this I would call attention to the circumstances that in the general contour of the country we have many indications that the upheaval has been in general gradual and slow.

By Sir John Herschel it is stated, in a treatise on Physical Geography,— " In the upheaval of any extensive tract of land from the sea hollows fitted for lake-basins cannot fail to be left. If the upheaval be rude and paroxysmal, resulting in the formation of mountain chains, and accompanied with fracture and dislocation of the strata, such hollows will be deep, precipitous, and narrow, in proportion to their length. Such is the general character of the lakes in mountainous regions—of the Swiss lakes for instance, those of North Italy, of Cumberland, Westmoreland, Scotland, &c. On the other hand, where the upheaving forces have acted more gently, and gradually, and have raised the country with more uniformity, producing extensive plains and low steppes, lakes will not only be more numerous, by reason of the less erosive power of running water to drain them by deepening the outlets, but will affect more rounded forms, and cover the country with shallow pools or ponds void of all picturesque beauty, as we see exemplified in Poland, and in the districts between the Gulf of Finland and the White Sea, which are almost connected by a chain of shallow lakes. Some of them (as those of Onega and Ladoga) very extensive." And such seems to have been the character of most of the sheets of water which covered South Africa, both in times more recent and in times more remote. The drainage of the lakes may in some cases have been sudden, but the formation of the lake slow, and the lake have been in its origin a product of the sea, rather than a product of the land. In the precipitous banks of most of the water courses we have indications of the upheaval having been continued to comparatively recent times, if it be not still continued ; and we see the result.

As the land rose the water would flow off. As the mountain ranges rose above the level of the sea the water would drain off from their summits and their sides. When water was retained in hollows by erosion waterfalls would be converted into rapids and rapids into waterfalls,—each successive change producing a state of things more favourable to the escape and flow of the water from the lake than was the state of things before. At the same time, these lakes and expanses of water, formed by the spreading out of water traversing a valley in its flow towards the lower level, would be silted up with the debris brought from a higher level, and the bottom of the outlet would be worn down ; and by the silting up of the one and the lowering of the other going on simultaneously a medium level would be reached by both, and the lake become a plain, while the river-bed now dry would remain a channel for the rapid conveyance of what might fall as rain, and draining off what might percolate through the soil, till the land became dry, and drier, and drier still.

This much is open and seen ; but the fountains, the hot-springs, both of which are numerous in the Colony of the Cape of Good Hope and subterranean rivers, which are not unknown, tell of the draining off or flow of water from the higher lying lands by other channels than the superficial river-courses. In other lands there is much of the rainfall carried off thus,

T

and there is abundance of indications, if not of evidence, that as it is in these so is it in this.

Marsh, citing Thomassy's *Essai sur l'Hydrologie*, says—"In the low peninsula of Florida, rivers, which must have their sources in mountains hundreds of miles distant, pour forth from the earth with a volume sufficient to permit steamboats to ascend to their basins of irruption. In January 1857 a submarine fresh-water river burst from the bottom of the sea not far from the southern extremity of the peninsula, and for a whole month discharged a current not inferior in volume to the River Mississippi, or eleven times the mean delivery of the Po, and more than six times that of the Nile. We can explain this phenomenon only by supposing that the bed of the sea was suddenly burst up by the hydrostatic upward pressure of the water in a deep reservoir communicating with some great subterranean river or receptacle in the mountains of Georgia, or of Cuba, or perhaps even in the valley of the Mississippi." And he goes on to say,—"Late southern journals inform us that the creek under the natural bridge in Virginia has suddenly disappeared, being swallowed up by newly-formed fissures of unknown depth in its channel. It does not appear that an outlet for the waters thus absorbed has been discovered, and it is not improbable that they are filling some underground cavity like that which supplied the submarine river just mentioned."

Sir John Herschel, writing of the Victoria Falls of the Zambesi, where "the river, 1000 yards in breadth, is suddenly swallowed up in a narrow perpendicular cleft, 100 feet deep, in a black basaltic rock directly across its course, which is prolonged from the bank 40 or 50 miles, in which the river takes its new course, compressed in a deep channel of 15 or 20 yards," goes on to say,—"The hydraulic system of the interior of South Africa, disclosed by Dr Livingstone's travels, is anomalous in the extreme, and is only compatible with the idea of a generally level plateau deluged with periodical rains, but not, like the plain of the Amazon, dominated by a great range of high-lands on one side, with a slope to the other, but as if the periodical rains fell on a gently rising convexity so as to leave the waters undecided by what channels to seek the main external drainage. It would seem very probable that the clift of the Victoria Falls has been of comparatively recent origin, and has determined a new system of drainage by which the water of these regions has been carried off more rapidly than heretofore, since the general tenor of Dr Livingstone's narrative points to what may be termed secular desiccation of the districts traversed by him."

By the consideration of such cracks and rents in the rock crust of the earth, thought is directed to the possibillity of a quantity of water being carried off by subterraneous as well as by superficial rivers. There are more than one *Zonder einde* river in South Africa—rivers which have no issue, but are apparently lost in the sand, as is the Kuruman.

One name of the Zambesi is Leeambye, both names mean the same thing —the RIVER—yet Livingstone writes in his *Missionary Travels in South Africa*,—"An untravelled gentleman who had spent a great part of his life in the study of the geography of Africa, and knew everything written on the subject from the time of Ptolemy downwards, actually asserted in the *Athenæum*, while I was coming up the Red Sea [on return from Africa], that the magnificent river the Leeambye had 'no connection with the Zambesi, but flowed under the Kalahari desert and became lost.'" To this I refer, not to call attention to the mistake, but to intimate that the phenomenon of the disappearance of rivers in Africa is one of such frequent occurrence that a student of the river system of the country publicly refers to this as the probable or certain termination of a mighty flowing river which he had failed to trace to the sea. And while rivers thus lost may have been evaporated or abstracted, or partly both, subterranean rivers are not unknown in South Africa—such is the Mooi river throughout a part of its course.

This Mooi river is formed by the commingling waters of some three or four streams, eight, ten, or twelve feet wide, and it may be sixteen inches deep.

In the Gatzrand there is an immense cavern called Wonder Fontein; and it is stated that chaff thrown into this cavern has come out in the Mooi river, some eighteen miles distant, conveyed by a subterranean stream. This information my informant, the Rev. Dr Murray, of Wellington, who had laboured as a minister over the whole of that region, gave me as he received it—without discrediting it—but vouching only for the fact, that it is said; and it is only in keeping with what the whole of the facts communicated to me in regard to that district or region would lead me to consider possible.

All fountains, indeed, may be considered outlets of subterraneous watercourses, of greater or lesser size, carrying away water from a higher level, and some of them must be of considerable magnitude. Such is the Kuruman, described by Mr Backhouse, at its source, as "A stream, which would turn a mill, issuing from under sand rocks." It is a clear permanent stream, but one which, unlike most, is largest at its source, and ceases about ten miles to the northwest, disappearing and reappearing at intervals, and at length terminating in a dry water-course, which is only filled in rainy weather. It is thus described by Dr Moffat :—

"It issues from caverns in a little hill, which is composed of blue and grey limestone, mixed with considerable quantities of flint, but not in nodules as found in beds of chalk. From the appearance of the caves, and the irregularity of the strata, one might be led to suppose they have been the results of internal convulsions. The water, which is pure and wholesome, is rather calcareous. It is evident that its source must be at a very great distance, as all the rains which fall on the hills and plains for forty miles round, in one year, could not possibly supply such a stream for one month. Although there are no sandstone formations nearer than thirty miles, great quantities of exceedingly fine sand come from it; it appears to boil up out of the smaller springs in front of the larger, and it is to be found in deposit in the bed of the river for miles distant. The substratum of the whole of the country, as far as the Orange River, is compact limestone, which in some of the Hamhana hills rises considerably above the neighbouring plain; but these only form the basis of argillaceous hills and iron-schist, on the top of which the compass moves at random, or according to the position in which it is placed. The strata of these schistose formations are often found to bend and curve into all shapes, frequently exhibiting an appearance of golden asbestos, but extremely hard. The common blue asbestos is to be found at Gamaperi, in the neighbourhood, the same as that found near the Orange River. The limestone extends to Old Lithako, where there are hills of basalt and primitive limestone; among which masses of serpentine rock of various colours, usually called pipe-stone, are to be met with. Beyond the Batlapi dominions, towards the Molapo, there is abundance of granite, green stone, etc., while the limestone foundation, towards the west, terminates among the sandy wilds of the southern Zahara. Fountains, throughout the whole extent of the limestone basin, are precarious, and independent of causes described in a preceding chapter; nor does that of the Kuruman continue to send forth the torrents it once did."

The mention of limestone, and the mention of its being so abundant and extensively diffused over the district, is in accordance with the supposition that there may be there numerous and extensive lines of caves, and in accordance with the fact of there being there this subterranean river, which only from its issue is called the Kuruman; and the Kuruman is only one of such.

There is, I am informed, a large plateau in the latitude of Delagoa Bay, 26° S., and extending from 28° to 30° E. long., from which the river systems of the Limpopo to the north, and of the Orange River on the south, take their rise. It may be about 7000 feet above the level of the sea. On this plateau, if I have understood my informant correctly, there are what can scarcely be called springs—they surpass so much in magnitude what are generally so designated—but streams, issuing like Minerva from the head of her father, in the full perfection of strength; not springs giving birth to rills and streamlets, spending their infancy and childhood in play amongst the hills, glancing or glinting in the sunshine, tumbling over stones, and playing such like childish freaks,—but streams in all the vigour of early manhood, like that of the Kuruman which has just been described. There are more than thirty such earth-born streams to the north of this plateau, and upwards of twenty to the south, but they do not all die in their bed like the Kuruman, some of them commingling themselves, and unitedly draining the valleys of the Limpopo and Gariep; and besides these there are many of a smaller size.

I am further informed that there are here and there scattered over the plateau hollows with somewhat precipitous sides, it may be 100 feet deep and from 100 to 200 feet across, which may have been formed by a swirl of water drawn off into a subterranean channel when the plateau was a waterbed, or may have been formed by a subsidence of superficial strata roofing a cavern, which I consider more likely to have been the case, but which, in either case, are indicative of subterranean hollows, which might serve as reservoirs or water-courses.

I may not ignore the existence of subterranean cavities of great extent into which water may escape by percolation or by rents in the rock, but I attach not importance to these as by themselves affecting the withdrawal of water from the surface of the land. I look upon them as bearing the same relation to subterranean rivers which lakes do to the rivers which flow through them, and estimate the drainage by the flow at the exit, not by the contents of the reservoir.

Besides these, the numerous hot springs—some of them such as those at Brand Vley near Worcester, at Caledon, at Balmoral near Uitenhage, and elsewhere, of considerable magnitude—and the water found, as it used to be found, by the divining rod [!], all tell of the draining off of water from higher levels by subterranean water-courses.

With so many fountains, hot springs, and subterranean rivers, within the region colonized, it is reasonable to suppose that many more may find an exit under the sea. When coming from a higher level they must flow freely, notwithstanding the depth of water above the orifice, as in the cases cited by Tomassy and by Marsh. Cases of such fresh-water springs under the sea are by no means rare; and not more rare are cases of fountains existing on islands at a higher level than that of the surface of the ocean, and of a greater flow than can be attributed to the percolation of a water from a higher level on the island itself,—leaving room for the supposition that it may have come from some more distant locality, and suggestive of the thought that we know not, and cannot know, the quantity of water which may thus be drawn off from the land.

Thus does it appear that from the higher position to which the land has been elevated over its surface, from it, and under it, water is constantly flowing off to the sea: and the channels thus created so facilitate the flow that apparently all the water that falls upon it—and other source it has none—finds its way, without let, or hindrance, or detention, to the same great reservoir. Does a thunder-storm pass over a district, deluging the district with rain, the water thus precipitated rushes headlong to the sea. Every year do the newspapers record the fact, and no phenomena enter so largely into the subjects of talk and conversation of travellers within and beyond the colony. Some of the water may escape by cracks and rents, but only to find another course to the same resting-place; and if the land be soaked and saturated by the rain, not a little of the water so retained for a time is drained off into some one or other of the water-courses leading to the sea. In view of all this it is that I attribute the desiccation of South Africa, primarily and principally, to its upheaval and elevation above the level of the sea. Thus have the waters which covered it been drained off; and thus have been drained off all the rains which have subsequently fallen upon it.

It would only be a controversy about the propriety of the phraseology employed which would be involved in the discussion, whether the relative position in regard to the elevation of the land and the sea—or the upheaval of the land—or the depression of the ocean-bed—or the cause of these disturbances—or the gravitation which brings the water from the higher to the lower level—should be spoken of as the primary cause of that desiccation: to the relative position in regard to the level of the land, of the bed of the ocean, and to the upheaval of the land as the cause of this, and to the drainage thus occasioned may be attributed, primarily and principally, the desiccation and consequent aridity of South Africa; and thus to the elevation of the land may be traced back the desiccation of the land.

But we meet with yet another class of phenomena connected with the desiccation of South Africa—the drying up of lakes from which there is no apparent outlet, and the drying up of these subsequently to the draining off of the waters to the level of the only outlet seen—the level of which may be somewhat, and in some cases is considerably, above the level of the lowest part of the bed of the lake; and to the cause or occasion of these phenomena we must next inquire.

CHAPTER II.

SECONDARY CAUSES OF THE DESICCATION AND CONSEQUENT ARIDITY OF SOUTH AFRICA.

THE rush of waters, whether from the lakes and inland seas of a former age or from districts on which the thunder-showers now fall, may be attributed to the upheaval of the land, and to this rush of waters may be attributed the fretting away or undermining and fall of barriers by which it was at one time restrained.

The removal of some of these barriers must have occurred long, long ago, and there are indications that the process of upheaval may be still going on, and thus may the rainfall be allowed to be carried off more rapidly, and in increased proportion, to the sea.

And thus the disturbance of level of the elevation of the land may be proved to have been the primary and principal cause or occasion of the desiccation of the land; but it is not the only cause or occasion of this. It does not account for all the phenomena observed. We have had under consideration lakes drying up after the surface of the water had fallen below the level of the outlet, and that expression—drying up—at once describes the fact and indicates the cause. Water exposed to the atmosphere dries up; the greater the heat and the drier the air the more rapid is the process: the water assumes the form of vapour, and it is said to evaporate or to evaporate away;—and to this, as a secondary cause or occasion of desiccation, may be attributed the aridity which prevails.

SECTION I.—*Phenomena of Evaporation, and Modifications of this produced by Atmospheric Moisture and by Shade.*

To such a process of evaporation may be traced all the supply of water brought to man, and bird, and beast, wheresoever in the wide, wide world man, or bird, or beast doth live.

While there are, in round numbers, about fifty millions of square miles of the earth's surface dry land, there are about an hundred and fifty millions of square miles of its surface covered with water. To evaporation from this is attributed the continuous supply of moisture, condensed into clouds, and precipitated as hail, and snow, and rain, and dew, all the world over, and to a portion of what is thus precipitated the formation and supply of all the streamlets, and streams, and rivers, and torrents, which fertilize and beautify, or tear up and destroy, the lands through which they flow. The supposition is not far from the truth, and it is in accordance with what was written by the Hebrew poets: "All the rivers run into the sea; yet the sea is not full: unto the place from which the rivers came, thither they return again. They go up by the mountains; they go down by the valleys, unto the place which Thou hast founded for them. Thou hast set a bound that they may not pass over; that they turn not again to cover the earth," having "placed the sand for a bound of the sea by a perpetual decree that it cannot pass it: and though the waves thereof toss themselves yet can they not prevail; though they war yet can they not pass over it."

The evaporation from such an extent of ocean must be great. From shallow water in warm and temperate regions it is probably proportionately greater. The annual evaporation from the Mediterranean, the Black Sea, and the Sea of Azov, is reckoned at 50 inches of their depth over the whole extent of their surface. This surface being equal to about 1,500,000 square miles, a simple calculation shows that, if the fact be as stated, the quantity of fresh water thus evaporated would measure upwards of 500 cubic miles of water; a corresponding estimate and calculation shows that the annual evaporation from the Red Sea must amount to 165 cubic miles of water. Of the evaporation of moisture from the sea, some idea may be formed from the quantity returned to it daily by rivers throughout the earth. This is calculated by Metcalfe to be 135,000,000,000 cubic metres per day, by Keith Johnston to be 175,000,000,000 cubic metres, by Elesèe Reclus to be 85,000,000,000 cubic metres,—quantities of which it is impossible to form an idea. From lakes situated inland and raised to a higher temperature, under a drier atmosphere, the evaporation may be expected to be greater still; and to this may be attributed the partial drying up of the lake Gnami, and the complete drying up of the salt-pans mentioned by Livingstone and by Chapman, and of others, which have been dried up within the memory of man, and the previous final drying up, at what may be called, in comparison with times which we have had under consideration, comparatively recent times, and of others of which mention has been made in the review which has been given of the hydrographic records presented in the geological phenomena and in the physical geography of the country.

When one breathes upon a cold sheet of polished steel, the condensed vapour seems to remain for a time confounded, knowing not what to do; after this it begins slowly to evaporate, and the process goes on with accelerating rapidity, until at last the dew-drops seem to run or fly as fast as feet or wings will bear them. So seems it to be with the drying up of a lake in a hot and arid atmosphere,—the rapidity of the evaporation increases as the depth and quantity of the water is diminished. With still greater rapidity is moisture evaporated from what is only moistened land. And it can not only be proved by experiment that the drier the atmosphere the more rapid will the evaporation proceed, but it can be shown how it comes to pass that such is the case.

First, In whatever way it be brought about—be it in accordance with the law of gaseous diffusion or through chemical affinity—when the two are in contact moisture is absorbed by the air of the atmosphere up to a point of saturation varying with the temperature; by adhesion, or it may be, by chemical affinity, but more probably the former, moisture is retained by the soil, but up to a certain point, varying with the composition of the soil, the absorbent power of the air is in general more powerful than is the retaining power of the soil; the excess of power of absorption manifested by the air over the power of retention manifested by the soil appears to diminish as the air approaches to saturation; and the statement that the drier the atmosphere the more rapidly will the evaporation proceed is only one which is the converse of this.

Marsh, citing *Der Boden und das Wasser*, by Wilhelm, a work published in Vienna in 1861, and *Het Klimaat van Nederland*, by Krecke, says:—" The relative evaporating action of earth and water is a very complicated problem, and the results of observations on the subject are conflicting. Schuebler found that at Geneva the evaporation from bare loose earth in the months of December, January, and February, was from two and a-half to six times as great as from a like surface of water in the other months. The evaporation from water was from about once and a-half to six times as great as from earth. Taking the whole year together the evaporation from the two surfaces was 199 and 8-12ths lines from the earth, and 536 and 1-12th lines from water. Experiments by Van der Steer, at the Helder, in the years 1861 and 1862, showed for the former year an evaporation of 602·9 millimètres from water, 1399·6 millimètres from ground covered with clover and other grasses; in 1862 the evaporation from water was 584·5 millimètres, from grass ground, 875·5."

"On the other hand," he says, citing *Saggio Idrologica sul Nilo*, by Lombardini, a work published in Milan in 1864, "the evaporation from the Nile in Egypt and Nubia is stated to be three times as great as that from an equal surface of the soil which borders it. The thermometrical conditions of land and water in the same vicinity are constantly varying, and the hydrometrical state of both is equally unstable."

Secondly, The power of absorption is increased with the temperature of the air; the air is raised in temperature by the sun's rays penetrating to the earth; these rays are compound, or produce at least the three correlated phenomena of light, heat, and chemical action; there are substances permiable by some but not by others of these constituent rays; glass of a particular colour is impermiable by the chemical ray, and photographers avail themselves of this to secure, without detriment to their work, the light necessary to manipulate their negative photographs; glass allows free passage to solar but not to reflected heat, hence its use in horticulture; and water allows not a free passage even to radiated heat; in accordance with this a cloud throws back the heat which falls upon it from the sun, lowering the temperature of a hot day wherever its shadow falls; and it throws back the heat radiating from the earth, and raises thus the temperature in a day of intense frost in the same way that a thin veil increases warmth by throwing back the heat radiated from the face which it protects; this it does whether it be in the solid, the liquid, or the gaseous state which it is in the air by which it is absorbed or held in a state of solution. And the more of it is thus held the greater will be the reflection; the less or the drier the air the freer the passage for the solar heat; the drier the atmosphere the greater will be the difference of temperature between day and night, and, it may be, between summer and winter; and the higher temperature of the air during sunshine will increase its power of absorption beyond what will be compensated by the diminished power of absorption during the night,—in this way also bringing to pass that the drier the atmosphere the more rapidly will the evaporation proceed.

But whatever may impede or reflect the rays of heat will, as does the moisture in the way now stated, retard desiccation; and the removal of anything that does so, will promote it—operating negatively.

Experience and observation have shown that desiccation, both of atmosphere and of soil, is impeded and prevented by vegetation. Throughout the whole period embraced by the memory of its inhabitants, and in earlier times, there has been carried on one continuous destruction of grass and herbage by fire, and partly by the hand of man, the effect of which must have been, as in some cases it has been seen to be, to facilitate evaporation, and thus to expedite the process of desiccation; and to this, as the immediate cause, I attribute the degree of aridity which now prevails.

Far more moisture, it may be, is carried off by drainage than by evaporation; and the increase of evaporation, attributable to the removal of vegetation it may be, bears but a small proportion to the evaporation which goes on irrespective of this, but yet the quantity of moisture thus withdrawn from the soil may be absolutely great; and whether it be great or small, seeing that it is this which has crowned or completed the process whereby the desiccation has been carried to the extent that it has been, it deserves, if it do not demand, attention; and when attention is given to it, it may be found that it is no less deserving of attention than are the indications of the former hydrographic condition of the country, and of water having been drained off extensively by the elevation of the land to the altitude it has attained.

That trees have some effect, whatever that effect may be, in attracting, or creating, or retaining moisture, is extensively believed; and therefore would I refer, first, to the great and extensive destruction of trees which has taken place in South Africa, and to the effect which this must have had upon the climate and soil as promoting the desiccation, and so producing the aridity.

The records of the colony of the Cape of Good Hope do not happen to supply evidence that this has been the case. But St. Helena, which, in connection with this discussion, may be considered a South African island, supplies illustrations of effects produced on the climate, both by the destruction of trees and by extensive sylviculture.

From a note appended by Emsman to his German translation of a work on meteorology, in relation to cosmical phenomena by Foissac,* it appears that in the beginning of the sixteenth century the forests of St Helena must have been extensive, for it is stated by him, on the authority of the introductory chapters in Beatson's *St. Helena,* that "it was the goats which destroyed the beautiful forests which, three hundred and fifty years ago, covered a continuous surface of not less than two thousand acres in the interior of the island, not to mention scattered groups of trees.

While I was at the Cape I wrote to St. Helena for information on the subject, and in reply his Excellency, H. R. Janisch, now Governor of the island, at once supplied me with the following information, embodied in notes published in the *Natural History of St. Helena* :—" Viewed from the sea the island offers little or nothing to the eye but an assemblage of lofty and barren hills, intersected in all directions with deep and narrow valleys, in many cases little better than ravines, and generally devoid of vegetation, excepting here and there patches of prickly pear samphire and profitless weeds, the wooded peaks in the interior being in most positions hidden from view by the almost perpendicular cliffs running down to the sea. But when first discovered, in 1502, it was in the valleys almost covered with trees

* *Meteorologie mit Rücksight auf die Lehere vom Kosmos. Deutsch von* A. H. Emsman, Leipzig, 1859.

right down to the water's edge. These trees appear to have been principally gum-wood, ebony, and red-wood." The gum-wood flourished nearest to the sea; the ebony and red-wood covered the slopes of the mountain; while the hill tops appear to have been covered with the cabbage tree and ferns—the former presenting from a little distance the appearance of a singular-looking tree bearing stocks of cabbage, or of broccoli, at the extremeties of its branches. While such was the state of vegetation, it must have been an island well watered everywhere.

But the earlier governors and settlers made sad havoc among the trees; and herds of goats and of swine being allowed to run loose on the land, young growing trees, which might have supplied the waste, were destroyed, and the island became almost denuded. All the ebony trees have long since disappeared; the last, a tree remarkable for its excessive hardness, size, and density, was found on Deadwood. The red-wood is now scarce, and, like the ebony, would altogether have disappeared, had not Governor Byefield caused two young trees to be set at Plantation House, from which two all at present on the island have been propagated. And a comparison of the cabbage trees of the present with the remains of those of the past tell of a stunted growth. What was the consequence of this extensive destruction of trees? "Incidentally we find," says my correspondent, "in the records of the last century, accounts of repeated and almost periodical visitations of very severe drought, occasioning ruinous losses of cattle and crops."

Towards the close of the last century, however, the denudation of the island had been carried so far that wiser governors saw it to be necessary to adopt some strenuous measure to restore the vegetation. Nurseries were made, and experienced gardeners were introduced by the Company, and trees from all parts of the world were introduced and flourished. Prizes were given for the number of trees reared, irrespective of their character. The cluster pine *(pinus pinaster)* was sown very extensively, and several plantations of this tree remain in a thriving condition. But a variety of other forest trees, greatly preferred both for beauty and use, were planted about the same period and have flourished well. Lists have been sent to me of 133 exotic trees and shrubs, and of 39 fruit-bearing plants, now growing on the island. And what have been the results? My correspondent writes:—"For may years past, since the general growth of our trees, we have been preserved from this scourge; and droughts, such as were formerly recorded, are now altogether unknown. We have no means, however, of otherwise comparing the rain-fall of the two periods, as no tables, or even estimates, of the rainfall can be had for the earlier dates. Our fall of rain now is equal to that of England, and is spread almost evenly over the year. The showers fall more heavily in two or three months of the year. But this period, though called on this account the rainy season, is in no way to be compared to what is understood by an inter-tropical rainy season."

Meteorological observations are or were kept at Longwood and at Plantation. I have at command only the record of the rainfall from 1841 to 1848. The amount of rain which fell in these years was:—

1841,	68·925	1845,	19·509
1842,	90·458	1846,	26·556
1843,	37·189	1847,	42·441
1844,	20·026	1848,	45·630

Giving as the mean annual fall 43·813 inches—a rainfall corresponding to that at Wynberg, at the back of Table Mountain.

In illustration of the importance of noting the locality in which such observations may be made, I give the following records of the rain which fell during a period of nine months in the first of these years (1841), at four stations, varying in altitude, but comprehended within a circle of little more than a mile radius :—

        At 414 feet of elevation   7·63 inches.
        At 1782   „   43·42   „
        At 1991   „   27·11   „
        At 2644   „   22·63   „

While proper corrections and eliminations may be necessary to make any series of meterological registers of great value, in the absence of these, general popular observations become of considerable importance. And the observations I have cited may command an attention which a bare record of observations—made by we know not whom, and instruments we know not what—cannot.

The statement furnished by Mr Janisch is not only in accordance with popular opinion, but in accordance with the testimony of others, in regard to what has been observed elsewhere in regard to the rainfall on mountains and forests.

" There is good reason," says Marsh, in his work on *The Earth, as modified by Human Action*, " to believe that the surface of the habitable earth, in all the climates and regions which have been the abodes of dense and civilized populations, was, with few exceptions, already covered with a forest growth when it first became the home of man. This we infer from the extensive vegetable remains—trunks, branches, roots, fruits, and leaves of trees—so often found in conjunction with works of primitive art, in the boggy soil of districts where no forests appear to have existed within the eras through which written annals reach ; from ancient historical records, which prove that large provinces where the earth has long been wholly bare of trees were clothed with vast and almost unbroken woods when first made known to Greek and Roman civilization ; and from the state of much of North and South America, as well as of many islands, when they were discovered and colonized by the European race."

In a foot-note he says—" The recorded evidence in support of the supposition in the text has been collected by L. F. Alfred Maury, in his *Histoire des grandes Forêts de la Gaule et de l'Ancienne France;* and by Becquerel, in his important work, *Des Climats et de l'Influence qu' exercent les Sols boisés et non-boisés.* Liv. II., C. I–IV." And he goes on to say— " We may rank among historical evidences on this point, if not technically among historical records, old geographical names and terminations etymologically indicating forest or grove, which are too common in many parts of the eastern continent now entirely stripped of woods,—such as in Southern Europe, Breuil, Broglio, Brolio, Brolo ; in Northern, Brueil, and the endings, dean, den, don, ham, holt, herst, hurst, lund, skaw, shot, skog, skov, wald, weald, wold, wood. The island of Madeira, whose noble forests were devastated by fire not long after its colonization by European settlers, takes its name from the Portuguese word for wood."

The name given originally to the island by the Portuguese was Materia, in allusion to the apparently inexhaustible materials it supplied for shipbuilding and for the construction of houses.

And in another foot-note, appended to a statement that the surface of

Palestine is composed in a great measure of rounded limestone hills, which were once, no doubt, covered with forests which were partially removed before the Jewish conquest, Marsh remarks,—"'Forests,' 'woods,' and 'groves,' are frequently mentioned in the Old Testament as existing at particular places, and they are often referred to, by way of illustration, as familiar objects. 'Wood' is twice spoken of as a material in the New Testament, but otherwise—at least according to Cruden—not one of the above words occur in that volume. In like manner, while the box, the cedar, the fir, the oak, the pine, 'beams,' and 'timber,' are very frequently mentioned in the Old Testament, not one of these words are found in the New, *except* the case of the 'beam in the eye,' in the parable in Matthew and Luke.

"This interesting fact, were other evidence wanting, would go far to prove that a great change had taken place, in this respect, between the periods when the Old Testament and the New were respectively composed; for the Scriptural writers, and speakers introduced into their narratives, are remarkable for their frequent allusions to the natural objects, and the social and industrial habits, which characterized their ages and their country."

And following up the statement in the text, he says,—"These evidences are strengthened by observation of the natural economy of our own time; for whenever a tract of country, once inhabited and cultivated by man, is abandoned by him and domestic animals, and surrendered to the undisturbed influences of spontaneous nature, its soil sooner or later clothes itself with herbaceous and arborescent plants, and at no long interval with a dense forest growth. Indeed, upon surfaces of a certain stability, and not absolutely precipitous inclination, the special conditions required for the spontaneous propagation of trees may all be negatively expressed, and reduced to these three:—exemption from defect or excess of moisture, from perpetual frost, and from the depredations of men and browzing quadrupeds. When these requisites are secured, the hardest rock is as certain to be over-grown with wood as the most fertile plain, though for drier seasons the process is slower in the former than in the latter case. Lichens and mosses first prepare the way for a more highly organized vegetation. They retain the moisture of rains and dews, and bring it to act, in combination with the gases evolved by their organic processes, in decomposing the surface of the rock they cover; they arrest and confine the dust which the wind scatters over them, and their final decay adds new material to the soil already half-formed beneath and upon them. A very thin stratum of mould is sufficient for the germination of seeds of the hardy evergreens and the birches, the roots of which are often found in immediate contact with the rock, supplying their trees with nourishment from a soil deepened and enriched from the decomposition of their foliage, or sending out long rootlets into the surrounding earth in search of juices to feed them."

But with all the provisions which have been made for the production of forests, and for the restoration of small portions which have been destroyed, it is possible for man to counteract these; and he has done so. But what have been some of the consequences which have followed?

According to a summary of some of these given by Marsh,—"With the extirpation of the forest all is changed. At one season the earth parts with its warmth by radiation to an open sky; receives, at another, an immoderate heat from the unobstructed rays of the sun. Hence the climate becomes excessive, and the soil is alternately parched by the fervours of summer, and seared by the rigours of winter. Bleak winds sweep unresisted over its suface, drift away the snow that sheltered it from the frost, and dry up its scanty moisture. The precipitation becomes as irregular as the temperature; the melting snows and varied rains, no longer absorbed by a loose and bibular vegetable mould, rush over the frozen surface, and pour down the valleys seawards, instead of filling a retentive bed of absorbent earth, and storing up a supply of moisture to feed perennial springs. The soil is bared of its covering of leaves, broken and loosened by the plough, deprived of the fibrous rootlets which held it together, dried and pulverized by sun and wind, and at last exhausted by new combinations. The face of the earth is no longer a sponge, but a dust heap; and the floods which the waters of the sky poured over it hurry swiftly along its slopes, carrying in suspension vast quantities of earthy particles, which increase the abrading power and mechanical force of the current, and, augmented by the sand and gravel of falling banks, fill the beds of the streams, divert them into new channels, and obstruct their outlets. The rivulets, wanting their former regularity of supply, and deprived of the protecting shade of the woods, are heated, evaporated, and thus reduced in their former currents,—but swollen to raging torrents in autumn and in spring.

"From these causes there is a constant degradation of uplands, and a consequent elevation of the beds of water-courses, and of lakes, by the deposition of the mineral and vegetable matter carried down by the waters. The channels of great rivers become unnavigable, their estuaries are choked up, and harbours which once sheltered large navies are shoaled by dangerous sand-bars.

"The earth stript of its vegetable glebe grows less and less productive, and consequently less able to protect itself by weaving a new net-work of roots to bind its particles together, a new carpeting of turf to shield it from wind and sun and scouring rain. Gradually it becomes altogether barren. The washing of the soil from the mountains leave bare ridges of sterile rock, and the rich organic mould which covered them, now swept down into the dark low grounds, promotes a luxuriance of aquatic vegetation that breeds fever and more insidious forms of mortal disease by its decay, and thus the earth is rendered no longer fit for the habitation of man."

In accordance with these views are the views of all the students of Forest Science whom I know to have given attention to the subject. "Almost everywhere," says Schleiden, Professor of Botany in the University of Jena, "in the great characters in which nature writes her chronicles, in fossilized woods, layers of peat, and the like, or even in the little notes of men, for instance in the records of the Old Testament, occur proof, or at least indications, that those countries which are now treeless and arid deserts, part of Egypt, Syria, Persia, and so forth, were formerly thickly wooded, traversed by streams now dried up or shrunk within narrow bounds; while now the burning glow of the sun, and particularly the want of water, allow but a sparse population. In contrast must not a jovial toper laugh indeed, who looks from Johannisberg out over the Rhine country, and drinks a health in Rüdesheimer to the noblest of the German rivers, if he recall the statement of Tacitus, that not even a cherry, much less a grape, would ripen on the Rhine! And if we ask the cause of this mighty change, we are directed to the disappearance of the forests. With the careless destruction of the growth of trees, man interferes to alter greatly the natural conditions of the country. We can indeed now raise one of the finest vines upon the Rhine, where two thousand years ago no cherry ripened; but on the other hand, those lands where the dense population of the Jews was nourished by a fruitful culture are in the present day half deserts. The cultivation of clover, requiring a moist atmosphere, has passed from Greece to Italy, from thence to Southern Germany, and already is beginning to fly from the continually drier summers there to be confined to the moister north. Rivers which formerly scattered their blessings with equal fulness throughout the whole year, now leave the dry and thirsty bed to split and gape in summer, while in spring they suddenly pour out the masses of snow, accumulated in winter, over the dwelling-places of affrighted men. If the continued clearing and destruction of forests is at first followed by greater warmth, more southern climate, and more luxuriant thriving of the more delicate plants, yet it draws close behind this desirable condition another which restrains the habitability of a region within as narrow, and perhaps even narrower, limits than before. In Egypt, no Pythagoras need now forbid his scholars to live upon the beans; long has that land been incapable of producing them. The wine of Mendes and Mareotis, which inspired the guests of Cleopatra,—which was celebrated even by Horace,— it grows no more. No assassin now finds the holy pine-grove of Poseidon, in which to hide and lie in ambush for the singers hastening to the feast. The pine has long since retired from the invading desert climate to the heights of the Arcadian Mountains. Where are the pastures now, where are the fields around the holy citadel of Dardanus, which at the foot of the richly-watered Ida supported three thousand mares? Who can talk now of the 'Xanthus,' with its hurrying waters? Who would understand now the 'Argos feeder of horses?'"

And so has it been elsewhere. It is said in Barbadoes and Jamaica the felling of forests has been attended by a diminution of rain.

The effect of the destruction of forests upon the climate has been questioned, but these facts remain. And so has it been seen again and again in the history of the nations. The term *savage*, from its etymological derivation, speaks of a sylvan life; and from the sylvan or savage life to that of the civilized or city life, the progress of man may be traced, to some extent, by the destruction of forests. The one has, until attention was given to consequences which have followed the destruction of forests, been the accompaniment or complement of the other, operating sometimes as a cause, manifesting itself sometimes as a consequence —if both be not con-sequences of a common cause. But it is possible that the destruction of forests may be carried too far. According to the testimony of Dr Hooker, cited in the preface, "In the estimation of an average Briton forests are of infinitely less importance than the game they shelter, and it is not long since the wanton destruction of a fine young tree was considered a venial offence compared with the snaring of a pheasant or rabbit. Wherever the English rule extends, with the single exception of India, the same apathy or inaction prevails. . . . In Demerara the useful timber trees have all been removed from accessible regions, and no care or thought of planting others; from Trinidad we have the same story; in New Zealand there is not now a good Kauri pine to be found near the coast; and I believe that the annals of almost every English colony would repeat the tale of wanton waste and improvidence."

In view of this waste, Schleiden, to whom I have already referred, writes, if not in the words, yet following the train of thought of one of the noblest veterans of our science, the venerable Elias Fries, of Lund : " A broad band of waste land follows gradually in the steps of cultivation. If it expands, its centre and cradle dies, and on the outer borders only do we find green shoots. But it is not impossible, it is only difficult, for man, without renouncing the advantage of culture itself, one day to make reparation for the injury which he has inflicted, he is appointed lord of creation. True it is that thorns and thistles, ill-favoured and poisonous plants, well named by botanists, 'rubbish plants,' mark the track which man has proudly traversed through the earth. Before him lay original nature in her wild but sublime beauty. Behind him he leaves the desert, a deformed and ruined land; for childish desire of destruction, or thoughtless squandering of vegetable treasures, have destroyed the character of nature; and man himself flies terrified from the arena of his actions, leaving the impoverished earth to barbarous races or animals, so long as yet another spot in virgin beauty smiles before him. Here again, in selfish pursuit of profit, consciously or unconsciously, he begins anew the work of destruction. Thus did cultivation, driven out, leave the East, and the deserts perhaps previously robbed of their coverings; like the wild hordes of old over beautiful Greece, thus rolls this conquest with fearful rapidity from east to west through America, and the planter often now leaves the already exhausted land, the eastern climate become infertile through the demolition of the forests, to introduce a similar revolution into the far west. But we see, too, that the nobler races, or truly cultivated men, even now raise their warning voices, put their small hand to the mighty work of restoring to nature her strength and fulness in yet a higher stage than that of wild nature; one dependent on the law of purpose given by man, arranged according to plans which are copied from the development of manhood itself. All this, indeed, remains at present but a powerless, and for the whole, an insignificantly small enterprise, but it preserves the faith in the vocation of man and his power to fulfil it. In future times he will and must, when he rules, leads, and protects the whole, free nature from the tyrannous slavery to which he now abases her, and in which he can only keep her by restless giant struggles against the eternally resisting. We see in the gray cloudy distance of the future a realm of peace and beauty on the earth and in nature, but to reach it must man long study in the school of nature, and, *before all*, free himself from the bonds of that exclusive selfishness by which he is actuated."

SECTION II.—*Denudation of South Africa by the destruction of Herbage and Trees.*

The destruction of forests in South Africa has been extensive. Ever since the discovery of Natal by Vasco de Gama in 1495, South Africa has justified the designation which he gave it of *Terra de fume*. The extensive burning of bush, herbage, and grass, the smoke of which procured for it that designation, has been continued by the native tribes, and by the European colonists; and thus have many trees been destroyed.

Dr Casilis, Secretary of the Paris Missionary Society, who was long resident at the Cape, in a work entitled "The Basutos, or Twenty-three years in South Africa," says, "The grass reaches such a height that it is necessary to destroy it every winter by means of fire; and it is perhaps to these annual conflagrations that we must ascribe the remarkable scarcity of trees. These are hardly ever to be found except on the banks of rivers, and in high mountain passes."

This conjecture of Dr Casilis is to some extent verified by an observation of Dr Livingstone, and his reasoning thereon. On one of his earlier expeditions he left at one place, suspended from a tree, the boat in which a part of the journey had been made, and which would be required again on the return of his party; but long ere their return it was consumed—burned! The natives in the vicinity of the locality were very desirous of persuading him that this had been the work of a hostile tribe; "but," says he, "on scanning the spot, we saw that it was more likely to have caught fire in the grass-burning of the country. Had we intended being so long in returning to it, we should have hoisted it bottom upwards; for, as it was, it is probable that a quantity of dry leaves lay in the inside, and a spark ignited the whole. All the trees within fifty yards were scorched and killed, and the nails, iron and copper sheathing, all lay undisturbed beneath. Had the Ajaiva done the deed, they would have taken away the copper and iron."

The reasoning is satisfactory; and we note the fact observed: "All the trees within fifty yards were scorched and killed."

To this conjecture and observation of Dr Livingstone, may be added the testimony of his father-in-law, Dr Moffat, who says explicitly "the natives have the yearly custom of burning the dry grass, which on some occasions destroys shrubs and trees even on the very summit of the mountains;" and he speaks, as of an unquestioned and unquestionable fact, of " the accidental destruction of whole plains of the *Olea similis* (wild olive), by fire near Griqua town," and of a gradual decrease of rain which succeeded in that region. But he also adverts to the destruction of forests by native tribes, effected otherwise than by fire. He relates that on his settlement at Latakoo "the natives were wont to tell of the floods of ancient times, the incessant showers which clothed the very rocks with verdure, and the giant trees and forests which once studded the brows of the Hamhana hills and neighbouring plains. They boasted of the Kuruman and other rivers, with their impassable torrents, in which the hippopotami played, while the lowing herds walked to their necks in grass, filling their *makukas* (milk sacks) with milk, making every heart to sing for joy." And he mentions that "independent of this fact being handed down by their forefathers, they had before their eyes the fragments of more fruitful years in the immense number of stumps and roots of enormous trunks of *Acacia giraffaea*, where now scarcely one is to be seen raising its stately head above the shrubs; while the sloping sides of hills and the ancient beds of rivers plainly evinced that they were denuded of the herbage which once clothed their surface. Indeed, the whole country north of the Orange river lying east of the Kalagari desert presented to the eye of a European something like an old neglected garden or field." He found no difficulty in accounting for this. "The Bechuanas, especially the Batlapis, and the neighbouring tribes," says he, "are a nation of levellers; not reducing hills to comparative plains, for the sake of building their towns, but cutting down every species of timber without regard to scenery or economy. Houses are chiefly composed of small timber, and their fences of branches and shrubs. Thus, when they fix on a site for a town, their first consideration is to be as near a thicket as possible. The whole is presently levelled, leaving only a few trees, one in each great man's fold, to afford shelter from the heat, and under which the men work and recline.

" The ground to be occupied for cultivation is the next object of attention. The large trees being too hard for their iron axes, they burn them down by keeping up a fire at the root. These supply them with branches for fences, while the sparrows, so destructive to their grain, are thus deprived of an asylum. These fences, as well as those in towns, require constant repairs, and indeed the former must be renewed every year; and by this means the country for many miles round becomes entirely cleared of timber; while in the more sequestered spots, where they have their outposts, the same work of destruction goes on. Thus, of whole forests, where the giraffe and elephant were wont to seek their daily food, nothing remains.

" When the natives remove from that district, which may be after only a few years, the minor species of the acacia soon grows, but the *Acacia giraffaea* requires an age to become a tree, and many ages must pass before they attain the dimensions of their predecessors. In the course of my journeys I have met with trunks of enormous size, which, if the time were calculated necessary for their growth, as well as their decay, one may be led to conclude that they sprung up immediately after the flood, if not before it."

Much of the information I possess in regard to forests and trees to the north of the Kuruman was derived from the late Mr Chapman. By him I was informed that around the mountains of Shoshong—the residence of Sekomé—which he passed in travelling from the Trans-Vaal State to the Victoria Falls, the most conspicuous product of the soil is the Kameel-Doorn or *Acacia giraffaea*.

At a distance of twenty or thirty miles from Shoshong the forests of this tree are dense, but within that distance so many have been cut down for use as fuel and for other purposes, and to remove shade from their gardens or cultivated ground, that there it is chiefly stumps that are seen.

He gave as the report of the natives, that the land around the village was formerly very prolific, but now rarely yields a good crop above once in five or six years; and that the rain seemed to fall all around, but to leave this locality dry.

I have learned much in regard to this district from the missionary resident at Shoshong, the Rev. John Mackenzie, of the London Missionary Society, who has given a story of every-day life and work among the South African tribes in his work entitled " Ten Years North of the Orange River." He alleges that the complaints of the natives in regard to the rain, and in regard to their crops, may be attributable in some measure to a disposition to grumble, which they share in common with others. But nothing learned from him, or from Dr Gustavus Fritsch, who penetrated thus far in the prosecution of ethnological and zoological researches, and from whom I learned much, affected the statement of Mr Chapman, regarding the existing evidence of the destruction of trees.

While the tribes of Bechuanas may have been influenced only by such motives as have been indicated in their destruction of trees, Kaffirs on the east coast, I have been informed by Mr White, who was for a very long time resident on the St. John's river (the Oomzimvooboo), maintain, and do so probably with reason, that the soil on which trees have grown is the best land for their gardens, and, therefore, every bush and tree disappears from around their place of residence. In illustration of the progress of destruction, he stated that there were numerous extensive patches of bush, and some of trees, in existence when he went to Natal in 1850, which, when I saw him in 1865, had entirely disappeared, and from the Oomtamfoona to

x

the Ibisi, scarcely a patch of bush was to be seen from the road to Maritzburg from the Oomzimvooboo.

This work of destruction has been going on for we know not how long. In an article having the initials of the late Mr Smith, who was overseer of the Government plantations on the white sands of the Cape Flats, which appeared in the "Cape Monthly Magazine" for June 1851, the writer says,—"Some years ago, I heard there was a tradition among the elder Hottentots, that the whole of this valley (the valley of the river Zonder-ende) was once covered with large timber trees, and that it was laid waste with fire during the wars of the early colonists with the natives. On examining the river banks for some miles, the truth of this tale became apparent, as I found numbers of large stumps and roots protruding from the banks where the current of the river had washed away portions of the soil, and laid them bare. A close inspection of many of them showed them to have been charred with fire. Those which I examined were principally Yellow Wood [*Podocarpus*], and Assegay [*Curtisia*], with some others I could not identify. Many of them when growing must have been magnificent specimens. One piece of a trunk measured 16 feet in length, with a circumference of 5 feet. The whole of one side was charred its entire length, but the remainder was perfectly sound, and of a beautiful red colour. The fires which occasioned this havoc must have happened far beyond the memory of any man now living—unless a landslip occurred in that neighbourhood—as a layer of clay, and several feet of alluvial soil now cover the stumps of the trees just mentioned; but as they are all evergreens, it might have been expected that the roots would send up abundance of young shoots to supply the place of the destroyed stems, and we may be sure that such did take place. At the same time, an abundance of rank grass and bushes would spring up, and the first 'grass-fire' that occurred in the vicinity would undoubtedly destroy the whole of the young plants. I can state this confidently, having seen a native forest of the same trees, and in this state, cut up three times in ten years by these 'grass-fires.'

"How long, under such circumstances, the roots will continue to send up shoots I cannot say. There can be no doubt that ultimately they must become exhausted, and cease to make further efforts, and, of course, to exist. In this latter case of the destroyed forest, there was evidence of the loss of the greater part of a spring of fine water, as a little further down the valley there is a large enclosed, but at present neglected, piece of ground, which, from numerous marks of old water-courses, had once been irrigated; and the present stream would not supply one-tenth of the enclosure."

It has been suggested that possibly the stumps seen by Mr Smith may have come from the Kloofs of the Zonder-ende mountains. I have not the means of determining this point; but even if it were so, evidence is thus obtained of the former growth of trees now destroyed.

I have not the means of determining the period at which these trees must have been destroyed; but, apparently, the further back we go, the more we find indications of the former existence of trees where now no trees are to be found. From the journal of Mrs M. E. Barber, extracts from which appeared in the "Cape Magazine" for 1871, we learn that the diggings in the diamond-fields have brought to light numerous flint arrow-heads and other stone implements, which indicate the former existence of a people in that district anterior to its being taken possession of by the

Kaffirs and the Bechuanas from the north, which may be said to be an event of yesterday, the traditional narrative being still preserved by the tribes; and, says Mrs Barber, who is a naturalist well known and highly esteemed at the Cape, and who is not likely to be rash in the assertion, "many circular incrustations of tufa lime which once enveloped the roots of trees, but are now filled with red soil, are scattered through the claims, in the Colesberg Kop." Such is the evidence we obtain when we go back to pre-historic times. Let us return to the present.

The South African practice of burning the rank herbage has been adopted by the European colonists. Extensive districts, once covered with grass, are now covered with the useless Rhinoster bush *(Elytropappus Rhinocerotis*, Less.), the down surmounted seeds of which, borne by the wind, had found an appropriate soil cleared for them by the fire; and, apparently, thus have plains been cleared of trees. The well-defined outlines of forests on their lower range speak not of forests spreading from the summit of the Kloof to the plain, but of forests driven to the Kloofs for shelter, and there making a stand for life; and even in these, their fastnesses, the work of destruction has been continued. In forest districts, I have been told of encroachments made on the forests thus :—the veldt has been burned, the flames have come up to the verge of the forest, and then been stopped, but not until they had scorched and killed a narrow strip or belt of brushwood and trees. The veldt was burned in the following season, and the brushwood and trees, previously scorched and killed, fell victims to the flames, and in burning scorched and killed a broader belt, which in a subsequent year met with a similar fate, with similar effects. And I have seen mountain sides now naked and bare, which some years ago were covered with trees, all of which had been destroyed by fire.

In the vicinity of Wynberg, some ten miles from Cape Town, are constantly to be seen extensive patches of Silver trees *(Leucodendron argenteum)*, and still more extensive plateaux studded thick with Sugar bush *(Protea mellifera)*, Kreupelboom *(Protea Conocarpum)*, and other arborescent shrubs, burned and blackened, killed by fire. Long before any one patch has recovered itself another is laid bare; and, times more frequent than I can now number, I have seen the mountains bright with a zone of fire, burning up herbage and bush, and imperilling plantations of considerable extent. I was told by a gentleman in the neighbourhood of Wynberg that on the abolition of slavery he anticipated a difficulty in obtaining the labour necessary to keep in cultivation extensive vineyards which were in his possession. He determined, therefore, to abandon the cultivation of the vine over a large portion of his property, and to plant that portion with the seeds of the Stone pine *(Pinus Pinea)*. The expense was trifling. Three muids, or nine bushels of seed, were sown by fourteen men in three days. Within fifteen years he had a revenue of about £300 per annum from the sale of spars, &c. But unhappily, through a neighbour burning the bush, the fire extended to his plantation, and reduced it to ashes; at that time the value of it was estimated at £10,000.

On the face of Table mountain are extensive plantations of the Cluster pine *(Pinus Pinaster)*: for years might be seen from Cape Town and from Table Bay a far-reaching broad belt of blackened trees killed by fire; and everywhere throughout the colony are the Crown forests subjected to a wasteful treatment, under which they are here and there gradually disappearing. The revenue is diminishing year by year. When I was in the colony, in the Zuurberg forest this had fallen short of the expense of conservation by an annual deficit of upwards of £100, and there was a corresponding deficit in the revenues derived from Olifants Hook, and of the Klein and Van Staden's rivers; and from some forests, such as the Cedar-tree forests of Clanwilliam, and others in the eastern province, no revenue whatever appears to be received.

In regard to the Cedarberg forests, Dr Pappe, in his " Silva Capensis," writes:—"Sir James Alexander in his exploring expedition into the interior of Africa (vol. i. p. 230 sqq.), in making mention of the Cedar tree, remarks that one of them was cut down in 1836 which was 36 feet in girth, and out of whose giant arms 1,000 feet of planking were sawn." He bitterly complains that this noble tree is fast disappearing in the Cedar mountains. Mr W. von Meyer (in *Reisen en Sud-Africa während der Jahre*, 1840 und 1841," Hamburg 1843, p. 131) says that "in former days the whole of the mountainous chain to which the Cedar mountains belong was studded with those trees; that of late the *axe* and *conflagrations* have done their utmost to destroy the valuable forests."

Under a system of forest management which, borrowing a term employed in works on forest science in France, I may call primitive *Jardinage*, the forests in the colony have been long gradually disappearing. The system followed was to cut down trees such as may be required, leaving others standing, but doing nothing to promote their growth or to replace those which are removed.

I have before me a chart of the forests of the Tzizi Kamma. From information supplied to me by Captain Harrison, the Conservator of forests in the district, I have gathered the following particulars, which I give, as illustrative of what I may call the first stage of the work of destruction under the treatment which I have called primitive jardinage.

On the west bank of Storm River, there is—or was at that time—a piece of what may be described as virgin forest, in which operations were begun about ten years ago. On the east bank of that river is a patch of scrub destitute of timber.

Below this is a large piece of ground in two divisions, which is mostly private property, and in which the Crown property had been denuded of timber previous to Captain Harrison entering on his duties as Conservator of forests in the district.

Continuous with this, and at the mouth of the river, is a patch in which wood-cutting has been actively carried on for years, and in which timber is consequently becoming scarcer, but Wagon-wood is still plentiful.

A little to the east of this is a patch which still contains some very large Yellow-wood trees; and half-way between this and the mouth of the Faure River, which is still further to the east, is a large patch from which an immense quantity of timber has been cut out of late years, and in which the work is now going on daily.

In the upper district of the Faure River, skirting its east bank, is a patch, the timber of which has been nearly exhausted, but in which there are an immense number of young trees. And half-way towards its mouth is a patch which has been nearly destroyed by fire. It is a patch of Kuerboom —*Virgillia capensis;* and there is valuable timber in it.

A small patch skirted by the Kruis River on the east, has a few Yellow-woods close to the river; but the other timber has been cut out.

To the north of this, near the source of a tributary of the Kruis River, is a larger patch, from which the timber has been cut out, but in which a few young trees are growing up.

Below the confluence of this tributary of the Kruis River, traversed by another shorter tributary stream, is a patch in which Stink-wood is becoming scarce, but in which Yellow-wood and Wagon-wood are plentiful.

Continuous with this, lying in the fork formed by the confluence of the Kruis and Eland's River, is a patch which was formerly private property, but which is now the property of the Crown, and which contains valuable timber at its lower extremity. Near the confluence of the rivers continuous with this, but on the eastern bank of the Eland's River, and extending towards its source, is a patch of valuable timber of all kinds, but the trees are growing in deep kloofs. Below this, and continuous with it to the banks of the Stinkwood River, and the confluence of this and the Eland's River, is a large portion of the same patch, containing valuable timber of all sorts, of more easy access. And continuous with this, on the eastern bank of the Stinkwood River, is Robbe Hoek, in which is sound, valuable timber, but it is difficult of access, in consequence of its growing in deep kloofs. In this patch Wagon-wood is plentiful.

Above this are three small patches in which no valuable timber has been left uncut, but in which a few young trees are growing up. Still higher, skirted on the east by the Witte-els River, and traversed in part by the upper bed of the Stinkwood River, is the Witte-els Bush, near to which is the residence of the conservator. It abounds in Witte-els and contains good Wagon-wood, but the Stink-wood and Yellow-woods have been nearly cut out.

On the south or seaward side of the Eerste River, where it follows a course parallel with the Eland, is a large portion of an extensive patch traversed by that river, in which there is plenty of Wagon-wood and some very large Yellow-wood trees, but little Stink-wood has been left in it.

On the north bank of this river and on the same side of the river, where it takes a southerly course, are three patches, from which all old timber has been cut, excepting such as is not generally used, and these patches are now closed to allow young timber to grow.

Such is the first stage of the work of destruction under the treatment which I have designated primitive jardinage, here arrested, it is to be hoped, by the judicious measures adopted by Captain Harrison. But the progress of the work can be traced a little further in an adjoining district in regard to one Crown forest, in which the forest warder wrote to me some time since : "I would suggest that Government should, without delay, get this portion surveyed, as ——— and ——— are appropriating the forest to themselves. No licences are exhibited, and to my knowledge, as much as £750 worth of timber has been removed within the last ten years, while for the cutting of timber out of the said forest I have only issued two licences [each for the removal of a single load.] The same amount of value in timber has been destroyed, through the reckless behaviour of these individuals, and those in their employment, igniting the grass, which has caused fearful destruction. There are a few other small patches and stripes of bush; but comparatively speaking, they are nothing, only adapted for fuel; most of the valuable timber has been removed, and by fire greatly destroyed. The great evils are men cutting without licences, and grass fires.

" To my knowledge, there is on an average 40 loads of *fuel, poles,* and *spars* removed weekly to Port Elizabeth from the forests between the Gamptoos and the Van Staden Rivers, for cutting timber in which I have never issued one licence for the benefit of Government. I feel convinced that it all comes from the Crown forest; but as it is a case of disputed boundary and licences, I am not empowered to move in the matter. If this state of things continues much longer, the whole of the forest will be eradicated and destroyed."

Such an issue as is thus indicated may be considered the second stage of the destruction of forests under primitive jardinage, the conversion of forests into *bush*. In Krakakamma, between the Zitzikamma and Port Elizabeth, there is a good deal of arborescent vegetation, but it can scarcely be reckoned forest; the same may be said of the Kadouw Bush, between Port Elizabeth and Grahamstown; and such, I am informed, is the present condition of what within the last thirty years was an extensive forest in the valley of the Kowie, in the neighbourhood of Bathurst: the old timber having been destroyed, but not replaced, the forest character has been lost.

But this second stage of the progress of the work of destruction is not unfrequently succeeded by a third, in which even the arborescent bush may disappear. From more than one of my correspondents I have heard of the mountainous country around Somerset having abounded in forest trees of various kinds—Yellow-wood *(Podocarpus)*, Iron-wood *(Olea)*, Assegai-wood *(Curtisia)*, but of these fast disappearing. Mr Leonard, of Somerset, in reply to a query issued from the Colonial Office in 1864, having remarked that the Yellow-wood tree forms a much less conspicuous element in the scenery than his memory pictured it doing some four-and-twenty years before, goes on to say,—" Of other forest trees there used to be an abundant supply in the forest that skirts our mountain here, but the large demand that rules in an age of bullock waggons for disselbooms and other waggon wood, is sure to clear out any but an inexhaustible supply of Assegai and Iron-wood trees, while the durability possessed by the olive post soon marked it out for the woodman's axe, in procuring timber for the ever memorable Hartebest house of the first pioneers; and subsequently the same durability in the nature of the wood caused the continuous destruction of the tree for fencing stakes, when advancing civilization demanded and gave way to buildings of brick and stone.

"Yellow-wood trees of any size, as well as Assegai, Olive, and Iron-wood trees are now becoming so scarce here that we may easily predict the speedy extirpation of them from amongst our natural productions; and, unless human care and culture produce specimens, when those of the kloof and the rivulet have disappeared, the next generation will have to refer to some botanical collection to see what they are like."

About the same time the late Rev. J. W. Pears, the minister of the Dutch Reformed Church at Somerset, previously professor in the South African College, Capetown, writing to myself on another subject, says :—" When I came to the frontier 38 years ago, there was grass everywhere in abundance, in the plains sweet, and in the mountains sour; and this, sometimes five or six feet high; now none, excepting near rivers or on the tops of mountains, is to be found. Formerly, also, the mountains were unoccupied, as no one chose to pay for them; the herbage was abundant; and the moisture was long detained, so that all the little streams continued to flow through the whole year. Now these mountains are all occupied, and generally burned annually, and the consequence is that the water has failed. For instance, the mountain behind my house, which rises to the height of 1,756 feet, was covered with high grass and thousands of beautiful bulbous flowering plants and shrubs, and its whole face and offshoots adorned with Yellow-wood or other valuable trees; now these are all gone; not a Yellow-wood or other tree worth anything left, and only a useless growth-of bushes occupy their place, and the consequence is that a stream that supplied my garden and some others, runs now only after rain. The whole face of the mountain, if planted with oaks, firs, and other useful timbers, might not only be valuable, but again it might protect the water. But almost every year, by the idle and reckless, the mountain is fired, and all is destroyed. It is now burning fiercely. In the kloofs there still stands the charred stumps of large Yellow-wood trees."

Such appear to be the only remains of the forests once flourishing in the neighbourhood of Somerset.

This may be considered as a third stage of the destruction of forests—the final—in which they entirely disappear. And to this those spoken of as being destroyed in the vicinity of the Gamptoos River are likely soon to come. I am informed that "the whole of the Crown Forest Reserve and vacant land in the ward of Van Staden's River, which comprises also the Field Cornetzy and ward of Eland's River, is to be disposed of on a twenty-one years' lease; other portions, not of great extent and value, are to be annexed to the properties adjoining them; and the office of Forest Ranger is to be abolished."

I have said that I have seen in the colony mountain-sides now naked and bare, which some years ago were covered with trees, which have been destroyed by fire; and that what I have stated has been confirmed by many of my correspondents.

The Honourable Mr Barrington, of Portland, New Belvidere, on the Knysna, besides confirming what I have stated in regard to encroachments having been made on the forests, wrote that what I had seen of mountain sides entirely stript of trees with which they were covered a few years before, I might also have seen in the neighbouring district of George. Another of my correspondents in the same district, writing to me of the destructing of the forest, says,—" One way in which the forests are greatly encroached upon and damaged is by burning them, which in spite of the Forest and Herbage Act cannot be prevented. Large tracts of land are for a time left untilled, until in the course of a few years quantities of rank grass, herbage, and underwood, have grown up in thick masses and partially decayed; then in a dry season, and generally when a northerly wind, or as it is here called a berg wind, is blowing, it gets ignited, and it sweeps off thousands of acres, including large patches of forest which otherwise would not have burned."

About the same time the late Mr Pullen, Ranger of the Crown Forests at Van Staden's River, wrote to me,—" There are many who burn the pasturage at an untimely season, for example, in the month of January when the bush leaves are dry; at such a time the least spark sets the forest in flames, and the veldt is adjacent to the bush leaves. A vagrant, it may be, in quest of game, or of honey, to clear a passage through the thick-set grass and dense bush makes use of his tinder-box; the result may be anticipated; the fire spreads and cannot be subdued and extinguished; consequently great tracts of forests are destroyed. The intense heat proves also pernicious to the tender plants at a distance where the fire never arrives; and, moreover, the bush-worker's oxen suffer materially thereby, and frequently die from the poisonous herbage which makes its appearance subsequent to the burning of the grass country.

"I attribute the calamitous drought that has been our visitation of recent years in a great measure to our unfenced forests being so denuded, for it is a notorious fact that the forests attract rain, and I am justified in affirming that there is not so much wood felled in ten years as I have seen destroyed and scorched in ten minutes by one single fire. I have had ocular demonstration of the facts, so I do not go by information, but by what I have experienced of that which is to me an eye-sore."

Within little more than a year after Mr Pullen had written this, viz., on December 13, 1865, a terrific fire in the forests of that district gave sad illustration of the fact that such forests are thus destroyed. Of the effects of this fire seen at a distance of upwards of one hundred miles the *Somerset Courant* gives the following account :—" On Wednesday evening last week a vast column of smoke was seen approaching Bedford from the south-west, and it was supposed that the grass was extensively on fire in the neighbourhood. The smoke was first blown towards the 'Schiet Rug,' between Bedford and Adelaide, and by a shift of the wind was brought up along the Hoggberg Range, and enveloped the mountain, over which it appeared to disperse. Inquiries were made next day, and each succeeding day, as to the origin of this extraordinary volume of smoke, which extended some seven or eight miles at least. As travellers came in, it was successively ascertained that it came in the same extraordinay manner, from a greater and greater distance—from Fish River—from Zuurberg, &c. Travellers affirmed that they had been nearly suffocated by it on the top of the mountain, and that it must have come from the Port Elizabeth side of the range. From the *Great Eastern* received this morning in Bedford, the origin of the smoke is found to have been the burning of some fifteen miles of forest at the Van Staden's River, beyond Port Elizabeth, on the Cape Town road; so that this extraordinary volume of smoke travelled in a compact mass for a distance of some one hundred and twenty miles, crossing the Great Zuurberg, range, and it is said to have passed over the Hoggberg, and to have traversed 'Daggaboer's Neck,' into the division of Cradock. News has come in that the smoke extended to the town of Adelaide, twelve miles distant from Bedford, and that the people of Adelaide were considerably alarmed at the sudden envelopment of their town in a dense cloud of smoke."

Mr Pullen, after making an official inspection of the scene of the fire, wrote of it :—" It was awful. I never could have thought that a forest would have burned so; it is one mass of fire. The fine view formerly to be obtained on coming down the Van Staden's River, is now among the things of the past. Not a green leaf is to be seen, and the whole of the trees are burned down. I counted no less than thirty bush-bucks roasted to death yesterday, and the quantity of game destroyed must be very considerable. I made an attempt to enter the forest, but the intense heat drove me back. The bridges are all burnt, and the waggons cannot pass with safety. I had to go round a long way to reach the regular road. The rocks on the other side of the river are quite bare, and the numbers of baboons and monkeys that must have perished, almost incredible. Van Halen's place had a very narrow escape, and the orange and fruit trees are entirely destroyed."

The following account was sent to one of the provincial newspapers from a station in the district, occupied at the time in connection with the execution of a trigonometrical survey of the Colony. After stating that "the havoc and devastation to the forest, and pasturage, &c., &c., are indescribable, and that the thermometer showed in the shade at 11 a.m. 110°," the writer proceeds :—" It will be a long time ere this part of the country regains its primitive state. Since the farms were granted in 1815, such a fire has not been known of, or witnessed by the eldest surviving residents of this part. For miles the country is denuded of copse and forest, even the rushes about the rivulets, vleys, and rivers are seared and scorched, the timely burns of August and September of the present year have been reburnt, and parched up, umbrageous trees are prostrated athwart the main roads, intercepting the traffic, the two main culverts of the Van Staden's Pass have fallen through, and the road could not be traversed for three days until temporary repairs took place. The fire ignited Mrs Cadle's stable by a spark, distant, as the crow flies, exactly a league, so you can imagine the ravages and scourge that have been inflicted on property. Pullen's farm, 'Augusta Park,' was in jeopardy, as the fences of Harrison, a lessee on the place, were fired from the flames of the adjacent farms, at a distance of exactly four miles. The sublime and picturesque scenery of the Van Staden's is absolutely destroyed, and bears an aspect changed from verdancy to opaqueness; roasted venison could be discovered everywhere; what have been found by the natives and Europeans exceeds 120; feathered game has been destroyed in great quantities, also vermin, and the whole landed property in this ward which has had the frightful visitation has deteriorated in value by the late fire. The ranger of this ward, Mr Pullen, puts down the destruction to Crown Reserve as at least £600; of private property on each farm as half of that value. The farm 'Kafir's Kraal,' advertised for sale in your advertisement columns, has been greatly injured, and the fences of the lands burnt, and the private groups of valuable bushes on the farm destroyed, orchard burnt, greater part of the orange grove is destroyed, and the leaves seared, and a great deal of mischief has been done by the late fire. It is to be hoped for the future more precautionary measures well be resorted to."

Captain Harrison, Conservator of Crown Forests in the district, estimated the value of the ward destroyed much lower, but this does not disprove what is said of the extent of the conflagration.

I made inquiry into the origin of the fire, and was informed by Captain Harrison that,—" Some four natives kindled a fire on the pasture-lands of Galger Bosche; the fire ignited the bush, and spread first into the private forests, and subsequently into the Crown Reserve. About a league of government forest has been destroyed, but of this great portions consisted of copse and underwood. There was not so much of umbrageous forest timber destroyed. I attribute the destruction of the forest in a great measure to the boundary of the government property not being properly defined, and no beacon being erected. There are a number of squatters on government lands bordering on the government reserve, being tenants of farmers whose lands are adjacent. These individuals, induced by the fertility of the soil, lay claim to the arable land on the precincts of the forest; the roots, stumps, and trees dug out are piled along the outskirts of the forest; and when such fires occur, on reaching this rubbish it finds fuel to strengthen it, and its fury is increased."

About the same time Captain Harrison had occasion to report a fire in the forest at the Zitzikamma scarcely less destructive. The following is his report:—" It is with regret that I have to report the occurrence of two fires in the forests,—one at Van Staden's River, the other in the Zitzikamma. I have carefully inspected the damage done at Van Staden's River, and it is with considerable satisfaction that I can state that the number of timber trees destroyed does not exceed twenty, and of these only five were sound. The bush destroyed was a scrub bush, mostly private property, containing spars and poles, with here and there an old yellow-wood tree, spared by the woodcutters on account of decay. The Crown forest lies at the back, towards the sea, and this has suffered but little. The fire in the Zitzikamma is a far more serious matter, and the damage done truly deplorable. What little work is going on I have confined as much as possible to the burnt forest, that the damaged timber may be worked up before it splits and becomes useless ; and I hope to save much of it from waste. This part of the forest had been closed for some years, to allow the young trees to grow up, and its destruction is a serious public loss. No human power could save the forest when once the fire caught the dense, dry, bushy veld of seven years' growth and ten feet in height by which the forests are surrounded. Science is opposed to veld fires, and justly so, if the practice could be suppressed ; but so long as our neighbours burn, we must, in self-defence, burn too, or the forests are destroyed by the very means we take to preserve them. Ten years' experience has enabled me to try both systems, burning and non-burning. On my first arrival here the veld was regularly burnt in winter, without any damage to the forests, but ensuring their protection against accidental fires. Science then said I was wrong, and burning was prohibited. The result is the late disastrous fire. Had the veld been kept burnt, such a fire could not have occurred, or, at all events, it might have been extinguished. Could any other means of protection be suggested, I would readily adopt it ; but the soil here is too stony and full of stumps to admit of ploughing round the forests. This calamity was caused by an old Hottentot herd, who lit a fire near the sea, on ground belonging to his employers, which, from the excessively dry state of the country at the time, and very high winds, was driven into the forest. The fire was not confined to Government property ; damage, estimated at £300, was done to the private forest at Oude Bosch."

A still more extensive fire, or rather a number of fires, originating in different centres, and spreading each in its own localitv, occurred on the 9th of February 1869, when "a tract of country 400 miles long, and varying in breadth from 15 to 150 miles, was desolated by a fire unparalleled in the annals of the colony. The weather had been unusually hot and dry for the previous six weeks. On the 9th February the temperature throughout the colony rose to more intense heat than any previously known. During the morning scorching hot winds blew from the NE., and in the afternoon a fire broke out at several places in the burned district, and wrapped millions of acres in an enormous conflagration. The cultivated land, farm buildings, native forest and bush, farm stock, and wild animals, shared the same fate. In a few hours hundreds of pounds worth of property was destroyed. The European colonists and natives alike suffered, and in the majority of cases the sufferers lost all they possessed. Several persons were burned to death. The casualties, in the majority of cases, occurred to the natives, and to the wives and children of the colonists. Those saved had to take shelter in the rivers, water dams, and wet ditches, where many of them were badly scorched. The calamity occurred just after the harvest—an unusually good one—and destroying its produce. This caused great distress in the district of Swellendam, Riversdale, Mossel Bay, George, and Oudtzboom, the Kingsna, Humansdorf, and Uitenhage."

Numerous accounts of the ravages, which appeared in the local journals, were sent to me. I may cite some of the more important of these, and in doing so I shall as much as possible avoid unnecessary repetition. A correspondent of the *Cape Argus*, writing from Humansdorp on the 10th ult., says,—" A calamity of unprecedented severity yesterday befell this district. A bush fire of such dimensions broke out in various places as to find no parallel in the recollection of the oldest residents. The result has been a large loss of life and property, many of the sufferers being left houseless and penniless. The morning of the 9th was very sultry, with the wind from the north—an indication which here always means something little short of a sirocco. The thermometer in the shade showed, at 8 A.M., a temperature of 93°; at 9 A.M., 101°; and at 2 P.M., 113°. The weather for some time before had been very dry, and the Veldt quite parched. Early in the afternoon a dense mass of smoke was seen in the western part of the Zitzikamma district, probably near Clarkson, but no danger was then apprehended. About 3 P.M., however, the wind chopped round to the southwest, blowing a perfect hurricane of dust and smoke, which completely enveloped the village. The imminence of the danger became painfully apparent as dusk came on. The church-bell was rung, and the villagers put on the alert. As seen from the village, the whole Zitzikamma, right away to Cape St Francis, seemed to be one intermittent blaze, whilst the hills to the north were also bathed in flame. It is impossible to give a strictly accurate account of the loss of life and property sustained, as full reports have not yet come in; but there can be little doubt that about twenty homesteads have been burned to the ground, including that of Mr W. S. G. Metelerkamp, of Zuurbron, that six Fingo children have been burned to death at the same place, twelve Fingoes in the Zitzikamma district, two coloured females on their way to Hankey, and a farmer's wife and servant somewhere in the same direction. One of the farm-houses destroyed is but one and a half mile to the south of the village, and another two miles to the north. so we have miraculously escaped this sad visitation. Much alarm was felt this morning, as the Veldt and bush were burning extensively about a mile off, when, fortunately, the wind veered to the south, and then to the southeast, bringing, as usual, a soaking rain, which lasted all forenoon."

A correspondent, writing from George, says,—"We have just received intelligence that the bush fires which have been raging here and elsewhere for the last month have found their way to the magnificent farms of Forest Hall, belonging to the Hon. Barrington, of Knysna; Restford, belonging to B. H. Darnell, Esq.; and Eastford, lately purchased by the British, all of which, it is reported, are completely destroyed, and the houses, etc., burned to the ground. Several other large farms, Barnard's, Gerber's, etc., between this and Knysna, are completely destroyed, the people saving their lives by rushing into the river, up to the banks of which the fire reached. One very rich old farmer (H. Barnard) had only time to drag his box, with some thousands of sovereigns, etc., in it, to the river, and throwing himself and box into the river, stood up to his chest in water for an hour or more, barely escaping being burned to death by the long rushes, etc., growing on the water's edge, and which the fire completely destroyed. Mr Darnell is a heavy loser (if report speaks true), thirty head of his valuable cattle being burned to death; and so we hear disastrous effects of the fire daily. The George and Knysna forests are very extensive—hundreds of miles in extent —and heaven knows where the fire will end."

The following letter from Mr B. H. Darnell, of the Knysna, presents a sad picture of the ravages of the fire in the neighbourhood of his house :—

"ASH-WEDNESDAY, 1869.—My dear ——, There will doubtless be a long catalogue of disasters by veld-fires to be chronicled in newspapers about this time; but as none of them can be more complete than that which has befallen myself and my nearest neighbours, I must give you a hurried account of it. The weather has been unusually hot and dry here for the last six weeks, but yesterday was such a day as will never be forgotten by those who went through it. On rising early in the morning I found the *berg-wind*, the sirocco of South Africa, blowing steadily from the north, the thermometer reaching one hundred degrees before eight o'clock. This wind, hateful to man and beast, fortunately rarely blows in the summer, and still more rarely for more than a day at a time, and is almost invariably followed by rain. Little did we dream of what was about to happen, when about nine o'clock in the morning we perceived there was a great fire raging on the flats above us, but a little to the leeward of us. Some wood-cutter on the way to his work, crossing the river higher up, probably knocked out the ashes of his pipe upon the grass. The grass was dry in the fields enclosed round about the house with ditch and mound; but I had made everything so secure outside by timely burning that danger from an ordinary fire was not to be thought of. My house was situated on an elevation near the head of a small valley, widening into the large valley of the Knysna River, and just opposite to its gorge, where, leaving the mountains and krantzes behind, it ceases to be a mountain stream, and pursues a more peaceful but not less romantic course to the ocean as a tidal river. No situation could be more beautiful, as those can testify who have ever looked down upon this valley from the neighbouring hills. As the morning advanced, denser and denser grew the smoke, and brighter the glare of the fire, whilst the thermometer rose higher every minute. The wind, too, increased rapidly in violence. Still I would believe nothing. I sat quietly teaching my children, and listening to occasional reports of the progress of the fire from my wife, to which I paid the usual amount of attention, until the washerman rushed up from the river and declared that the fire was coming down both sides of it upon us. Such a catastrophe was never heard of. A decent and well-intentioned fire makes a great splutter in the open veld, but stops respectfully at the edge of the forest, without doing too much damage. But I then went out. At first there was nothing to be seen but thick smoke, and nothing to be heard but the raging and roaring of the wind and fire. But presently above the smoke I saw the liquid fire pouring over the great wooded krantzes, and below it, in the fields, a great stream of fire surging along in the dry grass with inconceivable rapidity. Then I knew it was all up with Westford, Knysna, and rushing into my house, got out my household, who stood ready, and directed my wife, who alone retained any presence of mind, to fly with them through the garden and down to the dam. Had it not been for her courage and endurance I should never have got them to a place of safety. It is not an enviable billet at any time to be the sole guardian of thirteen women and children; but to conduct them, wholly distracted, and all pulling different ways, over a burning waste for nearly a mile, with the thermometer approaching boiling point, is an experience of Responsible Government such as I trust no colony may ever be called upon to pass through. I tarried a minute behind, but it was almost a minute too long. Instantaneously the whole of the buildings on the place were in a blaze, and at the same moment fire appeared all round, as well as above and below us. It was not merely sparks or flakes of fire that were flying so quickly, but firebrands. The Last Day itself can hardly present accessories more dreadful. We were literally at the mouth of a blow-pipe, as those who know the position will understand, and the danger rapidly decreased as we got away from it. We had hardly got through the garden and into the road, when the fire was half-way down, rampaging amongst the pumpkins and the fruit-trees. The fiery wind was so violent that it was only by making all cling together that they could be got along at all. Half their clothing blown away. But it would take too long to tell how it took us nearly two hours to get to the only house left by a miracle on the place. Inside it was a fire, which we did not want, and that we soon put out, but we found a bucket of water, which we did want. The inhabitants had taken refuge on the pontoon upon the river. Soon after we reached the house the wind changed suddenly to the westward, and there was an end to the hurricane of fire that we had gone through.

"Since writing the above I have visited the scene of this unparalleled disaster. No destruction can be more complete, nor can it be imagined without being seen. It was not such a fire as steals, in the middle of the night, upon a house surrounded by trees, and after blazing and crackling away for a few hours, lets the morning sun find out the ruin through the thick green leaves glittering with dew. This was a clean sweep of everything—houses, trees, gardens, orchards, forest, all gone—the labour and the pleasure of sixteen years swept away in a few minutes. Not a green thing in sight, except some rushes in the dam. Not a thing which the fire does not seem to have passed over or through except an old spade and a couple of white field gates *in situ*. All the rest black, dust and ashes—dust and ashes! Not only the natural beauties of the place, and they were great, have disappeared, but its very features seem to be changed. One might as well be on the barest Karroo place as on the banks of the Knysna. What will become of the pic-nickers I cannot imagine. The grass will grow again, and the whole farm will soon be one sheet of emerald green, and for grazing purposes will be as good or better than ever, but all that gave it value in my eyes is gone. Nature neither can nor will she restore the grand old trees, the pride of the forest, not a few of them thirty feet in circumference, that stood on the great haugh on the side of the river opposite the house. I took a walk along the river bank. Plenty of bush-bucks roasted alive, and I daresay an elephant or two, but not a sign of life, except an old baboon crooning over the desolation, and not another sound except the crashing of the mighty trees as they fell hissing into the water; and I turned away with a heavy heart, probably for the last time, from the blighted and blasted scene.

"But I cannot say that I felt the full extent of my loss until I had been to see my neighbours' places. I have lost everything I prized in the shape of books, furniture, plate, pictures, and the many memorials of a whole lifetime, which insurances can never replace ; but there are many people who have lost their all, and there is at this moment a great fire blazing cheerfully westward of the Knysna (which itself escaped by a miracle) towards George, and eastwards towards the Zitzikamma, which will furnish in due time many a tale of destruction and woe. Some other pen than mine must chronicle them. I can only concern myself at present with the fire which scathed me and burnt up my poor cows and calves, fowls, pigeons, and dogs, and which seems to have destroyed some half-a-dozen places. At Portland, Mr Barrington's place, there has been, I am sorry to say, a much greater destruction of accumulated property, and of the results of labour, than at Westford; but the damage done to the farm is not so considerable. At Barnard's, Buffels Vermaak, the farm-house is burnt down, and some of the money melted which they wisely kept in their own chests instead of trusting it to the coffers of the George Bank. Their silver spoons and forks are also melted down; but the loss these good people seem to feel most is that of their feather-beds! They are my two nearest neighbours, and I don't know or care much about the others. But I should not conclude this letter, which I feel is too much about myself and my own troubles, without expressing my gratitude for much practical kindness and sympathy from many persons in the Knysna from whom I had no particular reason to expect much consideration."

On the same day similarly destructive fires raged in the districts of Uitenhage and of Humansdorp, which are thus detailed in the *Eastern Province Herald*:—"It is our painful duty to have to record a catastrophe as appalling in its effects as it was unexpected. For the last three or four days an immense tract of country has been on fire—bush and veld being ablaze—the flames advancing rapidly, and destroying homesteads, crops, live stock, and, alas! several human beings. It is difficult to ascertain with correctness the particulars of such a wide-spread calamity, but, so far as we have been able to gather them, we publish the facts below. We have been careful not to exaggerate, and we have reason to fear that when the truth is fully known it will exceed what we have as yet been able to ascertain. The first intelligence came to hand on Wednesday last—the day after Tuesday, when the heat was so terrific—and we then learnt that the country in the vicinity of Van Staden's River had been devastated by fire. It is said by some that this fire originated at Captain Mallors's farm by burning weeds, but from others we hear that several parts of the country in that district were on fire simultaneously. Captain Mallors's homestead was totally destroyed, and the flames travelled onwards to Betshanger, the farm of Captain Boys. Despite every effort to avert the catastrophe, the thatched roof caught fire, and in a few minutes the house and all its contents were destroyed. Upwards of two hundred sheep were also destroyed, and the remainder of the flock scorched and charred in a dreadful manner. Captain Boys and his family have taken refuge in a small cottage on the homestead, which escaped the fire, but have literally lost all they possessed. It is said the house was insured for £1000, but this will not cover the loss, and the movable property was not insured. Mr Christian Heugh had a narrow escape. He has lost his stacks of grain, but the dwelling-house was saved. Captain Boys's sons came to his assistance, and they fortunately succeeded in saving the premises. The verandah was burnt and charred at the end, and all the kraals are destroyed. The grass burnt up to the very door. We publish below an extract from a private letter received by a friend yesterday, detailing some of the particulars of this fearful time. Further on other homesteads were destroyed. Mr Marthinus Mienaar's house, at

Sandfonteiu, is burnt down, and, sad to relate, on this place there was loss of life. Mrs Mienaar, with a child and native servant, took refuge in a ploughed field; but the servant and child were caught by the flames and burnt. Close by are the remains of a Hottentot woman and two children, also destroyed; so that on this homestead are five victims to the fury of the raging fire. A Mr Faver, in the same part of the country, had a water-mill, and went to look after it, and has not been heard of since. The mill was destroyed, and it is feared that he too has perished. Mr George Smith, of Nockton Park, and Mr Parkins, had a narrow escape. A waggon, with a load of goods sent from Port Elizabeth by Messrs A. C. Stewart & Co., a few days ago, has been burnt.—From the division of Humansdorp more disastrous tidings still have reached us. Zuurbron, the property of Mr Metelerkamp, has been totally destroyed, and everything lost. Ten or twelve homesteads besides have been destroyed, but it will be some days yet before we can learn the particulars. It would appear from the intelligence received that the destruction of property in the division of Humandorp has been much greater than along Van Staden's River, and we anxiously wait for further particulars. At this moment we have received a telegram from our correspondent at Humansdorp, who says that *twenty homesteads* have been burnt down, and twenty-six Fingo huts, and *twenty-one* lives have been lost. The damage is estimated at £25,000! Further particulars are promised us by post. This is, without doubt, the most serious calamity that has ever befallen the colony. We have had nothing like it before. Its very novelty is startling. We have had to mourn over losses by flood, by locusts, by drought, and by Kafir war, but, except in a minor degree, we have been preserved from the devastating effects of fire. Happening at a time when the crops had been gathered in, and the stacks, as was thought, safely secured, it was doubly felt.

"The following is an extract from a letter to a friend in this town, who has kindly permitted us to publish it. The writer is a lady, who herself witnessed the terrific scene described, and who narrowly escaped with her precious charge:—

"'The 10th day of February 1869.—After our merciful deliverance from a frightful death, I now sit down to write a few of the events. The day commenced very hot, and the heat increased towards the middle of it to a frightful degree; when we perceived a thick smoke approaching, with the wind, which commenced to rise. It grew more dense, and, as I had two children in my charge, I began to fear, and, hastily wrapping a blanket or kaross round each (four altogether, with my own), I started for my nearest neighbour's—Capt. Boys'; my husband and men-servants meanwhile starting for the stacks, which were composed of our corn and all our grain, as well as Capt. Boys'. That was all swept away, and my poor husband almost consumed beneath its fall. We reached our destination, and found our neighbours all alarmed, as the fire was almost all round the homestead. Every endeavour was made to save the house, but without avail, as the flames swept across the open space and ignited the thatch, which was instantaneously in a blaze. I took the children to the river, and we all sat in it, covered with blankets, as the cinders and burnt particles flew over our heads. I and they commended ourselves to God, but I expected every moment would be our last. However, the wind seemed to change, and we, with all the members of Captain Boys' family, escaped unhurt. They, poor things, have lost all—wearing apparel, bedding, and everything. Were it not for the kindness of the two young Boys, who at the commencement came over and beat the flames out which had encircled the house already, we should also this night have been homeless. All the clothes my charges had on were consumed. As they were too wet I was afraid of them taking cold, and removed them. We carried them home in blankets. The Lord, truly, is merciful and of great goodness in thus sparing us. I had quite given up all hopes of this life for myself and the poor little ones. . . . We have lost our all, and even our poor pigs were burnt to death in their styes. Two hundred of Captain Boys' sheep were consumed, besides a great many injured. As I now sit writing at nine o'clock P.M., *the whole country around* is smoking and sparkling. Oh! if it would only rain. The poor hares and wild bucks came to the houses for protection from the flames. It appears to me as if this day has been months long. Our only waggon is also consumed. I pray and wish that I may never witness such another day as this. I certainly thought that the last day had arrived. The sun appeared like blood through the dense smoke, and the air like fire. We were all perfectly parched, and could hardly speak. No one who did not see it could imagine this scene,—the fire coming from all directions, and the flames roaring like thunder, and the immense masses of black smoke hastening onwards. It was awful!'"

Not less graphic is the following account, given in the *Uitenhage Times*: —"Last Tuesday, February 9, will long be remembered by those who happened to be in Uitenhage on that day as the hottest day within their experience; and their memory will be no less charged with the terrible calamities which followed and were augmented, if not actually caused, by the intense heat of the atmosphere.

"There was a dense mist when the morning dawned, but as this wore away the heat began to increase. By nine o'clock A.M. a scorching hot wind blew from the northeast, and from that time till the afternoon it was almost impossible to breathe the heated air out of doors. It was like flame. People shut themselves up in their houses and excluded as much heat as they could. Our own compositors closed the printing office, and even then were unable to continue work; they took refuge from the oppressive atmosphere beneath the cases and benches, and we believe that in almost every house everything like work or exercise was suspended. Poultry ran gasping about and poked their heads into holes and crevices for relief.

"Such was the heat in the town. At noon the thermometer stood at 112 outside, in the shade. About halfpast five P.M., the wind veered round, and a regular hurricane blew from the southwest, bringing with it clouds of dust and smoke which completely obscured the sun. The thermometer then stood at 100 in the shade, and in a dining-room which had been darkened and shut up all day, at 90.

"It was evident that the smoke proceeded from a bush fire in the Van Staden's neighbourhood, but it was hoped it was only the bush; although for some time the thatched houses of the town were in a jeopardy, for now and then sparks were seen to fly overhead, and the thatch, already heated nearly up to combustion, would have almost exploded had a spark fallen on it, and been fanned by the wind which was then blowing. An 'old inhabitant' did take the precaution to throw water on his thatch; but fortunately no fire took place in the town. Later in the evening the wind subsided and a heavy dew fell; when it got dark the sky over Van Staden's mountain was lit up with the reflection of the fire which was still raging.

"Learning that the fire had been very destructive in the neighbourhood of the Maitland Mines, we started for the locality yesterday, in order to get an eye-witness's account for our readers. We had not got far on the Cape road before we came upon traces of the fire; indeed, it is almost a wonder that with the wind blowing full behind it, the fire did not continue its course along the dense bush which runs almost down to the river. On the hill behind Mimosadale the fire must have raged furiously, and had anyone been travelling on that road at the time, escape would have been utterly impossible.

"During Wednesday various reports were current in town, telling of farms, stacks, cattle, etc., swept away. Eager as everyone was to believe that rumour had as usual exaggerated, when the truth came to be ascertained it was found that she had erred on the other side, and had understated the mischief done.

"The homestead at Mimosadale had a narrow escape. The residents were greatly alarmed, and at one time prepared for flight. Fortunately, some 16- or 20 loads of firewood was the extent of Mr Kingwell's loss.

"We pushed on towards Captain Boys', having heard that his homestead had been destroyed and that the family had fled. On our way there we drove over miles of ashes; both the bush and the grass veldt had yielded to the fire. We came upon a few straggling sheep, yet alive, but with their wool burnt off close to their skins.

"On reaching the homestead we found that although the family were still there, the house and nearly everything in it had been destroyed. Notwithstanding the devastation and ruin which overspread the place, we could see that a more beautiful site for a homestead could scarcely be found in the Colony. It is situated in a sort of horseshoe-shaped kloof or valley, nearly surrounded by hills, which were densely wooded before the fire, but are now black and bare. The river runs partly round the place at the foot of the hill, entering at an opening which faces the sea and admits at the same time the bracing sea air. There were two other buildings within about fifty yards of Captain Boys' dwelling-house; and although covered with thatch, through almost superhuman efforts on the part of the captain's sons, they were saved, and into them the family have retreated for the present. The dwelling-house itself seems to have been unusually comfortable and commodious, and was furnished in accordance with refined taste and pretty liberal means. There was a good library, paintings—among which the old Dutch masters were represented, articles of vertu, family relics, and other household treasures which acquired an unappreciable extrinsic value from associations. These went with the rest; indeed, young Mr Boys' words were when we arrived, 'We've lost everything but what we stand in.'

"We will endeavour to give that gentleman's account of the fire. Early in the afternoon, while he was copying some music, he saw smoke in the direction of Mr C. Heugh's farm; and believing that place to be in danger went to render assistance. He found Mr Heugh vainly endeavouring to secure his stacks, but seeing that impracticable, he and Mr Heugh applied themselves to beating out the fire round the house. Mrs Heugh and her own family, with two little girls, visitors from Port Elizabeth, wrapped themselves up in blankets and fled to Captain Boys', miraculously escaping suffocation by the way. When they arrived at the homestead it was already on fire. But young Mr Boys, having rendered all assistance he could, was alarmed about his mother and sisters, who were left at the homestead, and made all haste back, arriving there before Mrs Heugh. The fire had already climbed up to the top of the mountain on the opposite side, and was flying along the summit. In a few seconds a gust of wind swept the flame down, and like a flash of lightning the whole mountain side was on fire. At this moment a 'spark' or piece of fire shot into the air, and fell upon the thatch of the dwelling-house. He gave the alarm, and was instantly on the roof, but too late; the thatch burst into flame all at once. The young ladies, at the imminent peril of their lives, endeavoured to save something, and did manage to get the piano and one small box away to the other building. Several other articles were got out to the front of the house and would have been saved, but the grass had already taken fire, and so the devouring element communicated to this property, and it was all destroyed. Personal safety now became the only consideration; the valley was heated like an oven; wild bucks from the surrounding bush came and crouched about, terror-stricken, and one, half scorched to death, took refuge on the stoop of the building. The ladies shut themselves up to exclude the hot air, expecting every moment, however, that the roof above them would burst into flame. Both Mrs Boys and her four daughters exhibited the most remarkable presence of mind, and made preparations, as a last resource, to wrap themselves in blankets (the building in which they had taken refuge was used for an occasional sleeping apartment) and run into the river. But, thanks to Providence and the efforts of the young men outside, the fire was kept off the house, although the grass had been burned to within five feet of it. The fire travelled and did its work so quickly that, like a wave or a tempest, it soon swept past and climbed the opposite mountain. At this time considerable alarm existed for the safety of Captain Boys, who had gone in the morning to meet the gentlemen of the Austrian expedition at a neighbouring farm. He was at length seen returning down the hill. The first sight that met his eyes was his house a mass of smoking ruins, but the joy of the family was unbounded when they saw him approach.

"We went with young Mr Boys up the mountain to look at the sheep which had been burned. It was a sad sight. About forty vultures retreated as we approached, and arranged themselves in a line at a short distance, eagerly watching the opportunity to return to the feast we had disturbed. Here there had been only long grass. This was burned to the roots, and between 200 or 300 sheep, all more or less charred, were lying dead—the ewe and lamb together in some instances, showing how to the last the one had clung to the other for protection. In some instances the brains had been boiled and seethed out of the head. Had these poor animals gone ten yards in the right direction they would have escaped destruction. From this hill a view of the surrounding homesteads was obtainable. It is remarkable that almost the only patches of green remaining were just round the houses. Whether the fire had been arrested there by the occupants, or whether grass, so to speak, civilized, is less inflammable, we don't know. Whatever the cause, the effect was to save many houses. The stacks at a little distance were all destroyed.

"Captain Boys' loss is not less than £2000, most of which is uninsured. Indeed the building only was insured. The valuable furniture, the wearing apparel, the crops of produce, the sheep, and the stores of provisions, linen, &c., which had just been laid in for the year, are all lost and are all uninsured. It is, indeed, a very hard case; a family living in refinement and comfort were in a few minutes rendered homeless and destitute. The way in which the ladies bear the misfortune is truly wonderful. Gratitude that the family are all spared to each other seems to be the prevailing feeling. We were informed that the Kaffirs on the place could not be induced to help to extinguish the fire.

"Sad as is the above case, we are assured it is not the worst. Every hour fresh reports of disasters come in. Last evening young Mr Niekerk, from Long Kloof, reached town, having passed through Humansdorp on his way. Other messengers have arrived, also a letter from a correspondent at Port Elizabeth, where telegrams have been received. All the reports agree in the following, and are corroborated by the last arrival, Mr Niekerk.

"At Zuurbron, the extensive buildings of Mr Metelerkamp have been swept away. Meyer's farm, Kromme River, Klipfontein; Zitzman's; Hendrik Meyer's, Zokoe River; Rondebosch; Johnson's farm, Witteklip; Du Plessis' farm, Misgund,—all destroyed.

"But the worst tragedies have yet to be told. At Suiker Kraal or Vlakte Plaats, inhabited by Messrs Gertenbach and Van Onselon, a life was lost. There Mrs Gertenbach ran out of the burning house with three children and was burnt to death; the children escaped. We have not fuller particulars.

"At Mauritz Kraal and Strandfontein, farms occupied by three brothers, Minnie, there has been further loss of life. Marthinus Minnie, of Strandfontein, saw the fire in the direction of Mauritz Kraal, and left his house to look. Before he got very far he discovered that his own house was in greater danger, and returned, but, in the meantime, a dreadful occurrence took place. He had left in the house Mrs Minnie, very near confinement, two of his own children, and a native servant with her two children. The house caught fire and the occupants escaped,—Mrs Minnie with one child, all that she could manage, to the mealie field, and the Kaffir woman with the other three children down to the river. Mrs Minnie and the one child with her escaped; but the Kaffir woman and the three children perished. The other Minnies at Mauritz Kraal packed up their goods in the waggons ready for trekking, but while they were gone for the oxen the fire came and consumed everything. At Galgebosch they had a very narrow escape, but managed to keep the fire away from the homestead.

"When we left Captain Boys' last evening the fire was still raging in the direction of Galgebosch, and we heard that considerable alarm existed all over the country yet unvisited.

"At Prentice Kraal, eight miles the other side of Uitenhage, there was also a large fire, so large as to alarm Mr Hartman, the hotel-keeper, and make him contemplate flight."

A Humansdorp correspondent to the *Eastern Province Herald* furnishes the following saddening particulars respecting the destructive fires in that division :—"It is with painful feelings that I have to record the lamentable events which took place on Tuesday the 9th instant,—a day never to be forgotten in the district. The morning of that day was ushered in with a hot northerly breeze, which gradually increased, until (at about eleven o'clock A.M.) the atmosphere felt more like a blast from a furnace than anything else. Fears were now being entertained for the safety of the village and surrounding farms, as fires were springing up in various directions, and about four P.M. the wind—which had veered round from N.W. to S.W.—increased to a perfect hurricane, which words can but faintly describe, while the heat, dust, and smoke were terrific in the extreme. About six P.M.

information was received that Mr H. Meyer's farm-house was burnt to the ground, and he himself greatly injured in trying to save his valuables. Immediately afterwards an express arrived from Zuurbron, the residence of W. S. G. Metelerkamp, Esq., with the doleful tidings that the homestead was in ashes—only a few books and papers saved—and about eight Fingo children burnt to death. On his way in, the messenger passed Wagoner's and Voslo's places, all in flames, and the whole country beyond, towards the Gamtoo's River, one mass of fire.

"Later in the evening, the flames were seen belching forth on each side of the village, to the great consternation of the inhabitants, as we every moment expected to see fire breaking out in the Dorp—the strong wind carrying the sparks and stubble hundreds of yards ahead, and hurling masses of burning palmiet and grass all over the country. At one point the fiery element had advanced to within a mile of the nearest house; but, providentially, its course was changed, and it passed on, leaving us unscathed.

"Next morning, 10th inst., we began to realize the havoc and desolation in the neighbourhood, as one messenger after another arrived with sad news, this farm was burned, and that, and so on—a list of which I send you herewith. The same day a poor young fellow of the name of Kamp was brought into the village, fearfully scorched. It appears he was on his way home from a 'tocht,' with his 'little all'—a waggon and fourteen oxen and a flock of sheep—and, when opposite the 'Vlak Plaats' (Gertenbach's) was obliged to halt on account of the fearful heat, and a dense volume of smoke and dust. A few minutes afterwards, he says, the country on each side was enveloped in flames, and he just had time to shelter himself behind an old wall when his waggon took fire, and in less time than it takes to tell it, the waggon, oxen, and sheep were one smouldering mass. He then went over to Mr Gertenbach's house, which was also blazing away, but could not find a soul. Mrs Gertenbach and a servant girl were subsequently found lying about 300 yards from the house burned to a cinder. It appears the poor creatures fled from the house towards Van Onelin's, about a mile further on, but were overtaken and destroyed, the husband being away from home at the time. From Swarts's place, after destroying everything there, the fire raged on towards Jeffrey's Bay, where it caught T. Kemp's house, which (together with a buck-waggon load of goods for Mr Steinman, of this place,) were soon in ashes. In the Zitzikamma Ward three large homesteads were burnt, together with about from 30 to 40 Fingo huts, which were standing in different parts of the Government grant. At the latter place some eight or ten women and children also miserably perished.

"Words cannot describe the fearful ruin and desolation on every side. Hundreds of people who were in comfortable circumstances have been reduced to the verge of starvation and nakedness, and are now wandering over the blackened ruins of their homes; and what makes it still worse is, that some thousands of muids of grain, besides stock innumerable, have been totally destroyed. The country in some parts, for miles and miles around, presents a most melancholy and desolate appearance, not a bush nor a blade of grass, not a drop of water to be seen anywhere, and the loss of stock which will consequently ensue will be something terrible.

"Inclosed is a pretty correct list of property destroyed :—Zuurbron, W. & R. Metlerkamp, nothing saved,—eight Fingo children burned to death; Zeeko River, P. Smart, nothing saved,—700 sheep and goats burnt;

Rondebosch, F. Wagner, nothing saved; Rondebosch, D. Vesloo and several others; Zeekoe River, H. Meyer, nothing saved; Misgund, C. du Plessis, nothing saved; Valk Plaats, Gertenbach, Mrs Gertenbach and servant burnt to death; Klein Vlatke, Van Onslin, nothing saved; Klipfontein, Coetzee, nothing saved; Lange Hoogte, Ferreira's, nothing saved; Krants Plaats, Terblan's, two children burnt to death, and one man fearfully scorched; Langefontein, du Plessis, everything destroyed; Oude Werf, Moolman's, ditto,—one woman and five children burnt to death; Fingo Locations, Zitzikamma, several lives lost; Geelhoutboom, several Fingo locations; Kromme River, L. Meyer, totally destroyed, together with 400 sheep.

"Another correspondent, writing to us from Humansdorp, under date 11th inst., says,—'Twenty-three farms in this division are known to be totally destroyed, with crops. No advice yet from Kromme River or Long Kloof, except that there was a fire at Avontuur. The damage is roughly estimated at £30,000; twenty-seven lives are lost. Hankey and Kruisfontein narrowly escaped. No news yet from Clarkston, and Moravian Station. The dorp was encircled with fire. The Civil Commissioner had all the Government money, stamps, books, etc., ready for a start: horses and cart in readiness. Had not a shower of rain fallen on Wednesday the fire would have reached us; it was then creeping up the kloof, and men were engaged trying to put it out.'

"From Humansdorp accounts have reached us that the district has also been visited by the devastating enemy. Mr Chiappini, telegraphing to Mr Metelerkamp on Wednesday last, states that on that day the whole of the surrounding country was in a blaze, and that the fire was working its way down to the Zitzikamma, in the direction of Combrink's place. The properties of Messrs Metelerkamp, Lucas, Meyer, Swart, Johnston, and Coetzee had been destroyed, as also the homesteads and produce on the farms Rondebosch, Klipfontein, Langhoogte, and Zitzikamma.

"The place of Mr Franz Gertenbach, situated near Humansdorp, has been destroyed. Mr John Gertenbach of this town received the following telegram yesterday morning:—'A fearful fire is raging through the district of Humansdorp. Your brother's place has been burnt down, and his wife and one servant have been consumed. The child is alive and well. Frans is away on *togt*. The report was sent in by his neighbour, Mr P. Hyffer. Fifteen other farms have been burnt.'

"Mrs Frans Gertenbach, whose untimely end we deplore, was interred on Wednesday.

"The following telegram has been received:—

"TELEGRAM.—Humansdorp, Friday, Feb. 12, 1869. Destructive fire on Tuesday over district. Twenty homesteads burnt down; also, twenty-six Fingoe huts. Twenty-one lives lost. Full report by post. Damage estimated at £25,000.

"From the *P. E. Telegraph*:—On Tuesday evening last considerable sensation was produced in this town by what at the time was considered to be a very unusual natural phenomenon. Soon after five o'clock the sun, as it gradually drew towards the hills to the west, was observed to change its usual bright golden tinge for a deep dark red, surrounding which was a wide circle of likewise very florid appearance. A large cloud was shortly seen gradually approaching the town so dense that at times it almost entirely obscured the sun. It reached here about half-past five o'clock, and then there burst forth such a gale of wind as had not been experienced for months previously. This raised clouds of dust as usual.; but mixed with the dust and wind was a close, almost suffocating vapour, evidently the steam and smoke of a very large fire. Had this occurred in more superstitious times, it is impossible to say to what cause such an unusual phenomenon would have been ascribed; as it was, it occasioned much apprehension, if not alarm, in the minds of some weak-minded people, and considerable speculation among the community generally. The wind continued through the greater part of the night to blow with unabated vigour from the northeast. The deep mist soon cleared away; but the unusual occurrence we have endeavoured to describe remained unexplained until near mid-day, when intelligence reached here that a very destructive fire had been raging at the Maitland Mines. News was reached the same day that another fire had devastated a large extent of country near Humansdorp, and that one had also been raging at Mimosadale, near Uitenhage.

"We have carefully collected all the particulars we have been able to get in reference to these most disastrous calamities; but the accounts vary considerably, and render anything like a connected narrative a very difficult undertaking. It appears that the fire in the locality of the Maitland Mines first broke out on the farm of Mr Mallers. That gentlemen wishing to clear out a watersloot, had set fire to some rubbish with which it was blocked up, not for a moment anticipating that by so doing he would bring upon himself and others the disastrous consequences which have resulted. The dry stubble burnt quickly, and the wind suddenly springing up blew the sparks on to the adjoining plots of dry grass, and in a very short space of time the whole was one mass of flame. Every effort made to prevent its advance was futile. It spread in every direction, and soon reached the homestead, the thatch of which becoming ignited, the whole structure in a very short space of time was burnt to the ground, with all it contained. The outhouses and a waggon were also consumed, the live-stock of the farm alone escaping. On spread the devouring element at a most surprising rate, the wind facilitating its movements by scattering the burning embers far and wide. In no direction did it advance so rapidly as towards the farm of Mr C. Heugh in a south-easterly course; but fortunately, owing to the strenuous exertions of those on the place, the homestead was saved; but a waggon and some other less valuable property were destroyed. The fire now sped in a north-easterly direction, and soon reached the hills above Capt. Boys' homestead. This fine old mansion, one of the best farm-houses in the neighbourhood, situated in a snug valley, was looked upon as quite safe. The grass around it was short, so that there was no fear of the fire being communicated in that way. Attention was therefore devoted to saving the live-stock grazing on the more exposed parts of the farm. Suddenly the wind swept from off the hills a lot of burning embers, which, falling upon the thatched roof, set the whole in a blaze. It was the work of a moment. All the hands rushed to save the house, but their efforts were fruitless, and now nothing remains of the fine old house but the four blackened walls. Even the furniture and clothing could not be saved. The only article rescued was a piano. A few oil paintings, prized as being heirlooms as well as from their intriusic value, were got out and placed in safety it was thought; but the grass becoming ignited, they too perished. A flock of sheep was surrounded by flames, and about 300 of them were burnt to death, or so mutilated as to necessitate their being killed. Another branch of the fire ran quickly up the Maitland Mines valley in a westerly course. Speedily reaching Hyland's place, it consumed a stack of from 20,000 to 30,000 bundles of oat-hay, leaving nothing in its place but a mass of ashes. The homestead on the farm escaped. The fire then crossing the valley made its way up to Mr Rice Smith's property. Here its advance was resisted inch by inch by a sturdy set of fellows determined to keep back the invader. Their efforts were almost superhuman. One young fellow, Henry Smith, we are told, particularly distinguished himself. Another had his shoes burnt off his feet ; still he battled with the flames. But they succeeded : the house was saved, though it very narrowly escaped, the trees surrounding it being burnt, as also all running along it. As our informant very forcibly described it, the fire completely 'licked the walls of the building.' The veldt is burnt for very many miles, and there is now no pasturage whatever for the cattle in these parts. Large patches of bush and even large trees in the kloofs are entirely destroyed, being now mere blackened ashes. The fire spread so rapidly that an eye witness describes it as flying along at the pace of a race-horse. As an instance of the force of the wind and the volume of flame, we are informed by Captain Stanbury, of the *Zephyr*, which arrived here on Wednesday, that on Tuesday evening when eight or ten miles off the land, particles of blackened embers were blown on to his ship from the shore, and the coast to an extent of fully forty miles was grandly illuminated by the burning bush and grass.

"By this sad calamity Captain Boys and his sons have lost all they possessed, as their property was only insured to the extent of £500 to cover a bond. They are now living in two small cottages near their homestead, which were spared by the fire. Mr Maller's, we believe, is wholly uninsured, as is also Mr Hyland.

"The most disastrous series of fires, accompanied as they are with melancholy loss of life, have yet to be recorded. These occurred in Humansdorp district the same day, and also on Wednesday, but whether it was a branch of the same conflagration is not known at present. It is believed not to be. The only particulars that have as yet reached town are through the electric telegraph, and are consequently very meagre. The whole of the buildings on the Zuurbron property, belonging to Mr Metelerkamp, an old and highly esteemed resident in the division, have been burnt to the ground. The properties of Messrs Meyer, Swart, Johnston, Lucas Meyer, Von Onselin, and Coetzee have been consumed, as also the buildings on the farms Klipfontein, Rondebosch, Zitzikamma, and Longhoogte, besides very many others. The farm house of a Mr Marthinus Minnie was destroyed, and a child and servant burnt to death. Mrs Minnie, it is said, saved herself and one of her children by rushing into the river and remaining there until the fire which was blazing all around had burned itself out. The fire had reached the Zitzikamma forest, and was, it is said, playing sad havoc amongst the noble trees there.

"A telegram was received yesterday by Mr John Gertenbach from Humansdorp, stating that his brother Franz's place has been completely destroyed, and that his wife, child, and servant had been burnt to death. A later telegram informs us that the child is not dead, having been placed somewhere in safety while the mother went to try and save some things in the house. She lost her life in the attempt ; but the child was afterwards discovered unhurt.

"A fire has also been raging in Mimosadale in the Uitenhage district, but does not appear to have done much damage. The smoke and soot from this were driven into Uitenhage, and falling on the washed wool laid out to dry has so discoloured much of it that it will be necessary to have it rewashed.

"LATER PARTICULARS.—The above was written last night, after collecting such particulars as were then current. This morning we have seen one or two farmers from the locality of Van Staden's River, who have informed us of further incidents connected with this fearful conflagration, which are of the most harrowing description. We mentioned above that a white child and a coloured servant had been burnt on Minnie's farm, but it appears that five lives have been lost on the place, viz., the two already mentioned and a coloured woman with her two children. The woman was found after the fire lying on her back on the ground, with one child strapped behind as the natives usually carry their children, the other lying upon and between her legs. She had most likely fallen with her children, and all three had become suffocated together. The farm Strandfontein, situated near the Gamtoos River, is occupied by the three brothers Minnie, viz., Daniel, Stephanus, and Marthinus. They are all married. The two first occupy the old and larger building, the latter a smaller one. On Tuesday, seeing the fire approaching the farm, every effort was made to divert it from the homestead, but in vain. Attention was then directed to the waggons and other property in the hope of saving at least something. Marthinus, whose house was furthest from the flames, ran to the assistance of his brothers, believing that his place was safe. His wife, children, and servants remained behind. He had scarcely got to his brothers' place, when, on looking round, he saw that the fire had advanced upon his residence from another direction, and that it was completely enveloped in flames. The veld, too, had caught fire between the two houses, so that it was impossible to proceed from one to the other. All had to look to their own dear lives. Both houses were burnt with all they contained, the only thing saved being one waggon. As soon as the fire would permit search was made for Marthinus' family. His wife with one child was found to be alive; but tied to her back was another —burnt to death! She had run out of the house, taking one child—the servant followed with the other. She rushed on to a place of safety; but her feelings may be imagined—they cannot be described—when on looking round for the girl and child neither were to be seen. As the fire would permit she retraced her steps, and came across the servant and child both dead. The latter she tied on her back, in the faint hope that the vital spark had not quite fled. The poor woman is very near her confinement, and this must have added very much to her sufferings.

"Mr George Smith, at Gamtoos River, only saved his property with great difficulty, the grass and bush all around being completely burnt off.

"Mr Wm. Parkin had all the crops, &c., on his property consumed; but the homestead is uninjured.

"A miller named Faver, who has a flour-mill worked by water-power near the Van Staden's River, is missing, and it is feared has been burnt to death. He was last seen proceeding in the direction of his mill, which was in danger of being burnt, and had not since been heard of.

"A waggon, laden with merchandize, proceeding into the country from this place was, we are told, burnt with its contents.

"Mr James Parkin, from whom we have obtained most of the additonal particulars, believes that the fire is still burning fiercely along the Gamtoos

River and up Baviaan's Kloof, and that much damage must have resulted in those parts.

"The resident magistrate proceeded out to the locality of the disaster this morning, to render what assistance he could to those in need. He took with him a quantity of clothing and comforts, contributed by the charitable of this town, for distribution amongst those who have lost their all by this disastrous conflagration."

This is by far the most extensive coincidence of bush fires in South Africa which has come under my notice. But view each of them apart, and it is only in keeping with what is of frequent occurrence on a lesser scale. I have had narrated to me not less exciting accounts of hair-breadth escapes with life, but with the loss of everything, occurring on the flank of Table Mountain. I have been in peril, both by night and by day, from such fires within ten miles of Capetown. I have roused a sleeping family, to whose house the flames were hurrying on, while there was barely time for them to escape before it was consumed. The following I find amongst my memoranda :—

"GRASS FIRES.—There have been serious grass fires on the frontier. By telegrams received on Monday it appears that in the Bedford division Mr R. Ainslie's homestead, etc., was destroyed; and that Mrs Ainslie, sen., had died from injuries received. Seven natives were burnt in their huts.

"The following is a telegram from the Fort Beaufort division :—' Grass fires at the Tyumie. Several farms and locations have been entirely denuded of pasturage. The forests took fire and burned for several days. Two sawyers and two little children were burned to death. Farmers compelled to trek. Great numbers of sheep burned, and the destruction of game immense.'"

"FIRE IN THE DISTRICT OF GEORGE.—A Port Elizabeth correspondent says,—' A pic-nic party in the district of George had a narrow escape. On Tuesday last, the 9th of February, the same day as that on which the great fire in Uitenhage and Humansdorp occurred, there was a festive gathering in the George district, when the grass caught fire, and a cart and harness had to be abandoned to the flames, and the company had to run for their lives. One man, a driver, was badly burnt.'"

The *Somerset Courant* says,—" The weather for the last ten days has been oppressively hot. We have not experienced such a continuance of warm, sultry days for a long time. Each day appeared to be warmer than another, until on Tuesday evening last the town was completely enveloped in a dense cloud resembling smoke, which some people believed came from the neighbouring mountain which was on fire. No fires having been heard of, others supposed it to be the peculiar state of the atmosphere. If so, it was a peculiar state indeed, for the smell of fire, like to burning grass, was very strong. From that evening, however, the weather became cooler, and at present there is every indication of rain, which we stand in need of.

"SMOKE.—We have heard an account of the extraordinary quantity of smoke with which the atmosphere was charged on the evening of Tuesday last. It appears that Mr Dixie, a farmer in the vicinity of Bedford, fired some portion of his veld, probably to reduce the long grass, in the meantime a high wind arose and carried the flames a much greater distance than was originally contemplated or intended; in fact, the fire communicated to the veld of Mr Henry Hutton and reached an out-station for sheep. The wind must have been very strong, as a kraal was entirely consumed and sixteen sheep were destroyed by the flames. The smoke from the fire extended almost to the Zuurburg, which gave rise to all sorts of rumours as to its origin."

These details justify my statement that the destruction of forests in South Africa has been extensive. They supply, in the case of those first given, indications that thereby the desiccation of the country by evaporation has been promoted; and by deduction from what has been ascertained by an extensive induction of facts observed elsewhere, it may be inferred that a similar consequence must, or may, have followed the destruction of forests, of which details have now been given. This subject next demands attention.

SECTION III.—*Effects of Denudation of the Country on Evaporation.*

In accordance with the prevalent opinion that trees have some influence in increasing or retaining moisture in the locality in which they grow, such destruction of trees as has been going on for such a length of time, and to such an extent, as these details embrace, it may be admitted, could scarcely fail to have tended to promote the dessication of the country by removing one hindrance to evaporation, and, in so far as this would effect it, allowing it to go on freely and unchecked.

It may have been remarked that simultaneously with this destruction of trees there has been going on a destruction of bush, and herbage, and grass, by the burning of the veldt, both by native tribes and by European colonists, and that the destruction of the forests has been to a great extent a consequence—and that an undesigned consequence of this practice—undesigned, and in some cases unheeded, in others deplored. This destruction of grass, and herbage, and bush has acted in the same way as the destruction of forests—in removing an important check upon evaporation, and so promoting the desiccation of the country.

To test some statements I made on this subject when I was at the Cape of Good Hope, Mr William Blore, M.L.A., Fellow of the Meteorological Society of London, and Secretary of the South African Meteorological Society, made some experiments at Wynberg Hill, about eight miles from Capetown, which I shall here detail, with the results obtained, premising that we have the means of comparing these results with others which have been obtained from similar experiments made in a forest and in open country.

From a report of such experiments made by Mathieu, one of the Directors of the Forest School at Nancy, prepared by orders of the General Superintendent of Forests, and published by the Government in the *Atlas Météorologique d l'Observatoire Imperial, pour 1867*,—which experiments were continued from April to October inclusive—it appears that during those months the evaporation from a vessel placed in the ground in a plantation of deciduous trees sixty-two years old was less than one-fifth of that from a vessel of like form and dimensions placed in the open country.

The quantity of water evaporated in the forest was 3·23 inches; the quantity evaporated from land clear of forests was 16·29 inches—about five times as much.

In April, before the development of leaves, if 1000 represented the evaporation from the open country, 623 represented the evaporation from woodland; but after the trees became clothed with foliage the amount of evaporation from the woodland was only 130, as against 1000 of open country evaporation. In October the woodland evaporation was to the open country as 90 to 100.

Mr Blore sunk two cylindrical jars of the same size in the ground to the depth of 4 inches, leaving them projecting an inch above the surface as a precaution against sand and other matters being blown into them, and covering each with wire gauze to keep out flies, &c. The one was placed where it was partially protected, but not covered by bush, the other was sunk in a newly cleared plot of ground, measuring about 60 feet in diameter, surrounded by sugar bushes, *Protea mellifera Thbg*, of a considerable height, and otherwise protected from the prevailing wind by a belt of pine trees, about 120 feet distant.

Into each of these jars was put 20 oz. of water on January 31st, at 10 A.M. On February 5th, at 5 P.M., the water remaining in each was carefully measured, and the evaporation was calculated. When it was found that the evaporation from the jar sunk in the cleared ground had been more than double the evaporation from that which was partially protected, though not covered by the bush; the former being 1·854 in.; the latter, ·863 in.; giving an excess of ·991 in. The experiment was repeated with similar results.

In reporting these results, Mr Blore remarked that had the experiment been made in a more arid district, the evaporation would have been greater; and that had it been made in the open country, the difference would have marked. But taking the results obtained as the basis of calculation, he arrived by the following process at a conclusion for which probably few who have not given attention to the subject are prepared.

The excess of evaporation from the more exposed jar above that from the jar partially shaded, but not covered, being one inch, more strictly speaking upwards of 99-100 of an inch of water, and more than double that of the latter, "An inch in six days," says he, "will give for 102 days, the ordinary duration of the hot windy and dry season in the district, 17 inches. This is equal to about three hundred and eighty-four thousand (384,000) gallons per acre, and supposing 1,000 acres to be burned, blackened, and dried—what with sunlight, fire, heat, and wind the evaporation would be an excess of three hundred and eighty-four millions of gallons of water above what would have been evaporated if the bush or grass had been left unburned."

In the prosecution of his researches, Mr Blore ascertained by experiment that on Wynberg hill, while the deposit of dew on a green surface amounted to 4·75, that on a white surface amounted only to 2, showing that the deposit of dew upon a green surface is more than double that upon a white; and he further ascertained that, while the difference of temperature in the water in the two jars employed in the former experiment was only a few degrees, the difference of temperature, between black ground and ground shaded by bush was about 25°, which would occasion a vastly greater difference in the amount of evaporation than that which occurred in his experiment.

Besides the promotion of desiccation, by removing an important check upon evaporation from the soil, consequent on the burning of the veldt, there has been reported a secondary effect produced in some cases which is at least worthy of notice.

Mr Horace Waller, F.R.G.S., who accompanied Bishop M'Kenzie and his party to the Zambesi, in 1861, in writing of their voyage up the Shire, says,—"The part of the river I am about to describe is singular for a species of canalization, which nature has arranged for it, as she tatoos fresh lines and wrinkles on Africa's face. Shortly after entering the Shire, one gets to a tract which, not many years since, was no doubt a lake. Time has altered this, and in the place of the lake there is a nearly grown-up marsh, for the river, a broad and shallow one before it, comes thus far to writhe and turn about it. When it gets to this part its whole character alters; it winds in countless turns, is narrow, and has a deep channel. One sees that in the gradual desiccating process (visible to so many African travellers) the current of this river has, in some unusually severe drought, lasting perhaps two or three years (and droughts often last that time), been reduced to a form which it still maintains with little alteration. It is true, that in ordinary seasons it would quickly have regained its original space, and the first heavy rains of the 'wet season' would have spread the waters as wide as ever; but, in the lengthened period of a drought a very important alteration takes place. The growth of rush and water-plants would now be most luxuriant along the edge of the river. Here the roots of the rank tropical vegetation are better watered than further away, where all is one hard, baked, black mass of earth sweltering in the sun. Here, too, a current of air is ever passing up or down the river; in short, vegetation can want nothing more, and is luxuriant beyond measure. It happens then, that when the fires, which every hot season pass over the whole country, crackle and roar across the space that was so lately a lake, they find more to consume along the banks than further away. Thus it is that the amount of debris left from the conflagration is larger on each side of the water, and also more solid in character; for, during the period of the fires, there is every afternoon a gale of wind for the most part blowing up the river's course, and this sweeps the flames so rapidly through the reeds that they do not get so thoroughly consumed as those that grow further away from its influence. The waters, in fact, cause and encourage an extra growth, and, when the fires come, they act as the 'navvies,' taking the excess of vegetation there is along the edge to make the dam. As my canoe drags its length beneath the bank, I can trace each year's quota in the strata of red ashes and charred reed-stalks. In places a hippopotamus' path causes an outlet for the water, and the river rushes through to try and regain its lost territory. It only wastes itself in the vast spongy marsh and the small lagoon, which give off more in evaporation than can be supplied by such means to counterbalance the effects of the sun. Throughout some thirty miles of the river in the Morambala marsh, this very interesting piece of natural engineering is to be seen."

In looking for the probable effect of this on the desiccation of the country, it may be well to bear in mind that to maintain the humidity of earth and air it is desirable that the rain which falls upon, or the water which passes through, it should be retained there and allowed to evaporate and to percolate through the soil, and should be kept from flowing away back again speedily or quickly to the sea, whence it had come.

By the confined channel the waters are carried off with increased velocity. A little escapes by breaches made by hippopotami, and this in circumstances favourable to evaporation, in consequence of which it is speedily and entirely taken up by the atmosphere; and so far so good; but it is indicated that the quantity thus retained is but a trifle compared with what, but for these embankments, would have spread out around, to be more slowly, but perhaps not less completely, absorbed by the atmosphere, to minister to the promotion of vegetation, and to arrest to some extent the rapidity of the process of desiccation which is going on.

It may appear paradoxical to speak of evaporation both as a means of desiccation and as a means of arresting desiccation; but it enters into the very nature of a paradox that the apparently conflicting facts are both facts though apparently conflicting; and in this case the solution of the paradox is not difficult. More water is carried off by gravitation than by evaporation, and evaporation is impeded by the humidity of the air; by the flow of the river more is carried off in a given time than would have been carried off in the same time by evaporation; and if this had not been so carried off it would have supplied humidity to the atmosphere, and so have impeded the evaporation whereby the land was desiccated while supplying moisture which, absorbed by that land, would have promoted vegetation, by which evaporation and desiccation would have been still further impeded. It is to some extent, though not invariably and constantly the case, that whatever tends to desiccate the country in any one way does so through so doing in many other ways beside; and conversely, whatever tends to increase the humidity of a climate in any one way, through so doing does so in many other ways beside. The fact observed by Mr Waller is a secondary result of the burning of the veldt. And while Dr Livingstone speaks as he does in regard to the drainage of the land by gravitation, so as to seem to teach that this alone may suffice to account for the desiccation and aridity of South Africa, there are others who have so spoken in regard to the promotion of desiccation by evaporation by the destruction of vegetation—arborescent and herbaceous, but chiefly the former—whereby the aridity under their consideration was brought about, that they have seemed to teach that this alone might suffice to account for the desiccation and aridity of the country. I hold with both, believing both to be correct in what they affirm in regard to the results which they severally report, and discriminating as I have done between the primary and the secondary cause of that desiccation.

I not only know of no one who has given so much attention to the study of the effect on the desiccation of South Africa of the destruction of trees, and bush, and herbage, and grass, as has Mr James Fox Wilson, of St Leonards, but I know of no subject connected with the desiccation of South Africa which has received such attention as has been given to this by him. The results he has embodied in a paper on the Water Supply in the Basin of the Orange River, and I have his permission to make free use of it in this compilation. I have already done so in describing the desiccation of the land, and I proceed to give his reply to the question—" Is there any cause besides the interior position of the country and the natural aridity of the soil which occasions the advance of drought?"

"WE ASSERT THAT THERE IS. . . The human inhabitants themselves are a prime cause of the disaster, to account for which we find only partial reasons in the central position and physical characteristics of these regions. THE NATIVES HAVE FOR AGES BEEN ACCUSTOMED TO BURN THE PLAINS AND TO DESTROY THE TIMBER AND ANCIENT FORESTS. The Bechuana, especially the Batlapi and neigbouring tribes, are a nation of forest levellers, cutting down every species of timber without regard to scenery or economy. The large traps or *hopos*, into which wild animals are driven for slaughter, must consume large quantities of trees in their construction, if we consider their immense size and the width of the avenues leading to them. Fuel, implements of war, husbandry, etc., make away with a large quantity of wood. Dwelling-houses, too, are chiefly composed of small timber instead of stone, and their fences of branches and shrubs. Thus, when a site for a town is fixed upon, the first consideration is to be as near a thicket as possible, the whole of which is presently levelled, leaving only a few trees, one in each great man's fold, to afford shelter from the heat. The ground to be occupied for cultivation is the next object of attention, and the large trees being too hard for their native iron axes, they burn them down by keeping up a fire at the root. These supply them with branches for fences, while the sparrows, so destructive to their grain, are deprived of an asylum. The fences, as well as those in the towns, require constant repairs; indeed the former must be renewed every year, and, rather than gather or quarry stones to raise a substantial fence, a man will take a forked stick, a thong, and his axe, and occupy nearly a whole day in bringing from a distance a bundle of the hook-thorn to fill up a gap in his cattle or sheep fold.

"By this means, the country for many miles around becomes entirely cleared of timber, while in the more sequestered spots, where they have their outposts, the same work of destruction goes on. Thus of the whole forests, where the giraffe and elephant were formerly wont to seek their daily food, nothing is now left but a few stumps of camel-thorn which bear a silent testimony to the wastefulness of the Bechuana. In some parts of the country, the remains of ancient forests of wild olive trees (Olea similis), and of the camel-thorn (Acacia giraffaea), are still to be met with; but when these are levelled in the proximity of a Bechuana village, no young trees spring up to take their place. When the natives migrate from a district, which may be after only a few years, the minor sorts of acacia soon grow, but the Acacia giraffaea requires an age to become a tree, and many ages must elapse before it can attain the dimensions of its predecessors.

"The natives of many tribes, even the Bakalakari of the desert have also the custom of annually getting rid of the tall dry grass by fire, which on some occasions destroys shrubs and trees to the very summit of the mountains, and must tend very much to produce an altered meteorological condition of the atmosphere, as well as to occasion that desolate and solitary aspect of the country which European travellers speak of so deprecatingly. In Namaqualand the field *(veld)* is seldom burnt, the fierce and powerful sun seeming to perform that office for the natives, and destroying, in a dry summer, an immense proportion of the young shrubs and trees which spring up in a wet one; the effect of drought in this instance becoming in its turn an auxiliary cause of drought; but there are vast regions in the basin of the Orange, and in the Cape Colony itself, bare of timber and bush, not only from the aridity of the soil, but from the pertinacity with which the natives, and even colonists of European descent, adhere to the practice of producing an annual conflagration in winter, in order that the flocks may find an abundance of pasturage as soon as the spring sets in. In these bare regions, trees are hardly ever to be found, except on the banks of rivers or in high mountain-passes, as the fire penetrates into all the kloofs or ravines where the most luxuriant vegetation is found, and destroys it.

"It appears certain that the farther we proceed westward from the mountains of Natal and Kaffirland, the less becomes the amount of rain bestowed by the clouds. The more denuded of trees and brushwood, and the more arid the land becomes, the smaller the supply of water from the atmosphere. The greater the extent of heated surface over which the partially exhausted clouds have to pass, the more rarefied the vapour contained in them necessarily becomes, and the higher the position which the clouds themselves assume in the atmosphere under the influence of the radiating caloric; consequently the smaller the chance of the descent of any rain on the thirsty soil beneath. And the more the short-sighted colonists and ignorant natives burn the grass and timber, the wider the area of heated surface is made; the further the droughty region extends, the smaller becomes the fountain supplies, and the more attenuated the streams, till they finally evaporate and disappear altogether. Thus the evil advances in an increasing ratio, and, unless checked, *must advance*, and will finally end in the depopulation and entire abandonment of many spots once thickly peopled, fertile, and productive.

"In the case of the fountains at Griqua Town, referred to at the commencement, as having formerly poured forth an abundant supply of water, the accidental destruction of whole plains of the wild olive-tree by fire near the town, and the removal of the shrubs on the neighbouring heights, are known to have preceded the diminution of rain, and subsequent diminution of the springs, the subterraneous caverns which acted as reservoirs in the bowels of the earth ceasing to be supplied from the clouds. There can be no question that, hitherto, vegetation, like animal life, has, in South Africa, been wastefully and ignorantly destroyed, in direct violation of physical laws, which can never be broken with impunity; and if we compare what is now taking place there with what has transpired in other arid countries, our conviction must deepen that it is not so much to the waywardness of nature as to the wilfulness of man that we must assign the recent extension of the Kalahari Desert.

"If we cautiously and carefully examine the subject, we shall find that in many temperate countries, and even in some cold ones, the felling of forests has been attended by a greater or less diminution of moisture, and an alteration of the climatic conditions. This has been the case in the Canadian settlements and the Eastern States of the North American Union, which, since being won from the primeval forest, have markedly improved in general salubrity and meteorological condition. Moreover, the general climate of Europe has undoubtedly undergone a great change since the destruction of the great belt of forest that, in the days of the old Romans, occupied its central portions. Not only has the climate of the old world become increasingly dry, but it has become warmer, the severe winters and heavy frosts described by ancient classical writers being now almost unknown in the South of Europe. In these cases the felling of timber, because productive of the removal of dank vegetation and unwholesome moisture, has operated to the improvement of the soil, increasing its producing capabilities, and occasioning it to be better fitted for the residence of man. The general character of ancient Europe, both insular and continental, whilst yet unreclaimed and overspread with forests, would naturally be more humid, and consequently colder. When cultivation and a vast increase of population occasioned the removal of the timber, the freezing of the Danube and Tiber would gradually become matter of history, and heavy frosts in Greece and Italy a cause of wonder.

"While the climate of our quarter of the globe has thus, we repeat, been ameliorated by the removal of the superabundance of wood, on the other hand, in the steppes of Southern Russia, in Northern Africa, in some parts of Italy, Greece, European Turkey, and Persia, many a bare tract exists which owes its origin to the folly or neglect of rulers, or subjects, who have removed, to the extent of absolute extermination, those natural protectors of humidity—the trees—and have thus turned fruitful gardens into a waste.

"In Greece and Asia Minor the traveller finds the reality fall far short of the description of the scenery given by the celebrated writers of olden time. The mighty streams so magniloquently described in the poems of antiquity are found to be mere rivulets compared with the grandiose accounts of the old epics. The sparkling cascades and fountains which, in enchanting the eye, also prompted the verse of the classic writers, have disappeared under the powerful influences exerted by ages of war, misrule, and oppression. Districts once covered with rich crops of corn, with olive and vineyards, orchards and groves, are at the present time mere expanses of sand or barren rocks, or arid flats. The same remarks are also true of Syria and Palestine, where the land 'flowing with milk and honey' has, under the iron heel of the obstructive and oppressive Turk, become in many parts a wilderness covered with stones and ruins.

"Proceeding still further to the East, perhaps there is no part of the world where evidence accumulates upon us of the evil effects resulting from the unwise destruction of timber, than in the more arid provinces of Persia. Here, under the ignorant government of the Shahs, whole tracts of country, once thickly peopled, well-watered, fertile, and extensively wooded, are little better than barren wastes, over which the traveller may pass and find no sweet bubbling fountain at which to quench his thirst, no solitary tree spreading its wide branches to produce a welcome shelter for his wearied limbs, no village or hostelry to which he can repair for hospitality. Instead of these, he will pass the remains of canals, bridges, and ornamental fountains, from which the water has been evaporated for centuries; he will encounter ruined houses, fallen walls of gardens, deserted villas, ancient churches and mosques, all baking in the fiery Persian sun, and testifying to the misrule which has so long prevailed here, as in other wretched countries of Asia. A late writer in 'Chambers' Journal,' on the subject of the failure of springs in the East, asserts that, as far back as the seventeenth century, a Persian nobleman, conversing with a European traveller (Tavernier), assured him that within a comparatively few years no less than four hundred springs had failed in the small province over which he himself ruled; a proof of the fatal consequences of permitting the destruction of timber for fuel without making provision for a fresh growth : for in the ancient days of Persia's greatness, before a Mahometan fatalism had begun to exert its baneful influence upon the Persians, a very different state of things existed. Then groves were planted on eminences; the streams were fringed with wood ; orchards and pleasure gardens, famous for their exquisitely scented roses, adorned the slopes of the hills ; and by careful irrigation through a thousand small canals, industry and energy were enabled to gather in an abundant harvest of the fruits of the earth. With the decadence of the political power of Islamism, however, the prosperity of Persia, such as it was under the caliphs, began to pass away : and ruined cities, aqueducts, palaces, and temples, standing in the midst of useless deserts, now offer their united testimony to the ignorance and incapacity of Mahometan princes.

"In our own British colonies of Barbadoes, Jamaica, Penang, and the Mauritius, the felling of forests has also been attended by a diminution of rain. In the island of Penang, the removal of jungle from the summits of hills by Chinese settlers speedily occasioned the springs to dry up, and, except during the monsoons, no moisture was left in the disforested districts. In the Mauritius it has been found necessary to retain all the lands on the crests of hills and mountains in the hands of Government to be devoted to forest, the fertility of the lower lands having been found by experience to depend upon clothing the hills with wood.

"In the steppes of Tartary we have abundant proof that physical changes of great magnitude, and similar in character to those which have been noticed on the Orange, have taken place within the historic period. Notwithstanding the present entire absence of trees, and the occurrence of a drought which regularly prevails for half the year, the beds of numerous rivers that once fertilized the country may be traced with the utmost facility to the sources from whence the waters originally flowed. In the time of Mithridates the Crimean steppe was famous for its fertility, and teemed with inhabitants, of which we have sufficient evidence, without referring to history, in the ruins of numerous towns and cities, and in the abundance of tumuli which strew the plains. Prince Woronzow, an enlightened Russian nobleman, assured the traveller Spencer that nearly the whole of western Tartary might be rendered a fertile and productive country by the adoption of judicious means. In his opinion, all that is wanted to change the entire character of the climate is to drain the marshes, dig artesian wells in the plains for the purposes of irrigation, and encourage the growth of timber. As the soil is generally of a dark loamy colour, and as, moreover, wherever the ground has been excavated, the roots of gigantic trees have been discovered, testifying to the former well-wooded condition of these now absolutely treeless plains, there can be little doubt that a paternal government might soon verify the truth of this enlightened nobleman's suppositions by a proper system of colonization.

"In Northern Africa, Egypt and Lybia have witnessed the advance of the desert since the decline of the Roman empire; and Algeria, although it has made rapid strides under its French conquerors, is still, in great part, the home of frogs, from the prevalence of marshes, and a nest of locusts from the barrenness of its plains. Algeria can only be rendered as fertile as it ought to be on condition that the French cover a third part of its surface with wood, and convert its rapid unnavigable rivers exclusively to the purposes of irrigation. The blindness of civilized states (who in this particular are little better than the uncivilized barbarians whose destructive practices we have been decrying), in foolishly laying the axe to the root of all trees, has been manifested in North as in South Africa; and until the carob, the olive, the cork-tree, the mastich, the oak, and the myrtle, are cultivated by the side of all waters, the rich harvests which rendered ancient Roman Africa the granary of the Imperial City need not be expected. Timber-trees, with roots which strike deep into the earth, it is worthy of remark, alone thrive here in summer, as they strike down into the humid soil under the parched crust; they should therefore be extensively encouraged for the shelter of water and of crops, since sheltered fields, according to an established fact, yield most corn.

"In this French colony, it must be noted further that the Wady-Kniss, called by Nicholas de Nicolai (1587) the Savo, used to be a large stream, and is now only a thread. It contains, however, many dry springs, the drying up having in all probability resulted from the stripping of the woods.

"Nor is the new world without evidence that the burning of prairies and pampas, and the wanton destruction of timber by Indian tribes and marauding Spaniards, has resulted in a deterioration of climate. Father Domenech, in his account of the Great American Desert, speaking of the celebrated Llano Estacado, or Staked Plain, says the prolonged drought, the nature of the soil, and the habit that the Indians have of *annually setting fire to the prairies*, account for its aridity. The country of New Mexico, since the invasion of the Spaniards, has become dry, arid, and deserted. Many of the Indian populations were suddenly deprived of both wood and water. Perpetual droughts followed the clearing of the forests. Both rivers and their sources dried up. A multitude of streams in Texas and New Mexico have ceased to flow—some for centuries, others only within a few years; and their banks, formerly gay with verdure, plants, flowers, and trees, now disappear under heaps of sand, and present everywhere a scene of desolation.

"On the banks of the Rio Verde, in the new territory of Arizona, abound ruins of stone dwellings and fortifications, situated in valleys where traces of former cultivation and of small canals for irrigation are yet visible. The traditions of the Indians, as under similar circumstances in Bechuanaland, point to a time when the elevated table-lands around were covered with magnificent and fruitful vegetation. But the timber was destroyed, the prairie-grasses were burnt off, and the Great Desert thereupon asserted its right to consider the newly-devastated lands as portions of its own territory, and evaporated the springs and rivers under the influence of its desiccating atmosphere.

"Turning to South America, Humboldt informs us that the Lake of Valencia in the state of Venezuela, is calculated, being destitute of an outlet, to gauge with the greatest nicety the increase or diminution of the rivers that pour their waters into it. From a careful examination, that accurate observer was convinced, both from the form of the surrounding hills, and from the occurrence of fresh-water shells in the heart of the country, that a great retrogression of the waters had taken place. No evidence, however, exists that any considerable diminution of them has taken place in very recent times, although within thirty years preceding Humboldt's visit the gradual desiccation of this great basin had excited general attention. This diminution is not to be accounted for, our traveller declares, by imagining the existence of subterraneous channels, as some suppose, but by the effects of evaporation, increased by the changes operated upon the surface of the country. Forests, he says, by sheltering the soil from the direct action of the sun, diminish the waste of moisture; consequently, when they are imprudently destroyed, the springs become less abundant, or are entirely dried up. Till the middle of the last century, the mountains that surround the valleys of Aragua, where the lake is situated, were covered with woods, and the plains with thickets interspersed with large trees. As cultivation increased the sylvan vegetation suffered; and, as the evaporation in this district is excessively powerful, the little rivers were dried up in the lower portion of their course during a great part of the year. The land that surrounds the lake being quite flat and even, the decrease of a few inches in the level of the water exposes a vast extent of ground; and as it has retired, the planters have taken possession of the new land.

"Five-and-twenty years after the visit of Baron Humboldt to Venezuela, M. Boussingault relates that, the country being desolated by the War of Independence, the lake was fuller than formerly, owing to the partial return of the land to a state of nature on the abandonment of many plantations. Hence, as timber was no longer felled to the same extent, rain fell in greater abundance, and the lake advanced in consequence. Another lake without an outlet, situated in New Granada, supplied Boussingault with a second and similar instance of the connection between the quantity of timber and the amount of rain. Here the recession of the waters was a matter of general notoriety, and coincident with the diminution had been the clearing of the surrounding forests, to afford fuel for the salt-works that exist in the neighbourhood. Nor could this have arisen from any change of climate; for in other places in the same neighbourhood, where no clearings have taken place, and where everything has continued to be left to nature, the level of the lakes has undergone no change from time immemorial.

"It being matter of notoriety in these instances that the removal piecemeal of forests, and the burning off of jungle from the summits of hills, has occasioned the uplands to become dry, and the lowlands to lose their springs, it becomes of extreme importance to our South African fellow-subjects, that the destruction of the arboreal protectors of water should be regarded as a thing to be deplored, deprecated, and prevented; and that public opinion on the matter should be educated.

"Up to the present the efforts made to employ irrigation in raising crops have been on the smallest scale, and little or no attention has been paid to the planting of trees for the purpose of protecting water, save at the Kuruman mission-village, where a considerable number have been planted by the veteran Moffat. Impelled by the best of motives, that of ameliorating the social as well as moral condition of the natives, whose tongue he himself reduced to grammatical rules, this gentleman has by precept and example been endeavouring to prevent that wholesale and wasteful destruction of timber which has prevailed from time immemorial. He declares his conviction that in process of time the natives will come to understand that trees are the true rain-makers, and to believe in the philosophy of encouraging their growth. He does not despair, he says, of eventually seeing the whole of the population—some of whom are now commencing the use of stone fences and brick houses—so fully satisfied on this point, that they will find it for their own interest, as well as contributing to the beauty of the country, to plant trees; more particularly as very few others, besides those indigenous to the soil, will grow to any extent.

"But we must not stop here. The evil is one of such magnitude, and likely to bear so abundant a harvest of misery in the future, that the authority of law, wherever practicable, should be invoked in order to institute preventive measures. Not only should fuel be economized, but the real interests of the British colonies and Dutch republics, for many long years to come, would most certainly be consulted by the passage of stringent enactments which should in the first place forbid, at any season or under any circumstances whatever, the firing of grass on field or mountain. The absolute necessity which exists for keeping as large a surface of the ground as possible covered with vegetation, in order to screen it from the solar rays, and thus to generate cold and humidity, that the radiation from the surface may not drive off the moisture of the rain-bearing clouds in their season, ought to compel the rigid enforcement of such a legal provision. Those colonial acts on this subject which are already in existence—for the Colonial Parliament at the Cape has found it necessary to pass restrictive measures—are not sufficiently stringent to be of much service, inasmuch as they are not entirely prohibitory, permitting the burning of the field at certain seasons of the year."

This paper was submitted to the British Association for the advancement of Science. Dr Livingstone, who had given his attention more immediately to the desiccation resulting from the upheaval of the continent, wrote to him in regard to the paper:—" Beith, 20th September 1864.—My dear sir,—I did not hear your paper, but heard Sir Roderick Murchison speak very favourably of its merits, and I quite agree in the view you take of the desirableness of planting trees and preventing grass-burning, as well as making Artesian wells. And I am, &c., DAVID LIVINGSTONE."

The paper was subsequently submitted to the Royal Geographical Society. It was published in their Transactions (Vol. xxxv. 1865); and the following account of the discussion which took place on its being read was published under the authority of the Council of the Society in the journal of proceedings:—

" The President, Sir Roderick I. Murchison, said that to a great extent he thought Mr Wilson's conclusions were correct. He regretted the absence from the meeting of Mr Cyril Graham, who could have thrown much light upon the present subject. In his description of the region of Hauran, to the east of Damascus, this distinguished traveller and scholar had showed how this country, which in Scriptural times was filled with towns and contained an immense population, had, without any geological change whatever intervening, become an uninhabitable desert from the same causes as those pointed out by Mr Wilson. He knew, from his own observations in Russia, that the Volga had diminished in volume in consequence of the cutting down of the great forests on the Ural mountains. Even in our own country the same process was in operation from the removal of timber and the drainage of lands. The remedies which Mr Wilson pointed out in reference to Southern Africa seemed reasonable. He would, however, call upon some of the African travellers present to state what they knew on the subject.

" Dr Livingstone could agree with the author of the paper on several points, and on others he must suspend his judgment. There could be no doubt as to the main fact of the drying up of the country to which reference had been made. The small stream on which he settled at Kolobeng was flowing very abundantly when he first laid out its waters in order to irrigate a garden; but in the course of two or three years it had entirely dried up. He ought to mention, however, that he had been informed since then that the stream had begun to flow again. In other cases, in that same district, fountains had dried up at such a remote period that no tradition existed of their ever having flowed, except in their names. No doubt these little streams did dry up and burst forth afresh; but the more general desiccation to which he referred left no doubt on his mind that the whole country had once enjoyed a much more humid climate than now. He had traced himself, in his earlier travels, for long distances, the dry beds of very large rivers which had a general course from north to south instead of east and west, the prevailing direction of existing rivers. In one instance he came upon the dry channel of a river two or three miles broad. It was remarkable that the natives still called these dried up water-courses by the name of rivers. In the dry bed of a large lake which he had discovered, as well as in the bed of the river just mentioned, he found large numbers of fresh-water shells, which were of the same species as those now living in the waters of the interior. The change in the state of the country, implied in the desiccation of these great streams and lakes, could not have been caused merely by the natives burning down trees and grass, though he admitted they did burn the grass extensively, so much. so in certain months of the year that there was quite a haze over the whole country, which in Western Africa is called 'the smokes.' One thing that struck him as very remarkable was this, that there must have been very large fresh-water lakes in the interior of the country, and that a very considerable difference of level had taken place since these lakes contained standing water. The only way in which he could account for their being drained off so completely is by the sudden opening of fissures by subterranean convulsion; and he believed these fissures were of a similar nature and origin to those which now form the Victoria Falls. The fissure into which this great cataract plunges was evidently not the result of wearing away by the action of water, as in the case of Niagara. The edge over which the water falls shows no signs of wearing away, and the rock is quite perpendicular for 310 feet on all sides. The rock consists of hard basalt, and a little to the east it has all the appearance of volcanic tufa. The author of the paper did not seem to know that many of his suggestions had already been adopted at the Cape, where immense quantities of *Eucalypti* were grown in the Botanic Garden for distribution among those who wished to plant trees. In four years the tree grew to a height of twenty feet. The general desiccation of the country he attributed not so much to the cutting down of trees as to the elevation of the country, more especially on the west side of the continent. The ancient streams on the western side had ceased flowing to a greater extent than those on the east, and he found the west coast had been elevated about 200 feet. He believed it was in the process of elevation that the fissures had let off the inland lakes.

"Dr Kirk said the writer of the paper pre-supposed a state of population different from that which is found in any part of Africa at the present day. In the tropical region that he visited, on the Zambesi, there was abundance of wood on the hill-sides, and the average amount of population; but he was sure the people alone could not complete the entire destruction of the forests. They used the wood for domestic purposes, but that did not in any way affect the average amount of vegetation in the country. Some other cause must be looked for to explain the progressing aridity of South Africa, but what that cause might be it was very difficult to point out. He was inclined to believe that the original aridity both of the Sahara in the north and the Kalahari in the south was due to atmospheric currents. Enormous volumes of air rushed towards the interior of Africa from both sides. This air must come down somewhere, after depositing its moisture in its ascent; and wherever it strikes the earth it will come down very dry. It was probable that in the north it came down on the Sahara desert, and in the south on the Kalahari.

"Mr Galton said the author of the paper had omitted to explain why the destruction of timber had progressed more rapidly in recent times. It was probably to be accounted for by two separate causes. A few centuries ago the population of that part of South Africa of which he spoke consisted mainly of Hottentots, now it consisted chiefly of the Caffre race. There is a considerable difference between the habits of the two races. The Hottentots are eminently natty and saving, the Caffres eminently wasteful; and from that cause we might conclude that more timber would have been cut down in recent times than formerly. Another cause of greater importance was the free introduction of iron. Axes are now to be had everywhere throughout South Africa, where formerly iron was a rarity; and the consequence is, that the wood is cut down much more readily than heretofore, for making camp-fires and protection for the cattle.

"Colonel G. Balfour stated that during the course of the investigation into the public works of India, on which he served twelve years ago, evidence was brought before the commission that the effect of cutting down trees was to diminish the moisture of the country. At the same time his brother, Dr Balfour (Deputy Inspector-General of Hospitals, Madras Presidency), undertook an investigation into the effect of cutting down trees on the sources of springs, and the notes, which he drew up, on the influence exercised by trees in inducing rain and preserving moisture, satisfactorily proved that in many instances springs which had dried up had been found to open again on the trees growing up. The Report was printed by the Government of Madras, and considered of such value that it was extensively circulated, with a view to further inquiries being made; but the results of these investigations have not yet been made public. He (Col. Balfour) had also observed the effect, on the rainfall, of the want of trees in different parts of southern India. He might mention a tract of country, the Ceded Districts of the Madras Presidency, as large as Ireland, where there is scarcely a tree to be seen, and that area has a smaller proportion of rain that any other part of India. When he passed through Aden in 1862 he was informed by the officer in charge of political affairs there, that in consequence of the opening of tanks the trees had increased considerably, and the supply of water for the use of the troops and people had also much increased. He had been informed that morning, that in the West Indies the Government of Trinidad had passed a law prohibiting the cutting down of trees near the capital, in order to ensure a supply of rain.

"Lord Stratford de Redcliffe, on being invited by the President to relate a circumstance which had come under his knowledge, said, most people who were acquainted with Constantinople and its neighbourhood were aware that the capital was supplied by water contained in reservoirs attached to streams that pass through a district called the Forest of Belgrade. Some years ago permission was given to cut down the timber in this forest: speculators took advantage of the Sultan's permission, to cut it down largely. The consequence was soon felt: the reservoirs began to fail, and the Government was obliged to interfere and to restrict its permission, in order to prevent the drying up of the springs, which seemed so inevitable a consequence of depriving them of the shade of trees.—The meeting then adjourned."

I accept most of the views thus expressed, and more than one of them are views which I have otherwise been led to embrace. I hold with Dr Livingstone, as preceding statements show, that the primary cause of the desiccation of South Africa has been the upheaval of the land. I am not prepared to question the statements of Dr Kirk in regard to the effect of atmospheric currents on the Sahara and the Kalahari; and I receive the testimony of Sir Roderick Murchison, Mr Galton, Colonel Balfour, and Lord Stratford de Redcliffe, to the observations cited by them, as in accordance with the views to which I have been led—first by vague statements brought under my attention, and then by deduction, or *a priori* reasoning—and in which I have been confirmed by explicit testimony. By Marsh, in his valuable treatise, an abundance of facts have been given in illustration of the influence of forests on the flow of springs being in accordance with these observations.

I have spoken of the drying up of lakes, and a diminished flow of streamlets and streams, as consequences which have followed the destruction of forests, and of herbage and bush by fire; but I attributed the same consequences, to some extent, to the destruction latterly of bush and herbage by sheep. The following statement on this subject occurs in an article by Dr Rubidge, of Port Elizabeth, on some of the evils of over-pasturing the country, which appeared in the *Eastern Province Monthly Magazine* :—" Sir Thomas Lyell says that Spain is fast being ruined by its large flocks of Merinos—he describes changes which the country has undergone, similar to those noted by the occupiers of recently settled districts in this country. Sheep, it is well known, crop the grass close; and in dry and sandy soils pull it up by the roots—thus laying the soil bare, and exposing it to be washed away by the heavy rains. Moreover, sheep tread much in the same tracks, and thus form little paths which serve as drains to convey the water away rapidly from the surface into the brooks, which, swollen into temporary rivers, wash away the sedges that impeded their course. The consequences of this too rapid drainage of the bared soil are, that little water sinks in to nourish the roots of the grasses and useful plants, and less soaks through the soil to replenish the springs,—so that in many overworked farms some of the springs no longer yield so much water as they formerly did, while others have entirely failed. The destruction of the grass and small bushes, and the quick drainage prevent the retention of the water on the surface, and its slow but continuous evaporation, thus probably diminishing the quantity of rain which falls. The rivers, as well as the smaller streams, undergo a change. In former times, the sedges and long grass which grew on the sides of the small tributaries of the Zeekoe and Sunday's Rivers afforded cover to the rhinoceros, the hippopotamus, and the buffalo,—whereas now a spring-buck could scarce hide himself. A farmer is, or lately was, living, who had seen palmiets in the Sunday's River, above Graaff-Reinet, where numerous large holes of water occurred in its bed. Those who have not visited districts either more recently occupied or less pastured by sheep, can scarce believe that Sunday's and Fish Rivers, which now flow in such deep channels, formerly ran almost level with their banks, which were fringed by a luxuriant growth of sedge and palmiet."

The same thing is referred to in a letter addressed to me while at the Cape by J. H. Davis, Esq., Colesberg, on grasses and herbage found in the Sour, the Sweet, and the Mixed veldts, and the Karroo, cited in a letter appended to Report of the Colonial Botanist for 1864, in which, speaking of the gentle undulating country extending from the Sneewberg mountains to the Orange River, reckoned by many amongst the prime sheep-walks of the Colony, he says,—" The most luxuriant grassy parts of the sweet veldt are generally plains nearly horizontal, which, not having a quick watershed, retain much moisture; and the light sandy soil, lying frequently but a few inches thick upon the hard Karroo soil below, is preserved from being washed away—for it may be observed almost everywhere, that where these plains are inclined, even at a low angle, the light top soil does get washed away, leaving the hard earth below exposed at the surface, and wherever this takes place the grass disappears, and the heaths, with other short scrubby plants, spring up. This change appears to me to be rapidly taking place in this part of the Colony; and it is promoted, perhaps often induced, by the feet of the sheep; they make little paths in every direction, and the water flows in these paths as so many little channels, washing away all the light earth, and then the grass roots get exposed and gradually disappear. Many farms which I remember fifteen or sixteen years ago to have been rich in grass are now almost bare of it, even in the most favourable seasons; and this process is, I believe, gradually but surely passing over the whole country, wherever sheep are introduced."

On the Continent of Europe an effect similar to what is here spoken of is found to be produced upon a larger scale by forest *slid pads*. These are occasionally converted into runnels and streams, and to the extent of their measure they tend to create torrents, against the production of which no better protection can be found, if better could be desired, than are forests and plantations of herbage and bush and trees.

SECTION IV.—*Effect of Denudation of the Country on the Rainfall.*

Thus far attention has been given to the effect of the destruction of forests, and herbage, and bush in promoting desiccation, by removing an important check upon evaporation. But this is not the only consequence affecting the hydrology of the country which must have followed the long-continued and extensive destruction of these which has been carried on. Amongst other consequences which must have followed may be reckoned the effect of this destruction on the rainfall, and the effect of it upon the soil.

Observations have been made which seem to show that over a great extent of country, and over an extended period of time, little effect has been produced on the total rainfall by very extensive destruction of forests. But this is not incompatible with these forests and the destruction of them having exerted an important influence on the distribution of the rainfall, both in time and space. And thus may be harmonized the observations referred to with observations which have given rise to prevalent popular opinions on the subject.

It is a prevalent opinion that trees attract rain, or attract clouds, and so increase the rainfall. I do not consider it probable that they do so; but this is a matter which must be determined by the testimony of the rain-gauge, and not by *a priori* reasoning on the subject. Such testimony we have not; and I do not see when or how we are likely to obtain the testimony required. The rainfall would require to be noted for years in the same locality covered with forests, and afterwards denuded of forests, or one bare of trees and afterwards covered with plantations,—and even then it might be questioned whether this would supply testimony sufficient of itself to establish the point.

The rainfall depends on the coincidence of a great many circumstances and combination of influences,—the absence or undue preponderance of any one or more of which may affect the result. And the observations which have been made up to the present are apparently, from want of attention to this, somewhat conflicting.

I think it not improbable that there will be a greater rainfall where there is abundance of forest, in consequence of the same moisture being precipitated and evaporated and precipitated again and again, as morning after morning the glass of a Wardian case is bedewed on the inside with moisture which is evaporated as the warmth of the day is increased, but only to be again deposited as the cold of the night comes on. This is something different from what can be called the attraction of clouds; but the rain thus occasioned would not be less efficient in promoting vegetation than would rain falling from clouds attracted from afar, and I attach much more importance to the abundant moisture indicated by repeated depositions of the same water than I do to any power which forests may have, or may be supposed to have, to attract clouds from any distance—great or small.

I find an opinion in exact accordance with that which I have formed on the subject expressed in the following statement by Marsh :—"The effect of the forest on precipitation then is by no means free from doubt, and we cannot positively affirm that the total annual quantity of rain is even locally diminished or increased by the destruction of the woods, though both theoretical considerations and the balance of testimony strongly favour the opinion that more rain falls in wooded than in open countries. One important conclusion, at least, upon the meteorological influence of forests is certain and undisputed,—the proposition, namely, that within their own limits, and near their own borders, they maintain a more uniform degree of humidity in the atmosphere than is observed in cleared grounds. Scarcely less can it be questioned that they tend to promote the frequency of showers, and if they do not augment the amount of precipitation they probably equalize its distribution through the different seasons."

In accordance with what is thus stated the following statements are subjoined in foot-notes :—" Among recent writers, Clavé, Schacht, Sir John F. W. Hershel, Hohenstein, Barth, Asbjoerensen, Boussingault, and others, maintain that forests tend to produce rain and clearings to diminish it, and they refer to numerous facts of observation in support of this doctrine ; but in none of these does it appear that these observations are supported by actual pluviometrical measure. So far as I know, the earliest expression of the opinion that forests promote precipitation is that attributed to Christopher Columbus, in the *Historie del S. D.'Fernando Colombo*, Venecia, 1571, Cap. LVIII, where it is said that the Admiral ascribed the daily showers which fell in the West Indies about vespers to ' the great forests and trees of those countries,' and remarked that the same effect was formerly produced by the same cause in the Canary and Madeira Islands and in the Azores, but that ' now that the many woods and trees that covered them have been felled, there are not produced so many clouds and rains as before.'

"M. H. Harrisse, in his very learned and critical essay, *Fernand Colomb, sa vie et ses Œuvres, Paris, 1872*, has made it at least extremely probable that the *Historie* is a spurious work. The compiler may have found this observation in some of the writings of Columbus now lost, but, however that may be, the fact, which Humboldt mentions in *Cosmos* with much interest, still remains, that the doctrine in question was held, if not by the great discoverer himself, at least by one of his pretended biographers as early as the year 1571."

And again,—" The strongest direct evidence which I am able to refer to in support of the proposition that the woods produce even a local augmentation of precipitation is furnished by the observations of Mathieu, sub-director of the Forest School at Nancy. His pluviometrical measurements, continued for three years, 1866–1868, showed that during that period the annual mean of rainfall in the centre of the wooded district of Cinq-Tranchées, at Belle Fontaine on the borders of the forest, and at Amauce, in an open cultivated territory in the same vicinity, was respectively as the numbers 1000, 957, and 853.

"The alleged augmentation of rainfall in Lower Egypt, in consequence of large plantations by Mehemet Ali, is very frequently appealed to as a proof of this influence of the forest, and this case has become a regular commonplace in all discussions of the question. It is, however, open to the same objection as the alleged instances of the diminution of precipitation in consequence of the felling of the forest.

"This supposed increase in the frequency and quantity of rain in Lower Egypt is, I think, an error, or at least not an established fact. I have heard it disputed on the spot by intelligent Franks, whose residence in that country began before the plantations of Mehemet Ali and Ibrahim Pacha, and I have been assured by them that meteorological observations, made at Alexandria about the beginning of this century, show an annual fall of rain as great as is usual at this day. The mere fact that it did not rain during the French occupation is not conclusive. Having experienced a gentle shower of nearly twenty-four hours duration in Upper Egypt, I inquired of the local governor in relation to the frequency of this phenomena, and was told by him that not a drop of rain had fallen at that point for more than two years previous.

"This belief in the increase of rain in Egypt rests almost entirely on the observations of Marshal Marmont, and the evidence collected by him in 1836. His conclusions have been disputed, if not confuted, by Jomard and others, and are probably erroneous." And he refers to Foissac *Meteorologie*, German Translation (pp. 634–639) in support of what is said.

Foissac, in his *Meteorologie mit Rüchsight auf die Lehere vom Kosmos*, translated into German by A. H. Emsman, and published in Leipzig in 1859—the work cited by Mr Marsh, Klöden, in his *Handbuch der Physischen Geographie*, and Belgrand, in a paper *De l'Influence des Fôrets sur l'écoulements des Eaux pluviales*, in *Annals des Ponts et Chaussées*, 1854, 1st Semiestre,—have all expressed opinions somewhat opposed to the opinions more generally received. But there is nothing advanced even by them at variance with what I have alleged. All that can be said at present is that the evidence is conflicting as to the fact whether forests do or do not increase the rainfall. If it be sufficient to established as a fact that they have done so, and that they do so in certain circumstances, there is a lack of evidence that they do so invariably and in all circumstances, or even generally, which is the matter in question.

But while that question remains undecided, awaiting the testimony of the rain-gauge through a series of years in the same locality, with and without a forest around, there are matters of more importance which can meanwhile, and that even now, be determined.

In connection with illustrations previously given of the aridity which has been attained in South Africa, I have cited deluges of rain as of occasional occurrence. I might have spoken of the extreme aridity and deluges of rain as being both of them characteristic of the meteorology of extensive districts of South Africa. These deluges of rain often are accompanied by thunder, the cause or occasion of both may be considered as the same, and the precipitation of the rain in torrents may be attributed to the disturbance of the electric equlibrium, though it owed not to this its deposition in the clouds.

From the occurrence of these it appears that there is even in the dryest atmosphere in South Africa sufficient moisture to produce such phenomena. Dr Moffat, writing of the effects in Namaqualand of winds from the north, says,—" These winds, I have learned from inquiry, come from within the tropics, where rain has fallen, and the cool air thereby produced rushes southward over the plains, filling up the space caused by the refraction of the air, owing to the approach of the sun to the tropic of Capricorn. The more boisterous these winds are, the more reason we have to expect rain. They cannot extend to any great height, as the thunder storms which follow, and which often commence with a small cloud in the opposite direction, increasing into mountains of snow, with a tinge of yellow, pursue an opposite course. These are preceded by a dead stillness, which continues till the tornado bursts upon us with awful violence, and the clouds have discharged their watery treasures. In such a case there are almost always two strata of clouds, frequently moving in opposite directions. The higher mountain-like masses, with their edges exactly defined, going one way, while the feelers, or loose misty vapour beneath, convulsed, and rolling in fearful velocity, are going another ; while the peals of thunder are such as to make the very earth tremble."

At this point I might close my quotation, but what follows has an important bearing on the subject :—" The lightning is of three descriptions, one kind passing from cloud to cloud; this is seldom accompanied with any rain. Another kind is the forked, which may be seen passing through a cloud, and striking the earth; this is considered the most dangerous. The most common, not always accompanied by rain, is what we are in the habit of calling stream or chain-lightning. This appears to rise from the earth in figures of various shapes, crooked, zigzag, and oblique ; and sometimes like a waterspout at sea : it continues several seconds, while the observer can distinctly see it dissolve in pieces like a broken chain. The perpetual roar of awful thunder on these occasions may be conceived, when twenty or more of these flashes may be counted in one minute. The lightning may also be seen passing upwards through the dense mass of vapour, and branching out like the limbs of a naked tree in the blue sky above. In such storms the rain frequently falls in torrents, and runs off very rapidly, not moistening the earth, except in sandy plains, more than six inches deep."

The whole phenomena, from the formation of the cloud at so great a distance from the sea, isolated and unconnected with clouds extending from the ocean thither, to the precipitation of the deluge of rain, appear to have been occasioned by a temporary disturbance and intermixture of the two aerial currents passing overhead between the equator and the poles.

The narrative recalls to me much that I heard of the breaking up of the drought in 1862. In particular am I reminded of an account which appeared in the colonial newspapers of the day, of the clouds and of the deluges of rain which in a time almost incredibly brief darkened and flooded the lands of the Lang Kloof. And what occurred there appears to have been but a type of storms which everywhere flooded the colony, carrying away bridges, destroying roads, undermining houses, and in other ways threatening to double the damage done to the colony by the preceding drought.

All the moisture was there, and there had been, it may be, as much throughout the whole continuance of the drought—but the aerial currents referred to pursued each its course undisturbed, and rain there was none. Now they dashed into each other, and the rain was deposited in a deluge. And the disturbance did not stop all at once, it was a year and more before the currents regained their stable force and direction.

These rains tell of the quantity of moisture which was in the atmosphere covering the regions of regular rain; and the torrents tell of the same in the same, or in the intermediate zone, of diminished rain. After such deluges of rain there comes rolling down the river-bed, or water-course, a wave which carries all before it, like the wave of an Alpine torrent; the waters which follow seem to swell as they flow—but this phenomenon is less impressive than the wave, and hence comes the form of expression in general use. The state of some of the rivers crossed by me in the tour I have referred to—for example, that of Tarka—flowing on for days from 20 to 25 feet in depth, where in general the depth is only, as it was immediately before, 16 inches, may give some idea of what is occasionally seen in South Africa, and prepare the reader for what might otherwise prove more astounding facts.

Captain Hall, in his *Manual of South African Geography*, states that he "has seen the bed of the Great Fish River perfectly dry, and within twenty-four hours a torrent, thirty feet deep and several hundred feet wide, was roaring through it. In February 1848 the Rat River suddenly rose upwards of fifty feet in a few hours, sweeping seventeen feet above the roadway of a stone bridge, at Fort Beaufort, supposed to have been built high enough to leave a clear way to the highest flood ever before remembered."

A gentleman engaged in civil engineering in Kaffraria, with whom I had an opportunity of talking over the subject of river-pumps, and who had given special attention to the flow of rivers in the Colony, informed me that the mean greatest rise in a number of rivers in that district was twenty-eight feet; but he told me of a maximum rise of sixty feet; and I have gone over the scene of devastation occasioned at Hankey, by the sudden rise of the Gamtoos River a short time before to a height of seventy feet above its usual level.

Whence come these waters? From clouds formed in a cloudless sky by a deposition of moisture, from transparent air occasioned by a slight disturbance and intermixture of the aerial currents passing overhead between the equator and the poles! All that moisture must have been there, as otherwise it could not have been deposited—there though invisible,—and destruction instead of fertility has been the consequence of its precipitation in a deluge, falling, it may have been, in the course of an hour and on a spot of limited extent,—whereas, had it been diffused over a district an hundred times more extensive, and fallen in genial showers at intervals extending over months, it had brought blessing both to man and beast. Now it is alleged, and that not without reason, that this is the normal state of the rainfall over a country covered with trees or other vegetation, and that that which makes the rainfall productive often of evil in South Africa is the characteristic rainfall of a country divested or devoid of vegetation. If such be the case, then has the extensive destruction of tree, and bush, and herbage, and grass, not only tended to promote that evaporation by which the desiccation of the soil has produced the aridity which exists, but it has tended to confine the rainfall, by which that desiccation might have been counteracted, to such limited times and limited spots, that almost the whole is carried off by gravitation to the sea, working destruction and ruin by the way, instead of causing it to be so diffused in time and space that the earth over an extensive district, "drinking in the rain coming oft upon it, should bring forth herbs meet for them by whom it is dressed."

To know the evil in its magnitude and its extent, and to know the producing cause and occasion of it, may lead to recovery. The Lord "turneth rivers into a wilderness, and the water-springs into dry ground; a fruitful land into barrenness, for the wickedness [or want of attention to his laws] of them that dwell therein." Again—"He turneth the wilderness into a standing water and dry ground into water-springs. And there He maketh the hungry to dwell, that they may prepare a city for habitation; and sow fields, and plant vineyards, which may yield fruits and increase. . . . Whoso is wise and will observe these things, even they shall understand the loving-kindness of the Lord."

SECTION V.—*Effect of Denudation of the Country on the Hydroscopicity of the Soil.*

The soil, exposed to the chemical rays of light, undergoes a change whereby its power of retaining moisture is greatly reduced; and thus also, as well as by its effect on the rainfall, may the destruction of forests, and bush, and herbage by fire, have promoted the desiccation of the country. Reference has been made to the absorbing power of the air being, in the specified circumstances, greater than the retentive power of the soil to prevent the desiccation of moist soil by a dry atmosphere. But it is also the case that several salts, such as carbonate of potash, muriate of lime, and even table salt, absorb moisture from what may seem to be a dry air—such as is the dry air in a house—and deliquesce or dissolve in the moisture they thus absorb. The same affinity for moisture in different degrees is exercised by different substances, and it can be shown that moisture is absorbed from the atmosphere, irrespective of rain or dew, by humus, a product of vegetable decomposition, and is retained by it in a state in which it is fitted to promote vegetation. But humus, it is alleged, is decomposed and eliminated from the soil, when this is exposed to the solar ray, one constituent of which induces chemical action.

In a paper on the Philosophy of Arboriculture, by the Rev Dr Macvicar, of Moffat, who was the original editor of the *Quarterly Journal of Agriculture*, issued by the Highland and Agricultural Society of Scotland, and subsequently resided in Ceylon, where he had opportunities for prosecuting researches upon which he had previously entered, the writer remarks, in regard to effects following the destruction of forests,—"The soil when stript of the clothing which the forest afforded, and exposed naked to the heat of the sunbeam, changes very rapidly from the rich mould which the long-continued fall of the leaf in the forest had made it, and becomes very unproductive. Had occasional trees in the forest been left to give shade during part of the day, the destination of the carbon in the mould would have been to have been slowly converted into carbonic acid, and so to supply food to the successive crops growing on the soil, as they required it. But when the sunbeam is left to break in its full force on the soil all day long, it burns the carbon in the soil with great rapidity into carbonic acid; and this gas, unless there be in the soil some oxide having an affinity to it to retain it, goes off in gas, injuring the salubrity of the air perhaps, and at all events wholly impoverishing the soil,—for carbonic acid is the principal food of all plants. The same course of things, it might be shown, happens with regard to ammonia; and thus, both as itself the immediate food of plants and as that which by oxidation yields nitre, ammonia is lost. Thus the indiscriminate destruction of forest over any great breadth of country, if that country have plenty of sunshine, is a great evil."

If it be so, then would it appear the thinness of the superficial layer of soil covering the pot clay throughout extensive districts of the Colony of the Cape of Good Hope and of regions beyond, subjected to the solar rays falling through a dry atmosphere, cloudless and singularly transparent, and the small store of humus in that soil, cannot be held as evidence that no forests ever covered these districts if there be counter indications that the contrary must have been at one time the case.

In correspondence with Dr Macvicar on the subject, he wrote to me,— "As to the point to which you refer—the rapid generation in the soil, and the vaporization from it of ammonia and carbonic acid, under the impact of the tropical sunbeams and breezes,—I do not remember to have seen it dwelt upon by any writer, though both in the writings of Boussingault and of Liebig it is implied; and it is an inevitable consequence of the eremacausis or the slow combustion of organic matter. It is familiarly verified by the process of bleaching. Even with such sunshine as we have in this country the organic matter which imparts colour to tissues is carried off much more rapidly in the sunbeam than out of it; and it can only be carried off as carbonic acid and ammonia: that is, it is not merely changed from coloured to colourless, as is proved by the loss of weight which the web has sustained when it is bleached. In this country we have generally less sunshine than we require, and, except in fallows, the surface of the soil is never left bare. Hence the effect of the impact of the sunbeam has been but little considered. But from what I have observed in the tropics, I am persuaded that its power of affecting plant food in the neighbourhood, by the destruction of the fertility of every surface that is left bare, is very great. It intensifies to a wonderful extent that action of the incumbent atmosphere by which the carbon and hydrogen in the soil unite with the oxygen and nitrogen of the air, and give moisture, carbonic acid, and ammonia almost immediately after, if they be not utilized on the spot where they are generated, dispersing all but that quantum which the soil can retain at a temperature of perhaps 140 or 150 F., which is not much."

Thus can we account for the fact that the destruction of trees not only deprives the land of the shade which they afford, but, if the ground be not speedily covered again with vegetation, the soil is impoverished. Under favourable circumstances a forest destroyed by fire renews itself rapidly and permanently. This was the case after an extensive destructive fire which occurred at Miramichi in 1825; but it is not always the case. Marsh says, "Between sixty and seventy years ago, a steep mountain with which I am familiar, composed of metamorphic rock, and at that time covered with a thick coating of soil and a dense primeval forest, was accidentally burned over. The fire took place in a very dry season; the slope of the mountain was too rapid to retain much water, and the conflagration was of an extraordinarily fierce character, consuming the wood almost entirely, burning the leaves and combustible portion of the mould and in many places cracking and disintegrating the rock beneath. The rains of the following autumn carried off much of the remaining soil, and the mountain side was nearly bare of wood for two or three years afterwards. At length a new crop of trees sprung up and grew vigourously, and the mountain is now thickly covered again. But the depth of mould and earth is too small to allow the trees to reach maturity. When they attain to the diameter of about *six inches* they uniformly die, and thus they will no doubt continue to do until the decay of leaves and wood on the surface, and the decomposition of the subjacent rock, shall have formed, perhaps hundreds of years hence, a stratum of soil thick enough to support a full grown forest. Under favourable conditions, however, as in the case of the fire of Miramichi, a burned forest renews itself rapidly and permanently."

In this way does the destruction of forests, and more especially the desstruction of forests by fire, tend to promote the desiccation of a country, so far by combustion and further by exposure of the humus to decomposition by the sun's rays, destroying one of the constituents of the soil which exercises great retentive power on its moisture.

The effects of forests on evaporation, absorption, and infiltration of water is a subject which has engaged much of the attention of students of forest economy in France engaged in the employment of *reboisement* and *gazonnement*, or the replenishing denuded districts with forest, and herbage, and bush, as means of preventing the occurrence of the devastating effects of mountain torrents and inundations, and their conclusions are in accordance with those now advanced; but enough has been adduced for my present purpose.

PART III.—ARIDITY OF SOUTH AFRICA AND WATER SUPPLY.

The primary and principal cause of the desiccation and consequent aridity of South Africa appears to have been, and to be, the elevation of the land, and the consequent flow of the water which falls upon it as rain, by gravitation to the sea. The secondary cause of that desiccation and consequent aridity appears to have been, and to be, the evaporation of remaining water, by which the aridity has been brought to the degree it has attained,—the desiccation thus completed having been promoted by the long-continued destruction of forests, and bush, and herbage, and grass, chiefly but not exclusively by fire. And I would now renew an attempt to communicate information in regard to the degree of aridity which has been the result.

CHAPTER I.

ARIDITY AND WATER SUPPLY BEYOND THE COLONIZED PORTION OF SOUTH AFRICA.

Section I.—*Aridity beyond the Colonized portion of South Africa.*

We have a description given by Dr Livingstone of the terrible drought that interrupted his initiatory labours as a Christian missionary when he established himself on the Kolobeng River, in the Bakwain territory, before he set out on his extensive journeys in the land to the north. This description may give some idea of the aridity which has followed the desiccation of the country, and of the consequences of long-continued drought. After describing his dam-making and other operations during the first year of his residence there, he proceeds,—" But in our second year again no rain came. In the third the same extraordinary drought followed. Indeed, not ten inches of rain fell during these two years, and the Kolobeng ran dry; so many fish were killed that the hyænas from the whole country round collected to the feast, and were unable to finish the putrid masses. A large old alligator, which had never been known to commit any depredations, was found left high and dry in the mud among the victims. The fourth year was equally unpropitious, the fall of rain being insufficient to bring the grain to maturity. Nothing could be more trying. We dug down in the bed of the river deeper and deeper as the water receded, striving to get a little to keep the fruit-trees alive for better times, but in vain. Needles lying out of doors for months did not rust; and a mixture of sulphuric acid and water, used in a galvanic battery, parted with all its water to the air, instead of imbibing more from it, as it would have done in England. The leaves of indigenous trees were all drooping, soft, and shrivelled, though not dead; and those of the Mimosæ were closed at mid-day the same as they are at night. In the midst of this dreary drought, it was wonderful to see those tiny creatures, the ants, running about with their accustomed vivacity. I put the bulb of a thermometer three inches under the soil in the sun at mid-day, and found the mercury to stand at 132° to 134°; and if certain kinds of beetles were placed on the surface, they ran about a few seconds and expired; but this broiling heat only augmented the activity of the long-legged black ants."

Mr Helmore, who afterwards was stationed at Likatlong, made a journey with his wife and family into a region much further to the north—a journey undertaken in the prosecution of their Christian enterprise, but a journey from which they never returned. Some idea of the aridity of the land may be formed from the following accounts of their sufferings from thirst, given in letters from his noble-hearted wife—the first a letter addressed to the sister of her husband, the second one addressed to her daughter in England, in school—the last she wrote. To her sister-in-law she wrote from Latlakane:—" I write this in a pretty little hut, 14 feet by 12, built by your brother. The walls are of palmyra wood, and it is thatched with palmyra leaves, so it answers literally to the name we have given it—*Palmyra Lodge*, and though rough-looking on the outside it forms a delightful shelter from the scorching rays of the sun. I should tell you that it is 'hartebeest' shape, and has a window at each end, with thin calico instead of glass. I only wish I were in a hut of similar description, but of larger dimensions, north of the Zambesi, instead of being still 200 miles south of it, with the prospect of another six weeks' journey; but I must be patient, and leave fearing for the future to record the mercies of the past.

"The last stage of our journey has been without exception the most trying time of travelling I have experienced in Africa. We are now within the tropics, and on a journey we are more exposed than in a house; the heat during the day is intense, 102° in the shade, and it often affects me with faintness and giddiness; but the early mornings are still pleasantly cool. We may expect rain this month, and are longing for it, as those only can long who have travelled through a dry and parched wilderness where no water is. Our poor oxen were at one time four, at another five, days without drink. It was quite painful to see how tame they were rendered by thirst; they crowded round the waggons, licking the water-casks, and putting their noses down to the dishes and basins, and then looked up to our faces, as if asking for water. We suffered very much ourselves from thirst, being obliged to economize the little we had in our vessels, not knowing when we should get more. We had guides, but they either could not or would not give us any information.

"Tuesday the 6th inst. was one of the most trying days I ever passed. About sunrise, the poor oxen, which had been painfully dragging the heavy waggons through the deep sand during the night, stopping now and then to draw breath, gave signs of giving up altogether. We had not gone as many miles as we had travelled hours. My husband now resolved to remain behind with one waggon and a single man, while I and the children and the rest of the people went forward with all the oxen, thinking that we should certainly reach water by night. We had had a very scant supply the day before; the men had not tasted drink since breakfast until late in the evening. We divided a bottleful among four of them. There now remained five bottles of water; I gave my husband three, and reserved two for the children, expecting that we should get water first. It was a sorrowful parting, for we were all faint from thirst, and of course eating was out of the question; we were afraid even to do anything lest exercise should aggravate our thirst. After dragging slowly on for four hours the heat obliged us to stop.

"The poor children continually asked for water; I put them off as long as I could, and when they could be denied no longer doled the precious fluid out a spoonful at a time to each of them. Poor Selina and Henry cried bitterly. Willie bore up manfully, but his sunken eyes showed how much he suffered. Occasionally I observed a convulsive twitching of his features, showing what an effort he was making to restrain his feelings. As for dear Lizzie, she did not utter a word of complaint, nor even asked for water, but lay all the day on the ground perfectly quiet, her lips quite parched and blackened. About sunset we made another attempt, and got on about five miles. The people then proposed going on with the oxen in search of water, promising to return with a supply to the waggon, but I urged their resting a little and then making another attempt, that we might possibly get near enough to walk on to it. They yielded, tied up the poor oxen to prevent their wandering, and lay down to sleep, having tasted neither food nor drink all day. None of us could eat. I gave the children a little dried fruit, slightly acid, in the middle of the day, but thirst took away all desire to eat. Once in the course of the afternoon dear Willie, after a desperate effort not to cry, suddenly asked me if he might go and drain the bottles. Of course I consented, and presently he called out to me with much eagerness that he had 'found some.' Poor little fellow! it must have been little indeed, for his sister Selina had drained them already. Soon after he called out that he had found another bottle of water. You can imagine the disappointment when I told him it was cocoa-nut oil melted by the heat.— But this is a digression: I must go back to our outspanning about nine P.M. The water was long since gone, and, as a last resource, just before dark, I divided among the children half a teacupful of wine and water, which I had been reserving in case I should feel faint. They were revived by it, and said, 'how nice it was,' though it scarcely allayed their thirst. Henry at length cried himself to sleep, and the rest were dozing feverishly. It was a beautiful moonlight night, but the air hot and sultry. I sat in front of the waggon unable to sleep, hoping that water might arrive before the children awoke on another day. About half-past ten I saw some persons approaching: they proved to be two Bakalahari bringing a tin canteen half-full of water, and a note from Mrs Price, saying, that having heard of the trouble we were in from the man whom we had sent forward, and being themselves not very far from the water, they had sent us all they had. The sound of water soon roused the children, who had tried in vain to sleep, and I shall not soon forget the rush they made to get a drink. There was not much, but enough for the present. I gave each of the children and men a cupful, and then drank myself. It was the first liquid that had entered my lips for twenty-four hours, and I had eaten nothing. The Bakalahari passed on, after depositing the precious treasure, saying that though they had brought me water they had none for themselves. They were merely passing travellers. I almost thought they were angels sent from Heaven. All now slept comfortably except myself; my mind had been too much excited for sleep. And now a fresh disturbance arose: the poor oxen had smelt the water, and became very troublesome; the loose cattle crowding about the waggon, licking and snuffing, and pushing their noses towards me, as if begging for water.

"At two o'clock I roused the men, telling them that if we were to make another attempt to reach water no time was to be lost. They were tired and faint, and very unwilling to move, but at last they got up, and began to unloose the oxen and drive them off without the waggon.

"I remonstrated, but in vain; they had lost all spirit, 'lipelu li shule,' as the Bechuanas say. I was obliged to let them go, but they assured me I should have water sent as quickly as possible, and the cattle should be brought back again after they had drunk. They knew no more than I did the distance to the water.

"When they left us, I felt anxious at the thought of perhaps spending another day like the past; but they had not been gone more than half-an-hour, when I saw in the bright moonlight a figure at a distance coming along the road. At first I could not make it out, it looked so tall; but on coming nearer, who should it prove to be but my servant-girl Kionecoe, eighteen years of age, carrying on her head an immense calabash of water! On hearing of our distress she volunteered to assist us. She had walked four hours. Another servant had set out with her, but as he had driven the sheep the day before a great distance, without either food or water, he became so exhausted that he lay down under a bush to rest, and on the girl came alone, in the dead of night, in a strange country infested with lions, bearing her precious burden. Oh, how grateful I felt to her! Surely *woman* is the same all the world over! She had only lived with me since June, was but an indifferent servant, and had never shown any particular attachment to the children; but this kind act revealed her heart, and seemed to draw us more closely together, for her conduct since then has been excellent. I made a bed for her beside me in the forepart of the waggon; and the children having slacked their thirst with the deliciously cool water, we all slept till six o'clock. I made coffee, and offered some to Kionecoe and her companion, who had now come up. At first they declined it, saying the water was for me and the children. I had now the happiness of seeing the children enjoy a meal of tea and biscuits; and then once more filling up my two bottles, I sent the calabash with the remainder of its contents to my husband, who by this time stood greatly in need of it. The distance was about twelve miles. Another hot day had now commenced, and I had only the two bottles of water. About noon a horseman rode up, leading a second horse with two water-casks, and a tin canteen on his back. This was a supply for your brother, sent by our kind fellow-travellers Captain and Mrs Thompson, who had heard of our distresses from the Prices. . . . While we were preparing the coffee, up came a pack-ox sent by Mr Price, with two water-casks for me, and soon after some Bakalahari arrived with a calabash; so we had now an abundant supply, and my heart overflowed with gratitude to our Father in heaven, who had watched over me and mine, as over Hagar of old, and sent us relief. I related that and other instances of God's care to the children the day before, and exhorted them to pray to their heavenly Father, and rest assured that He would send us help; they now referred to the subject, saying, 'it was just as I had said.' . . . Captain and Mrs Thompson rode up to the waggon in the afternoon, to see if they could be of any further assistance, and brought a little milk for the children. . . . A span of oxen passed me in the middle of the day, going to fetch my husband, and about half-past nine on Wednesday night a span arrived for us. Next morning we reached the water, where Mrs Price had kindly prepared a substantial breakfast. My husband did not come up till the evening."

To her child, she wrote:—" North of Kamakama, Nov. 24th 1859.—MY DARLING,—It is now your turn to get a letter from me; but I fear that it will be a long, long time before you receive it, for their are few opportunities of sending or receiving letters. We have had none from you since the May ones which overtook us at the Matlwaring, just beyond Kuruman. . . However, we must be patient, and the letters will perhaps be doubly sweet when they do come. Although I long to hear of you, I do not feel anxious about you, my dear girls. We daily commit you to the care of your Heavenly Father, and He never disappointed those who trust in Him. I hope that you, dear ——, are setting the Lord always before you. As the eldest of the family, you will have a strong influence over the rest. O seek especially to guide your sisters, dear —— and ——, in the way of life. I look forward with delight to the time when we shall be all united again; but still I think it is your duty to remain in England as long as you can. You may never go there again.

"You see we have not yet got to our journey's end. It is a long journey indeed; but we have had so many hindrances from waggons breaking, cattle wandering, fatigue, drought, and other causes. We have been already twenty weeks on the road, and shall be three or four weeks yet. Six weeks ago, on the river Zouga, dear little Willie was taken ill with fever, and for several days we scarcely thought he would recover; fever was very high, with delirium. He is now getting well again, and to-day is playing on the bed with Selina and Henry for the first time. He is, however, still so weak in his legs that he has to be carried about like an infant. A fortnight after Willie had been taken ill, dear Lizzie was seized with fever and erysipelas in the back, but she too is getting well now; so you see, dearest ——, you have much to be thankful for, as well as to pray for. Selina and Henry are well, and all send their love to you all. I need not tell you much about our journey as you have papa's journal. . . We meet with some beautiful flowers. I often wish it were possible to transport them to you. Few of them have much scent alone; but about sunset their united fragrance is delicious.

"Monday, Nov. 28.—Yesterday dear little —— —— was baptized by your papa. We had a pleasant English service. It was quite a treat in the wilderness. The Bechuanas were present as spectators, and seemed interested. Papa has service in Sechuana regularly every Sunday. . . Our cattle, at least some of them, have been lost ever since last Monday. Four men were seeking them three days and nights, and returned with some of them—without having tasted food all that time. They lost their way, which it is very easy to do, as the country is covered with forests and thick bush. Now another party is out after the rest of them. This is their third day. We have had no road for many weeks. Some of the party have to go before, sawing down trees, and chopping bushes to make room for the waggons to pass, and after all we frequently become entangled; so it is very slow work. There are no wild beasts here except elephants, and occasionally troops of zebras. The latter we sometimes manage to shoot. They are excellent eating; so is the gnu.

"Dec. 26.—A happy Christmas to you, my children! It is now nearly a month since I laid down my letter to you, dear ——; yet, strange to say, we are only *five miles* nearer our journey's end than we were then. I told you that a party of our men had gone out in search of some of our oxen, which had been stolen by the Masarwa, or Bushmen. They returned on the fourth day with all but three; one had been left sick on the road; the other fine large hind oxen the Masarwa had killed and eaten. It was a great loss, but there was no redress for it, and as our pool of water was almost dried up, we were glad to go forward. As we proceeded we found the country more and more dry, and at last we were brought to a complete stand-still for want of water. Our waggon was unpacked and sent back with all the casks, Mackintosh bags, and vessels we could find, to bring water. All the oxen and sheep, and all the men, excepting two, were sent back likewise, and what little water still remained was divided amongst us who stayed. This was only enough for drinking, there was none to cook with, and before the waggon arrived, which was two days and nights, we were so weak from want of food that the children and I could scarcely walk. The weather was at the same time extremely hot, the thermometer at eight o'clock in the morning stood at 96°, and in the middle of the day at more than 105°. Papa and the two men who remained went out in the evenings in search of water, and walked about all night, but they could find none. I forgot to say that Tabe stayed with one of his men, and they too searched for water; for we were unwilling to go back if there was a possibility of getting on. However, all the pools were empty, so we were most reluctantly obliged to retrace our steps. But by this time the ponds we had left were dried up too; so, after travelling a day and a night, and until nine the next morning, the poor cattle were so exhausted with thirst that they could go no farther, and we were compelled to unyoke them and send them on with the sheep, and most of the men, to the nearest water. We hoped that they would return that night and take us on; but day after day and night after night passed and neither men nor oxen came, and our sufferings were again very great. I was most anxious about Lizzie, who was still weak from her recent illness. I thought she would have fainted when I had not a drop of water to give her.

"One afternoon about four o'clock papa set out with two men, taking our Mackintosh bags, and returned about half-past nine next morning with a supply of water. When they arrived they were so exhausted that they dropped on the ground unable to speak. Papa looked so ill that I was quite alarmed. They had walked thirty-eight miles, and carried the water fifteen miles. Having found water, parties were sent in succession each night to return the following one. Fancy every drop of water we had for drinking, cooking, or washing ourselves brought a distance of thirty miles going and coming! At length, on Sunday, December the 11th, we were roused very early by a heavy rain. We spread out a sail and caught enough to replenish our water-vessels. This was indeed a shower from Heaven; it revived our languid spirits, and filled us with thankfulness to Him who had remembered His promise to His servants (Isaiah xli. 17). We now hoped to go on, but the clouds passed away, and the pools remained empty.

"When the oxen returned we rode back fifteen miles to the pool from which we had been obtaining water. It appeared that on leaving us with the oxen and sheep the men had set off for Kamakama, but losing their way did not get their till the following night; and our two little calves, unable to walk so far in such hot weather, were left behind to perish; and also our entire flock of twenty-four sheep and lambs were lost through the carelessness and indolence of the man who was driving them, and have not been heard of since. This is a very heavy loss indeed.

"I must now say a few words about your coming out, for there are so few opportunities of sending letters to you now that I do not like to delay writing on that subject... Lizzie says I am to tell you to bring some comfits, little baskets, etc., that we may have a Christmas-tree the first Christmas you are all at home. Your sisters and brothers send warmest love; so does papa. The God of Love be your Friend and Portion, my dear child.!—Your affectionate mamma, ANNE HELMORE."

I could not find in my heart to do otherwise than give this letter entire. It was the last she wrote. Shortly after it was written *the whole family perished!*

Of drought and aridity such as this betokens I have little expectations of conveying an adequate conception. It has been remarked that no one knows what hunger is who knows where food is to be found. I avail myself of the formula to say, No one knows what thirst is who knows where water is to be had. And drought such as this must be experienced to be known. Of cold, of heat, of damp, some experience may be had in Europe, but of drought like this *none*: of such drought—long continued, widely extended drought—and the consequent aridity of earth and atmosphere, and, as a consequence of this, the suffering of man and beast, NONE.

Another of my friends, Mr M'Kenzie, a missionary to the heathen, subsequently travelled in the same track. Of the earlier part of it he writes,—"The country through which we were now travelling was exceedingly monotonous and uninteresting. The hollows which contain pools of water in summer were now dried up, and along the 'mokoko' or ancient river-bed on our left, we were told there was not a drop of water. Without a single hill in sight, we found ourselves traversing an undulating prairie, whose gentle sloping ridges of sand followed one after another like the waves of the sea. The long ripe grass, of a lightish yellow colour, gave to the landscape something of the appearance of one immense harvest field. A solitary camel thorn, with fantastically turned branches, was here and there seen in the distance, while a variety of small shrubs and bushes was distinguishable only in our neighbourhood from the tall white grass, gently bending to the afternoon breeze, or standing droopingly in the breathless stillness and dazzling glare of noonday.

'A region of emptiness, howling and drear,
Which man hath abandoned from famine and fear;
Which the snake and the lizard inhabit alone,
With the twilight bat from the yawning stone.

A region of drought where no river glides,
No rippling brook with osier'd sides,
Where sedgy pool, nor bubbling fount,
Nor tree, nor cloud, nor misty mount,
Appears to refresh the aching eye;
But the barren earth and the burning sky,
And the blank horizon round and round,
Spread—void of living sight or sound.'—*Thomas Pringle*.

Not a living creature was to be seen for miles; but, once outspanned, we found that even here life was not entirely extinct. More frequently than snake or lizard, we found near to our waggon a little cricket industriously making what noise it could; and in the dreariest places we observed a little bird, about the size of a lark, which, like that bird, rose from the earth to give forth its song. But its soaring and its song were of short duration. It rose only some fifteen or twenty feet from the ground, uttering meanwhile its one plaintive note, which again subsided as it descended to the ground. After a brief interval this lonesome bird would repeat its desert dirge. In the distance we sometimes descried the shy khama (hartebeest), or the kukama (gemsbuck or oryx), fleetest of the antelopes; an occasional herd of springbucks cropping the short thick grass of the hard river-bed; and once or twice we saw in the distance troops of elands and giraffes, roaming at will and without thought of water. After leaving a fountain, our cattle when unyoked usually grazed well for the first twenty-four hours; but thirst afterwards took away inclination to eat, so that, although surrounded by the rich sweet grass of the prairie, as soon as they were out of the yoke they sought the shade of a neighbouring tree, and there remained till brought again to their place before the waggon.

"I was told by the Bakalahari at Nkowane that they kept one of the wells shut because it was easy of access, and if it had water the lions would come and drink there, and infest their dwellings and their sheep and goat pens at night. The second well was in the hollow of a limestone rock—its sides abrupt, and the water accessible only by means of a sort of ladder. There was a conviently shaped rock near the mouth of the well, into which the water for the oxen was poured. For a small piece of tobacco each, the Bakalahari assisted us to clear away the mud from the second well; but after all our trouble I found that the supply of water from both was not sufficient to allow all my oxen to drink at once. So I separated the party on Monday, sending on in advance the two waggons which were driven by the Hottentots. The rest of the party left Nkowane on Tuesday. On Wednesday night, while toiling diligently through the deep sand, we came unexpectedly upon one of the waggons which had started a day before us, its solitary guardian in the desert was its Hottentot driver. He explained that he had sent on his oxen with the other waggon, as they would pull no longer."

And again :—"It was here also I heard of the extreme sufferings which my friends, upon whose track I was proceeding, had endured in the country north of Maila and Kamakama. When I asked for guides to go with me in that direction, not a single Bushmen would consent to accompany me. To go without guides I felt to be quite out of the question. Pointing northwards, they shook their heads, and exclaimed, 'Yonder there is no water; nothing but sun; nothing but sun! That land causes the cattle to stray from the waggons; the men, too, who venture thither wander about in vain search for what is not, and hasten southward to the fountains which they had left. All these things,' they said, 'did we see last year in the case of the white men who went to the Makololo. Both they and their oxen, and we who accompanied them part of the way, had well-nigh perished with thirst. If you are determined to travel on that path you go alone.'"

SECTION II.—*Water Supply beyond the Colonized portion of South Africa.*

While the desiccation and aridity in the districts specified are such as has been represented, further into the interior it is a land abounding with water. The journeyings of Stanley in search of Livingstone tell more of difficulty in travelling over districts covered with water, than of sufferings from drought. One of the first confirmations received by Livingstone and Oswell and Murray, of statements they had received from Bakwains who had been into the interior with Sebituane, in regard to what they had seen, was an answer which they received to a inquiry relative to whence came the Tamunak'le, a large stream flowing into the beautifully wooded Zouga. On their inquiring whence it came, the answer was, "Oh, from a country full of rivers, so many no one can tell their number, and full of great trees." And of that country they themselves give the following account:—"A hundred miles from the point where the waggons stood to the river Seseheké, we saw no hill higher than an ant-hill. The country is intersected by numerous deep rivers, and adjacent to each of these, immense reedy bogs or swamps stretch away in almost every direction. Oxen cannot pass through these swamps,—they sink in up to the belly, and on looking down the holes made by the legs, the parts immediately under the surface are seen to be saturated with water. The rivers are not like many in South Africa, mere "nullahs," containing nothing but sand and stones. All of those we saw contained large volumes of water. The period of our visit happened to be the end of an extraordinary dry season, yet on sounding the Chobe we found it to have a regular depth of fifteen feet on the side to which the water swung, and of twelve feet on the calm side. The banks below the lowest water mark were more inclined to the perpendicular than those of a canal. It was generally as deep at a foot from the bank as in the middle of the stream. The roots of the reeds and grass seem to prevent it wearing away the land; and in many parts the bank is undermined and hangs over the deep water. Were its course not so very winding a steam vessel could sail on it. The higher lands in this region are raised only by a few feet above the surrounding level. On these the people pasture their cattle, make their gardens, and build their towns. The rivers overflow their banks annually. The great drought prevented the usual rise of the water while we were in the country in July, and the people ascribed the non-appearance of the water to the death of their chief. But when the rivers do fill, the whole country is inundated, and must present the appearance of a vast lake, with numerous islands scattered over its surface. The numerous branches given off by each of the rivers, and the annual overflow of the country, explain the reports we had previously heard of 'Linokanoka' (rivers upon rivers), and 'large waters' with numerous islands in them. The Chobe must rise at least ten feet in perpendicular height before it can reach the dykes, built for catching fish, situated about a mile from its banks, and the Seshéké must rise fifteen or twenty feet before it overflows its banks; yet Mr O. and I saw unmistakable evidence of that overflow reaching about fifteen miles out."

Of the quantity of moisture deposited in central Africa some vague conception may be formed from the magnitude of rivers flowing thence. The Zambesi, the Nile, and the Congo, in regard to which it was stated, in a lecture on the discoveries of Dr Livingstone, delivered by Sir Henry Rawlinson, President of the Royal Geographical Society, that "no soundings were obtainable in it at 200 fathoms; its current could be seen 300 miles out at sea, into which it discharged 1,800,000 cubic feet of water per second."

In accordance with these intimations of abundance of water, we find in Arrowsmith's detailed map of Dr Livingstone's route across Africa an entry of,—"The plains of Lobale are impassable during the rainy season." And writing of a district still nearer to the equator, he writes:—"We entered on an extensive plain beyond the Leeba, at least twenty miles broad, and covered with water, ankle deep in the shallowest parts. We deviated somewhat from our N.W. course by the direction of Intemese, and kept the hills Piri nearly on our right during a great part of the first day, in order to avoid the still more deeply flooded plains of Lobale (Luval ?) on the west. These, according to Intemese, are at present impassable on account of being thigh-deep. The plains are so perfectly level that rain-water, which this was, stands upon them for months together. They were not flooded by the Leeba, for that was still far within its banks. Here and there, dotted over the surface, are little islands, on which grow stunted date-bushes and scraggy trees. The plains themselves are covered with a thick sward of grass, which conceals the waters, and makes the flats appear like great pale yellow-coloured prairie lands, with a clear horizon, except where interrupted here and there with trees. The clear rain-water must have stood some time among the grass, for great numbers of lotus-flowers were seen in full blow; and the runs of water tortoises and crabs were observed; other animals also, which prey on the fish and find their way to the plains.

"The continual splashing of the oxen keeps the feet of the rider constantly wet, and my men complain of the perpetual moisture of the paths by which we have travelled in Londa, as softening their horny soles. . . . We made our beds on one of the islands, and were wretchedly supplied with firewood. The booths constructed by the men were but sorry shelter, for the rain poured down without intermission till mid-day. There is no drainage for the prodigious masses of water on these plains, except slow percolation into the different feeders of the Leeba, and into that river itself. The quantity of vegetation has prevented the country from becoming furrowed by many rivulets or 'nullahs.' Were it not so remarkably flat, the drainage must have been effected by torrents, even in spite of the matted vegetation.

"That these extensive plains are covered with grasses only, and the little islands with but scraggy trees, may be accounted for by the fact, observable everywhere in this country, that, where water stands for any length of time, trees cannot live. The want of speedy drainage destroys them, and injures the growth of those that are planted on the islands, for they have no depth of earth not subjected to the souring influence of the stagnant water. The plains of Lobale, to the west of these, are said to be much more extensive than any we saw, and their vegetation possesses similar peculiarities. When the stagnant rain-water has all soaked in, as must happen during the months in which there is no rain, travellers are even put to straits for want of water. This is stated on native testimony; but I can very well believe that level plains, in which neither wells nor gullies are met with, may, after the dry season, present the opposite extreme to what we witnessed. Water, however, could always be got by digging, a proof of which we had on our return when brought to a stand on this very plain by severe fever: about twelve miles from the Kasai my men dug down a few feet, and found an abundant supply; and we saw on one of the islands the garden of a man who, in the dry season, had drunk water from a well in like manner. . . . The plains of Lobale, to the west of this, give rise to a great many streams, which unite, and form the deep, never-failing Chobe. Similar extensive flats give birth to the Loeti and Kasai, and, as we shall see further on, all the rivers of an extensive region owe their origin to oozing bogs, and not to fountains."

Further on he writes,—"In the afternoon of this day we came to a valley about a mile wide, filled with clear fast-flowing water. The men on foot were chin deep in crossing, and we three on oxback got wet to the middle, the weight on the animals preventing them from swimming. A thunder-shower descending completed the partial drenching of the plain, and gave a cold uncomfortable 'packing in a wet blanket' that night. Next day we found another flooded valley about half a mile wide, with a small and now deep rivulet in its middle, flowing rapidly to the S.S.E. or towards the Kasai. The middle part of this flood, being the bed of what at other times is the rivulet, was so rapid that we crossed by holding on to the oxen, and the current soon dashed them to the opposite bank; we then jumped off, and, the oxen being relieved of their burdens, we could pull them on to the shallower part. The rest of the valley was thigh deep and boggy, but holding on by the belt which fastened the blanket to the ox, we each floundered through the nasty slough as well as we could. These boggy parts, lying parallel to the stream, were the most extensive we had come to—those mentioned already were more circumscribed patches, these stretched for miles along each bank; but even here, though the rapidity of the current was very considerable, the thick sward of grass was 'laid' flat along the sides of the stream, and the soil was not abraded so much as to discolour the flood. When we came to the opposite side of this valley, some pieces of the ferruginous conglomerate, which forms the capping to all other rocks in a large district around and north of this, cropped out, and the oxen bit at them as if surprised by the appearance of stone as much as we were; or it may have contained some mineral of which they stood in need. We had not met with a stone since leaving Shinte's. The country is covered with deep alluvial soil of a dark colour and very fertile.

"In the afternoon we came to another stream, Nuana Loke (or child of Loke) with a bridge over it. The men had to swim off to each end of the bridge, and when on it were breast deep; some preferred holding on by the tails of the oxen the whole way across. I intended to do this too, but, riding to the deep part, before I could dismount and seize the helm the ox dashed off with his companions, and his body sank so deep, that I failed in my attempt even to catch the blanket belt, and if I pulled the bridle, the ox seemed as if he would come backwards upon me, so I struck out for the opposite bank alone. My poor fellows were dreadfully alarmed when they saw me parted from the cattle, and about twenty of them made a simultaneous rush into the water for my rescue, and just as I reached the opposite bank one seized my arm, and another threw his around my body. When I stood up, it was most gratifying to see them all struggling towards me. Some had leaped off the bridge, and allowed their cloaks to float down the stream. Part of my goods, abandoned in the hurry, were brought up from the bottom after I was safe. Great was the pleasure expressed when they found that I could swim like themselves, without the aid of a tail, and I did, and do feel grateful to these poor heathens for the promptitude with which they dashed in to save, as they thought, my life. I found my clothes cumbersome in the water; they could swim quicker from being naked. They swim like dogs, not frog-fashion, as we do."

Such is South Africa, in regard to water supply, in the trans-colonial regions referred to.

CHAPTER II.

ARIDITY AND WATER SUPPLY WITHIN THE COLONY OF THE CAPE OF GOOD HOPE.

It may be alleged that the statements made have been made in regard to different parts of the country, and both of them parts of the country far distant from the colonized portion, which is what is generally known as South Africa, in contradistinction to Southern Africa, which is more comprehensive, and may be legitimately applied to all the continent lying to the south of the equator. But if so, this may be said in reply, The physical geography and arborescent productions of the intermediate land south of the scenes described, and north of the European colonies extending from the Cape, make it to some degree probable that such as these watery plains are those arid plains must have been not long before those aged trees began to grow. And what is more to the point in hand, in the Introduction I have stated facts illustrative of the colony, at the Cape of Good Hope, being throughout much of its extent subject from time to time to have the same locality suffer for a lengthened time by drought similar in character, though not equal in degree, with that from which Mr Helmore and his family suffered so much, and then be deluged in a similar way, though not to the same extent, as the district traversed by Dr Livingstone, described in the extracts from his journal which I have cited. And I have corresponding testimony to adduce in regard to the abundance of the water supply at command to counteract the evils induced by the drought within the colony.

I have never experienced, nor have I ever heard of anything experienced by others equal to that within the colony of the Cape of Good Hope. But some of the details I have given of what was experienced in 1862 are in keeping therewith, and the colonists are not unacquainted with long-continued as well as excessive droughts. Neither have I ever experienced, or heard of others having experienced, a long-continued drought so excessive as is indicated by some of the observations made by Dr Livingstone at Kolobeng; but I have read of an observation made within the colony which may be placed side by side with these.

Amongst other paradoxes connected with evaporation and heat, it is stated in scientific treatises, that the finger slightly moistened may with impunity be plunged into molten lead, the evaporation keeping the finger cool, and the produced atmosphere of vapour preventing contact; and that a little water projected into a plantinum crucible at a white heat has by the evaporation of one portion converted the other portion into a lump of ice. It is more generally known that by the rapid evaporation of a portion of water under the exhausted receiver of an air-pump another portion may be frozen, and that, by appropriate arrangements, ice is produced in India by the rapid evaporation produced by the heat. The same thing has occurred in South Africa through rapid evaporation, induced by the aridity of the atmosphere.

Mr Andw. Wylie, in his notes of a journey in two directions across the colony, made, as geological surveyor to the colony, in the years 1857-58, with a view to determine the character and order of the various geological formations—writing of the Narrows on the Orange River about twenty miles from Colesberg—says,—"The night spent here on the banks of the Orange River was one of the coldest I have ever experienced in the colony. Inside of a tent, in which three persons slept, bowls of hot coffee and a compound liquid of still more potent character were converted into a solid mass of ice.

"While in the neighbourhood of Hopetown, a gallon of water in a tin bucket was sometimes frozen quite solid during the night, and yet the ice on the dams was never more than a quarter of an inch thick. This discrepancy evidently arises from the water of the latter [and the earth] receiving so much heat during the day as to prevent its freezing at night except to a very limited extent; whereas the water in a small vessel, exposed on all sides to the cold wind, is soon reduced to atmospheric temperature, or *even below it*. The freezing power of the air is greatly assisted by its dryness, which causes rapid evaporation to take place, even in solid ice itself."

Notwithstanding the aridity of the atmosphere which is thus indicated, the quantity of moisture in the atmosphere, though it be relatively small, must be very great. Frequently have I witnessed the phenomena described in the Scripture narrative of a cloud the size of a man's hand appearing in the sky, and ere long the whole heavens being black with clouds, and the earth darkened: the clouds not being blown thither, but formed there of moisture then existant, and the deposit being occasioned by a current of cold air lowering the temperature of an upper stratum to a temperature below the dew-point; and sometimes, while expecting such a rainfall as Elijah foretold, the whole has dissolved away, like the vapour of a locomotive steam engine, leaving the heavens as transparent and clear as before. But sometimes it is otherwise, and from that dry arid air the rainfall has been tremendous.

I have in the Introduction given some accounts of the drought and the rainfall; the former of which preceded and the latter followed my return to the Cape in 1863. Notwithstanding the abundance of the rain which fell in that year, the drought was again severe in 1864; the same was the case in the year following, 1865, and yet again in 1866. Towards the close of 1867 there were torrents of rain; and so has it been ever since, alternate torrents and drought; and at one and the same time drought in one part of the country, torrents in another, the waters of which not only rushed away to be lost in the sea, but wrought mischief and devastation by the way.

At Port Elizabeth, in November 1867, I find there fell in the course of six hours, between Wednesday 20th at 9 P.M., and Thursday 21st at 3 A.M., 6·5 inches of rain. In the month of July preceding there was a fall of rain in London, in a report of which, presented by Mr Bazalgette, chief engineer to the Metropolitan Board of Works, he says,—"A fall of rain such as has not been recorded in London for the last twenty years, and stated in the Registrar-General's return of July 27 to have been unprecedented at the Greenwich Observatory, fell between midnight of the 25th July and nine on the following morning. During these nine hours 3·25 in. of rain fell." From this it appears that the fall of rain at Port Elizabeth during these six hours was double what fell in these nine hours in London —that is, three times as much in the same space of time as the heaviest recorded rainfall at London or Greenwich. But this can convey no such idea of the torrents of rain as do the details given of its disastrous effects.

Of these the following details were given in the journals of the time:—

"Port Elizabeth, November 21, 1867.—This part of the Colony has lately been rejoicing in an amount of rain exceeding even the most extravagant desires of the most 'thirsty souls,' and last night from nine o'clock for several hours a deluge of rain fell, creating such a flood, and bringing such disasters in its train, as will not be soon forgotten by any of the inhabitants of Port Elizabeth.

"For the benefit of such of your readers as may not know this town I will briefly describe the locality, the better to enable them to understand the effects produced by the floods.

"The town of Port Elizabeth consists of a long line of streets running parallel with the beach, from north to south, at a distance varying from two to three hundred yards, the intervening space being occupied by intersecting streets, chiefly composed of poor dwellings and shops. Immediately behind the 'Main Street' on the west side, rises 'The Hill,' very steep for some hundred yards or so, and then more gradual in its ascent for a similar distance, and stretching out eastward—a nearly level plain, and now occupied by quite a second town, where a large portion of those engaged in commercial pursuits, from the merchants downwards, reside. On each side of this hill were formerly two kloofs, which were filled in, and two splendid roads constructed, on the south side White's Road, and on the north side Russell Road, each having stone drains which have hitherto been sufficient to carry off the water of all ordinary rains. On the south side of White's Road is another hill, very precipitous, and beyond that, the Baaken's River runs into the sea, flowing generally sluggishly enough through 'the valley.'

"On the south side of the Baaken's River is another town, composed almost entirely of dwellings of the poorer class, a large number being the very poor. These are built to a great extent upon sand, by which small kloofs had been filled up.

"On the north side of the Russell Road is the 'Hospital Hill,' so called from the hospital which is built on the summit.

"The kloofs which formerly took the place of the two roads referred to were the natural outlets for the water collected on the hills on either side. These roads were therefore now the receptacles for much more than could be carried off.

"Down the Russell Road the water came with irresistible force, quickly destroying the drains and excavating the road in some places to the depth of ten or twelve feet, and in its course undermining the foundations of a few good houses so seriously that the inhabitants have been compelled hastily to remove from them, lest they should be buried in their fall, which seems imminent.

"'White's Road' presents a very similar spectacle. The gas pipes—twisted into strange shapes—lying only, supported here and there, across huge chasms, laying bare the rocks of the old kloof. This road leads direct into the market-square. At the bottom, the deepest chasm of all is made.

"Between the two roads just described, and parallel with them, is Donkin Street, the bottom part of which is similarly destroyed; an immense quantity of the dislodged earth being carried into the Main Street, forming a heap of six or seven feet in height, through which a way had to be dug to the doors of one or two of the shops. All the houses, shops, and stores on the west side of the Main Street were more or less flooded from behind, in some instances the astonished proprietors finding the mud level with their counter tops. On the opposite side, some houses most exposed to the fury of the descending waters are totally demolished, while all the stores are more or less damaged by the water and mud carried into their cellars,—sugar, rice, flour, &c., &c., lying in a state giving bright prospects for the auctioneers.

"Great as is the destruction of property, public and private, so far described, the worst remains to be told. On the south side of the Baaken's River the scene of devastation beggars all description, and must be seen to be *believed*. About twenty-four houses are completely demolished. In some instances the fronts of the houses are carried away, leaving the other half tottering on the brink of a deep hollow, which reminds one of a railway cutting, and is almost as regular, in many parts eighteen or twenty feet deep. It seems incredible that a good 'metalled' street in a few hours could be transformed into this ravine; but it is explained to some extent by the fact that all beneath the crust is sand, to the depth I have stated, and which appears to have been sometime or another drifted into various small kloofs, which probably formerly existed. As might be expected, the course of the torrent did not always lie in the middle of the streets, and consequently many houses have entirely disappeared, not even so much as a bit of timber marking the spot; all being hurried down to the sea. One poor Irishman describes his being awaked by a noise and finding the front of the house demolished, the rooms being open to the street, and it was with difficulty he and his family escaped before the rest of the house followed.

"It will easily be imagined that a fearful amount of distress is the result here. A large number of families have lost everything except the clothes they had on.

The Baaken's River, which has of late joined the sea in a little stream that a lady could easily step over, soon cut itself a channel of fifty feet wide through the sand, which it carried before it, seriously filling up (it is feared) the space inside the breakwater. Twelve or thirteen boats, of various sizes, were swamped, the masts of some of which are just visible above the water. It is marvellous that all these catastrophes have resulted in the loss of only two lives. One child was carried down to the sea and was found with only its legs visible above the sand on the shore. The second was a man, a servant of the Harbour Board, who was foolishly endeavouring this morning to save a piece of timber, and was drawn in by the current of the Baaken's River and disappeared in a moment. Although numbers of people hurried along the side in the hope that he might be rescued, he was never seen again, nor has the body yet been recovered.

"Some few instances there are of very narrow escapes. Our Colonial Chaplain, Mr Pickering, was dining on the Hill, and about twelve o'clock the rain having somewhat abated, set out for his residence, near the bottom of White's Road. Having, of course, no idea of the liberties the water had taken with the road, and the darkness being extreme, he was precipitated unsuspectingly into six feet of water, not by any means stagnant. He escaped drowning; and fortunately was, I believe, not much hurt. One gentleman was saved by his companion catching him by the tail of his coat just as he was making a plunge into a kloof by the side of the Military Road.

"The amount of rain which fell during the night (by the rain-gauge) was 6·36 inches. The damage done is estimated at £25,000."

From recorded observations it appears that on the Tuesday at 9 A.M. and at 5 o'clock the wind was S.E.; on Wednesday at 9 A.M. and at 1 o'clock it was the same, at 5 o'clock it was S.S.E.; on Thursday at 9, and at 1, and at 5 o'clock it was S.W. At all these times, and it may inferred throughout all that time, generally blowing from the sea, and it may be surmised charged with moisture, though transparent and clear. And we have the data necessary to enable us to determine the maximum quantity of moisture with which it could be so charged, as Mr Hammond, the Meteorological Observer at the light-house, whose observations I have quoted above, has recorded also his observations on the state of the barometer and the thermometer throughout the period of the storm. His full record is as follows:—

		Bar.	Ther.	Wind.
Nov. 19—9 a.m.	... ...	30·086	68·0	S.E.
1 p.m.	... ...	30·055	62·2	S.E.
5 p.m.	... ...	30·076	64·9	S.E.
20—9 a.m.	... ...	30·064	62·1	S.E.
1 p.m.	... ...	29·980	62·6	S.E.
5 p.m.	... ...	29·981	63·1	S.S.E.
21—9 a.m.	... ...	30·119	61·7	S.W.
1 p.m.	... ...	30·109	63·5	S.W.
5 p.m.	... ...	30·157	63·7	S.W.

With these data it is possible to calculate what was the greatest quantity of moisture which the air could possibly have held in solution. That the air was so saturated does not appear, but assuming that it was, the rainfall supplies an indication of how great the quantity of moisture thus suspended in solution must have been, more impressive than any array of figures would do; and, if the atmosphere was, as it is reasonable to suppose was the case, not fully, but only partially saturated with moisture throughout its forty-five miles of depth, it may be admitted that the deposit from a full saturation would have been proportionally more.

What fell was only the surplus moisture in excess of what could be sustained, suspended in solution, or otherwise, in a portion of the atmosphere limited in extent and in depth.

Moisture in the air is invisible, as cloud, or fog, or rain, until the lowering of the temperature of that air renders it incapable of sustaining it in solution. It is then deposited from the solution in the form of cloud, or fog, and precipitated to the earth by electricity, or gravitation, or the combined action of both. And the meteorological observations of Mr Hammond enable us to tell of how the clouds and the rain were formed of this surplus moisture in the atmosphere.

According to the statement of Mr Hammond, the meteorological observer, the wind ranged from S.E. to S.S.E. and S.W. during the storm. "But," says the *E. P. Herald*, "it will be observed in the above statement that the direction of the wind *during the night* is not given, but we are assured by those who were up and watched the storm, that about nine o'clock the wind veered to S.W., then to W., and for an hour or two blew strong from N.W.

It afterwards went round to N., subsequently to E., and in a few hours—that is before daylight—to S.W. again, from which quarter it was steady yesterday. It will thus be seen that the storm went round the compass. The points from which it blew most violently were S.W. and N.W."

In this may be found information needed to enable us satisfactorily to account for the remarkable rainfall that occurred at that time at Port Elizabeth, a whirlwind either originating there or passing over the town in its progress from another, and that it may be a distant point—a whirlwind similar in character to those of tiny dimensions seen sometimes twenty at a time, raising the sand or dust in tiny pillars, in the interior of the colony; and similar at the same time to those vast cyclones, the study of which has enabled meteorologists to determine the law of storms, but intermediate between these in magnitude. By this, air near the surface of the ground, charged with what quantity of moisture it might be, was raised to an elevation at which the reduced temperature there induced unfitted it for holding so much or nearly so much in solution. This surplus was thrown off and deposited in form of clouds. These were unceasingly increased by the continuous fresh supply, and what was set free fell in torrents of rain, being the surplus only of what the air could contain in solution at its lowered temperature.

Vivid flashes of lightning and the roar of thunder are spoken of as accompaniments of the storm. These I attribute to the same cause, and reckon them consequents of the disturbance of electric equilibrium, occasioned by changes of temperature; and this electric disturbance, though it added nothing to the quantity of moisture set free, may have occasioned the more rapid precipitation of what had been set free, in accordance with what is reported,—"The rain, which came gently at first, increased by degrees until it fell down in sheets."

At the time it was intimated that it would be interesting if meteorologists would track the storm in its course through the country. I do not know whether this has been done by any in the colony. From statements in the journals of the day it appears the storm had not by any means been confined to one locality. From Humansdorp it was reported that the bridge over the Van Stadens River had been swept away, and that the mails had to be got across by means of ropes. Some portions of the road in the neighbourhood had been so much cut up that the mail bags had to be carried on men's backs. The lighthouse of St Blaize had been so considerably damaged that an officer of the Public Works Department had to proceed to the spot for the purpose of reporting upon the extent and nature of the repairs required.

Mr Molteno, the present premier of the colony, happened to be journeying at the time from Beaufort to Capetown, and the following narrative of what he witnessed between George and Swellendam was transcribed from a hastily given verbal account of his adventure:—"He first encountered stormy weather with heavy rains in Montagu Pass, and on arriving at George found the river very much swollen, and remarked that the bridge looked very queer. It seemed as if it had been twisted by the stream. Half an hour after he had passed over it was broken to pieces and swept away like a toy!

"We may mention, before going further, that Mr Molteno was travelling with a gentleman and a man servant in an ordinary colonial cart, with two horses, and being an old traveller was pretty well prepared for the vicissitudes incident to colonial travellers. After passing George it continued raining almost continuously, indeed, from the Tuesday morning to Wednesday and Thursday it scarcely stopped. One hour from George was a small bridge, which had been partially carried away. The river was quite impassable. The deck planks were torn up in many places and the causeway removed. The water had previously risen some ten feet above the bridge. The party, after resting awhile, went to work with a will, taking up some of the planks and contriving to make a rough road over the stream just wide enough to receive the cart, which was unspanned and wheeled by hand carefully over the tumble-down structure. The horses were then led over, and with great difficulty got across, one narrowly escaping a broken leg.

"The Witte Elsjes River Bridge was next reached, and it was in a still worse plight than the last. Gaps were cut right through it in all directions, and it was covered with drift wood and splintered fragments. No one, it must be known, had, before Mr Molteno, essayed to cross the rivers all along the route since the flood was at its height. The river, too, was literally choked with palmiet, torn up and borne down with the rush of the river. Finding the task a serious one, Mr Molteno assembled a considerable force of farmers and labourers, who began clearing the bridge and making a temporary thoroughfare with spars in the same manner as before. After great labour the cart was wheeled across in safety. But the horses could not be moved in the same way, the bridge was too rickety and the decking too open. What was to be done? A drift was tried higher up, where it was thought the horses might be swum across. But after one or two hazardous trials the attempt was abandoned for the night, and the horses sent to a neighbouring farm-house. During the night the flood sensibly abated, and it was looking brighter over head. The next morning the whole party got over safely, but not without great difficulty.

"On again the party went, wondering what was coming next, until the Brak River heights were reached. Here they came upon a number of weather-bound travellers. Waggons were stuck in the mud, and oxen and mules straying whither they listed. The pass was in a most dangerous state, the land having slipped both above and below the road, rendering it almost impassable. As the party descended into the valley the Brak River bridge looked a scene of desolation. The river was fairly blocked up with the *débris* of the bridge and drift wood, and the water was rushing through a narrow channel on the further side. Here waggons and their living freight had cast anchor to await the subsiding of the flood. On Mr Molteno's arrival, all united as before in making a temporary way across the ruins of the bridge, and succeeded in getting over. The toll-house by the river-side narrowly escaped destruction, the water rising to the ceiling of the first floor. If it had not been built of stone it would probably have been carried away. The tollman and his family only escaped drowning by getting into the loft. When Mr Molteno arrived, he was drying his furniture, beans, and other provisions. The out-houses to the building were completely swept away. Those who know the road will form some idea of the height of the water when they are told that the house known as Ferreira's Hotel was completely submerged.

"From Brak River to Mossel Bay the country was flooded in all directions. The post had to diverge from the main road to get along at all. Here and

2F

there were waggons stuck in the mud, with the water up to the axles, and the attendants in the most bewildered condition. The oxen had strayed, enjoying the fun rather than otherwise, and had left no spoor to guide their masters in the pursuit.

"The Hartebeest River was passed with nothing worse than a wetting for the cart and its contents; and at the Gouritz River there was fortunately a boat big enough to take the cart over bodily, while the horses were able to swim across.

"Passing the Vette River and Kafirkuils River which were just fordable, the party hastened to cross the Heidelberg River, that they might reach without delay the Duivenhok's River, which they had heard was just passable. But it proved quite otherwise. The post cart was on the bank, and every effort was being made to get it across. The mail bags were put into a boat and conveyed safely over, and the cart was floated across, with the aid of casks and a tow line hauled by a number of people on the other side. The stream was still very strong, and Mr Molteno not being on Her Majesty's service deemed it prudent to wait until the next day. He then got over in precisely the same way as the post-cart had done, compelling the horses to swim through the flood. From that point the journey was without great adventure. The roads were everywhere cut up, as far as Swellendam, beyond which the severe effects of the flood were not felt."

This may or it may not have been in the course of the cyclon. I think it not impossible that it was. Be this as it may the whole of what has been stated is suggestive of much that might be stated in regard to the loss of property; the risk of life occasioned by such torrents of rains; the compensation which is found in the fertility which is thus produced on farms which are at other times sterile; and the importance of measures for retaining such waters when they fall. Such a rainfall had not occurred for twenty years before, and all was allowed to run off to the sea, carrying destruction and desolation with it in its course, while it might have been to a great extent retained to clothe the fields with verdure and flowers and fruit. But the point to which I direct attention at present is, that all that water was in the atmosphere while that atmosphere was cloudless, transparent, and clear; and thus it supplies an indication of the vastness of the water treasures which are stored up there.

It may be surmised that the proximity of Port Elizabeth to the sea may have tended to increase the rainfall; but so far as Georgetown at least the rainfall was of a corresponding character, produced, it is maintained, not by clouds carried thither by the wind, but formed there by the whirlwind. The rain may have come previously from the sea, the great reservoir whither all surplus water returns, but which is never the fuller because of the evaporation from its surface. But though it may have come previously from the sea, it was not spray but rain—it was not salt water but fresh, and it fell from the sky,—that sky, a few days before, was, I doubt not, clear and cloudless as is generally the sky in that sunny clime; yet from that sky it came. And there it was, notwithstanding the clear transparent blue of its hue,—if that blue were no itself the consequence of its presence and its abundance there.

Within a year a similarly destructive rainfall occurred at Natal. Of this the following details are given in the newspapers of the day:—"Durban, 9th Sept. 1868.—Since 'The Flood' of 1856, no disaster has befallen the

Colony to compare with that which has has just befallen us from the same cause. On Friday afternoon, the 28th ultimo, the rain began to fall, with squalls from southwest, and continued throughout, almost without intermission, until the forenoon of Monday, a space of about sixty-five hours. During a great portion of this time, in fact from two P.M. on the Saturday, the wind came from the south and southeast, from which quarter our heaviest, although by no means most frequent, rains come. On the Monday the clearing up was heralded by the wind going gradually round to the northward of east, and by the breaking up of the clouds, showing blue sky. On the morning of the first day the barometer stood at 29 90·7 ; on the following day at 30·20, at which it continued on the third day; the two days following, when the storm was passing and past, indicating 30 10·5. The rain which fell during the continuance at Merebank, Mr Lamport's sugar plantation, amounted, as stated by that gentleman in an interesting letter to the *Mercury*, to 17·11 inches. On Sunday the rising of the rivers, and especially of the Umgeni, indicated that heavy rains had fallen in the upper country as well as on the coast, and fears began to be entertained for the safety of the bridges. At the Queen's Bridge on the Umgeni, about a mile and a half from the sea, reeds, sugar-canes, trees, and at length two little timber bridges from feeders of the main stream, were constantly being carried down, and as the level of the water approached the girders of the bridge, this *débris* began to be arrested and to accumulate. About midnight a large portion of the Queen's Bridge itself gave way,—how much could not, of course, be known in the darkness and the storm ; and about four A.M. the remainder was swept off. Daylight showed the approach on the Durban side crumbling into the torrent, and a thousand feet distant, on the further side of the roaring gulf, the extremities of the white handrails were all that could be seen of the Queen's Bridge. Injuries to the railway prevented trains running ; but as soon as the weather moderated many persons from town went to witness the scene. I reached the spot about midday. The water was then said to have fallen five feet, a statement I saw some reason to doubt ; but the tops of three of the circular piers, and a fragment of the roadway hanging down into the stream were all that was then to be seen of the bridge. Far down the stream, towards the sea, in more than one place, curled huge foaming waves, as if caused by portions of the structure obstructing the channel it had so lately spanned. Altogether, it was a grand and terrible sight. Through a gorge some thousand or twelve hundred feet wide, with high precipitous banks clothed with wierd-looking euphorbias and other trees, hurried on the angry waters, discoloured with the soil of many a hill and field over which they had been spreading devastation. But a month before I had ridden along the low sandbank which barred up the mouth of the river and made it discharge itself three quarters of a mile to the northward. Now this had disappeared, flowed over, it seemed, and thrust out by the headlong force of the torrent which rapidly wore it down. But for an embankment placed across a narrow part of a low-lying marsh on the landside of the sandhills known as the Barkbeach Bush, the river would undoubtedly have poured down into the bay, carrying, as in 1856, devastation into the very town of Durban. As it was, the rainfall had been far too great to be carried off by such drains as exist, and much injury was done in some of the lower-lying parts of the town. A large body of water, which could not be taken by one of the principal drains, was dammed back by the embankment of the Pine Terrace extension of the railway; and had the rain continued but a few hours longer, there is much reason to believe the embankment must have yielded, carrying devastation through the very heart of the town.

"As it was, the damage done in the town, although serious, is far less than was anticipated. But it is on the roads and bridges, and in the sugar and coffee plantations, and the smaller estates and farms, that the greatest amount of damage has been done. For days the mails were stopped altogether, or delayed; and even now, a week after, intelligence has not yet been received from some of the more remote parts of the Colony. The great Mulas Flat, extending from the head of the bay to the Isipingo, fifteen miles distant, and to a considerable extent cultivated for sugar, was under water, and much damage has been done, although the extent is not yet known. The two Mulas bridges, the public one, and that to the Reunion Estate, were carried off, and the river flows 2000 yards on the hither side of its former channel. Lower down the coast, as well as up northward, similar damage has been sustained both by individuals and by the community. Sudden torrents and landslips have hurried acres of cane and coffee plants, with the soil that bore them, down to the sea. Bridges have gone with them; yawning gullies have opened across the main roads, or rocks and masses of earth from above have blocked them up. It is impossible, as yet at least, to estimate at all accurately the extent of damage that has been done. That to public works has been set down at about £50,000; while private persons are variously estimated to have sustained an aggregate loss of £50,000 to £100,000. Altogether, the calamity, widespread and vast as it is, is probably less than was at first supposed, and the lower estimate may turn out to be the more correct. The rainfall at Maritzburg, or the neighbourhood, according to Dr Sutherland, was 12·75 inches, considerably less than in the vicinity of Durban; and in the direction of the counties of Klip River and Newcastle, it is not even said to have been excessive or more than acceptable. No statement has yet appeared of the losses among the stock and sheep-farmers in the upper country, but it will probably turn out to be considerable wherever the rain has reached.

"The railway embankment near the Queen's Bridge was in two or three places undermined and swept off; a bridge on the Point line destroyed, and the line otherwise so injured as to put a stop to all traffic for a week. It is now, however, resumed, although the repairs have not been quite completed.

"On the very day on the morning of which the Queen's Bridge was destroyed, the Colonial Engineer, who happened to be in Durban, took measures to have boats placed on the Umgeni near the site of the late bridge. Thus the passenger traffic has not been interrupted even for a day. On the day following Mr Paterson proceeded to Maritzburg to lay before the Lieut.-Governor a plan for a temporary bridge, which could be got ready in six weeks, so that the whole sugar-crop of Victoria county, now just beginning to be got in, should suffer no unnecessary delay in being brought to market. The Chamber of Agriculture promptly met, and passed resolutions expressing their conviction that the planters would cheerfully pay a toll to avoid the delay which must otherwise be sustained.

"I again visited the Umgeni on the seventh day after the destruction of the bridge. The river although greatly fallen—fallen, indeed, at that spot to about its ordinary level—was still pouring an immense volume of water at a rapid rate into the sea. The channel, which ten days ago was perhaps barely twenty inches in depth, by scouring away of the sand, was now running twenty feet deep. Many hundreds, indeed thousands, of tons of rubbish from the Government quarry, where stone for the harbour works was being wrought, had been swept away down stream. On the same spot where I had stood about a month before in the quarry, a couple of hundred yards from the edge of a softly-flowing stream, with waving reeds and sedge, I now found myself on a cliff of rock, looking right down a swirling torrent thirty feet below. A spot across which I had then ridden was now on the opposite side of the river, which had there added many acres of bare sand, while on the other side where I was it had swept as many off into the ocean, and now hurried along close under the steep wooded extremity at the Berea, in one spot confined in a channel in a gorge barely sixty yards across, in another widening out to nearly four hundred. Two sections or ledges of the bridge, each of a hundred feet, lay in the stream; a third, the northernmost, still hung from its abutment; the other four sections were nowhere to be seen. On proceeding to the north of the river, I found it discharging itself right out to sea, having scoured away the broad sandbank, while the opening to the lagoon, through which it had lately flowed to the northward, was now closed up.

"There has been much controversy as to the height to which the Umgeni has risen as compared with the occasion of 1856, but no clear and thoroughly reliable record appears to have been kept of the rise in either case. In the papers of the day the flood of 1856 is stated to have risen 22 feet above the previous level. But prior to that event the river had been flowing in a channel only 208 feet in width, while since then it has been much wider, filling the whole space of 700 feet spanned by the late bridge. A rise of the same number of feet in so much wider a channel would therefore indicate a vastly greater rainfall. The amount of rain which fell on the first two days of the flood in April 1856 is stated at 19 inches, and the total rainfall in four days at 27 inches; but I feel very distrustfull of the accuracy of those figures.

"Eight years before, namely in April 1848, heavy floods had been experienced, although not equal to those of 1856, and native tradition spoke of other floods at the same season. People had therefore come to regard April as the month when danger was to be apprehended from this cause. Yet we have not been without warning in the month of August. Only three years ago almost to a day, namely on the 24th of the month, heavy rain fell, continuing with little intermission for three days, on which occasion the Umgeni rose to within eighteen inches of the roadway of the Queen's Bridge. It had not then been erected twelve months, for the day of its destruction was only four years and eight days from that which witnessed its formal opening.

"Amid all the disasters of these eventful last days there is one thing for which we have to be greatly thankful,—the comparatively small number of lives which have been lost. The only white man known to have perished is a youth of the name of Barr, an only son, who, with two companions, attempted to swim the river Umhloti, to his father's sugar mill. The other two succeeded in getting across, but young Barr, although a good swimmer, was carried off, and his body has not, I believe, yet been found. Of Coolies and Kaffirs some six or eight are known to have perished. The Swedish brig *Vaeringer*, the only vessel in the outer anchorage at the time, had a narrow escape. She lost one anchor and dragged the other for upwards of a mile until she got among the breakers not very far from the mouth of the

Umgeni. Whether the strong flow from the river enabled her to hold this position, or whatever may have been the cause, she succeeded in weathering out the storm, and after recovering the proper anchorage ground, has now come happily inside. From the greatly increased cultivation within the last twelve years the amount of damage done to crops, mills, and country buildings generally is much greater than that sustained by the Colony in 1856. On the other hand, the town buildings are now generally, at least at Durban, of a much more substantial character than they were in 1856."

Of a rainfall mentioned as occurring in April 1857, possibly the same as is spoken of here as occurring in 1856, Dr Mann in a paper read before the Royal Geographical Society, and printed in the society's journal of proceedings in 1867, gives the following particulars:—" It is said that 27 inches of rain fell at Durban, and between 10 and 11 inches at Maritzburg, between the fourteenth and sixteenth days of the month. I was not in the Colony at the time, and cannot vouch for the accuracy of this estimate; but at any rate there is no doubt that the Umgeni River rose about 28 feet above its usual level near its mouth, and burst quite across the sand flats on which Durban stands to the inner bay. The water was at one time within 12 feet of the level of the principle street of the town. The Tongaati River rose 30 feet above its usual level. The Umvoti River rose 16 feet, and spread a bed of sand 4 feet deep over the neighbouring pastures. Even the Maritzburg River, the Umsundusi, where the fall was so much less, carried away its bridge, and cut off the communication between the city and the port for several days. The sea beach was covered by trunks of trees and beds of reeds brought down by the rivers. 200 dead oxen were counted on one place on the beach, within a distance of 10 miles."

In the following year 1869, the Western Province was the scene of similar torrents. The following is a notice taken from one of the local papers:— "After a month of almost uninterrupted fine weather, on the 19th of June rain began to descend in Capetown and neighbourhood, and continued to pour down, in tropical fashion, almost without intermission till the night of Wednesday the 30th, doing great injury to buildings in Capetown and neighbourhood, and causing a serious accident on the Wellington railway. To give our English readers some idea of the quantity of water falling from the clouds upon us during the fortnight, Mr Blore, a meteorologist residing a short distance from Capetown, but in a situation where, from various causes, the temperature is more moist than in the town itself, reports that from the 19th June, at one P.M., till the 29th June, at 4 P.M., the fall was 18·252 inches, giving an average of ·075 inch per hour, and that during eight hours of the 20th June 2·185 inches fell, being at the rate of ·273 inch per hour. The same gentleman also reports that the rainfall during the past six months amounted to 33·890 inches, 31·951 of which fell during May and June. Mr George Maclear, of the Royal Observatory, reports that in the past half-year 20·179 inches have fallen, 17·51 inches being registered for May and June. In another direction from Capetown, Mr J. J. Steytler, of Sea Point, reports the quantity to have been 15·219 inches, 13·28 of which fell in May and June. All the reports given agree that if May and June be taken together, more rain has fallen this year than is recorded for the same months in any previous year. If we take the first six months, the rainfall has been greater than in any year since 1838."

The rainfall varies greatly with locality in Capetown and its vicinity. Mr Martin, resident in Capetown, gives the following as his observations:—
"SIRS,—I beg to forward the following account of rainfall at Rouwkoop Place, upper end of Caledon Street, from the 1st January to the 30th June, 130 feet above the sea:—

January,	...	...	...	0·330	inch.
February	...	...	...	0·010	,,
March,	...	...	...	0·590	,,
April,	...	...	...	1·795	,,
May,	...	...	...	7·465	,,
June,	...	...	...	7·495	,,
				17·685	,,

"The above measurements are from a gauge standing on a wall 18 feet 6 inches higher than another on the ground about 70 feet distant, from which I obtain at every rainfall an increase of 20 per cent.; the total for the past six months has been 21·222 inches.

"Taking the mean of our temperature for the last six months to be 66° Fahrenheit, the daily evaporation, according to experiments by Mr Crichton, of Glasgow, and Mr Dalton, from a space equal to the mean surface of the large reservoir, Capetown, will be 27,947 gallons, or 5-8th inch in depth.

"With a vessel of 12 inches diameter, from constant observation, I record 90 inches evaporated, exclusive of rain-days, which, if added, will give as near an approximation to Dalton's table as need be. I have, &c.,

"Rouwkoop Place, 1st July 1869." "W. MARTIN.

The destruction of property was considerable; not the least remarkable was the destruction of a railway bridge, in regard to which Mr Watson, the general superintendent, wrote to a local paper,—" The accident seems to have been caused by the embankment having become completely saturated with water during the previous night. An immense quantity of rain had fallen in that locality, and all the water courses were filled and overflowing. The water on the mountain or upper side of the line runs for some distance along the embankment before making its exit by the girder bridge at the Wellington end of the hollow, and as the water appears to have reached a great height against the railway, there is reason to believe that the portion which gave way became gradually so thoroughly soaked and perforated by the flood as to render it quite incapable of resisting the heavy pressure of a passing train."

Two public trials arose out of this accident, one a criminal trial before the Resident Magistrate at the Paarl, for culpable homicide, an accident to the railway train under which the bridge gave way having been followed by fatal consequences; another, a trial before the Supreme Court for damages, laid at £5000, sustained by one of the passengers; and there were elicited facts which were thus summarized by the Chief Justice in the delivery of his judgement:—" The chasm in the railway was undoubtedly produced by water which had accumulated on the upper side of the railway. The water had come from the higher grounds on that side, and also from the Berg River which flows on the lower side of the railway. The river had overflowed its banks and sent a volume of water to the upper side of the railway, underneath a bridge of 24 feet span, called the Sandhills Bridge, which was rather less than a mile nearer Capetown than the scene of the accident. This bridge, therefore, instead of relieving the railway from water, helped on this occasion to increase the water which was coming from the higher lands. The only exit for the water thus accumulating was through a culvert of six feet span, situated between the Sandhills Bridge and the scene of the accident, and by a bridge of twenty feet space on the further or Wellington side of the site of the accident. The accident occurred within six chains, or about three hundred feet of this last mentioned bridge, between that bridge and the culvert. When the train passed the twenty feet bridge on the morning of the 30th the water was above the girders of the bridge, these being of open, not close, construction. The girders, therefore, operated so far as to dam back the water, and to allow only that to pass which would escape under the girders. As the higher ground on the upper side of the railway converged towards the railway, and met it at a point a little beyond the twenty feet bridge on the Wellington side of it, the accumulated water had got into a sort of corner, from which what the bridge would not allow to pass could only escape by the six-feet culvert I have mentioned. While waiting for this escape the water seems to have worked its way through the railway at a point, as I have before mentioned, between the culvert and the bridge, and to have opened the chasm of at least thirty feet wide into which the train fell. Several theories were suggested by the scientific witnesses to account for the making of this chasm. One was that the embankment was made of sandy material; that the water while it was rising had saturated the sand; that the water rose till it flowed over the embankment through the cross channels in the ballasting upon the top of the embankment; that it then gradually cut its way through till it had opened a course sufficiently large to give a force of current equal to carrying away the extent of embankment which I have before mentioned. Another theory treated the embankment as having sufficient clay mixed with the sand to make it tenacious, and therefore of good material, provided its sides, if exposed to the action of water, had been faced with clay or stone. In other respects this theory coincided with the first I have mentioned. A third theory coincided with the second in regard to the goodness of the material of which the embankment was composed, but suggested that the accident was attributable to mole-holes in the embankment, which had weakened it, and had allowed water to get entrance. In the view I take of the case, I do not feel it necessary to consider which of these theories is the more correct, neither do I consider it necessary to deal with another matter, which occupied much attention during the evidence and much discussion at the bar,—to wit, whether there had been sufficient provision made at the time the railway was constructed for carrying away the water which might be expected to accumulate on its upper side. It seems that when the plans for the railway were submitted to the Colonial Engineer, he thought the water-way insufficient, and suggested that it should be increased, so as to afford at that part of the line a drainage of thirty-eight square feet; that this suggestion was carried out by making a water-way equal to fifty square feet, and by changing the line of the railway so as to make it pass along a higher level than was originally contemplated. Notwithstanding this apparent careful provision against the accumulation of water, the result has shown that, although the water-way has been sufficient since the year 1862, when the line was constructed, it has proved insufficient in the year 1869, when, as seemed to be admitted, the fall of rain, within a given time, during the night of the 30th June, from one to three o'clock, was greater than had been known for many years."

The fact to which attention is called is, that in connection with severe and long-continued droughts there occur within the Colony occasionally deluges of rain, working disaster and destruction even after every precaution deemed necessary has been taken.

In the same year, at Beaufort West, a deluge of rain washed down a large dam which had been erected by the municipality for the storage of water for the supply of the inhabitants; and in the year following the town was flooded by the waters of the Gomka; of this a correspondent writes:— "This town was visited on Monday, 7th instant, with a heavy rain, which commenced in the afternoon, and continued without intermission during the whole night. The river Gomka, on the one side, overflowed its banks, carrying away the parapet walls constructed for preventing its running into the town. At the same time the Springfontein, on the other side of the town, was full, and not having vent sufficient through the gap in the dam made by the breakage some time since, both rivers flowed uncontrolled into the town, flooded many houses, causing losses of a very considerable extent, blocked up the water furrows, and left the streets in a deplorable plight. The principal losers are Messrs P. J. Alport & Co., who had their stores washed through by a body of water of about two feet, filling a large underground cellar, containing quantities of bags, sugar, &c., and wetting a large amount of goods of all descriptions. Many families had to fly from their houses and take refuge with their neighbours."

In the next year, 1871, Victoria West was the scene of disaster. The following is a summary of the details collected by the *Capetown Argus*: The beginning of the storm is thus described in a private letter:—" Above the village, on the farm Patrysfontein, occupied by Mr Frans Hugo, at 5 o'clock on the afternoon of the 27th February, heavy low thunder-clouds were seen approaching, while the lower masses flashed vivid lightning, accompanied by but little thunder. Clouds, as it were, of steam rolled in volumes along the ground. An hour before sunset it got so dark that one could scarcely see an object just in front of him, and rain in torrents began to fall, accompanied by immense hailstones. About 8 o'clock Mr Hugo's family heard a loud crash as if of falling iron in the sky. Mr Hugo on opening the door exclaimed, 'Woman, let us fly!' And scarcely was she outside with her children when on came a mountain of water which swept away the whole of the buildings, so that scarcely a trace of them could afterwards be found. But that was not the worst. Before they could get away the flood came down, and poor Hugo had to see his wife and four children swept away and drowning, himself barely escaping with the infant in his arms. All his stock, big and little, was carried away and drowned. The flood then took its course towards the village, and about 9 o'clock began the work of destruction."

Of what took place in the village itself the following is a brief description by one who was there:—" On Monday night, about 9 o'clock, rain commenced to fall, and at ten o'clock our whole village was flooded. I was reading a newspaper in my bedroom. The next moment my wife heard a scream and went out, but came running back, and cried out 'We will be drowned.' A heavy knock then came at the window. I asked 'Who is there?' The reply was, 'Mrs Laws, let me in, we are **drowning.'** We threw open our French window which leads to our parlour, and the poor woman rushed inside. It was awful to hear my children screaming, sometimes 'Father,' and sometimes 'Mother, we will be drowned—we will be drowned.' Our shop stands very high—our stoep stands about five feet higher than the opposite, which is the lower side of the street—which saved us from the ruin. Now, what could we do? The screams from the opposite side of the street were something terrible, and it was as dark as pitch. I flew to the shop, put all the lamps I could lay my hands on in the window, opened my shutters, and threw out all the light into the street. All that could find their way to my stoep did so. The sight was most lamentable. Bales of wool by the hundred floating down the middle of the street in the flood. Door-frames, window-frames, roofs of houses, sheep, goats, mules, and horses were like feathers in the water. You may imagine what it was in the river which runs behind the houses and shops opposite me. They screamed from the opposite side to throw a rope across. When Mrs Laws opened her door the water rushed in. She screamed out to Mr Laws and three other gentlemen that were sitting having a chat. She rushed across to our place, which took her up to her knees, and before they got to the door it was impossible for them to cross. Luckily, I had a coil of rope in my back store; I got it out, and succeeded, with the assistance of Mr Palgrave, who was drenched to the skin, in getting it across. He had been through the water, up to his chest; he worked like a nigger. By his contrivance we got the rope across. They made it fast to the rail above the door. We held on tight, and all four succeeded in getting across safe. By this time the back of the building had fallen, which leaves Mr Laws a heavy loser,—a place that was all but finished. The opposite corner to Mr Laws was still more distressing. Here lives a Mrs Dodds. I think the number this evening was seven in the house, and with the rope we succeeded in getting them all across; but before getting them all across the whole of the house fell in, barring a little piece of the front, which held on; but a fine young lady, eighteen years old, who was to be married the 15th of next month, got struck on the forehead with a brick, which caused her death about an hour after they got her across. Behind Mrs Dodds' place stood that of John M'Donald, baker and butcher, close to the river. We concluded they were both gone,—I mean his wife also,—as the building was gone. But for a willow tree he planted in front of his house they would have been washed away. When the bricks began to fall in they flew to the tree, and when the water went down a little they got on the top of the ruins. They had screamed till they were tired; but nobody heard them for the roar of the water. When the water fell enough to enable us to get over to their place, we heard a voice from among the ruins, and found John M'Donald and his wife almost in a state of nudity. They had only been in bed a quarter of an hour when part of the place fell in. We got them across to our place, and had them dressed at once. The next up the street was Mr Smith, who had a very narrow escape of his life. I think he will save the most of his stock, as his place fell in after the water fell. It has hurt him very much; not quite recovered yet. Mr Adams, his brother-in-law, will be the heaviest loser in the village, as a great many houses belonging to him are gone. Opposite this stands the Commercial Hotel, which had three feet of water inside; they are afraid to sleep in the place. I think it will fall. The next place was Mr Jacobsohn's. The screams from both of them were terrible. They stood on a table till the place began to fall in. He is a heavy loser. He had about 400 bales waiting for transport. He may get it all, but fancy some of it two or three miles off. Skins, you need not look for them. Opposite is the magistrate's office; all their books and papers are in an awful state. Mr Garcia, our worthy magistrate, also Mr Rawstorne and Mr Munnik, worked until they were actually worn out. Rawstorne and Munnik's landlady is gone, and everything they had. You can hardly see the foundation of the house. Marcus and Mrs Armstrong went down the river with her, holding fast to one another. Tell Elsner and Lewis that Schoombom's place is completely gone,—in fact, part of the foundation is away. Hanna and Hoffa will lose, I think, seven or eight hundred pounds in wool and buildings. A farmer, called Frans Hugo, living about six miles from the village, lost his wife and four children, and his farmstead is left the same as the veldt—bare. Mr A. L. Devenish, three miles from the village, has lost four hundred of his best sheep, and a splendid dam he was making, which was supposed to cost £2000 when finished. As near as possible twenty-five houses have completely gone. Up till six o'clock this evening (1st March), fifty-three dead bodies have been discovered and buried; but we are afraid we shall hear of a great many more, as this river runs a long way."

On the same day similar destructive effects were produced by the rainfall near Oudtshoorn. Of this a correspondent of the *Cape Argus* writes:— "Not having as yet seen an account in any of the papers of a severe hailstorm accompanied with torrents of rain, which was experienced on the farm known by the name of 'Schoemanshoek,' at the entrance of the Cango Poort, distant about ten miles from this village, on Monday, the 27th ult. —the same day on which the calamity occured at Victoria West,—I send you particulars of the storm. The weather looked gloomy on the date mentioned; there were several heavy showers in this village, and dark clouds appeared in the direction of the Cango. The Grobbelaars River, on the banks of which Oudtshoorn is situated, was almost stagnant, but swelled into a torrent towards evening, and almost became impassable. Nothing, however, was known by the villagers of the hailstorm, or the damage occasioned by it to the proprietors of the farm 'Schoemanshoek,' until the following day. It appears that at about 2 o'clock P.M. it commenced to rain in torrents at 'Schoemanshoek,' accompanied with hail, which lasted about an hour, and in that short space of time the whole of the tabacco plantations, for which the above farm is celebrated, were completely destroyed; the greater portion of the crop, which was unusually fine, was ready for gathering. The leaves were battered to pieces; in fact, nothing remained after the storm was over but the bare stalks. The storm was confined to 'Schoemanshoek' only, and did not extend to the adjoining farms. All the kloofs and gullies running down to the Grobbelaars River in a remarkably short time became foaming torrents, and quite impassable while the storm lasted. The watercourses on the farm were found, after the storm had passed over, to be silted up with sand and stones; there was a great rush of water on the homestead between the houses of the several proprietors. All the manure from the kraals was swept into the river, and the roads in the locality were washed into deep chasms, so that traffic was stopped to and from the Cango, until the farmers in a body turned out to repair damages, which was no easy task as regards the roads. With respect to the tobacco their losses are very heavy. The following is a statement of the losses sustained; the estimate, I was assured by my informant, one of the Messrs Schoeman, whose statement may be relied on, is considerably below the mark :—H. P. Schoeman, 3000 lb. tobacco; L. M. Schoeman, 7000 lb. do.; Estate late P. J. Schoeman, 3000 lb. do.; H. S. N. Schoeman, 4000 lb. do.; H. S. Schoeman, 7000 lb. do.; P. Schoeman, 2000 lb. do.; Jan Schoeman, 2000 lb. do.; Jacs Schoeman, 2000 lb. do.; Jan Schoeman and Jacob van Antwerp, 2000 lb. do.; Christoffel Spies, 3000 lb. do.—total, 35,000 lb. do. Reckoning the price of the tobacco at 5d per lb., the losses sustained by the proprietors of the farm Schoemanshoek will reach about £725."

In the *Cape Argus* of 4th June 1872 it is mentioned :—" Heavy rains have fallen in all parts of the Colony. In Capetown they caused a flood which for a time turned several of the streets into rivers. Many houses and stores had water in them to the depth of four feet."

Such details seem to tell that it is not want of rain which is the cause or occasion of the drought. They seem to tell that "it never rains but it pours." They remind one of what has been written in regard to St. Swithin, of popular fame; and of what has been told of St. Dunstan's brother Peter of the Inglesby legends,—rain, rain, raining as if it would never cease. And they remind one of the feeling of the ancient mariner,—sea, sea, sea, everywhere sea, and not a drop to allay his thirst. Water, water, water, everywhere water, and not a hundredth part to be retained to fertilize the ground; all rushing in torrents to the main, where there is no lack.

Whatever may be the aridity of South Africa there is moisture in the atmosphere, for all this superabundance of water has fallen thence, and fallen from what was, shortly before the collision and intermingling of aerial currents preceding the down-pour, a cloudless sky.

I had almost said scarcely does a newspaper come to me from the Cape in which mention is not made of drought. While some of the preceding pages were passing through the press I have received several. In one of these I read :—" A gentleman who has very recently travelled from Murraysburg to Graaff-Reinet, writes to a contemporary :—'You can form no idea of the dreadful state of the country between this (Graaff-Reinet) and Murraysburg; water is failing; pasturage is completely dried up, and covered with locusts. At Murraysburg I paid two shillings a bundle for forage. If we don't get rain soon I don't know what will become of us.'"

"A Fraserburg correspondent, writing on the 19th inst., [Nov. 1874] says: —'While I write, the rain is coming down in torrents—a blessing which we have not enjoyed here for the last eight months. That scourge to the country, the spring-bucks, are said to be in the neighbourhood in countless numbers.'" These animals are generally driven into the Colony by the lack of water and of pasturage in districts beyond.

The same post which brought the newspaper from which these quotations have been made, brought me a letter from the District Surgeon of Fraserburg, the place mentioned, in which he writes, amongst other things, of a journey of about a hundred miles which he made to visit a patient :—" We left about mid-day, pushed slowly on with weak, poor horses, for the whole **land suffers** from drought, and all the cattle are poor and dying, the waters giving up, and general distress impending. We pushed on all night [with changes of horses] as that is much cooler for the horses, and the next day before sunset we reached our destination." Thirty-two hours of continuous travelling for a journey of one hundred miles! He goes on to say:—" I have been writing this morning since before sunrise and a fine thunderstorm has been coming in from the north. Little ——'s morning greeting was, ' Kind God, making the *tunder* and send the nice rain.' Thus you see how early God's blessings are appropriated here! This is indeed a dry and thirsty land, and everyone in the village and neighbourhood is anxiously, hopingly watching the clouds."

In another part of the newspaper I have cited is a communication from a correspondent at Burghersdorp, in which is said:—" We had a heavy thunderstorm on Saturday (7th November), accompanied with great hailstones, as large as hens' eggs, which caused considerable damage amongst the glass, especially the windows of the Masonic Lodge. Most of the blue gums here have a very peculiar appearance. The heavy frosts during the winter killed all the foliage, and many are now without leaves. They are, however, shooting out round about the stem and branches, which at a distance has the appearance of immense clusters of bees. Strange to say, one or two in the town escaped, and have not suffered any injury. The Port Jackson willows are all dead; the blackwood trees also. Fruit will be scarce this season. Our market is badly supplied—some mornings not a single thing, not even an egg! Butter, when there is any, 4s 6d per lb. The country round about is as dry as a chip, the hills bare and brown."

Any other newspaper taken at random at any other time would probably have been found to contain similar accounts of drought. But in these notices of drought there are, as probably would also be found to be the case in notices of the state of the weather elsewhere, at some other time, references to rain; and to form a correct conception of the state of things to be remedied to this also attention must be given.

The beginning of November is, at the Cape, the beginning of summer. Hail in summer is not unknown elsewhere in connection with thunderstorms, but to some who reside elsewhere it may be supposed that a description of " great hailstones, as large a hens' eggs," must be an exaggeration. I cannot say it is not, but I have no reason to suppose it is; and from what I have seen and learned in the district of Burghersdorp I am led to accept the statement as correct.

When at the Cape, in travelling from King Williamstown to Burghersdorp, I visited Queenstown, the principal town of an adjoining district, about the same season of the year, a little later, with summer more advanced, and I was told that the week before there had been there *a heavy fall of snow*; stores, banks, and public offices were closed that the men of business, clerks and principals alike, might have the sport of snowballing. I there heard of a storm of hail which, falling in a slanting direction, had cut off the cobbs of Indian corn almost as regularly, over extensive plots, as if it had been done with a hedgebill. And on the same journey, near Riversdale, I saw a house the wall of which was defaced with numerous marks like such as might be made with a pick-axe, and was told it was the effect of a hailstorm, or storm of ice, which had occurred some six weeks before. And large as the hailstones falling at Burghersdorp were said to be, in this there is nothing incredible.

Of men of science no one stands higher in general reputation at the Cape than does Sir John Herschel. On the subject of hail he wrote:—"In a balloon ascent, performed by Messrs Green, Rust, and Spencer, on September 4th, 1838, after mounting to an altitude of 19,185 feet, during which ascent the thermometer, at 12,000 feet, marked 46° Fahrenheit, they found on descending again to the last mentioned level a temperature of 22° Fahrenheit only, or 24° colder than in their ascent. At the same time they found there a heavy fall of *snow* in progress. It is evident that this arose from the condensation of vapour *at* that level, and that, from the intrusion of some current, a mass of intensely cold air had been introduced, which, finding vapour near saturation, converted it into snow. It is equally evident that had the latter condition prevailed not at the level in question, but at a somewhat higher, where the condensation might have been into *rain* very near freezing point, the drops in descending would have been frozen solid and fallen as *hail*. It might have been so equally, had the precipitation been so copious as to allow the coalescence of a great number of minute particles in a nascent state into drops frozen together instanter, since there is good reason to believe that the solid forms is never assumed without transition through the liquid, however momentary.

"The generation of hail seems always to depend on some very sudden introduction of an extremely cold current of air into the bosom of a quiescent, nearly saturated mass. Hail-storms are always purely local phenomena, and never last long. They often mark their course by linear tracks of devastation of great length and very small breadth. In the hail-storm of July 13th, 1788, which passed across France from south to north, two such tracks were marked, of 175 and 200 leagues in length respectively, parallel to each other, the one four leagues broad, the other two, and separated by a track five leagues in breadth, in which only rain fell. A similar character is very common, though not to such an extent. Such linear hail-storms are always attended with violent wind, sudden depression of the barometer, indicating a great commotion in the air, and probably mingling of saturated masses of very different temperature. To attribute to hail, as is often done, an electrical origin, because hail is often accompanied with thunder and lightning ('hailstones and coals of fire'), seems to us to be putting the effect for the cause.

"Hail may be very properly distinguished into single hailstones and aggregated masses. Single stones have generally a crystalline structure, radiating from a centre, if large forming spherical, oval, or rounded masses, often marked out (on making a section) into concentric layers, like the rings in the section of a branch. They fall from the size of small peas to that of an egg, an orange, or a man's head, and weighing from a few grains up to fourteen pounds and upwards. Dr Thomson, in his *Introduction to Meteorology*, a work in which the reader will find assembled a most extraordinary collection of the recorded marvels of meteorology, gives many instances of the fall of large hailstones. One described by Capt. Delcrosse, as having fallen at Baçoniere, July 4, 1819, fifteen inches in circumference, had a beautiful radiated structure marking it as a single stone, formed in passing through two distinct regions of condensation. Dr Buist stated to the Bombay Geographical Society that in India the hailstones are from five to twenty times larger than those in England, often weighing from six ounces to a pound, seldom less than walnuts, often that of oranges! These storms are almost always accompanied by violent wind and rain, thunder and lightning, and are frequent in the delta of the Ganges, especially in the low country within fifty miles of the Bay of Bengal.

"Great hail-storms are often preceded by a loud clattering and clashing sound, indicating the hurling together of masses of ice in the air. The recent experiments of Professor Tyndall, in the re-uniting of broken ice by 'regelation,' or a sort of welding, fully explains the formation, under such circumstances, of large masses of ice of irregular forms in this aerial conflict. Such are recorded to have fallen of almost fabulous magnitude. In Candeisch, in 1826, in a hail-storm which perforated the roofs of houses like small cannon-shot, a mass fell which took some days to melt, and must have weighed more than a hundred-weight.—(Malet). On May 8, 1832, a mass fell in Hungary a yard in length, and nearly two feet in thickness.—(Thomson). And if it be true, as stated in the *Rosshire Advertiser* in 1849, that a block of irregular shape, nearly twenty feet in circumference, fell in August of that year on the estate of Mr Moffat, of Ord, immediately after an extraordinarily loud peal of thunder, Heyne's relation of a hailstone as large as an elephant, at Seringapatam, in the reign of Tippoo Sultan, may perhaps find believers. The Rosshire mass is stated to have been composed of lozenge-shaped pieces, one to three inches in size, firmly congealed together."

I have before me the *Introduction to Meteorology* by Dr D. P. Thomson, a work published in Edinburgh in 1849. I have read the extraordinary collection of details to which Sir John Herschel refers, with the statement of the authorities upon which the details of extraordinary hail-storms are given, and I consider no one after doing so would see anything incredible in the statement sent from Burghersdorp.

According to views advanced by Espy, a distinguished American meteorologist, the two parallel lines along which the hail-storm advanced in the case mentioned by Sir John Herschel can be satisfactorily accounted for. According to one of the laws regulating storms, many of these advance, as does a wheel, rotating and progressing horizontally—as a wheel does vertically in advancing along a road—as is made visible in a small advancing whirlwind of dust, or leaves, or straw, or chaff. The cyclon, a whirlwind of such extent as to create a storm, is fed with air as it advances; this, raised to a great height, expands, cools, precipitates the moisture it contained, and throws this off in a frozen state—as does a twirled wet mop throw off drops of water,—and by gravitation it falls. As the rotating whirlwind advances the motion of the air forming the forefront will cross the breadth of the circle from left to right, or from right to left, as the case may be; the air forming the rear will cross the breadth of the circle in the opposite direction, and scatter the hailstone or rain over the whole breadth traversed in two showers, minutes, hours, or days apart; but at the sides the wind blows in but one direction on the right of the circle, and in one direction, the opposite of this, on the other, and along the lines followed by these the hail or rain falls continuously in greater abundance.

Of Natal Dr Mann writes in a paper read before the Royal Geographical Society, and published in their journal for 1867,—"Very heavy hail-storms occasionally happen in connection with thunder-storms. The hail for the most part sweeps on in the midst of a torrent, a distinct drone or humming is heard to herald its approach for one minute, or even two minutes, before it arrives. Hailstones as large as pigeons' eggs are sometimes seen; masses of ice weighing three-quarters of a pound have, in rare instances, been noticed. The fall of the hail is always limited to a very narrow zone. The path of the hail-storm is accurately marked out over the country by a long narrow line of devastation."

And in a letter from Natal by Mr Dunn, a geologist there, on a special exploratory expedition to the Transvall, for which he was now about to leave, are given the following details of a hail-storm there witnessed by him:—" Pietermaritzburg, 18th April 1874.—The climate here is something out of the ordinary run, if yesterday is a sample of it; for we then witnessed one of the most extraordinary hail-storms I have ever even read of, and I am sure even you would think I am romancing unless I assure you to the contrary.

"Yesterday afternoon, about 4.25 P.M., I was walking with a friend up ——— Street when suddenly the wind—such an usual precursor of storms—began to blow the dust about; at the same time I observed that the S.W. portion of the sky was filled with an exceedingly black cloud, contracting upwards to a point. Presently a few drops fell, then heavier ones, and then solitary great lumps of ice. On the sight of these we dashed under an iron verandah, and none too soon. A loud rushing sound came from the S.W., which rapidly became more distinct, and then suddenly the most terrific display took place of Heaven's artillery. Hailstones poured down with great violence and rapidity; liberally mingled with the stones were great masses of ice of very irregular forms. The hailstones were seldom less than one inch in diameter; the average was from one and a half to two inches in diameter. These were of very regular spherical form, and consisted of a nucleus of white snow, with an envelope of hard transparent ice. Sometimes they presented when broken through a concentric arrangement of zones, alternately white and opaque and transparent.

"The irregular masses were formed of a nucleus generally longer in one direction than the others, from two to four inches in diameter; projecting all over were stalactites, each one about the thickness of a little finger, and presenting when broken across an agate-like structure, as though segregation had built them up. Of these masses I weighed a few with the following results: Three weighed over 8 oz., two over 6 oz., and one over 4 oz. The last, which was the largest, I found myself, and it was weighed sometime after the storm was over. Those below were weighed by others, but I saw some, and know the others are right from the parties who took the weights. One weighed $7\frac{1}{2}$ oz., one 8 oz., and one 6 oz. This last was weighed fully fifteen minutes after the storm had ceased, and it had suffered much from melting. It was an irregular mass, with projections all over it. The storm raged with fury for seven or eight minutes, the great lumps could be distinguished as they descended, and then as they fell on the road they broke into fragments, scattering all around. In about two minutes from the commencement the whole road was completely covered, and appeared as though covered with snow.

"The hail as it came down smashed the tiles in a terrible manner; pieces as they were broken off ran down the roof into the road, while the thuds of the stones against the galvanized iron threatened to destroy even it. Ground beneath trees was strewn with severed twigs.

"On looking round afterwards the damage was enormous. On many roofs fully half the tiles were broken, not merely cracked, but very frequently the masses went right through into the houses. None have escaped. Fortunately for windows there was no wind, or the damage would have been much heavier. Many of the corrugated iron roofs are dented all over, and have a pock-marked aspect, while some *corrugated iron* roofs are *completely riddled*, the stones went *right through*, as though they had but paper to encounter. I have made a point of examining the iron roofs, and therefore can vouch for the above. The mischief done will not be covered by £2000, or anything like that sum.

"Soon after the downpour ceased the drains were running swiftly with water; most had disappeared by dark."

This narrative is in keeping with the communication from Burghersdorp which I have cited; and all of the details given by Dr Mann are in accordance with what has been stated above, the parallel line of hail or rain, corresponding to the long narrow line of devastation mentioned by him, may have been ten or a hundred miles, or less or more, to the right or to the left of it. With fuller details, this and much more in regard to any such case could be determined. But all goes to show that there is moisture in the atmosphere, that it is not only not absolutely devoid of moisture, but the quantity of moisture suspended in it is absolutely great—a fact of which the occasional flooding of the country by rainfall and overflowing rivers thus fed supplies additional, and it may be more satisfactory, evidence.

The communications from the midland districts, from Fraserburg, and from Burghersdorp, I have quoted from a Cape paper published towards the end of November of last year [1874], all tell of drought, of severe and long-continued drought, but of a promise of rain. A newspaper received by the next mail contained the following announcement, which showed that the hopes awakened had not been disappointed:—"BREAKING UP OF THE DROUGHT.—The Colesberg paper of the 20th ult. says,—On Friday evening of last week, a heavy thunder-storm burst over this neighbourhood, and extended for a considerable distance towards and along the Orange River. On the following day heavy rain again fell. On Sunday the weather was fine, but heavy rain fell on Monday, Tuesday, Wednesday, and Thursday. The heaviest and longest down-pour occurred on Wednesday afternoon, when rain continued to fall during some seven hours. We are glad to learn the rain has extended far and wide, and that there is now every reason to believe that a favourable season has set in both for stock farmers and agriculturists, to which the greatest drawback will be the locusts, countless swarms of *voetgangers* being reported in all directions. Here the grass is growing rapidly, and, unless destroyed by locusts, will soon be in fine condition."

But it was the old story over again—after a drought a deluge! The same paper contained the following:—"The following extract from a private letter, dated Jansenville, 26th ult., has been kindly handed to us for publication:—On Monday a severe thunder-storm, accompanied by smart showers of rain, passed over the village, and the whole sky in the direction of Graaff-Reinet presented an appearance as dark as night, giving evidence that no ordinary storm was being experienced in that quarter. During the whole of Tuesday it continued to pour almost incessantly, and on Wednesday morning, at three A.M., the Sunday's River came down with a rush never before experienced within the recollection of the oldest inhabitant. The noise was like distant thunder, but quite near enough to make things uncomfortable. By six A.M. the river, which for many months past could have been crossed without wetting one's feet, was now running mountains high, and was still rapidly rising. By ten o'clock it began to overflow, and the width of the water at the place where the Jansenville bridge is being constructed was 250 yards or more. Large trees floated down like so many pieces of cork, and bales of wool, pigs, sheep, oat sheaves, and pieces of fencing, all came down in quick succession. The lower parts of the gardens at the north top of the village were all covered with water, amongst others, that of our worthy resident magistrate. At one time it was feared that the barracks occupied by the immigrants constructing the bridge would have been flooded, the water having come to within a few feet of their houses, and orders had been given to be ready for any emergency. Fortunately the flood subsided towards the evening, and the inhabitants of Jansenville returned to their beds satisfied that for the present there is no necessity for removing on to the numerous hills which surround the village. As I write this it is still raining, but all fear of a flood is over. The box in which the mails are conveyed across the river has been washed away, and I have no idea when this may reach you. Notwithstanding the flood, the bridge works stood the test well, and no damage has been done to any part of the works."

The *Cradock Register*, of Nov. 27th, says,—" Yesterday intelligence was received in town of a sad case of drowning in a small sloot between Blauwhoogte and Plankfontein Poort, about eight miles from Cradock, on the Tarkastad road. The particulars are as follows:—On the previous day (Monday) four Dutch farmers, named Jan Coetzer, Barend de Lange, Andries de Lange, and P. Jordaan, left Cradock for their homes. On arriving at the sloot in question, which is deep and narrow, they found it very full. Jan Coetzer started first and got through safely. He then called to the others to wait and he would drive back his horse, which is a strong animal and accustomed to water, and they could use it in turn. They took no heed of the offer, however, but all plunged into the stream, and were all in a moment swept down by the force of the current. Two of them—Barend de Lange and his companion, Piet Jordaan, scrambled out by means of some bushes. The three men then ran down the banks in hopes of saving Andries, who could be seen for a while struggling in the water. Unfortunately, after they had followed the poor man for about 450 yards, they saw him disappear over a steep descent in the stream, and there can be no doubt but that the unfortunate man was drowned. They followed the course of the stream to where it joins the Tarka River, but were unable to find any traces of him. The brother of the drowned man suffered a heavy pecuniary loss by the accident, for on reaching firm ground he found that by some means or other a courier bag, which he had slung around him, containing £200 in gold and silver and £100 in notes, had been torn from the straps and was nowhere to be seen. The deceased was about thirty years of age, and leaves a wife and three children to mourn their loss.

"We hear also that Mr Gert Venter (son of Mr Field-Cornet Venter) had a very narrow escape on the same day. He was crossing a drift that was swollen with the rains, when he was swept from his horse. By great good luck he and the horse managed to scramble out."

These notices were only, like those which have been already cited, the precursors of others of greater moment which were to follow. In another paper received by the same mail it was stated,—" In the Eastern province the rains have been very heavy, and the damage to the public works is estimated at £350,000. Telegraphic communication east of Algia Bay was stopped, the poles having been washed away."

From another paper I cite the following :—"There is something not merely exceptionally, but extremely sensational, in the telegram which we publish to-day. The bridges reported as washed down by the recent floods, and the damages resulting therefrom, cannot be estimated at much less than £300,000! There are the Klaas Smit River, near Queen's Town, gone; the Koonap River Bridge, ditto; the Carlisle Bridge over the Fish River, ditto; the Fort Brown, also over the Fish River, ditto, though the piers may still be available; the Kookhuis Bridge, the Tarka Bridge, the Cradock Bridge, with the new Buffalo Bridge damaged at King William's Town, and the Port Beaufort Bridge, injured, though now being repaired, across the Kat River. In addition to this, Fort Beaufort itself has been to a considerable extent destroyed by floods. Alice has been more than half under water, from the small neighbouring stream of the Chumic; and lives were saved only by the pluck of the inhabitants. The Committee's Drift Bridge, in course of buiding, was forty-five feet under water, and quite swept away. On the principle that it is an ill wind that blows nobody good, or an ill flood that sweeps nobody fortune, we find that at East London the bar has been swept quite clear, and the *Florence* was able to discharge her cargo inside. But, *per contra*, there were some eight wrecks, more or less, outside."

The *Friend of the Free State*, of 26th November, gives the following details of what occurred there :—"From 4.30 A.M. till noon, on the 24th instant, the rain descended unceasingly and literally in cascades. The accompanying thunder and lightning roared and gleamed at intervals during the lengthened period of seven and a half hours. The first intimation we had of the unparalleled nature of the down-pour was the tidings that our big dam, which had been completely empty for several months, was filled to overflowing, and that, moreover, 2000 square yards of the flats beyond it were submerged. What made this the more surprising was that thousands of loads of mud had recently been removed from the bed of the dam, which was thereby very level, capable of holding at the deepest part upwards of thirteen feet of water. From 8.30 A.M. the rain put on a spurt, during which period the water was precipitated to the ground in one solid, unbroken sheet. The effect of this was to cause Bluim Spruit, which had already been running like mad, and roaring like a thousand bulls of Bashan, to go altogether beside itself; it broke bounds and continued to rise, and to rise, till it rose to an unprecedented height, at least so our authority the oldest inhabitant affirms, and it is not for us to impeach his word."

"Next, it was reported that the Spruit had burst barriers intended to prevent its destroying the fountain; and shortly thereafter that the bridge in Green Street was swept away in sight of scores of spectators who had lined the banks of the raging torrent. "Then a horseman came tearing up and announced that the bridge in Fraser Street had taken to the water as naturally as a duck, and was sailling away beautifully to——no one knows where. All eyes were now intently fixed on the only remaining bridge, that in Church Street. Presently the shout arose, 'She's gone,' and shortly afterwards she parted in the middle and sailed down the stream as saucily as ever did the *Arethusa*, which called forth tears from some of the spectators. Meanwhile the incorrigible Spruit continued to swell in a most alarming manner. Several houses were one after another surrounded by water, and suffered considerable damage. One of these, the dispensary of Dr Keiller, which, says the report, "was alike a credit to himself and an ornament to the town, is internally a heap of ruins. The water gained access to the cellar by forcing a hole through the back-wall facing the Spruit, and the disastrous effects of this fissure was to cause the flooring above the cellar to give way, and then down came partition walls and shelving with a tremendous crash, smashing the bottles containing the doctor's drugs and chemicals to shivereens. It was a piteous sight to behold. The place where order and regularity, cleanliness and good taste, reigned supreme but a moment previously was, in the twinkling of an eye, converted into a scene of inextricable and utter wreck. While the events we have been depicting were transpiring, Fountain Street became the bed of a roaring boiling torrent, and great fears were entertained for the inmates of houses"—which are specified. In one of these "the women and children were removed from their perilous position, but not before the water had attained a depth of two or three feet" in the houses spoken of; and many such minor details are given. The large dam, which had been repaired some time before, stood its ground, but the park dam succumbed. Happily no lives were lost.

Such, in regard to water supply, is South Africa within and beyond the regions colonized by Europeans ! Much that I have seen of it has reminded me of a description I got in America, from a Kansas man, of the state of Kansas as one frequently given of that state. It is said to be the richest and the poorest, the hottest and the coldest, the wettest and the driest state in the Union, in America, or in the world !

Similar contrasts may be seen in South Africa : diamonds and rubies, and copper and gold in some districts, but some of these so devoid of vegetation as to recall, by the appearance they present, a remark of John Campbell, cited by Moffat, and well remembered by his few surviving friends, 'Hech, sirs, it would take a good pair of spectacles to see a blade of grass here ;' vineyards and orchards in one district, others, heard by, covered with the rhinoster bush, or other plants as profitless ; districts covered with waving corn, others with arid sand ; spots in these, to which water is conveyed, yielding crops a hundred fold in quantity to the seed sown, and all around a barren waste. Livingstone tells of the heat experienced at Kolobeng : I have suffered more from cold in South Africa than I ever did during a residence of seven years in Russia. There are districts flooded with waters, as was found to be the case by Livingstone and Stanley, and districts dry as Livingstone found Kolobeng to be, and as that in which Mr Helmore and his family perished.

Within the Colony of the Cape of Good Hope there are rains and torrents such as have been described and referred to, and, as often it happens within an hour or two after torrents of rain the sky is cloudless and serene, so, frequently within a month or two after, all is as arid as before ; and the traveller listening to details of what had happened hears them with a feeling of incredulity and a disposition to ascribe much of what he hears to a fervid fancy, and to liken much of what he hears to what Moffat tells of his experience in his first journey to Griqua Town of visions of water—but visions of water which had no corresponding existence. The passage I shall give entire, as a picture of the aridity which prevails, notwithstanding the abundance of moisture in the atmosphere, and the occasional deluge and torrent by which it is carried off to the sea :—

"On the seventh day (says he) we reached that part of the river called Quis or Kwees, from which we intended to go in a direct course to Griqua Town, leaving the Orange River far to the right. We had previously made inquiries about the country which lay between; some said there was water; others, that we should find none. We had eaten a small portion of meat that morning, reserving only enough for *one* single meal, lest we should get no more, and drank freely of water, to keep the stomach distended, and felt tolerably comfortable. At night we came to some old huts, where were remains of tobacco gardens, which had been watered with wooden vessels from the adjoining river. We spent the evening in one of these huts; though, from certain holes for ingress and egress, it was evidently a domicile for hyenas and other beasts of prey. We had scarcely ended our evening song of praise to Him whose watchful care had guided and preserved us through the day, when the distant and dolorous howls of the hyena, and the no less inharmonious jabbering of the jackal, announced the kind of company with which we were to spend the night; while, from the river, the hippopotami kept up a blowing and snorting chorus. Our sleep was anything but sweet. On the addition of the dismal notes of the hooting owl, one of our men remarked, 'We want only the lion's roar to complete the music of the desert.' 'Were they as sleepy and tired as I am,' said another, 'they would find something else to do.' In the morning we found that some of these night scavengers had approached very near the door of our hut.

"Having refreshed ourselves with a bathe and a draught of water, we prepared for the thirsty road we had to traverse; but before starting, a council was held, whether we should finish the last small portion of meat (which any one might have devoured in a minute), or reserve it. The decision was to keep it till evening. We sought in vain for ixia bulbs. Our only resource, according to the custom of the country, was to fill ourselves with as much water as our bodies could contain. We had no vessels in which to carry it; and if we had, our horses were not equal to more than the carriage of our persons. We were obliged to halt during the day, fearing our horses would give up from the excessive heat. When the evening drew on we had to ascend and descend several sand-hills, which, weary and faint from two days' fasting, was to us exceedingly fatiguing. Vanderbyle and myself were somewhat in advance of the rest, when we observed our three companions remaining behind; but supposing they staid to strike light and kindle their pipes, we thoughtlessly rode forward. Having proceeded some distance we halted and hallooed, but received no reply. We fired a shot, but no one answered. We pursued our journey in the direction of the high ground near the Long Mountains, through which our path lay. On reaching a bushless plain, we alighted and made a fire: another shot was fired, and we listened with intense earnestness; but gloomy desert silence reigned around. We conversed, as well as our parched lips would allow, on what must be done. To wait till morning would only increase the length of our suffering,—to retrace our steps was impossible: probably they had wandered from the path, and might never overtake us: at the same time we felt most reluctant to proceed. We had just determined to remain, when we thought we would fire one more shot. It was answered—by a lion, apparently close to the place where we stood. No wood was at hand to make a fire, nothing but tufts of grass; so we ran and remounted our horses, urging them on towards a range of dark mountains, the gloom increasing as we proceeded; but as our horses could not go much above a walking pace, we were in dread every moment of being overtaken. If we drew up to listen, his approach in the rear was distinctly heard. On reaching the winding glen or pass through the mountains, despairing of escape from our enemy, we resolved to ascend a steep, where, from a precipice, we might pelt him with stones; for we had only a couple of balls left. On dragging ourselves and our horses up the steep, we found the supposed refuge too uneven for a standing-place, and not one fragment of loose stone to be found. Our situation was now doubly dangerous; for, on descending to the path, the query was, on which side is the lion? My companion took his steel and flint to try, by striking them, if he could not discover traces of the lion's paws on the path, expecting every moment that he would bound on one of us. The terror of the horses soon told us that the object of our dread was close to us, but on the right side, namely, in our rear. We instantly remounted, and continued to pursue the track, which we had sometimes great difficulty in tracing along its zig-zag windings among bushes, stones, and sand. The dark towering cliffs around us, the deep silence of which was disturbed by the grunt of a solitary baboon, or the squalling of some of its young ones, added to the colouring of the night's picture. We had not proceeded very far before the lion gave a tremendous roar, which echoing from precipice to precipice, sounded as if we were within the lion's den. On reaching the egress of the defile through which we had passed, we were cheered by the waning moon, rising bright in the east. Descending again we would gladly have laid our weary limbs down to rest; but thirst, and the possibility of the lion's resolving to make his supper on one of us, propelled our weary steps, for our horses were completely jaded.

"We continued our slow and silent march for hours. The tongue cleaving to the roof of the mouth from thirst, made conversation extremely difficult. At last we reached the long-wished-for 'water-fall,' so named, because when it rains, water sometimes falls, though in small quantities; but it was too late to ascend the hill. We allowed the poor worn-out horses to go where they pleased, and having kindled a small fire, and produced a little saliva by smoking a pipe, we talked about our lost companions, who happened for their comfort to have the morsel of meat, and who, as Jantye thought, would wander from the position in which we left them towards the river. We bowed the knee to Him who had mercifully preserved us, and laid our heads on our saddles. The last sound we heard to soothe us was the distant roar of the lion, but we were too much exhausted to feel any thing like fear. Sleep came to our relief, and it seemed made up of scenes the most lovely, forming a glowing contrast to our real situation. I felt as if engaged, during my short repose, in roving among ambrosial bowers of paradisaical delight, hearing sounds of music, as if from angels' harps; it was the night wind falling on my ears from the neighbouring hill. I seemed to pass from stream to stream, in which I bathed and slaked my thirst at many a crystal fountain, flowing from golden mountains enriched with living green. These Elysian pleasures continued till morning dawn, when we awoke speechless with thirst, our eyes inflamed, and our whole frames burning like a coal. We were, however, somewhat less fatigued, but wanted water, and had recourse to another pipe before we could articulate a word.

"My companion then directed me to a projecting rock, near the top of the hill, where, if there were water at all, it would be found. I took up the gun to proceed in that direction, while he went in search of the horses, which we feared might have been devoured by the lion. I ascended the rugged height to the spot where water once was, but found it as dry as the sandy plain beneath. I stood a few minutes, stretching my languid eye to see if there were any appearance of the horses, but saw nothing; turning to descend, I happened to cough, and was instantly surrounded by almost a hundred baboons, some of gigantic size. They grunted, grinned, and sprang from stone to stone, protruding their mouths, and drawing back the skin of their foreheads, threatening an instant attack. I kept parrying them with my gun, which was loaded; but I knew their character and disposition too well to fire, for if I wounded one of them I should have been skinned in five minutes. The ascent was very laborious, but I would have given any thing to be at the bottom of the hill again. Some came so near as even to touch my hat while passing projecting rocks. It was some time before I reached the plain, when they appeared to hold a noisy council, either about what they had done, or intended doing. Levelling my piece at two that seemed the most fierce, as I was about to touch the trigger, the thought occurred, 'I have escaped, let me be thankful;' therefore I left them uninjured, perhaps with the gratification of having given me a fright.

"Jantye soon appeared with the horses. My looks, more expressive than words, convinced him that there was no water. We saddled the poor animals, which, though they had picked up a little grass, looked miserable beyond description. We now directed our course towards Witte Water, where we could scarcely hope to arrive before afternoon, even if we reached it at all, for we were soon obliged to dismount, and drive our horses slowly and silently over the glowing plain, where the delusive mirage tantalized our feelings with the loveliest pictures of lakes and pools studded with lovely islets, and towering trees moving in the breeze on their banks. In some might be seen the bustle of a mercantile harbour, with jetties, coves, and moving rafts, and oars; in others, lakes as lovely as if they had just come from the hand of the Divine Artist, a transcript of Eden's sweetest views, but all the result of highly rarefied air, or the reflected heat of the sun's rays on the sultry plain. Sometimes, when the horses and my companion were some hundred yards in advance, they appeared as if lifted from the earth, or moving like dark living pillars in the air. Many a time did we seek old ant-hills excavated by the ant-eater, into which to thrust our heads, in order to have something solid between our fevered brains and the piercing rays of the sun. There was no shadow of a great rock, the shrubs sapless, barren, and blighted, as if by some blast of fire. Nothing animate was to be seen or heard, except the shrill chirping of a beetle resembling the cricket, the noise of which seemed to increase with the intensity of the heat. Not a cloud had been seen since we left our homes.

"We felt an irresistible inclination to remain at any bush which could afford the least shelter from the noonday's sun, the crown of the head having the sensation as if covered with live coal, and the mind wandering. My companion became rather wild. Having been anxious to spare him all the toil possible, I had for a long time carried the gun; he asked for it, apparently to relieve me, but his motions were such that I was glad to recover possession of it.

"My difficulties and anxieties were now becoming painful in the extreme, not knowing any thing of the road, which was in some places hardly discernible, and in my faithful guide hope had died away. The horses moved at the slowest pace, and that only when driven, which effort was laborious in the extreme. Speech was gone, and everything expressed by signs, except when we had recourse to a pipe, and for which we now began to lose our relish. After sitting a long while under a bush, oh! what a relief I felt when my guide pointed to a distant hill, near to which water lay. Courage revived; but it was with pain and labour that we reached it late in the afternoon. Having still sufficient judgment not to go at once to drink, it was with great difficulty I prevented my companion doing that, which would almost instantly have proved fatal to him. Our horses went to the pool, and consumed nearly all the water, for it appeared that some wild horses had shortly before slaked their thirst at this spot, leaving for us but little, and that polluted.

"Becoming cooler after a little rest, we drank, and though moving with animalcules, muddy, and nauseous with filth, it was to us a reviving draught. We rested and drank, till the sun, sinking in the west, compelled us to go forward, in order to reach Griqua Town that night. Though we had filled our stomachs with water, (if such it might be called, for it was grossly impure,) thirst soon returned with increased agony; and painful was the ride and walk, for they were alternate, until we reached at a late hour the abode of Mr Anderson.

"Entering the door speechless, haggard, emaciated, and covered with perspiration and dust, I soon procured by signs, that universal language, for myself and my companion, a draught of water. Mr A., expecting such a visitor from the moon as soon as from Namaqua-land, was not a little surprised to find who it was. Kind-hearted Mrs A. instantly prepared a cup of coffee and some food, which I had not tasted for three days; and I felt all the powers of soul revive, as if I had talked with angels—it was to me a 'feast of reason and a flow of soul.'

"Retiring to rest, the couch, though hard, appeared to me a downy bed. I begged of Mr A. just to place within my reach half a bucket of water: this he kindly and prudently refused, but left me with a full tumbler of unusual size: such, however, was my fevered condition, that no sooner was he gone than I drank the whole. After reviewing the past, and looking upward with adoring gratitude, I fell asleep, and arose in the morning as fresh as if I had never seen a desert, nor felt its thirst. We remained here a few days, in the course of which our lost companions arrived, having, as we rightly supposed, wandered towards the river, and escaped the thirst which had nearly terminated our career in the desert."

In a foot-note he adds:—"The following remarks on the general appearance of the mirage, taken from Belzoni's *Narrative of his Operations and Researches in Egypt*, will not be uninteresting:—' It generally appears like a still lake, so unmoved by the wind, that every thing above is to be seen most distinctly reflected by it. If the wind agitate any of the plants that rise above the horizon of the mirage, the motion is seen perfectly at a great distance. If the traveller stand elevated much above the mirage, the apparent water seems less united and less deep; for as the eyes look down upon it, there is not thickness enough in the vapour on the surface of the ground to conceal the earth from the sight; but if the traveller be on a level with the horizon of the mirage, he cannot see through it, so that it appears to him clear water. By putting my head first to the ground, and then mounting a camel, the height of which might have been about ten feet at the most, I found a great difference in the appearance of the mirage. On approaching it, it becomes thinner, and appears as if agitated by the wind, like a field of ripe corn. It gradually vanishes as the traveller approaches, and at last entirely disappears when he is on the spot.'

"This phenomena is called by the Bechuanas, 'Moénéne;' and, therefore, parched ground, in Isaiah xxxv. 7, translated 'glowing sand,' by Dr Lowth and others, I have rendered by this term in that language. It is produced, as Dr Hartwell Horne correctly remarks, in his *Introduction to the Critical Study of the Scriptures,* 'by a diminution of the density of the lower stratum of the atmosphere, which is caused by the increase of heat, arising from that communicated by the rays of the sun to the sand, with which this stratum is in immediate contact.'"

CONCLUSION.

Much that has been stated in the preceding pages is applicable, with a slight change in the phraseology, to what has occurred or been seen in other lands. While the compilation has been made chiefly with a view to the help and encouragement of the colonists of South Africa in prosecuting the execution of measures which they have it in contemplation to carry out, with a view to counteracting the aridity which prevents the full accomplishment of their desires and purposes in developing the agricultural capabilities of the country, the publication of it may subserve the accomplishment of similar purposes in other Colonies and newly settled territories; and in view of both objects I desire to indicate the remedial measures which a state of things such as has been depicted seems to render desirable.

In view of what has been stated, the desiccation and consequent aridity of South Africa may be considered to be the combined results of the elevation of the land above the level of the sea, and the consequent flow, or draining off by gravitation of much of the water which falls upon it in the form of rain, and of the evaporation which may be traced to the law of gaseous diffusion, but is increased by the solar heat, and has been promoted by the destruction of vegetation removing an important screen which throws off or absorbs the direct rays of the sun, and one which in other ways conserves the humidity of soil and of the atmosphere.

If the escape of water by gravitation and evaporation combined be greatly in excess of the supply from the atmosphere, the desiccation will go on with rapidity; if the disproportion between the escape and the supply be lessened the desiccation may still go on continuously, but with diminished rapidity; if they be equalized the desiccation will be arrested; if the escape of water be reduced below an equality with the supply the process of desiccation will be reversed, and a degree of humidity such as previously prevailed may be restored.

From all this it seems to follow that any measure, and every measure, which has the effect of preventing the escape of water by gravitation or evaporation will, in its measure, tend to arrest the evil and promote the good; and it so happens that some, if not all, of the more important measures which suggest themselves as calculated to have the effect of arresting the desiccation are such that they may remunerate the outlay required for their execution by immediate profit.

The counsel given by a Hebrew prophet in other circumstances, "Cease to do evil; learn to do well," is not inapplicable here, as counsel whereby the greatest amount of benefit may be secured. Abandon, if possible, the practice of burning the veldt; carry out an enlightened conservation and extension of forests; and introduce, wherever it can be done, irrigation and the construction of dams, together with such other measures as may be likely to retain and utilize the water supply.

I care not to discuss here the relative importance of these several measures. The adoption of all of them is necessary if we would have a full reward; but any one of them, carried out to any extent, however limited may be the measure of that extent, would tend to secure the end desired.

The measures spoken of are all of them measures which have commanded more or less effectively the attention of the colonists. I may differ from some in regard to the relative importance of some of these measures, but I do not consider the absolute importance of any of them to be over-estimated by its most sanguine panygerist or partizan.*

Apart, however, from the desiccation and consequent aridity of the country, though intimately connected therewith in the relation of cause and effect, is the torrential character of the rivers.

Much attention has been given on the Continent of Europe to the study of torrents, with a view to the prevention of them and of the disastrous consequences which often follow them. In some respects South Africa is in the very condition which it is sought to prevent in the Alps. And the South African torrents are in some respects homologous with the torrents which threaten devastation there. In the Alpine torrents the different characteristic portions—the basin drained, the channel, and the deposit of earthy materials—are compressed longitudinally, supplying thus facilities for the study of them. In the South African torrents the channel is elongated, and the deposit of earthy matter is in the sea; but the homology is complete.

In France it has been found that the best and most efficient means, and this an effectual one, of preventing the forming of torrents, and of bridling and extinguishing them when formed, is planting the basin drained by them with grass, and herb, and shrub, and tree; and that by such an appliance the torrential rivers of South Africa might be controlled, and much of their waters retained to fertilize the soil, I have no doubt. But to accomplish this might require operations so extensive as to startle and to forbid the attempt being made.

The precipitation of rain in torrents instead of drizzling showers, and the drainage of the land by short-lived torrents instead of equably flowing rivers and streams, are characteristics of land divested or devoid of vegetation.

In the High Alps the designation torrent is given to the channel of what we call mountain torrents. These are there to be seen in various stages, and it has been remarked that in the forests there are none; that the deepest and most dangerous are in mountains devoid of wood; that old torrents, now always dry, are found where the woods have extended themselves over what is called the *bassin de réception*; and that lately formed torrents are found

---

* Along with the abstract of the Memoir, of which this is an expansion, there were appended to Report of Colonial Botanist for 1866 the following:—

1. Abstract of a Memoir prepared on Irrigation and its application to Agricultural Operations in South Africa; with Notices of the Water Supply of South Africa: Its sources, its quantity, the modes of irrigation required in different circumstances, the facilities for the adoption of these in different districts, and the difficulties, physical and other, in the way of works of extensive irrigation being carried out at the Cape, and the means of accomplishing these which are at command

2. Abstract of Memoir prepared on Arboriculture in South Africa, with details of what has been done, and of what might be done in planting trees in the Cape Colony, with notices of the natural history of Australian and European trees which have been recommended by arboriculturists for plantation there.

3. Abstract of Memoir prepared on the Forest and Forest-lands of Southern Africa: With details of the extent and contents of the different forests of the Colony of the Cape, of Kaffirland, of Natal, and of the regions beyond to the mouth of the Zambesi, and to a corresponding latitude on the west coast, with the intermediate districts.

4. List of South African Trees and Arborescent Shrubs, upon the natural history, botanic characteristics, and economic uses of which a report had been prepared.

5. Abstract of Memoir prepared on the Forest Economy of the Colony.

where the forests have been of late years destroyed. And in consequence of this the French Government have been carrying on for years extensive operations of *reboisement*, replanting with woods the Alps, the Pryenees, and the mountains of Central France, with a view thereby to prevent the occurrence, or the destructive effects and consequences, of torrents.

It would be both more difficult and more expensive to carry out such measures in South Africa than in France. But the secondary advantages—climatal and economic—might compensate for this; and an outlay far short of the value of property, to say nothing of lives, destroyed by such torrents as have been described might accomplish much. I have given Colonial estimates of the loss occasioned by fire and flood during the last eight years, which would show that loss to have been about £100,000 per annum.

THE END.

PRINTED BY JOHN CRAWFORD, HIGH STREET, KIRKCALDY.

www.ingramcontent.com/pod-product-compliance
Lightning Source LLC
Chambersburg PA
CBHW032116230426
43672CB00009B/1759